ACHIEVING ENVIRONMENTAL JUSTICE

A cross-national analysis

Karen Bell

First published in Great Britain in 2014 by

Policy Press
University of Bristol
6th Floor
Howard House
Queen's Avenue
Clifton
Bristol BS8 1SD
UK
Tel +44 (0)117 331 5020
Fax +44 (0)117 331 5367
e-mail pp-info@bristol.ac.uk
www.policypress.co.uk

North American office:
Policy Press
c/o The University of Chicago Press
1427 East 60th Street
Chicago, IL 60637, USA
t: +1 773 702 7700
f: +1 773-702-9756
e:sales@press.uchicago.edu
www.press.uchicago.edu

© Policy Press 2014

British Library Cataloguing in Publication Data
A catalogue record for this book is available from the British Library

Library of Congress Cataloging-in-Publication Data
A catalog record for this book has been requested

ISBN 978 1 44730 594 1 hardcover

Cover design by Policy Press
Front cover: image kindly supplied by Mamani Mamani
Printed and bound in Great Britain by CPI Group (UK) Ltd, Croydon, CR0 4YY
The Policy Press uses environmentally responsible print partners

This book is dedicated to my sister, Jenny

To Alison and Flo,
Great being in the
choir with you.
Solidarity for ever!
Karen xx

Contents

List of figures and tables   vi
Acknowledgements   viii
List of abbreviations   x

one	Introduction: fighting for humanity	1
two	The concept and measurement of environmental justice	15
three	The causes of environmental injustice	33
four	'Killing yourself is no way to make a living': environmental justice in the United States	65
five	'The world has been deceived': environmental justice in the Republic of Korea (South Korea)	79
six	'Regulation means bad': environmental justice in the United Kingdom	97
seven	'We have always been close to nature': environmental justice in Sweden	119
eight	'The rich consume and the poor suffer the pollution': environmental justice in the People's Republic of China	141
nine	'Recuperating all that we have lost and forgotten': environmental justice in the Plurinational State of Bolivia	161
ten	'Socialism creates a better opportunity': environmental justice in Cuba	181
eleven	Achieving environmental justice	213

Appendices   237
References   247
Index   295

List of figures and tables

Figures

1.1	Capitalist/socialist spectrum	6
2.1	Arnstein's 'Ladder of Participation'	26
5.1	Guryong and Gangnam	88
5.2	The Yeongheung coal plant	92
6.1	Overhead pylons in Lockleaze, Bristol	105
6.2	Polluting factory in a low-income area of Glasgow	108
6.3	Lockleaze Community Market	111
7.1	After the riots in Rinkeby, a Stockholm suburb	127
9.1	Consultation on new cable car public transit system for La Paz	176
10.1	Urban agriculture in Moa, Holguín	188
10.2	Integrated Neighbourhood Transformation Workshop, Principe Barrio, Havana	203
11.1	Environmental Justice Indicator scores in seven countries	215

Tables

2.1	The Environmental Justice Indicator Framework	31
3.1	Causes of different aspects of environmental injustice	63
11.1	Policies that could advance environmental justice	220
A1.1	The Environmental Justice Indicator Framework for seven countries	237
A2.1	International economic datasets	240
A2.2	International environmental datasets	241
A2.3	International socioeconomic datasets	242

... it takes a lot of things to change the world:
Anger and tenacity, science and indignation,
The quick initiative, the long reflection,
The cold patience and infinite perseverance,
The understanding of the particular case and the
understanding of the ensemble:
Only the lessons of reality can teach us to transform
reality
– Bertolt Brecht, *Einverständnis* (1929)

Acknowledgements

This work is the result of the contributions and support of many people, including all those who have inspired me over the years among my family, friends, neighbours, teachers and fellow activists; as well as the wider world of journalists, authors, politicians and campaigners. Some will never be acknowledged, since much of what we learn is through informal osmosis. Others are already referenced in this book and I would like to take this opportunity to express my gratitude to them. In addition, I would also like to specifically mention some of those who have been particularly helpful in bringing this book to fruition. Of course, those named do not necessarily agree with all, or any, of what I say here and all mistakes and omissions are my own.

Firstly, thanks for the considerable support, advice, encouragement and practical help given to me by colleagues at the University of Bristol, especially David Gordon, Simon Pemberton, Sarah Cemlyn, Min Young Lee, Yedith Guillen Fernandez, Di Qi, Taewook Huh and Young Jun Lee; as well as the University cleaners, administrators and other support staff, especially Jane Bakowski. Also thanks to the anonymous reviewer of this book and the colleagues and friends, in Bristol and around the world, who have given me valuable feedback on the book chapters, including Hosuk Lee, Tammy Alfred, Ann Singleton, Suet Ying Ho, David Sweeting, Ian Wright, Mark Ellingson, Laura Dickinson, Karolina Isaksson, Hannah White and Daniel Faber. I would also like to specifically thank some of the various people who helped me during the fieldwork for this book, especially Mikael, Maritza, Caridad, José, Alfredo, Justin and Julie, for their help and support. I am also very grateful to all those who agreed to participate as interviewees for this study, for their time and their trust in me.

I also wish to thank all my friends for their moral and practical support during the period of writing this book, especially Helen Fielding, Jane Bowen, Lani Parker, Julie Boston, Lynn-Marie Sardinha, Rossana Vanni, Clare Paine, Jafar Sahari, James Bond, José Sagarnaga and Adelia Quique. In addition, I am grateful to the Lockleaze community of Bristol for being such great neighbours and inspiring me to work on the issue of environmental justice, in particular, Grace, Patricia, Katherine, Donna, Carol, Ellen, Joyce and Dave. I would also like to thank Rosalie Coleman, my teacher at Lowestoft College, for opening my eyes to the importance of the environment and encouraging me to pursue further education.

I would also like to thank the staff at Policy Press, especially Emily Watt, Jo Morton and Laura Vickers, for their helpfulness and efficiency, but most of all for giving me the opportunity to disseminate the ideas and information contained in this book. In addition, I wish to acknowledge and express gratitude to the Economic and Social Research Council, which awarded me with the funding that enabled me to work on the Master's thesis and PhD that formed the basis of this book. I must also thank Santander Bank for awarding me a travel grant that enabled me to carry out the fieldwork in Bolivia. Many thanks, also, to the Bolivian artist Mamani Mamani for kindly giving me permission to use his image *Pachamama* (Mother Earth) for the cover of this book. Also, thanks to Bolivia's Ministry of Environment and Water for facilitating this.

Lastly, I also would like to thank all of the members of my family, especially my sister, Jenny, and my brothers – John, Philip and Armando – as well as my nieces and nephews for their love and support. Finally, this book is thanks to my Mum and Dad, who taught me, without telling me, to love nature and hate injustice.

List of abbreviations

ALBA	The Bolivarian Alliance for the Peoples of Our America
BME	black and minority ethnic
CIDOB	Confederación Indígena del Oriente Boliviano (Indigenous Federation of Eastern Bolivia)
CITMA	Ministry of Science, Technology and Environment (Cuba)
COB	Bolivian Workers Central
CPCC	Chinese People's Consultative Congress
CPPCC	Chinese People's Political Consultative Conference
CTC	National Trade Union Council (Cuba)
Defra	Department for the Environment, Food and Rural Affairs (UK)
DHED	Damaging Hegemonic Environmental Discourse
EIA	Environmental Impact Assessment
EJ	environmental justice
EJI	Environmental Justice Indicator
EPA	Environmental Protection Agency (US)
GATT	General Agreement on Tariffs and Trade
GDP	Gross Domestic Product
GGGI	Global Green Growth Institute
GIS	Geographical Information System
GMO	genetically modified organism
IMF	International Monetary Fund
LCGG	Low Carbon Green Growth
NPC	National People's Congress (China)
OECD	Organisation for Economic Co-operation and Development
PCB	polychlorinated biphenol
PM	Particulate Matter
REDD	Reducing Emissions from Deforestation and Forest Degradation
SEPA	Swedish Environmental Protection Agency
WHO	World Health Organization
WWF	Worldwide Fund for Nature

ONE

Introduction: fighting for humanity

In the beginning I thought I was fighting to save the rubber trees. Afterwards I thought I was fighting to save the Amazon rainforest. Now I realize that I am fighting for humanity. (Chico Mendes)

Environmental justice (EJ) is relevant to the health and survival of all natural beings and systems, though it particularly emphasises how assaults on nature adversely affect humans. It incorporates many different aspects but is, fundamentally, about achieving a healthy environment for all, now and in the future. This book intends to contribute to debates regarding how this might be done, based on an analysis of the extent, form and causes of environmental justice and injustice, in seven very different countries – the United States, the Republic of Korea (South Korea), the United Kingdom, Sweden, China, Bolivia and Cuba.

As well as aspiring to a healthy environment (substantive environmental justice), environmental justice (EJ) aims for an equitable distribution of environmental 'goods' and protection from environmental harms for all socioeconomic groups (distributive environmental justice); and fair, participatory and inclusive structures and processes of environmental decision making (procedural environmental justice). According to this definition, most people in the world do not currently experience environmental justice and, despite the many policies and programmes designed to address the issue, the situation continues to worsen. Climate change appears to be one of our most serious and immediate challenges because of its wide-ranging consequences. Yet it is but one environmental crisis of many resulting from human overuse of resources, production of waste and disruption of natural systems, as numerous reports are now highlighting. For example, in 2009, the Stockholm Resilience Centre reported that, as a result of human activities, we have now either crossed, or are imminently in danger of crossing, nine earth system 'planetary boundaries' within which humanity can safely live (Rockström et al, 2009). These boundaries relate to the nitrogen and phosphorous cycles, global freshwater, land use, biodiversity, atmospheric aerosol loading, chemical pollution, climate change, ocean acidification and stratospheric ozone depletion. The authors warned that, if we continue to go beyond these boundaries, we will cross 'tipping-points', bringing a risk of irreversible and abrupt environmental change that would destabilise the planet, resulting in sudden, deleterious or even disastrous consequences for humans. In order to avoid reaching these tipping-points, we need to restore planetary balance as soon as possible, and certainly within the next 20 years.

These spiralling environmental problems have been paralleled by a corresponding, and some would argue related, surge in the global morbidity and mortality rates of non-communicable diseases, in particular, cardiovascular diseases, diabetes, cancer and chronic respiratory diseases. For example, worldwide, cancer incidence rates have increased to the extent that there is now an 18.6% chance of developing the disease before the age of 75 (29.9% in the US, 26.3% in the UK) (Ferlay et al, 2008). We are often told that these increases in cancer rates are primarily the consequence of an aging population (for example, Macmillan Cancer Support, 2013). However, though there is some evidence for this, it is not the only reason, as reflected in the escalation of age-adjusted incidence rates (see for example, Pellegriti et al, 2013; SEER, 2013). Furthermore, increased longevity does not explain the rise in childhood cancers (see, for example, Kaatsch, 2010). In general, we are repeatedly told that the reasons for the global increase in all these diseases are to be found in our life-styles, our genes and our increasingly long lives, as well as better methods of diagnosing these diseases. The role of the environment is minimised or ignored, as a recent UK cross-party inquiry highlighted, stating:

> Poor air quality probably causes more mortality and morbidity than passive smoking, road traffic accidents or obesity. Yet it receives little or no attention in the media and scant attention in Parliament and within Government. (Environmental Audit Committee, 2010, p 21)

This is in spite of the numerous studies that have linked these non-communicable disease epidemics to toxic substances in the water we drink, the food we eat, the products we use and the air we breathe. For example, the following illnesses have been linked to air pollution, alone:

- heart disease (Ware, 2000; Samoli et al, 2006; Tofler and Muller, 2006; Naess et al, 2007; Silverman et al, 2010)
- cancer (Knox, 2005; Naess et al, 2007; Grant, 2009)
- strokes (Tsai et al, 2003; Wellenius et al, 2005; Tofler and Muller, 2006; Kettunen et al, 2007)

- pneumonia (Knox, 2008)
- respiratory illness (Pope, et al, 1995; Ware, 2000; Samoli et al, 2006; Knox, 2008)
- adverse birth outcomes (Shah and Balkhair, 2011)
- impaired cognitive development (Ranft et al, 2009; Grandjean, 2013)
- diabetes (Andersen et al, 2012; Raaschou-Nielsen et al, 2013)
- depression and suicide (Kim et al, 2010).

The World Health Organization (WHO) suggests that 23% of global deaths are attributable to environmental factors (WHO, 2006) but this may still be an underestimate as only a fraction of the potential risks have been adequately investigated. For example, we still remain largely ignorant as to which synthetic chemicals are toxic to humans; what the safe levels of exposure are; and what the synergist and long-term effects will be (UNEP, 2012). Their impacts on health are often far from immediate or obvious and detecting these against a background of variability in exposure and human susceptibility poses significant scientific challenges. Medical history shows that caution is appropriate. Some materials and chemicals, such as asbestos and polychlorinated biphenyls (PCBs), were used for years before they were found to cause adverse health effects (see, for example, McCulloch and Tweedale, 2008, regarding asbestos). These environmental threats to health are in our homes, our workplaces and our communities. Some of us may be able to avoid them by moving house, changing jobs or adopting a 'healthy life-style', but most of us are, tragically, unable to protect ourselves from them. Hence, the International Labour Organisation reports that, globally, a worker dies from a work-related disease or accident every 15 seconds, amounting to more than 2.3 million deaths a year (ILO, 2013).

As well as considering these environmental 'bads', environmental justice focuses on the positive benefits of environmental 'goods'. For example, EJ analysis draws on studies showing that contact with natural environments has a beneficial effect on people's self-reported physical and mental health, as well as physician-assessed morbidity (de Vries, 2001; Takano et al, 2002; de Vries et al, 2003; Maas et al, 2006; 2009). In general, then, the environment is central to our chances of living a long and healthy life.

Therefore, when we work to achieve environmental justice, we are, indeed, 'fighting for humanity'. However, environmental justice particularly focuses on exposing the injustice that occurs when the distribution of environmental goods and bads is uneven for different socioeconomic groups. For example, while wealthy people can generally access the environmental resources they need, poorer people and communities continue to lack a whole range of environmental necessities. Approximately one in three people globally are still without basic sanitation services (UNICEF/WHO, 2012); one in six lack access to electricity (IEA, 2013); and one in eight are without clean water (UNICEF/WHO, 2012); safe cooking fuels (IEA, 2013); or enough food to meet the minimum daily energy requirement (FAO, 2013).

There is also often a 'double injustice' (Gough, 2011), whereby the social groups that are most likely to be negatively affected by environmental problems are those least responsible for causing them. For example, the world's richest 8% of people emit half of the world's carbon dioxide emissions (Pacala, 2007). In addition, there is frequently a 'triple injustice' (Cook et al, 2012) that arises when environmental policies, themselves, further exacerbate negative social and distributional consequences for groups that are already disadvantaged. In the UK, for instance, some of the policies designed to address climate change are being financed by increased household energy costs, exacerbating the plight of low-income householders who already struggle to heat their homes sufficiently (see Chapter Six).

Despite significant social movement and governmental efforts to address environmental injustice in many countries, these initiatives appear to have been insufficiently effective, as this book will illustrate. To some extent, this seems to be because there is still no agreement about what the causes of the problems really are. Previous research on this from within the field of environmental justice has been minimal and those studies that do exist offer unclear or contradictory explanations. Consequently, the policy response and campaign focus are muddled, since it is not clear where our efforts should be applied. Therefore, this book addresses this deficit, focusing on the causes of environmental injustice and, thereby, proposing strategies to overcome the problem. Broadly speaking, EJ analysts tend to view environmental injustice in terms of one of five possible theoretical causes: discrimination; market dynamics; a lack of citizen power; industrialisation; and capitalism. Two other possible causes, frequently discussed in the mainstream environmental literature, could also be added: individual behaviour/ life-style choices; and an environmentally harmful dominant culture. This book will discuss all seven of these causal factors but emphasise capitalism as a root cause of environmental injustice. At the same time, I will reject outright economic determinism, arguing that cultural processes are also important in shaping environmental justice outcomes.

Although there is a growing body of literature linking the origin of environmental problems to capitalism (for example, Magdoff and Foster, 2011), comparatively few analysts make this link to the wider question of environmental justice, with its distributive and procedural components (with some notable exceptions, for example, Faber and O'Connor, 1993; Harvey, 1996; Schnaiberg and Gould, 2000; Berry, 2003; Williams, 2005; Pellow, 2007). This may be because, at least in Western countries, it has, for some time, been considered rather 'extremist' to criticise capitalism and 'idealistic' to believe that it could ever be overcome. Intellectuals from all disciplines seem to have convinced many of us that 'there is no alternative' because capitalism will last forever; human beings are genetically programmed to be greedy; and the market is usually right (for example, Spencer, 1864; Hayek, 1933; Fukuyama, 1992). Therefore, most of us living in the West have come to accept the capitalist backdrop to our lives without question, or even mention.

Recently, however, the invisibility of capitalism has begun to change. A series of crises (the collapse of the banks, increasing recognition of the seriousness of climate change, a global recession and austerity measures in many of the wealthier countries) have focused mainstream attention on the issue. There are now popular books (for example, *The Selfish Capitalist* – Oliver James, 2008) and even films (for example, *Capitalism: A Love Story* – Michael Moore, 2009) on the topic. Alongside the increased visibility of capitalism, there has been a growing recognition that capitalism is not a force of nature but an ideological choice. In the context of this widened debate, it now seems important to also consider the role of capitalism in relation to environmental injustice.

However, some might argue that it is not possible to generalise about capitalism (or what is often considered its only alternative, socialism), as there are overlaps and varieties of both typologies. Both capitalism and socialism embrace a diverse array of political philosophies. For example, socialism ranges from 'state socialism', which emphasises the nationalisation of the means of production, to 'libertarian socialism', which opposes state ownership. A number of analysts also critique the tendency to present the economy as a singular system, arguing that it is, rather, a contested zone of multiple economic forms (for example, Gibson-Graham, 2006). Most capitalist countries maintain a significant role for the state, while most socialist countries usually have components of capitalism within them, and all regulate the environment to some extent, so that there are no purely free-market or state-controlled economies. For example, in recognisably capitalist countries, the means of production are mainly under private ownership and the accumulation of capital is the fundamental driver of economic activity. Yet, capitalist governments also use fiscal and monetary policies to manage the economy, support social welfare, protect the environment and maintain competition. Furthermore, citizens of these countries spend a great deal of their economic lives in non-capitalist activities, working for the public or voluntary, community and cooperative sectors, or in unpaid activities in the home, in caring and in exchanging goods and favours (Gibson-Graham, 2006). However, I believe that the predominant economic system of a country, whether capitalist, socialist or otherwise, is what dominates our lives, even when we are engaging in forms of activity that appear to lie outside that system. For example, within capitalism, cooperatives still have to earn a profit and compete with other capitalist firms to survive. Thus, I follow other studies of comparative political economy, which, while recognising the limitations of simplistic typologies, such as 'capitalist/socialist' and 'market/state' have often used these categories as starting-points for subsequent, more nuanced analysis (for example, Gough, 1994), and this is my intention here (further discussion on defining capitalism can be found in Chapters Three and Eleven).

Approach to the research

In order to understand capitalism in relation to environmental justice, the book explores the intra-national (within country) environmental justice situation in seven countries. These countries were selected, not only to cover a wide variety of state/market forms, but also because they have all achieved some positive recognition for their environmental or EJ policies, as the chapters that follow will explain. Acknowledging that every country in the world today is, to a greater or lesser extent, a mixed economy, I have positioned them on a spectrum, from more socialist/state directed to more capitalist/market directed (see Figure 1.1). Their positioning reflects their own constitutional declarations and government statements regarding their capitalist/socialist orientation, as well as their overall public policy as indicated by, for example, the proportion of public sector workers, the level of corporate taxation and the percentage of state spending on welfare (see individual country chapters for more justification of their positioning). The spectrum was

Figure 1.1: Capitalist/socialist spectrum

| United States | Rep of Korea | UK | Sweden | China | Bolivia | Cuba |

More capitalist/market based ⟷ More socialist/state based

Source: Bell, 2013

used to help me consider whether the degree of environmental justice in a country varied according to the extent of capitalist orientation.

This continuum should be considered a heuristic device that can allow us to think more systematically about the processes involved. It should not be viewed as implying that capitalism equates with 'markets' or that socialism is equivalent to 'state control', only that capitalism favours markets, while socialism (as it is currently practised at a national level) emphasises the state. The spectrum should also not be read as implying that socialism is the only possible alternative to capitalism. As I will discuss later, there are other possible alternatives, but socialism is the main alternative that currently exists at a national level.

The research for this book spanned six years, including work for a Master's dissertation and a PhD, and fieldwork in Bolivia, Cuba, Sweden, the United Kingdom and the United States. Data was collected using a diverse range of techniques, including participant observations, document reviews and semi-structured interviews. Participant observations involved visiting areas, projects and communities where there were potential environmental justice issues; taking part in activities that constituted the everyday lives of the people experiencing the environmental justice or injustice; and attending public meetings where environmental decisions were being made.

The interviews totalled 140 over the period and included a diverse range of actors, such as state representatives, civil society organisers, local 'experts', academics, workers and residents. Interviewees were selected using 'purposive' (because they had particular knowledge or experience) and 'opportunistic' (because they were available) sampling methods. I took care to include a diversity of voices in each country, in terms of varieties of opinion as well as demographic characteristics such as class, age and ethnicity. Where I could not carry out face-to-face interviews, I used Skype or telephone to speak to research participants. All the interviews were undertaken by myself, either in Spanish or in English. Although interpreters were used for some of the Chinese and Korean interviews, I was not, otherwise, accompanied in any of the interviews. Almost all the dialogues were digitally recorded, except on a few occasions where the settings made it difficult and notes were taken instead. With regard to confidentiality, I have identified only those participants who represented an organisation, and only where they agreed to be named in the subsequent research outputs.

Before and during data-gathering on the specific countries, I developed a structure as a basis for analysing the material, that is, a list of environmental justice indicators. Together, these formed an 'Environmental Justice Indicator Framework' (discussed in detail in

Chapter Two and Appendix 3). I recognise that some environmental justice analysts would reject the use of such a framework on the grounds of the subjectivity, breadth and complexity of EJ claim making. However, I felt that a vision of justice was necessary to provide a solid base for the research, acting as the structure for a detailed series of research questions. Once all the data had been entered into the framework, an 'Environmental Justice Indicator' (EJI) score was calculated for each country. In order to increase the reliability of the EJI score, the framework for each country was checked by at least one expert from the country being examined. The EJI scores were then used as a basis to analyse the countries according to their apparent level of environmental justice.

However, because a good level of intra-national environmental justice can be achieved by creating problems elsewhere, for example, by 'outsourcing' pollution and waste,[1] Ecological Footprint data (Wackernagel and Rees, 1996) was also incorporated into the EJI Framework. This ensured that the international, intergenerational and interspecies dimensions of environmental justice were taken into account. The Ecological Footprint is a measure of human demand on the Earth's ecosystems. It represents the amount of biologically productive land and sea area needed to regenerate the resources consumed and to absorb, and render harmless, the corresponding waste (Wackernagel and Rees, 1996). It can be used to illustrate the consumption of a group, people or nation in relation to the Earth's resources. The total Ecological Footprint (EF) for humanity, as a whole, is currently estimated to be 1.5 planet Earths (Global Footprint Network, 2012). Individual countries currently have EFs as high as 11.7, that is, they use ecological services 11.7 times faster than the Earth can sustain. As we only have one Earth, this is evidently problematic.

The underlying philosophical basis for my approach is Critical Theory, which, while not representing a single cohesive theoretical viewpoint, tends to be normative, desiring to effect positive social change. Critical Theory links to a post-structuralist approach, where social processes are seen as determining economic outcomes, as well as the reverse being true. It encompasses, yet goes beyond, a Marxist analysis by investigating the connections between the economic, nonhuman, societal, political, cultural and psychological realms. Unlike Marxist economic determinism, cultural processes are viewed as having as much significance as economic processes, though the balance is seen to lie predominantly with the economy. Hence, the critical perspective used in this book stands in contrast to the dominant discourses on environment and environmental justice, which tend to be managerialist and market-based, whereby environmental problems are seen as issues that can be fixed with new technology and smarter economic incentives within current societal structures. Swyngedouw (2007) has described this managerialist approach as part of the 'post-political' condition, whereby solutions are framed within the current organisation of society and economy, largely relying on technical knowledge and deliberation among supposedly impartial individuals.

From this Critical Theory perspective, I will argue in this book that it is, not only capitalism that lies at the root of environmental injustice, but also a particular conglomeration of beliefs that are carried in 'Damaging Hegemonic Environmental Discourses' (DHEDs). Discourse carries the culture of societies and reveals the taken-for-granted beliefs about reality that define what is regarded as natural, normal, right and good, in addition to what is considered to be bad, other, undesirable and wrong. Consequently, discourse reveals the collective worldview that is woven into the social fabric and inherited by all members of a social group. The most relevant, taken-for-granted Damaging Hegemonic Environmental Discourses appear to be the beliefs that ever-expanding growth is 'good' or 'necessary'; that the environment is separate from humans and needs to be controlled (or 'mastered'); that the environment is of minimal importance for human health; and that complex, modern or 'high' technology is preferable to more basic or traditional technology (see Chapter Three for more on each of these).

The concept of 'hegemony' is critical to a discussion of environmental justice. While there have been numerous different meanings ascribed to the term (see Prys, 2004), hegemony is generally seen to be a form of structural power that works by using institutions and ideas to present the interests of the globally powerful as universal interests. Therefore, rather than use coercive power, a consensus about ideas, norms and values is created among powerful elites and/or states. Dominance is obscured by achieving an appearance of 'natural order' (Cox, 1996, p 66). In this book, informed by Critical Theory, I use the Gramscian understanding of the term, which can be distinguished from the more deterministic Marxist approaches. This perspective asserts that there are temporary historical structures that frame action, understood as combinations of thought patterns, material conditions and institutions (Cox, 1996, p 96). Though these structures do not determine actions in a mechanical sense, they provide the context for 'habits, expectations, and constraints ...' (Cox, 1996, p 97). These structures are considered to be partly constituted by the consciousness and actions of individuals and groups (Gill, 1993). The existing hegemony works to the continuing benefit of the powerful groups in society who support the hegemonic ideology because it justifies and legitimates them (Taylor, 2000).

Therefore, hegemonic environmental discourses shape and support our culture and values and, in turn, our actions. Yet, the assumptions that they encompass often lack robust evidence and are rarely inspected or challenged, having been handed down to us as taken-for-granted knowledge. Hegemonic discourses provide conceptual frameworks that have power, in terms of shaping our view of the world and enabling us to accept some policy measures as 'realistic' and others as far fetched. They are difficult to challenge because of their seeming invisibility and the extent to which people come to identify with them, as will be evident throughout this book. This does not imply that the there is no role for resistance and that people are merely duped into accepting these discourses. Indeed, there is a great deal of resistance. However, these DHEDs, alongside the structural constraints of capitalism, create confining conditions within which agencies operate. One of the tasks of the environmental justice movement is to construct a counter-hegemony in order to overcome the likelihood that many people (including possible supporters) might accept the dominant hegemonic frame as normal (Taylor, 2000). Thus, a community protesting about a specific 'development' is also fighting general societal discourses, values and norms.

Scope and limitations

This comparison of policy in different political, economic and cultural contexts draws upon a tradition of comparative method. Such comparative studies have been used to test or develop theories or hypotheses, to construct models, to challenge the apparent inevitability of particular policies and to promote the 'borrowing' of policies or practices (for example, Esping-Andersen, 1990). They provide access to a wide and varied range of data, but the non-equivalence of the data can be a major issue. National conditions may be idiosyncratic and there can be variance in the conceptual frameworks used. Some might argue that attempts to develop general theories for countries with such a wide range of socioeconomic and political structures, as examined in this book, are therefore misguided. However, I approach these issues as considerations, rather than as insurmountable obstacles. Therefore, for example, I elaborated a very clear concept of 'environmental justice', as Chapter Two outlines, to help me cope with varying cross-national conceptual frameworks. In addition, I have taken into account the relevant variations in context in the analysis, as discussed in Chapter Eleven.

There are also a number of other criticisms that can be made about the approach taken in this book. In particular, it could be argued that analysis at a national level has become redundant because of the dual processes of globalisation and fragmentation (for example, Lash and Urry, 1987; Sklair, 2002), leading to a 'hollowing out' of the state (Jessop, 2004). However, I have taken the view of Kennet (2001), who argues that that the nation-state continues to be a useful unit of analysis, as it still provides the administration and infrastructure through which social policy is delivered. Even so, it has been important to distinguish between the influence of local, regional, national and international policies and contexts in the analysis.

It could also be argued that, despite the wide scope of the work, seven countries is a small sample of cases on which to base any general statement about the causes of environmental justice. However, the argument I make in this book should be seen in the context of the wider literature that relates to the causes of environmental injustice (see Chapter Three). The ideas developed are intended to have 'theoretical generalisability' (Hammersley, 1992) to the extent that they provoke thought and aid understanding of ideas and debates. Because of the lack of previous research on environmental justice in the majority of the countries looked at, this enquiry has, necessarily, been exploratory, and there is much more to learn. In addition, the whole notion of grading countries according to a snapshot moment is, to some extent, flawed, because environmental justice issues often relate to long-term processes. Hence, I make no claim to be comprehensive but, rather, to convey an overview of the economic, political and ecological conditions that pertain to EJ in each complex country at a particular time. However, my confidence in the position I take is based, not only on the data from my primary research, but also on the evidence from the prior studies that I draw upon. Even so, numerous ideological obstacles impeded a thorough examination of the countries. It was difficult to know what could be considered to be reliable information at all stages of data gathering. Although I have done my best to be authentic, meticulous and transparent, I encourage readers to build on this work and help to establish the credibility (or otherwise) of the research for themselves.

The structure of the book

Following this introductory chapter, Chapter Two covers the history of the concept of environmental justice and gives a brief overview of current debates on how EJ should be defined, analysed and operationalised. Chapter Three examines current explanations for environmental injustice, particularly focusing on capitalism and Damaging Hegemonic Environmental Discourses. Chapters Four, Five, Six and Seven look at environmental justice in the capitalist countries – the United States, the Republic of Korea, the United Kingdom and Sweden. Subsequently, Chapters Eight, Nine and Ten look at environmental justice within the context of socialism – in China, Bolivia and Cuba. Chapter Eleven summarises the apparent causes of environmental injustice and justice in the countries examined and discusses whether capitalism can completely explain environmental injustice, also considering the role of culture. It ends by highlighting specific policies and strategies that could be adopted, demanded or invented.

Environmental justice from the inside

Lastly, it may be useful for you to know something about my background. I have been an environmental and social activist my entire adult life, mainly working for peace (Greenham Common Women's Peace Camp, Campaign Against the Arms Trade, Stop the War); environmental justice (Friends of the Earth, Bristol Green Bike Scheme, Lockleaze Environment Group); and international solidarity (Cuba, Bolivia and Venezuela Solidarity Campaigns). I come from a manual working-class family (with some Romany gypsy heritage) and have lived almost all my life on council estates, including now. For almost 20 years I was employed as a community development worker in deprived areas of Bristol focusing on environment, participation, health and equalities until I began working on the PhD that forms the basis of this book. This life experience has left me with an engaged approach to research, rather than one that attempts to be, or purports to be, 'neutral'. Instead, I strive to be honest and authentic. It is, in any case, difficult to be neutral while we live through what is perhaps the most critical period in the history of humanity. We have a window of opportunity of only about 20 years to resolve the environmental crises. The more people that fight for environmental justice from an informed and optimistic position, the greater will be our chance of success. Therefore, I hope this book will inspire, provoke and inform.

Note

[1] For example, Davis and Caldeira (2010) report that the United States outsources 10.8% of its CO_2 emissions abroad, and European nations outsource up to 50%, most of it to developing countries. Consequently, over 25% of China's CO_2 emissions are the result of manufacturing goods for other countries.

TWO

The concept and measurement of environmental justice

Individually and collectively, people around the world have opposed environmental injustice for hundreds of years.[1] However, most commentators agree that the conceptualisation and use of the term 'environmental justice' first emerged in the 1980s, out of resistance to the siting of toxic facilities in black and other minority ethnic communities in the United States. A defining moment was the publication of research that reported that hazardous installations, such as toxic waste dumps, were often located in areas with higher percentages of 'people of color' (UCC, 1987). This study was followed by further investigations that confirmed that poor and minority ethnic communities in the US were disproportionately exposed to environmental hazards (for example, Bryant and Mohai, 1992; Adeola, 1994; Cutter, 1995) and received unequal protection under environmental law (for example, Kratch, 1995). These findings led to accusations of 'environmental racism' and the growth of an environmental justice movement made up of tenants' associations, civil rights groups, agricultural workers, religious groups, non-governmental organisations (NGOs), academics, trades unions and other civil society organisations. However, unlike previous environmental groups in the US, which had focused on the protection of wilderness and endangered species, this movement focused on the environment in the workplace and the community.

Therefore, the term 'environmental justice' was originally applied to the socio-spatial distribution of pollution within national borders and, in particular, environmental racism in facility siting. It has since been taken up in other parts of the world and, over the past decade, the concept of environmental justice and its associated research methodologies have begun to be used in other countries around the globe, though more often by political and academic elites than by local activists (Walker, 2012). In the process of expanding its boundaries, environmental justice has become a somewhat contentious term. In general, it seems that activists have tended to promote a wider, and often more radical, use of the concept, applying it to more diverse contexts and issues, while policy makers and most academics have clung to a narrower definition. For example, the principles adopted by delegates of the First National People of Color Environmental Justice Summit (1991) embody perhaps the widest conception of environmental justice, including that:

> Environmental Justice affirms the sacredness of Mother Earth, ecological unity and the interdependence of all species, and the right to be free from ecological destruction … Environmental Justice calls for universal protection from nuclear testing, extraction, production and disposal of toxic/hazardous wastes and poisons and nuclear testing that threaten the fundamental right to clean air, land, water, and food … Environmental Justice demands the right to participate as equal partners at every level of decision-making, including needs assessment, planning, implementation, enforcement and evaluation … Environmental Justice affirms the right of all workers to a safe and healthy work environment without being forced to choose between an unsafe livelihood and unemployment … Environmental Justice opposes the destructive operations of multi-national corporations … Environmental Justice opposes military occupation, repression and exploitation of lands, peoples and cultures, and other life forms. (First National People of Color, 1991)

Several authors point out that when environmental injustice occurs, it is within the context of particular economic, societal and state relations. For example, in the US, environmental racism can be perpetrated because of high levels of racial segregation (Martinez-Alier, 2003). By extension, some activists and academics assert that environmental justice should be defined so as to pose a challenge to these relations (for example, Scandrett, 2007). However, mainstream use of the term has tended to avoid such a comprehensive and radical analysis. This wish to maintain a narrow focus for environmental justice may be partly, or wholly, based on a desire to contain or undermine its radical implications. For example, Scandrett argues that in Scotland, the term has 'narrowed in favour of certain social interests, especially the interests of capital', so that 'mainstream policy discourse has increasingly restricted environmental justice to policy areas which do not challenge economic growth' (Scandrett, 2007, pp 1–4). This has meant a shift in policy emphasis towards 'street level incivilities', in other words, issues such as litter, graffiti, dog mess and vandalism, rather than major polluters and infrastructure projects which may threaten economic interests. This emphasis also diverts attention away from the neglect of the state (that is, in terms of poor and inappropriate housing, transport and planning) (Scandrett, 2007).

It has also been suggested that, because there are such diverse notions, appropriate to different practical and analytical contexts, and reflecting interests, it is not possible (for example, Debbané and Keil, 2004), necessary (for example, Walker and Bulkeley, 2006), or useful (for example, Foreman, 1998) to absolutely define environmental justice. Therefore, 'environmental justice should be seen more as a discourse, embedded in social movement, always provisional and contested, and reflecting interests' (Scandrett, 2007, p 1). However, some analysts argue that we need a definition of environmental justice because, if we accept that there are different concepts of justice, for example, appropriate to different cultural contexts, the whole notion of justice becomes meaningless (for example, Low and Gleeson, 1998). These analysts imply that, without universal standards of justice, we are without moral benchmarks. This debate reflects the intellectual discussion around the wider notions of justice, with the various strands of thought – utilitarianism, communitarianism, liberal equality, libertarianism, Marxism and so on – containing different assumptions about the merits and possibility of defining justice.[2]

I have taken a pragmatic approach to this issue, as I felt that I needed a vision of justice as the basis for my research in order to have a framework against which I could determine the extent to which environmental justice had been achieved in each of the seven countries. In addition, I felt a definition to be important because it is clear that the way environmental justice is defined has important implications for the kind of solutions that are considered. A widely framed definition enables more wide-ranging proposals for change. Therefore, considerable space is given here to establishing a working definition of the concept.

In general, debates around how environmental justice should be defined and analysed have centred on whom the term should be applied to; what environmental issues are relevant; which elements of justice should be considered; and whether to move beyond equity issues, to a general critique of the right to pollute. These issues will now be considered in terms of three overlapping and interrelated facets of EJ – distributive, procedural and substantive justice.

Distributive justice[3]

As a number of researchers note (for example, Stanley, 2009), most studies in the field equate environmental justice with distributive justice that is, distributional patterns among social categories. The categories for inclusion differ, with some activists and academics focusing on environmental racism (for example, Bullard, 1990; 1993; Bryant and Mohai, 1992), and others widening this to include inequity based on income, class or, more recently, gender and age (for example, Buckingham and Kulcur, 2009). It is important to note, however, that these categories are always linked in the experiences of individuals and groups, in what critical race theorists have termed 'intersectionality' (Crenshaw, 1994).

Some analysts focus on international and intergenerational environmental justice (for example, Hofrichter, 1993; Escobar, 1996; Shiva, 1998; Stephens et al, 2001; Newell, 2005). With this emphasis, the emerging 'climate justice' movement reminds us that people in low-income countries and future generations are likely to be adversely affected by climate change caused by high-income countries and previous generations. Similarly, the global movement for environmental justice focuses on issues such as the effects of consumption in the global North, for instance, the disposal of hazardous wastes in the low-income and middle-income countries of the South. These movement activists now argue that the industrialised, high-income countries of the North have accrued a large 'ecological debt' for over-use of resources and contamination of the environment over the past few centuries (for example, Acción Ecológica, 2008).

Studies of distributive justice vary, not only according to their interest in different social categories, but also with regard to their focus on different aspects of equality, such as equality of primary goods (for example, Rawls, 1971), of resources (for example, Dworkin, 1993), of capabilities (for example, Sen, 1985), of welfare outcomes (for example, Smith, 2000) or of the distribution of environmental risks (for example, Schlosberg, 2004). In addition, distributional environmental justice campaigns and studies are interested in a diverse range of environmental issues. Some are primarily concerned with environmental 'bads', while others include access to environmental 'goods', such as energy, water and green space (for example, Heynen, 2003; Lucas et al, 2004), or vulnerability to 'natural' risks (for example, Walker et al, 2006). Several analysts also include non-material factors, such as cultural contexts and values. For example, Warren (1999) points out that with the environmental destruction and loss of indigenous land comes the demise of traditional ways of life – oral traditions, ritual, myths, art, music and stories; often leading to the loss of traditional values, such as sharing and reciprocity.

Distributive environmental justice studies have the advantage of generally providing clear and mappable evidence of environmental outcomes, often using GIS (Geographical Information Systems) software to measure the proximity of environmental hazards to various demographic groups. Yet, as a number of analysts have pointed out, a study that considers only distributional justice is severely limiting (for example, Faber, 1998; Walker and Bulkeley, 2006; Stanley, 2009). If we focus solely on inequitable distribution, the solution would seem to be to share environmental burdens evenly, rather than eliminate them altogether. The debate over whether to focus only on distributive justice or to include, or replace it with, other notions of justice reflects discussions in the wider justice literature. While some justice philosophers, such as Dworkin (1993), for example, advocate a focus on outcomes (distributive justice), others consider that this is insufficient. Young (1990), for example, argues that a distributive model limits understanding, since it tends to focus thinking on the allocation of material goods. Even when non-material social goods are included (for example, power, opportunity, self-respect), she argues, they are treated as static entities, rather than as processes. Thus, she claims: 'distributional issues are crucial to a satisfactory conclusion of justice, [but] it is a mistake to reduce social justice to distribution' (Young, 1990, p 1). Therefore, so as to lessen environmental harm in general, and not merely achieve an equal spread of it, and to take into account the non-material realm, procedural justice should also be included as an essential component of EJ.

Procedural justice

Procedural justice refers to the fairness and transparency of the processes by which decisions are made. Some researchers highlight the importance of the justice that stems from the interpersonal behaviour of decision makers, which they refer to as 'interactional justice' (for example, Greenberg, 1993), and justice that is based on acknowledgement of culture and identity, that is, 'recognition justice' (for example, Young, 1990; Schlosberg, 2007). However, while I acknowledge that interactional and recognition justice are important underpinnings to the achievement of procedural justice, I have included them here under procedural justice for the purposes of organising this discussion.

Habermas (1984) argues that justice occurs when everyone affected as a participant in rational discourse freely agrees on a course of action, regardless of the outcome. He uses the concept of ideal speech and the ideal speech situation to describe the conditions for dialogue which will lead to this consensus. It is considered that the preferred outcome will be decided in the process of discourse. However, several feminist analysts argue that Habermas's conditions for discourse are utopian because society does not currently equip people with the necessary information, rationality or equality required to participate in the ideal way (for example, Mansbridge, 1990; 1992; Young, 1990; Benhabib, 1992; Fraser, 1992). They describe the ways in which the more powerful group can subtly control proceedings. Benhabib (1992) notes, for example, that the concerns of non-dominant groups, such as matters that primarily affect women, are often deemed inappropriate for public discussion. Therefore, projects which aim to find a 'general will' and the 'common good' tend to overlook difference and to manufacture consent. In this way, power is shifted from a repressive mode of domination to a hegemonic one so that 'deliberation can serve as a mask for domination' (Fraser, 1992, p 119). Especially where there are low levels of participation, participatory models can reinforce existing inequalities between groups of citizens because they give privileged groups yet another channel of influence, while marginalised groups remain side-lined. This enables a hegemonic discourse or dominant perspective to reproduce itself.

Yet, despite the difficulties of challenging the dominant hegemony, procedural justice should not be rejected. It is difficult to imagine how we can be successful in our demand for environmental justice of any kind without some procedural justice. If there were no information, no way of expressing our point of view, no way of influencing decisions through the democratic process, it does not seem likely that we would be able to mobilise people to join environmental justice campaigns. Social movement literature has found that people are more likely to get involved in a campaign when they feel a combination of anger (about the issue) and hope (that they can achieve change). As one study concluded:

> people need to feel both aggrieved about some aspect of their lives and optimistic that, acting collectively, they can redress the problem. Lacking either one or both of these perceptions, it is highly unlikely that people will mobilize, even when afforded the opportunity to do so. (McAdam et al, 1996, p 5)

Anger is suppressed by restricting controversial information and hope is crushed where oppressed people have no power. Therefore, control over information and decision-making processes is vital for environmental justice. Without these, we are always in the position of having to ask/ demand/hope that the powerful will give us what we want.

Some also argue that procedural justice gives us only the most favoured, rather than the best, solution. For example, there is an argument that the public are unlikely to make decisions that would benefit the environment, so that democracy may be an impediment to environmental improvement. James Lovelock, for example, has asserted that democracy should be put on hold in order to deal with climate change because most people are 'not sufficiently evolved' to adequately respond (Lovelock, cited in Hickman, 2010). However, this argument is contradicted by several studies of international variations in environmental quality which show that better environmental conditions correlate with greater citizen power in environmental decision making, as measured by indicators such as political and civil rights (Barrett and Graddy, 2000). However, environmental quality depends on citizens being able to acquire information about their environment, to assemble and organise and to state their preferences; as well as depending on governments having an incentive to satisfy these preferences (Barrett and Graddy, 2000).

Therefore, procedural justice, with a strong voice from poor[4] and marginalised groups, is necessary to bring about environmental justice. With procedural justice 'There are no guarantees that people will make wise decisions, but they have an incentive to do so: they must live with the consequences' (Kann, 1986, p 253). However, even moving from distributional justice to include procedural justice would still only guarantee that we may participate in the equitable allocation of environmental problems. Therefore, in addition to distributional and procedural justice, we also need substantive justice.

Substantive justice

Substantive environmental justice is usually discussed in terms of an individual's right to a healthy environment. While there is considerable evidence that the environment affects our health (see Chapter One), exactly what constitutes a healthy environment is highly contested. In many cases, there is a lack of an agreed minimum threshold for the environmental goods and bads that impact on health. Even standards for an aspect that is as measurable as air pollution, for example, are disputed. Though there are internationally agreed air quality standards, harmful effects have been shown below these thresholds (Barnett et al, 2006). However, despite the difficulties in strictly defining standards, it is important to include substantive justice, as a healthy planet is the basis of our survival as a species. Linked to substantive justice, but subsumed under it here, is 'productive justice', which goes beyond a demand for procedural and distributional equity and the right to protection from environmental harm, towards explicitly questioning the production of hazardous materials at all (Faber, 1998; Choi, 1999). Proponents of this idea argue that productive justice will enable substantive, distributive and procedural justice. This is an approach that goes to the root of the problem and is increasingly becoming the perspective of environmental justice campaigners (Agyeman and Evans, 2004) as they begin to demand 'Not here, not anywhere'.

Therefore, the working definition of environmental justice for this book incorporates these three aspects:

- a healthy environment (substantive environmental justice)
- an equitable distribution of environmental 'goods' and protection from environmental harms for all socioeconomic groups (distributive environmental justice)
- and fair, participatory and inclusive structures and processes of environmental decision making (procedural environmental justice).

Measuring environmental justice: the Environmental Justice Indicator Framework

In order to make an assessment of the seven countries examined in this book, it was necessary, not only to have a working definition of environmental justice, but also to have a precise set of indicators. Since indicators reflect the way a concept is understood and which dimensions are emphasised, both defining and operationalising an issue, their potential power in formulating policies is substantial. Indicators can also be applied as tools for environmental campaigning in many different contexts. However, despite all the debates around definitions, there seemed to be virtually no sets of indicators within the environmental justice literature against which I could evaluate the extent of environmental justice in the seven countries (though there have, more recently, been some attempts to do this at a local level, for example, Lakes et al, 2013). Therefore, I developed the Environmental Justice Indicator (EJI) Framework for this purpose. According to Pastille (2002), indicators can be 'citizen oriented', with a principal purpose to be used in dialogue with the citizens; 'expert oriented', relating to performance assessment and measuring effectiveness; and 'objective setting', helping to set goals. The EJI Framework intends to address all of these dimensions, but primarily the first.

The EJI Framework was based upon a Marxist ideal of justice, which requires the distribution of benefits on the basis of 'to each according his needs' (Marx, 1969 [1875], p 160). Some theorists might consider this problematic on the grounds that a universal and objective definition of 'needs' is not possible and/or appropriate, since needs are socially constructed (for example, Schutz, 1965) and relative (for example, Townsend, 1987). Attempting to define needs for others is considered to be undesirable, since this could lead to cultural imperialism and the dismissal of expressed needs that are 'inconvenient'. However, I take the view of Doyal and Gough (1991), who argue that universal and objective human needs *do* exist and that they can be identified. They assert two basic needs – health and autonomy – that they argue are 'common to all humans, irrespective of culture' (1991, p 91). Doyal and Gough (1991) argue that self-defined needs are not enough, since people are not always the best judge of their wants because of limits to knowledge and to rationality. Also, wants can be shaped by institutions, for example, through advertising and socialisation.

This is a difficult debate to resolve. The matter is particularly difficult when applied to environmental justice because so many justice claims are context related. It could be argued that it is not appropriate to assess and compare entire countries using a universalistic list of indicators because some issues are more important in certain countries, or even regions and localities, than in others. This links to the concept of 'fungibility', that is, the idea that all green acts are interchangeable, that whatever is achieved environmentally accomplishes the same, wherever or whatever it is. This is a faulty rationale, though widely embedded in current discourse, enabling people to describe themselves as environmentalists purely because, for example, they recycle, even though they may also drive a 4x4 or consume meat regularly.

There is a necessary relativism that is inherent in environmental issues. For example, in one area a community might be opposing electric pylons because of the health risks from electric and magnetic fields (EMFs), while elsewhere people might be demanding pylons so they can be connected to the electricity grid. Therefore, Dobson (2003) suggests that the criteria for sustainability should include, not only scientific testimony, but also values, since environmental standards are inherently normative.

Because of the inherently subjective nature of EJ, environmental justice academics and campaigners generally prefer not to use lists of indicators, subscribing to the idea that injustice is in the eye of the beholder. There is certainly scope for such frameworks to be misused. For example, the United States Environmental Protection Agency's (EPA) environmental justice framework is used 'to determine whether or not an environmental justice situation appears to exist or may be avoided altogether' (US EPA, 2004, p 73). Therefore, this tool could be used to deny claims of environmental injustice. It would clearly be unfair to establish my own definition of environmental justice and use that to judge the policies and practices of another country without taking into account local ideas of need and justice. For that reason, the Environmental Justice Indicator Framework developed here was devised to be easily open to influence and verification by ordinary citizens. At the same time, the EJI Framework links to recognised standards, thereby drawing on the expert, democratic and participatory ways of defining environmental justice.

I was convinced by the debates within the literature, as outlined above, that such indicators should be based on a wide, multi-faceted and interrelated notion of justice. Therefore, inclusion of procedural, distributive and substantive aspects was considered necessary for a meaningful examination of environmental justice. In addition, it was considered that the international, intergenerational and inter-species dimensions of EJ could be covered by reference to the Ecological Footprint.

The indicators for substantive justice were based on the current scientific understanding of environmental impacts on health, as well as the subjective criteria of the interviewees and informants. When deciding on the distributive justice indicators, I focused primarily on income as a distributional category, while including other social categories where relevant to the particular country. This decision was informed by Critical Theory, which acknowledges that there are multiple forms of power, including race, gender and sexual orientation, but regards economic factors as integral to other kinds of oppression (Kincheloe and McLaren, 1994). With regard to procedural justice, an extensive literature has examined this topic in a variety of organisational, legal and social settings. However, no indicators for procedural justice have formerly been developed in the context of environmental justice. The list of procedural environmental justice indicators developed for the Environmental Justice Indicator Framework was, therefore, based on a synthesis of ideas from a range of disciplines. These included the following theories, models and principles. Together, they advance important and distinct, though often overlapping and contradictory, criteria for fairness in communication, decision making and politics.

Early studies of procedural justice tended to focus on the criteria that citizens apply. The seminal work within the literature on citizens' assessments of procedural justice was conducted by Thibaut and Walker (1975), who found that people consider procedures fair according to the extent that they give them outcome and process control over decision making. Later, Leventhal (1980) expanded the list to include: consistent procedures, across persons and over time; lack of bias, self-interest or prejudice; availability of accurate information; 'correctability', that is, the possibility to modify and reverse decisions that reflect errors or oversights; representativeness of concerns, values and outlook of those affected by the decisions; and 'ethicality', that is, compatibility with the ethical and moral values that are held by the people affected by the decisions. Developing these ideas, Pops and Pavlak (1991) proposed a model for a fair decision-making process, including equality of access, neutrality, transparency, efficiency and right to appeal. In addition, emphasising the interpersonal aspects of decision making, Bies and Moag (1986) found that fairness judgements are affected by whether decision makers are truthful, treat people with respect, refrain from improper questions and justify decision outcomes.

The EJI Framework procedural justice indicators were also based on Arnstein's 'Ladder of Participation', a brilliant and simple model of degrees of citizen participation in decision making. Each rung of the ladder describes a level of participation, from 'non-participation' up to full managerial control (Figure 2.1).

Manipulation occurs when the public are 'educated', and participation is in fact a public relations vehicle for power holders. *Therapy* focuses on curing citizens of their personal problems, rather than addressing the issues that cause these problems. *Informing* citizens of proposals and their rights is a step up, but tends to be a one-way flow of information, often at a late stage. *Consultation*, if not combined with other modes of participation, offers no assurance that citizen concerns and ideas will be taken into account. At this stage participation would be measured by how many people come to meetings or answer a questionnaire. At the level of *placation*, citizens begin to have some degree of influence but it is quite tokenistic. This occurs, for example, when there are a few hand-picked 'worthy' residents on local partnerships. They are generally unaccountable to a constituency in the community and are usually outnumbered by power holders. Power holders reserve the right to judge the legitimacy or feasibility of the advice given by these token residents. At the level of *partnership*, power has been redistributed between citizens and elites and decision making is shared. It works most effectively when there is an organised power base in the community and

Figure 2.1: Arnstein's 'Ladder of Participation'

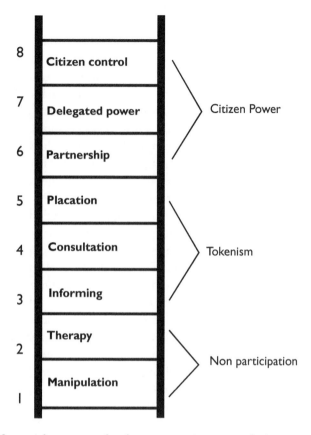

when there are financial resources for the community to pay their own technicians, lawyers and community organisers. *Delegated power* occurs when citizens achieve dominant decision-making authority, and *citizen control* when participants or residents can be in full charge of policy, programmes and management. Arnstein identifies the most significant blocks to participation as racism, paternalism and resistance to power redistribution. There are also 'inadequacies of the poor community's political socioeconomic infrastructure and knowledge-base' and difficulties in organising a representative and accountable citizens' group 'in the face of futility, alienation, and distrust' (Arnstein, 1969, p 3).

In establishing the indicators for the EJI Framework, I also used some ideas from deliberative democracy, a system of collective decision making based on inclusive public discussions (Dryzek, 1990; Mansbridge, 1992). Theorists of deliberative democracy argue that traditional representative democracies, which tend to limit citizen participation to voting, leaving actual governance to politicians, are very limited. They assert that democracy is realised through the experience of deliberation, which enables increased understanding and self-development. Ideally, Dryzek argues (1990), deliberative communication should be free of domination, strategising and self-deception; and all actors should be fully capable of making and questioning arguments. Related to this, Habermas's 'ideal speech situation' focuses on the interactions that would occur for procedures to be considered fair. According to his idea, there would be no restrictions, either inner (for example, prejudices) or outer (for example, ideologies, lack of time, insufficient knowledge), determining the outcome of discourse. Only the force of better argument would determine the outcome (Habermas, 1984). Several principles of Habermas's ideal speech situation are as follows: use of language that is mutually understood; truthfulness; sincerity; freedom and right of speech; right to question and give answers; and accountability.

However, Young (2002) cautions us with regard to attempting to put the ideals of deliberative democracy into practice in societies where injustices or social harms are based on structural inequalities. According to deliberative democracy principles, agreement should be reached on the basis of reason, rather than force. But, from an activist perspective, because it is not possible to bracket the influence of power differentials, deliberative processes would probably be biased toward more powerful agents. Swyngedouw (2007) also argues that the idea that consensus can be achieved through rational dialogue is problematic, since it leaves little space for dissent or politics. He considers that this marginalisation and denial of politics, which he refers to as the 'post-political condition', is bound up with the modern capitalist socioeconomic order, characterised by consensus, technocratic management and problem solving. Scientific knowledge plays a role in this. By being portrayed as a superior, objective, value-free and factual form of knowledge, it limits the possibility of debate and decision making based on values, experience and needs (Latour, 2004). Science is also often constrained by the availability of research funding, which generally reflects the interests of elite groups. For example, Faber (2008) describes how corporate interests, working through think-tanks, lobbyists and public relations firms, have influenced the production and evaluation of environmental science in the US. Therefore, it might be considered necessary to engage in oppositional activity (picketing, demonstrations, occupations, boycotts and so on), rather than to attempt to negotiate with those who benefit from existing power structures. This use of power is justified on the grounds that the activist is committed to a universalist, rather than partisan, cause. As Young (2002) argued, respectful argument in formal meetings is fine in the ideal world that the deliberative democrat theorises, but, under circumstances of structural inequality, citizens should be protesting outside these meetings.

Further indicators of procedural environmental justice for the EJI Framework were derived from participatory politics (parpolity), which proposes practical ideas as to how decision making could be organised. It builds on the ideas of participatory economics (parecon), and the two (parecon and parpolity) are envisioned as running alongside each other (Shalom, 2005). Parecon is a proposed economic system that uses participatory decision making to guide the production, consumption and allocation of resources. It has been described as an anarchistic economic vision, and an alternative to capitalist or socialist economic structures (see Albert, 2003; Hahnel, 2004; 2005). Parpolitics is based on the values of freedom, self-management, justice, solidarity and tolerance (Shalom, 2005). The main decision-making principle is that every person should have a say in a decision, proportionate to the degree to which she or he is affected by that decision. This is clearly not easily definable but would, presumably, be worked out through these deliberative bodies. There would be a system of nested councils, which would include every adult member of a given society. Decisions would be achieved either through consensus, majority vote or through other means compatible with the principle. There would be a minimum of hierarchy and a maximum of transparency. The features of such a system would also include liberty without intruding on others' desires; equal treatment; participation to help define and create preferences; promotion of cooperation and diversity; a diverse media; and rotation and sharing of jobs so that everyone develops their highest level of political efficacy (Shalom, 2005).

With regard to the environment, parpolity allows people in different regions to choose different trade-offs between less pollution and more consumption or development. This would seem to encourage worse environmental distributive justice through a 'race to the bottom'. However, Hahnel (2004) argues that it would not, since parpolity assumes that there are no significant differences in income and wealth between communities, so that there will be no poverty-stricken local communities who acquiesce to the hosting of unsafe toxic waste because they are desperate for income. Thus, parpolity intends to create an equal society, but also needs an equal society in order to function properly.

The EJI Framework also incorporated two existing environmental process mechanisms – the Aarhus Convention and the Precautionary

Principle. The UN Economic Commission for Europe (UNECE) Aarhus Convention, which came into effect in 2001, states:

> in order to contribute to the protection of the right of every person of present and future generations to live in an environment adequate to his or her health and well-being, each party shall guarantee the rights of access to information, public participation in decision making and access to justice in environmental matters in accordance with the provisions of this Convention. (UNECE, 1998, Article 1)

The provision on 'access to information' not only entails passive obligations on behalf of the public authorities to hand out available information upon request but also obliges governments to actively disclose and disseminate environmental information. The Convention also states that information must be presented in an easy-to-digest format. There are also detailed requirements for public participation (Articles 6, 7 and 8) at all levels of decision making, creating an obligation on decision makers to ensure the 'early involvement' of the public 'at the appropriate stage, and while options are still open', when consulting on environmental matters. Access to legal justice must be granted where a person deems that his/her rights concerning information or participation have not been respected. However, the need for financial resources makes the costs of legal actions one of the most important barriers to environmental justice (Capacity Global, 2007). This underlines the need for free access to legal redress.

The Precautionary Principle, another useful mechanism, is defined in Principle 15 of the Rio Declaration (1992) in the following way:

> Where there are threats of serious or irreversible damage, lack of full scientific certainty should not be used as a reason for postponing cost-effective measures to prevent environmental degradation. (UNEP, 1992)

According to this principle, reasonable evidence of potential damage, rather than absolute scientific proof, would be enough to secure cost-effective environmental protection. This shifts the burden of proof that an activity is not harmful onto those taking the potentially problematic action. It implies that there is a social responsibility to protect the public from exposure to environmental harm. However, clearly, the words 'cost-effective' are problematic here in terms of justice, as justice requires doing what is 'right' and 'fair', which may, or may not be, cost-effective. In practice the principle can be interpreted strongly or weakly. A strong precaution requires regulation whenever there is a possible risk to health, safety or the environment, even if the evidence is speculative and even if the economic costs are high (for example, as in the Wingspread Consensus Statement, see SEHN, 1998).

Therefore, the above ideas have formed the basis for the substantive, distributional and procedural elements of the EJI Framework. In addition to this, the Ecological Footprint was used as a proxy indicator for intergenerational, inter-species and international environmental justice (see Table 2.1) (for further discussion on the development and use of the EJI Framework, see Appendix 3). In the following chapters, the complete EJI Framework has been applied to the seven countries selected so as to build a greater understanding of the patterns and causes of environmental injustice as well as a stronger conception of what actions are required to unravel these injustices.

Notes

[1] For example, the 1932 Kinder Scout trespass in the UK, which led to the establishment of National Parks, long-distance footpaths and the Countryside and Rights of Way Act 2000.

[2] Communitarians, for example, argue that justice cannot be absolutely defined because it depends on the cultural context and the specific issue (Sandel, 1982). Libertarians, however, hold that the market is inherently just, allocating resources in the optimal way (Nozick, 1974; Hayek, 1976).

[3] Some authors use the term 'substantive' as an alternative to the term 'distributive', but 'substantive' is used here to refer to the quality of the environment, and 'distributive' is used to refer to disparities in environments.

[4] My use of the term 'poor' corresponds with Townsend's idea of relative deprivation, in which he states that 'People can be said to be deprived if they lack the types of diet, clothing, housing, household facilities and fuel and environmental, educational, working and social conditions, activities and facilities which are customary, or at least widely encouraged and approved, in the societies to which they belong' (Townsend, 1987, p 126).

Table 2.1: The Environmental Justice Indicator Framework

Substantive justice indicators Universal access to sanitation Universal access to adequate waste disposal Universal access to safe drinking water Universal access to adequate and sufficient food and nutrition Universal access to clean air Universal access to adequate and safe transport Universal access to green space for recreation and leisure Universal access to sufficient energy for cooking and heating Adequate housing for all Safe working and living environments for all Universal protection from environmental disruptions (for example, hurricanes, flooding) Universal protection from potentially hazardous substances: harmful chemicals, genetically modified organisms (GMOs), radiation, electric and magnetic fields (EMFs)
Distributive justice indicators Equal access to sanitation Equal access to adequate waste disposal Equal access to safe drinking water Equal access to adequate and sufficient food and nutrition Equal access to clean air Equal access to adequate and safe transport Equal access to green space for recreation and leisure Equal access to sufficient energy for cooking and heating Equally adequate housing for all Equally safe working and living environments for all Equal protection from environmental disruptions (for example, hurricanes, flooding) Equal protection from potentially hazardous substances: harmful chemicals, GMOs, radiation, EMFs
Procedural justice indicators All parties that were affected by environmental decisions were invited to contribute to the decision-making process The relevant rules and procedures were applied consistently, with regard to different people and at different times Those affected received accurate and accessible information – that is, timely, honest, easy to understand, digestible and easily available A fair outcome resulted from the process, in terms of substantial and distributional EJ There was authentic, accessible and honest communication All parties were accountable, that is, responsible to answer for their actions and decisions and to remedy them if necessary All parties would have access to sufficient material resources to enable them to participate on an equal footing Those affected were included in all stages of decision making Sufficient skills and personal resources have been available for those affected to participate on an equal basis All participants in the environmental decision-making process were treated with equal respect and value All environmental decisions were made publicly The environmental decision-making process was open to all questions and alternatives All affected had an equal right and an equal chance to express their point of view There was a lack of external coercion Decision making was deliberative, that is, free from any authority of prior norms or requirements Freedom of association Right to peaceful protest Those affected had control of the outcome of decisions (ideally, proportional to how much they would be affected) Consensus decision making was carried out, whenever this was practical Use of a strong precautionary principle Free access to legal redress
International, intergenerational and inter-species indicator The above criteria have not been met through undermining the EJ of other species, nations and generations, as evidenced by the Ecological Footprint

THREE

The causes of environmental injustice

The environmental justice literature broadly offers five competing explanations for environmental injustice: discrimination; market dynamics; lack of citizen power; industrialisation; and capitalism. The wider environmental literature, which corresponds to the 'substantive' aspect of environmental justice, emphasises some of the same themes and, in addition, includes a further two causal themes, those of 'individual behaviour or life-styles' and 'culture'. This chapter outlines the debates relating to each of these themes but focuses on capitalism, which, I argue, is a root determinant of environmental injustice.

Discrimination

'Discrimination', on the basis of income or race, is the explanation for environmental injustice favoured by black and other minority ethnic (BME) communities in the US (Bullard, 1983, 1994a; Bullard et al, 2007). According to this view, discrimination can be inferred from studies that show the socio-spatial correlation between particular demographic groups and the location of toxic facilities, without the necessity to prove discriminatory intent. However, some analysts argue that the studies which support this view only provide snapshot analyses and do not look at the social make-up of the neighbourhood when the facility was first established. Therefore, they argue, such correlations do not necessarily signify discriminatory intent, and, therefore, more direct evidence of intent is required (for example, Been, 1994; Hamilton, 1995).

It is certainly difficult to find evidence of overt discriminatory decision making with regard to the location of toxic facilities or access to environmental goods. This may be because discriminatory intent would, in most circumstances, be perceived as immoral or deemed to be illegal, and so reports of this may remain hidden. Polluting industries have repeatedly stressed that their siting decisions are not based on the demographic make-up of the proposed location, and can almost always offer some alternative justification for their decisions (Kiniyalocts, 2000). However, there has been some documented evidence of discriminatory decision making where industry has intentionally located in low-income or minority ethnic communities (for example, Viereck, 1993; Center, 1996). For example, discriminatory intent is illustrated in the following excerpt from a US nuclear waste negotiator's speech to an indigenous conference:

> Because of the Indian's great care and regard for nature's resources, Indians are the logical people to care for nuclear waste. Radioactive materials have half-lives of thousands of years [and] it is the Native American Culture and perspective that is best designed to correctly consider and balance the benefits and the burdens (1991, cited in Viereck, 1993).

At an international level, a classic example of discriminatory intent is apparent in the following, now infamous, 1991 memo by Lawrence Summers, then Chief Economist of the World Bank (later to become United States Secretary of the Treasury in 1999):

> Just between you and me, shouldn't the World Bank be encouraging MORE migration of the dirty industries to the LDCs [Less Developed Countries]? ... The demand for a clean environment for aesthetic and health reasons is likely to have very high income elasticity. The concern over an agent that causes a one in a million change in the odds of prostate cancer is obviously going to be much higher in a country where people survive to get prostate cancer than in a country where under-5 mortality is 200 per thousand. (Summers, 1991, cited in Pellow, 2007, p 9)

However, discrimination can also occur without deliberate intent, such as through a lack of understanding of equalities issues, often embedded in historic, cultural and institutionalised practices. For example, one US study shows that Environmental Protection Agency managers were reluctant to positively target environmental justice communities because they were concerned that they should treat all communities the same, believing that equal treatment is the way to avoid racism (Holifield, 2004). Institutional discrimination includes when environmental policies distribute the costs of controls in a regressive pattern, imposing disproportionate costs on those with lower incomes. As will be discussed in Chapter Six, a major element of the UK government's low-carbon energy policy does just that, involving an increase in energy bills that will have a proportionately much higher impact on poorer people.

In general, institutional racism, sexism, classism, disablism, ageism and so on, inherent in wider society, provide the basis for environmental injustice. Distributive environmental injustice in the US, for example, could not occur without housing segregation on the basis of race, often a result of the institutional discrimination of letting agencies, housing authorities, mortgage lenders and so on, though economic inequality and self-segregation also underpin the pattern (Fosset and Warren, 2005).

However, though discrimination can evidently be a cause of environmental injustice, focusing only on individual acts of intentional discrimination ignores the structural factors that create wealth and status inequalities. For example, low income reduces choices about where to live or which jobs to take, so that it can become impossible to avoid toxic facilities, whether located on the basis of discriminatory intent or not. This links to the issue of 'market dynamics', the focus of the next section.

Market dynamics

Neoclassical economic critiques of environmental justice, such as those offered by Been (1994) and by Lambert and Boerner (1997), contend that correlations of black and other minority ethnic communities with LULUs (locally unwanted land uses) are the result of 'market efficiency'. From this position, disparate environmental burdens originate from supply-and-demand market forces, with rational actors weighing up costs and benefits. Governments and corporate actors are seen to be simply making economic decisions, rather than intentionally discriminating. The rational firm seeks to lower costs and will locate to poor areas because the land is cheaper. Householders who do not like a new polluting facility will move away if they can afford to. Diminished willingness to move into the area will mean that property prices decline, making the area affordable to those on low incomes, often black and minority ethnic (BME) groups, who will then move in (Been, 1994; Lambert and Boerner, 1997). This 'move-in' hypothesis is well illustrated by Been's study of landfills in Houston (Been, 1994). She found that, when the sites were first established, there was little evidence of a disproportionate number of these sites being placed in BME communities. Rather, the BME community began to form after the construction of the waste sites, suggesting that it is the dynamics of the housing market that leads to the pattern, rather than the process of corporate or governmental decision making.

However, Been's study has since been criticised on the grounds that it omitted some of the landfills and did not take into account the concentration of BME populations living in the most toxic areas that were nearest to the site (Bullard, 1994b). In general, research on discrimination versus move-in shows mixed findings, though slightly favouring the discrimination argument. While Lambert and Boerner (1997) also found evidence of low-income and BME move-in, Pastor et al (2001) found that disproportionate siting decisions mattered more than housing-market dynamics. Other studies found there was more likelihood of out-migration by BME groups after toxic facilities were located in their communities, or a mix of in and out migration in the same area (Pastor et al, 2001; Talih and Fricker, 2002). Oakes et al (1996), however, found that neither of these processes existed in their study.

However, as with the discrimination argument, there seems to be a key element missing in the explanations that point to the rationale of the market, since they fail to recognise the larger societal context that limits individual choices. People on low incomes, including many BME people, find their mobility limited through financial constraints that link to educational and employment disadvantage, as well as urban segregation and housing discrimination. Market-efficiency explanations de-contextualise and depoliticise individual decisions. Therefore, it is important to look at social conditions, rather than just individual decisions, and to understand how these constrain individual choices.

Lack of citizen power

Some analysts argue that the most important reason for environmental injustice is the issue of economic, political and social powerlessness (for example, Boyce, 2001; Pastor et al, 2001; Berry, 2003). Because a powerless community is less able to defend itself, it becomes host to unwanted facilities and fails to preserve or gain environmental resources. Industry and government are aware that many communities will actively oppose the placing of polluting facilities in their locality, so, in order to avoid delay and expense, they seek to avoid the communities that are the most capable of mounting an effective opposition, that is, those with abundant resources and political power. Low-income and BME communities are an easier target because they are not well represented in the decision-making structures and have fewer resources, so, unlike their wealthier counterparts, they cannot afford to employ lawyers, lobbyists and experts to support their cause. Low-income and BME communities opposing toxic facilities are almost always less powerful than the governments and companies they oppose. Such groups tend to be less involved in political processes and under-represented on governing bodies, and so relatively deprived of information and the ability to influence decisions (Kiniyalocts, 2000). Environmental disparities can occur when corporations and governments intentionally take advantage of this situation, or when they merely follow the path of least resistance in their decision making.

Low-income communities are economically powerless, not only in the sense that they struggle to find sufficient economic resources to defend themselves, but also because they may be more in need of any economic benefits that the toxic industries claim to bring. These communities are often desperate for jobs, revenue or facilities and are more likely to accept a toxic facility, regardless of its implications. Because of the threat of unemployment, or, sometimes, their legal status, many low-waged and minority groups are forced to choose between unemployment and a job that may threaten their health, their families' health and the health of their community. The pressure faced by poor communities to accept hazardous industries into their midst has been described as 'environmental blackmail' (Bullard, 1992). Bullard and Johnson (2000) have shown that, at least in the US, this economic inducement is often false, as there is frequently little or no correlation between new industrial plants in the community and more jobs for nearby residents. Furthermore, compensation schemes that, on the surface, offer the possibility of benefiting poor communities may mean an increase in the siting of toxic facilities in these areas. When there is a desperate need for income, offers of compensation can weaken or divide resistance (Bailey et al, 1993). Therefore, in the US, for example, indigenous communities have often accepted toxic or radioactive waste on their reservations in order to offset poverty (Churchill and La Duke, 1992; Gedicks, 1993), though there has also been much dissent among these groups (Goldtooth, 1995). Similarly, in the Republic of Korea, communities initially united in opposition to toxic developments in their locality have eventually been divided by such payments, enabling the contested development to go ahead anyway (Lee, 2009; see Chapter Five).

Power differentials do, then, seem to explain environmental injustices. However, the literature that focuses on how unequal power enables environmental injustice often does not acknowledge that these relationships are integral to the functioning of a capitalist system. While poor people are often excluded from environmental decision making, corporate economic interests are usually very well represented. Because of the relative power of the companies, the issues being debated come to focus on a very narrow set of concerns, in particular, economic growth and corporate freedom. This increase in corporate power amplifies injustices because, unlike the state, the corporations have no remit to work on behalf of citizens.

Beck (1999) argues that the extreme wealth of large corporations and the ease with which they have been able to relocate their operations has led to a shift in power from the nation-state to corporations. Others suggest that there has not been a loss of state power but, rather, a blurring of boundaries between the state and corporations (for example, Pellow, 2007). Lake and Disch (1992) report the problematic ways in which the state (both national and local) mediates between the polluting businesses and the communities that receive the pollution. The state controls the agenda in three ways. It controls the timetable, often only allowing reaction to decisions that have already been made. It restricts the debate to the issue of siting, ensuring that public opinion can be expressed only in terms of self-interested local opposition. Lastly, it allows argument over technical issues only, excluding principles and emotions. Sometimes, seemingly inclusive, government participation policies may be disguised attempts to control communities and to legitimate decisions that have already been made. Business interests will often cooperate with politicians and government officials, so forming a 'hegemonic bloc'. Structurally weak groups tend to be excluded from this bloc unless they are willing to adopt a non-critical view of economic growth or have something of economic value, for example, land rights.

This imbalance of power might be partially offset by the support of environmental campaign groups. However, it is often the case that mainstream environmental NGOs do not focus on the issues that are important to poor communities. At the same time, people in deprived areas do not join environmental organisations because of their lack of local presence and insufficient provision of accessible information (Burningham and Thrush, 2001).

However, though poor and low-income groups lack power in terms of their structural positions and may be manipulated, they have been able to enforce positive change through determination, coalition building and solidarity, as this book will describe. Heightened global awareness of environmental pollution, risk and justice, as well as easier access to support and resources through modern communication systems, may have resulted in enhanced social and political power for local communities. In some cases, communities have exercised sufficient power to delay or block corporate and government decisions. For example, Pellow and Brulle (2005) note the successes of the US environmental justice movement at a local level in shutting down major incinerators and landfills; preventing polluting operations from being built or expanding; and relocating residents from polluted areas. Even more dramatically, mass protests in Bolivia between 2000 and 2005 over the privatisation of water and hydrocarbons led to reversal of these policies, two presidential resignations and the election of a new government that prioritises national control over natural resources (see Chapter Nine).

Industrialisation

Another factor that is considered to be a cause of environmental injustice is industrialisation. It is associated with extensive environmental degradation, as well as threats to human health from occupational hazards and waste production. These problems are now most evident in rapidly industrialising countries like China but are, to some extent, analogous to those of earlier industrialisations, such as that of early industrial Europe. There is a major difference, though, in that the industrialisation of Europe spanned nearly 200 years; whereas recent industrialisations have meant undergoing similar changes in just a couple of decades. Industrial wastes are also now more varied, more noxious and more difficult to dispose of or decompose (as in, for example, e-waste) (UNEP, 2004).

However, industrialisation is also widely perceived to be a positive process, the driver of economic growth and the provider of many social benefits, including electricity, heating, jobs, better diets and an overall improved standard of living and material progress. Consequently, controlling industrial emissions, or resisting industrialisation, can be seen to interfere with economic development and greater well-being. Industrialisation is viewed as a phase for poorer countries or localities to pass through, and it is assumed that the attendant problems must be tolerated because 'the economy needs' the risky production processes. As a result, there are numerous examples, as described later in this book, where governments have given approval for toxic installations or harmful developments on the basis that they would create jobs, enable economic growth and improve general well-being. In the context of industrialisation, environmentalism can be perceived to be a threat. This thinking was evident in the drawing up of Cuba's first framework environmental law, for example, where there were different perspectives within the government about the impact of the proposed legislation on economic activity, with some taking the position that the laws would obstruct economic development, claiming that 'environmental protection is a game for the rich' (Houck, 2000, p 18). From this perspective, activists who are against industrial developments at a local level are accused of being 'NIMBYS', selfish parochialists who are preventing the attainment of societal goals.

The assumption is that industrialisation equals development and development equals progress. However, research casts doubt on the idea that there is a simple relationship between industrialisation, development and progress. For example, though the Industrial Revolution in the UK generally brought immense wealth for some, there were social costs, not least in terms of the impact on health. One indicator of this is that the first two generations of adults who lived during that period lost nearly an inch in height (Steckel and Floud, 1997). More recent rapid industrialisation tells a similar story. For example, the Republic of Korea and China's recent rapid industrialisations, though bringing some obvious benefits, have not clearly improved social and environmental conditions overall (see Chapters Five and Eight).

In particular, there is some debate over whether industrialisation really creates jobs, since it seems simultaneously to destroy them. In the UK, for example, when employment in manufacturing was declining in the 1980s, manufacturing output increased, indicating that technology was taking over the production output (Rumberger, 1984). Often, it seems, 'the productivity index is really an automation index' (Grossman and Daneker, 1977, p 2), because technology is replacing jobs. Neither the theoretical nor the empirical literature has been able to resolve this issue, but it seems that different technologies have different effects at different times. For example, during the industrialisation of Europe, when technology displaced labour in certain occupations and industries it often created economic growth, so that there were enough jobs in other sectors of the economy to offset those lost. However, technologically driven increases in productivity have since created crises of over-production that have led to a reduction in employment. Therefore, industrial and technological progress can exacerbate the plight of poor and marginalised people because they must compete more frantically for scarcer jobs.

In any case, industrialisation is not inherently necessary for the creation of jobs. We could employ people in many more necessary jobs that would not harm the environment, such as in healthcare (especially that which uses natural medicine), teaching (enabling smaller class sizes), social care, dance and fitness training, arts and culture and so on. All these jobs are labour intensive, satisfying to do and useful, yet they are often limited under capitalism because they do not create sufficient profit. For example, a coalition of leading UK charities have recently published research showing that a third of disabled people in England aren't now getting enough support with their basic needs like washing, dressing or eating because of insufficient funding to employ the workers required (Brawn et al, 2013).

Moreover, as an explanation for environmental injustice, while industrialisation may account for the substantive aspect of the problem, it does not explain distributional patterns. These patterns appear to be better explained in terms of the combination of capitalism and industrialisation, as some analysts propose (for example, Beck 1992; Lake, 1993; Schnaiberg and Gould, 2000; Pellow, 2002; 2007). From this perspective, it is argued, industrial facilities:

> are needed not by society but rather by capital, and by a state striving to reproduce the capital–labor relationship … the local protectionism characterized as NIMBY represents a barrier not to societal goals but to the goals of capital (Lake, 1993).

Therefore, industrialisation appears to contribute to environmental injustice, but is often driven by the requirements of capital.

Individual behaviour or life-style

The dominant thrust of much mainstream environmental discourse, especially in relation to climate change, has been to encourage individual consumers to change their behaviour. According to this perspective, consumer choice is seen to be the reason for the production of excessive and toxic goods, and a bottom-up reform of these choices is the way to encourage corporate producers to change. Therefore, individuals are encouraged to engage either in 'green consumption' or in 'voluntary simplicity', that is, to consume differently or to reduce consumption and live more simply. Green consumption has taken off massively in the last decade with, for example, rocketing sales of ecological light bulbs, organic food and eco-travel. Yet, even if consumers do manage to create sufficient pressure that company owners and managers decide they would be willing to 'green' their production processes, they may not necessarily be able to do so if this would prevent them making a profit. Industry has been quick to establish and/or sign up to a number of voluntary environmental codes, such as the UN's Global Compact, and voluntary standards, such as ISO 14000. However, though they may have tried to be greener and sometimes gone 'beyond compliance', these companies have only generally been able to make marginal improvements. It is difficult for corporations to make socially and ecologically rational decisions, as they must act according to company interests, whether or not these coincide with the interests of the environment or wider society. Some can do no more than present a green façade, 'green washing' their business by using the language of environmentalism without the corresponding action (Parr, 2009). Where companies do actually adopt cleaner production methods, it is often beside the point, since the product itself is toxic, harmful or unnecessary, not the process of producing it. For example, a Swedish manufacturing company is now marketing lead-free 'green' bullets (Nammo, 2012) for military use.

Therefore, producers' choices are constrained by capitalism. Similarly, consumer options are limited. The choices that are available tend to be restricted to those that enable profit to continue while reducing individual guilt, such as replacing an old car with a new 'green' one. Yet, so-called 'green cars' are a marketing invention, since electric/hybrid vehicles, while using less energy, cause other ecological problems related to their production. A recent study found that, compared to petrol or diesel-fuelled cars, electric cars 'exhibit the potential for significant increases in human toxicity, freshwater eco-toxicity, freshwater eutrophication, and metal depletion impacts, largely emanating from the vehicle supply chain' (Hawkins et al, 2013). As in this case, virtuous acts of consumerism can actually create more environmental problems than they solve.

Voluntary simplicity, as an alternative to 'shopping our way to sustainability' (Szaz, 2007), is also problematic. If we 'reject consumerism' within a capitalist economy, where most jobs are linked to consumer sales and, therefore, depend on consumption, it seems likely that unemployment will soar. Therefore, not only capitalists, but also workers and governments, are locked into the consumption drive in order to maintain profits, jobs and tax revenues.

Moreover, these individualistic approaches to the environmental crises tend to mask the bigger environmental harms such as unsustainable agricultural, transport, housing and health policies; and to encourage an overemphasis on individual action, at the expense of systemic or regulatory action. The individualistic emphasis also implies that everyone has the same ability to carry out these virtuous acts, even though many people do not have sufficient income to engage in green consumerism or sufficient time to engage in some acts of 'voluntary simplicity', such as growing their own food. At the same time, these ideas make invisible the fact that some individuals are more responsible for environmental harm than others and that not everyone equally suffers the consequences of these harms.

Because low-income groups in the UK are less able to engage in green consumerism, some have concluded that these groups are not concerned about the environment. This is often explained in terms of the 'post-material values thesis' (Inglehart, 1990), which suggests that poorer people are too preoccupied with meeting their basic needs for food, warmth and security to be able to think about, or be active on, environmental issues. However, there is now a growing body of evidence that is challenging this view, suggesting that income levels make little difference to people's concern about environmental issues (for example, Jones and Dunlap, 1992; Fairbrother, 2012). Rather than having more important things to worry about, poor people and poor countries prioritise environmental protection as much as do their wealthier counterparts.

Hence, it does not seem very useful to consider environmental injustice as resulting from individual behaviour choices, since, in many cases, such choices are very limited, and more limited for some than others.

Culture

The literature on environmental justice barely touches on the role of culture, though this is a key theme in the more general environmental literature. Here I focus on discourses (that is, written and spoken communication) in order to understand culture. There are a number of particularly pervasive discourses that are detrimental to the achievement of environmental justice. I call these Damaging Hegemonic Environmental Discourses (DHEDs). They are important because they directly affect the attitudes, beliefs and values of the general public. It is vital that public opinion supports environmental justice – or at least, does not undermine it – because, to some extent, public opinion does influence policy makers (Johnson et al, 2005; Franzen and Meyer, 2010). DHEDs undermine public support for EJ through disseminating and maintaining the following interconnected ideas, assumptions and values:

1. There is a linear rationality to the universe.
2. Complex, modern or 'high' technology is inherently preferable to more basic or traditional technology.
3. The environment is, or can be, separate from humans.
4. The environment is of minimal importance for human health.
5. Growth is 'good' and/or 'necessary'.
6. The environment needs to be owned and controlled.

Each of these DHEDs will now be briefly outlined to explain how it might contribute to environmental injustice.

DHED 1: There is a linear rationality to the universe

This DHED assumes a type of linear rationality that does not take into account the complexity of the natural world and fails to understand or respect the interconnectedness of ecosystems. Such assumptions are evident in the technical fixes that are now being proposed by some scientists and corporate bodies to address the environmental crises. These proposals to 'solve' the 'problem' of the Earth's limits are sometimes wildly adventurous, though given a façade of credibility and respectability through complicated scientific modelling. For example, the various geoengineering projects that are now being developed to deliberately alter the earth's temperature in order to combat climate change are not based on full consideration of the consequences. Numerous scientists are deeply concerned about this and have advised caution. The ETC group (2010), for example, strongly recommends a moratorium on geoengineering, warning:

> The geoengineering suite of technologies affects outer space, the atmosphere, the land, the oceans and fresh water bodies, the weather, the production of food, the protection of health and livelihoods, and national sovereignty. It entails risks that we know about and many more that we cannot yet predict. Until there has been a full debate on the course all countries wish to go, there must be a moratorium on all geoengineering activities outside the laboratory. Anything else is folly, putting the planet and its peoples at tremendous and unjustifiable risk. (ETC, 2010, p 40)

As well as encouraging the notion that the vital work of reducing carbon emissions may be unnecessary, such an approach appears to disregard the complexity and interconnectedness of the natural world that makes it impossible to predict the impacts of radically manipulating the global atmosphere or oceans. Though justified by a Damaging Hegemonic Environmental Discourse, there are economic incentives behind such projects, however. Unlike social policies to address environmental issues, specific technical fixes are amenable to marketing and can reap large financial rewards. This economic motivation was revealed when a UK geoengineering experiment, part of the Stratospheric Particle

Injection for Climate Engineering (SPICE) project, was postponed in 2012 because of a disagreement over patents.

DHED 2: Complex, modern or 'high' technology is inherently preferable to more basic or traditional technology

Some high technologies may be useful and appropriate, but others appear to be pursued, however socially and environmentally risky, on the assumption that new and complex technology must inherently be better than traditional or basic approaches. Hence, appropriate technologies (ATs) that fit local conditions and are easily and economically utilised from readily available resources have struggled to take off, despite their potential to improve millions of lives around the world with minimal environmental impact (Zelenika and Pearce, 2011). Research and development investments in AT have declined over the decades relative to that in high technology, largely because they are viewed as 'inferior', a poor person's technology, only be used for an interim period until a more high-tech solution can be afforded.

DHED 3: The environment is, or can be, separate from humans

The compartmentalisation of the human and environmental realms is manifest throughout academia and government agencies around the world, denying or minimising the interrelationships between humans and the ecological system as a whole. This division is embedded in Western culture, which has a long history of dualistic thought that some trace to the Greek philosophers and the Judaeo-Christian tradition. Such ideas promoted a dualistic severance from nature, with human beings placed above because they possess mind and soul, and nature situated below, existing only to serve human needs. Christianity, in particular, promulgated the conviction that humans, being made in God's image, are superior creatures. The biblical concept of dominion appears to give divine authorisation for the exploitation of nature. However, these philosophies and sets of beliefs are complex, leaving much scope for interpretation. For example, the Greek philosophers also conceived of a world soul that included all nature, and many Christians argue that 'dominion' does not mean domination, but should be interpreted as care and stewardship. Hence, it is particular interpretations of Western philosophies, those that divide us from and denigrate nature, that have been fostered. As a result of this division, it has been possible to demonise environmentalism as a philosophy that does not care about people and that holds up or prevents development.

The same arguments are made against environmentalists as against those who pointed out in the 1980s that smoking was bad for health; that is, that jobs and business would be affected by public acceptance of these ideas. The fact that we need to care for the environment in order to care for ourselves has been obscured. Even the sustainable development concept did not manage to break down this compartmentalisation. A recent Report of the High-Level Panel of Eminent Persons on the Post-2015 Development Agenda admitted that:

> the MDGs [Millennium Development Goals] fell short by not integrating the economic, social, and environmental aspects of sustainable development as envisaged in the Millennium Declaration, and by not addressing the need to promote sustainable patterns of consumption and production. The result was that environment and development were never properly brought together. People were working hard – but often separately – on interlinked problems. (UN, 2013, p 7)

This perceived division between humans and nature may have contributed to the lack of unity between mainstream environmental organisations and organisations that mobilise for social justice, such as trade unions. Though 20 years ago, in the Agenda 21 proposals from the 1992 Rio Earth Summit, trade unions highlighted how environmental issues are bound up with health and safety issues and how workers should be involved in decision making on sustainable development, in the work environment and the production process there has been little subsequent interaction between trade unions and environmental organisations (Rathzel and Uzzell, 2011).

Fortunately, though, this DHED is now being challenged at many levels. For example, a number of academics, such as Tony Fitzpatrick (2011; 2014) and Ian Gough (2013), are now writing on environmental issues from within the field of social policy. In addition, social movements, particularly indigenous groups of the South, have been very active in proposing counter-hegemonic environmental discourses that emphasise the reciprocal relationship between humans and nature.

DHED 4: The environment is of minimal importance for human health

Linked to the assumption that humans are separate from nature, is the belief that the environment is of minimal importance with regard to human health. This is manifest in public health discourse that continually plays down the importance of the environment. For example, at a UK conference, eminent academic and former health policy advisor to the New Labour government, Professor Julian Le Grand, claimed that the environment influenced only 3% of health outcomes, way below the impact of personal behaviour choices (Le Grand, 2012). To some extent this perception is understandable, because it is often difficult to 'prove' the relationship because specific details, such as levels of exposure, for example, are often uncertain or unknown as a result both of a lack of detailed monitoring and of inevitable variations within population groups. Overall, long latency times, the effects of cumulative exposure to toxins, and multiple exposures that could act synergistically, all make it difficult to unravel associations between environmental degradation and health. However, as was explained at the beginning of this book, the evidence, taken overall, shows that there is a major link between the environment and health. Environmental factors can degrade health, both directly, by exposing people to harmful agents, and indirectly, by disrupting the ecosystems that sustain life. The perceived division between the environment and health has been a major block for environmental justice campaigners, who struggle to convince others of the impacts of toxic facilities and commodities on their health. Hence, Rachel Carson, author of *Silent Spring* and a prominent early Western environmentalist who emphasised the link between synthetic chemicals and human health problems, was, for many years, accused of apocalyptic fear mongering (Sideris, 2012).

DHED 5: Economic growth is 'good' and/or 'necessary'

Over 20 years ago, 1,700 of the world's leading scientists, including the majority of Nobel laureates in the sciences, issued an appeal that said:

> The earth is finite. Its ability to absorb wastes and destructive effluent is finite. Its ability to provide food and energy is finite. Its ability to provide for growing numbers of people is finite. And we are fast approaching many of the earth's limits. Current economic practices which damage the environment, in both developed and underdeveloped nations, cannot be continued without the risk that vital global systems will be damaged beyond repair ... The developed nations are the largest polluters in the world today. They must greatly reduce their over-consumption,

if we are to reduce pressures on resources and the global environment. (Union of Concerned Scientists, 1992)

Yet, at climate change negotiations from Kyoto to Cancun, governments have all made it clear that they do not want to sacrifice growth for the environment. They argue that the two are compatible and even that growth will ultimately be good for the environment. This notion is often justified with reference to the 'Environmental Kuznet's Curve' (EKC) thesis. This predicts that, though pollution increases as a poor country becomes wealthier, after a certain point, as more resources become available for environmental improvement, there is a reversal of this trend, leading to an inverted U-shaped curve of environmental degradation over time. There is some evidence for this, in that rising gross domestic product (GDP) levels in already affluent countries have been accompanied by reduced emissions of certain pollutants (notably nitrogen dioxide, carbon monoxide and sulphur dioxide) at a local scale (Grossman and Krueger, 1995). However, for a number of other environmental impacts, the evidence is fragile or contradicts the hypothesis, for example, with regard to resource use (Spangenberg, 2001; Kumar and Aggarwal, 2003); biodiversity (Dietz, 2000); energy use; and carbon dioxide emissions (Azomahou and Van Phu, 2001; Galeotti et al, 2006). In addition, some studies indicate that, in the longer term, the EKC tends to be N-shaped instead of the inverted U-shape (Friedl and Getzner, 2003; Martinez-Zarzoso and Bengochea-Morancho, 2004). It seems that pollution levels increase as a country becomes less poor, then begin to decrease, but rise again with greater wealth, so that total pollution emissions tend to rise with increasing income, rather than to follow the predicted inverted U-shaped curve (Stern, 2004). It is misleading, in any case, to plot a decline in the emissions of a specific pollutant as wealth increases, as there may have been a change in technology, resulting in a switch to a different kind of pollutant. Moreover, reduced emission levels in wealthier countries are likely to be a result of outsourcing polluting industries to poorer countries.

It is also argued that, even if growth is not good for the environment as a whole, it is necessary because it contributes to human well-being and reduces poverty. Deaton's (2008) analysis of Gallup World Poll data for 123 countries provides some key evidence that growth enhances well-being, concluding that each doubling of GDP is associated with a constant increase in life satisfaction. However, Easterlin (2013), in a separate study that looked at subjective feelings of well-being over time, found that although in the very short-term well-being may increase with growth, in the longer term, for rich, poor, and transition countries, whether pooled or analysed separately, there is no evidence that a higher growth rate increases the rate of improvement in life satisfaction; rather, the evidence is that it has no significant effect at all. (Easterlin, 2013, p 4)

Certainly, for poor countries, growth sometimes helps to provide necessary services, such as sanitation and clean water (Galeotti et al, 2006). However, growth has generally proved inefficient as a means to reduce poverty and has often contributed to increasing inequality (Harvey, 2006; Woodward and Simms, 2006; Melamed et al, 2011). In wealthier countries, quality of life may begin to deteriorate if growth continues beyond a threshold level without redistribution (Max-Neef, 1995; Wilkinson and Pickett, 2009). The implication is a strong case for redistribution of wealth, instead of overall economic growth, as a means both to meet basic needs and to improve quality of life. Therefore, Næss and Høyer (2009) argue that economic growth should be promoted as part of a sustainability strategy only in the poor countries and regions of the world, while in the rich countries there should be a replacement of economic growth with degrowth.

There have been some policy initiatives in this direction. For example, calls for 'contraction and convergence', a proposed global agreement that consists of every country bringing its greenhouse gas emissions, per capita, to a level that is equal for all countries, leading to a contraction for some countries and an overall convergence (Meyer, 2000). Also there is some work on moving away from GDP as a measure of progress (see Chapter Eleven). The main problems with traditional GDP are that it only rarely takes into account the economic costs associated with environmental problems; and that it counts investment in environmental abatement measures as an addition to GDP but does not consider losses caused by environmental destruction as a deduction (Wang et al, 2011). The degrowth movement has been particularly advanced in providing a counter-hegemonic discourse in relation to the DHED around growth. Key figures such as Georgescu-Roegen (1971) and Daly (1977) predict that, without degrowth, the increasing use of resources and production of waste means that there will be accelerated, irreversible decay. Degrowth (or no growth) will mean that people will live at a significantly lower level of consumption than the middle classes but, though 'poorer' in terms of individual material goods, they will be richer in terms of health, public goods and human relationships (Jackson, 2009; Magdoff and Foster, 2011).[1]

DHED 6: The environment needs to be owned and controlled

Another DHED is the idea that nature needs to be owned and controlled. Garret Hardin's 'Tragedy of the Commons' (1968) typifies this perspective, conceiving of public goods as scarce commodities that need either privatisation or strong state control. Hardin assumes that herders follow their own self-interest, trying to graze as many cattle as possible on the common land and destroying the resource for all. This parable is often used to justify the need for private property and, thereby, increased privatisation. The counter-argument to this is that, in an environmentally just society, decisions would be made collectively, so that everyone would have their needs met in so far as the resource allowed. It is only rational to over-use a common pool when resources are privately held because users will tend to compete for, rather than share, what they produce.

This DHED is used to justify the increasing 'commodification' of nature, a process of converting goods and services that are not currently bought and sold into the market. Commodification reduces people and nature to a supplier of resources and a repository of wastes, with little concern to preserve any aspects that are not deemed to be useful. The commodification of natural resources has increasingly occurred with the privatisation of (formerly) publicly controlled natural resources, what Harvey (2003) terms 'accumulation by dispossession'. Both natural resources, as inputs to production, and natural processes, as environmental services, are now being commodified. The belief in the need to own and control nature increases opportunities for profit making and so is highly useful for capitalism.

Therefore, these six Damaging Hegemonic Environmental Discourses have come to pervade much of the debate about environmental issues. The next section looks at the role of capitalism as a determinant of environmental injustice and how this intersects with these discourses.

Capitalism

The last and, arguably, most important theoretical explanation for environmental injustice is that it is an outcome of the capitalist economic system. The term 'capitalism' has been applied historically in numerous ways with varying attempts to discern its essence (for example, Marx, Weber, Sombart, Schumpeter). There is still no consensus on its meaning and usage because definitions reflect underlying theoretical frameworks. For example, while Sombart (1902) conflated the concept of capitalism with free and competitive markets, Marx referred to the 'capitalist mode of production' to distinguish a social relationship within which labour was commodified and exploited through the appropriation of surplus value. This book, based on the theoretical tradition of Critical Theory, draws on the Marxist analysis of capital, emphasising the interrelated and defining features of commodification, the profit motive, competition and growth.

A number of environmental authors have argued that it is capitalist processes which are chiefly responsible for environmental degradation (for example, Commoner, 1972; O'Connor, 1998; Kovel, 2002; Pepper, 2010; Magdoff and Foster, 2011). O'Connor (1998), for example, describes environmental limits as the 'second contradiction of capital', since accumulation is dependent upon, and rooted in, the unsustainable consumption of nature. In addition, some, though relatively few, EJ analysts see capitalism as responsible for environmental injustice, on the grounds that modern capitalist societies produce intense ecological harm at the same time as extensive social hierarchies, principally those of race, class, gender and nation (for example, Schnaiberg, 1980; Marable, 1983; Faber and O'Connor, 1993; Schnaiberg and Gould, 2000; Pellow, 2007; Faber, 2008; Harvey, 2010). This position is also now growing among indigenous, socialist, anarchist and anti-globalisation social movements.

One of the most influential of these analyses has been the 'treadmill of production theory', originally developed by Schnaiberg (1980) and later revised and extended (for example, Gould et al, 1996). This stresses the inherent need of capitalist businesses to grow, to replace costly labour with advanced technologies and to increase the use of resources through a self-reinforcing mechanism of ever more production and consumption. The theory clarifies how a powerful coalition of capital, state and labour develops in support of continued growth, making it difficult, if not impossible, for environmental advocates to halt the resulting 'treadmill'. When resources are limited, the treadmill searches for alternative sources, rather than reducing production and consumption. Beck's (1992; 1995; 1999) 'risk society' proposed a similar model, though with more emphasis on knowledge and culture, for example, pointing out how private institutions strongly influence scientific research programmes.

Though seemingly more relevant to international, rather than intra-national, studies of environmental justice, the integration of Dependency Theory (Frank, 1967) and World Systems Theory (Wallerstein, 2004) can also advance our understanding of the relationship between capitalism and environmental injustice within states. Dependency Theory argues that the Western core of world capitalism could develop only by distorting the development of the peripheral poorer nations, thereby 'under-developing' them (Frank, 1967). World Systems Theory asserts a similar process, though it introduces a semi-peripheral position of states that have partly industrialised (Wallerstein, 2004). According to this perspective, the modern world system, though stable in terms of structure, is dynamic in that different nations have occupied different positions over time. The economies of the core nations tend to be based on lucrative manufacturing, with the peripheral nations (and, increasingly, the semi-peripheral nations) providing the raw material and cheap labour to maintain them. Environmental issues were not considered in the original formulation of Dependency Theory and World Systems Theory but are now increasingly being considered from these perspectives (for example, Bunker, 2003). These studies tend to find that core nations contribute disproportionately to global levels of environmental degradation through outsourcing their polluting industries and hazardous waste to peripheral nations, and through importing excessive natural resources from the peripheral nations.

One of the most problematic aspects of capitalism is that a constant stream of new commodities must be produced and sold so as to maintain profits and be competitive against rivals. If there is insufficient demand, 'needs' are artificially created. Advertising aims to convince people that they need certain consumption goods and want to replace those they already have, even when they are still functioning perfectly. There is also 'built-in obsolescence', so that goods either stop working or must be replaced because they have gone out of fashion. The pressure on people to consume begins at an early age, with small children in capitalist countries being exposed to hundreds of advertisements on a daily basis, learning to associate these 'goods' with all that is culturally defined as positive. With the easy availability of credit and the short life of consumer goods, people are induced to shop at every opportunity, whether or not they can really afford it. 'Luxury consumption' and 'symbolic consumption' are encouraged and a culture of consumption takes hold, where consuming constitutes a large part of social existence, leading people to search for meaning, contentment and acceptance primarily through the consumption of goods and services. Insidiously and cumulatively, advertising encourages us to believe that consumer goods are the route to happiness, status, recognition, acceptance and belonging (Leonard, 2010; Simms, 2013). Though people come to develop knowledge of marketers' persuasion tactics and, in doing so, become better able to avoid manipulation, the more invasive (for example, internet tracking to create a consumer profile) and subtle (for example, adverts that bypass the conscious mind) methods that are now being used make it much more difficult to do this (Shrum et al, 2012).

Therefore, production and consumption are driven so that capitalism can survive, rather than for the purposes of meeting human need. The environmental consequence of this is that natural resources are depleted to feed the system and there is increased waste. There are also social implications because these consumption patterns can be maintained only through the appropriation and destruction of the resources of poorer nations and communities. When resources or markets are depleted or saturated in one area, capital moves on. One recent example of this is 'land grabbing' where private capital and national governments rush to gain control of acres of land in other countries to produce food and/or biofuels (see Chapter Five).

Moreover, the drive for profit encourages cost cutting, putting pressure on corporations to choose the cheapest, rather than the most sustainable, processes. This means that there is a clear and direct conflict between environmental protection and corporate profits. For example, investigators alleged that cost cutting had been behind the BP oil spill off the US coast in the Gulf of Mexico in 2010 (National Commission on the BP Deepwater Horizon Oil Spill and Offshore Drilling, 2011). The Committee on Energy and Commerce of the US Congress explicitly stated:

> BP appears to have made multiple decisions for economic reasons that increased the danger of a catastrophic well failure ... it appears that BP repeatedly chose risky procedures in order to reduce costs and save time and made minimal efforts to contain the added risk. (Letter to BP Chief Executive, 14 June 2010 in Freudenburg and Gramling, 2011: 47)

Gibson-Graham (2006) argue, however, that we cannot assume every company is interested in maximising profits because there are such a wide range of ownership structures of companies, and a diversity of social actors who are involved in them. Even so, across the board, if a company does not make a profit for its shareholders, then it is unlikely to survive. Business owners and their management teams have to focus primarily on the short-term. Unfortunately, while they make short-term decisions based on what will help their business to survive, they may make decisions that collectively harm society and the environment.

However, market environmentalists argue that capitalism is, or can be made to be, entirely compatible with environmental protection. They consider that 'green capitalism' will marry the pursuit of environmental protection with the power of the market (for example, Mol, 1995; 2003). Under green capitalism, environmentally friendly businesses are seen to offer eco-efficient solutions, as well as being more profitable, flexible and innovative (Hawken et al, 1999; Gore, 2000; Porritt, 2005). There is a strong belief that 'ecological modernisation' processes will solve our environmental problems, through improved efficiency and technological innovation (Mol, 1995; 2003).

However, 'risk society' (Beck, 1992; 1995; 1999) and 'treadmill of production' (Schnaiberg and Gould, 2000) theorists point out that technology and efficiency measures have achieved little, since, in general, modern industrialised nations are becoming increasingly less sustainable, producing more toxic waste and depleting resources at an accelerated rate. Their view is backed by considerable evidence of greatly increased environmental damage in recent times, including an exponential increase in the production and use of hazardous and potentially hazardous synthetic chemicals (see www.CAS.org). While there may appear to be environmental improvements in wealthier nations, this is often the result of the increased use of poorer nations as supply depots and waste repositories.

Although some technologies may increase the efficient use of resources, there is often a 'rebound effect', whereby efficiency in the use of a particular resource often leads to a greater overall use of that resource (the so-called 'Jevons Paradox') (Jevons, 1866). Technological innovation is, of course, an important element in helping us to achieve environmental justice. However, under capitalism it is pushed at the expense of other measures because there is the possibility for profit, even if it solves one problem by creating another. For example, some environmentalists who focus on climate change see nuclear power as a viable option for rapidly reducing greenhouse gas emissions (for example, James Lovelock). Yet, nuclear power has the potential to create significant environmental and social harm through uranium mining; the construction and decommissioning of reactors; toxic leaks; the risks of accidents; the potential for use of its by-products in nuclear weapons; and the need for storage of potentially lethal material that will last for thousands of years. Moreover, it will take some time to develop the necessary capacity and, in the meantime, will limit the possibility of investing in alternatives that could begin to reduce carbon emissions much more quickly. There appear to be powerful interests driving the take-up of this technology, as nuclear power is not even financially competitive against other energy options (Du and Parsons, 2009).

Meeting the needs of the population is often the justification given for developing these risky technologies. This argument ignores the social factors that militate against needs being met. For example, transgenic agricultural technology is justified on the grounds that it is the only way to feed the world's poor (for example, Foresight, 2011). Yet, food shortages generally occur, not because insufficient food is grown but, rather, because poor people cannot afford to buy it. Even in wealthy countries, such as the UK, there has been an explosion of food banks, soup kitchens and school breakfast clubs since 2010 as a result of the impact of government austerity measures on the living standards of low-income families. Those who argue that there are better ways than the invention of endless new technologies to address such needs are cast as anti-modern, anti-scientific, 'Luddites'.

Market environmentalists also argue that there is no need for radical social change in response to the environmental crises because advanced industrial societies are 'dematerialising' (that is, their economies are increasingly based on services, culture and information), and this will mean that there will soon be less environmental harm from industry (for example, Bernardini and Galli, 1993). Dematerialisation is a potentially useful strategy in terms of increasing our capacity for remanufacturing, zero-waste, closed-loop systems (where waste products are reused), producing more durable and repairable goods, and using human labour, rather than mechanical labour. However, a number of analysts have shown that the supposed environmental benefits of dematerialisation, in the sense of becoming a service-based economy, are not occurring (Duchin, 1998; Martinez-Alier, 2003). For example, although the expansion of the finance sector created the illusion that growth was becoming delinked from the material world, in reality, these activities require an energy-dependent economy (Kovel, 2002). Forms of production and consumption may differ, but resource use remains high. Duchin's (1998) analysis of household life-styles, for example, reveals the high material needs in the consumption patterns of those employed in the 'post-industrial' sector.

As well as focusing on technology and 'dematerialisation' to solve environmental problems, market environmentalists also advocate the use of market mechanisms. An important aspect of this market-based vision is the financialisation of nature. It is argued that market externalities must be 'internalised', so that firms should have to pay the full costs of the pollution they cause. Environmental problems are seen to be an outcome of the fact that the expense of destroying the earth is largely absent from the prices set in the marketplace (Hawken et al, 1999). It is considered that, once natural capital is 'valued' on the balance sheets, managers and governments will have to adopt more environmentally sound practices. Many companies support these policies because they are seen to be preferable to regulation and because they pose no limit to growth. However, such schemes have generally been used ineffectively by governments, who have not been keen to undermine the competitiveness of their industries by imposing additional financial burdens and who have succumbed to industry lobbyists, who have pressured them for higher caps and lower taxes. Moreover, as David Harvey (2011) asserts, if capitalists are forced to internalise all of the social and environmental costs they generate, the expense will be so great that they will go out of business.

However, the most worrying aspect of this financialisation is not so much its ineffectiveness, but the social and ecological damage that it could do. The increased use of pricing mechanisms requires that nature be quantified ('given value') to enable its reduction into tradable commodities. This creeping privatisation, commodification and monetisation of nature is embodied in the policies that promote 'payments for ecosystems services' (PES). Ecosystems services include both provisioning services (for example, water, agriculture, wild plants) and human life-supporting services (for example, the recycling of nutrients, the assimilation of waste, the regulation of climate and the control of pests/diseases). Arguments for placing monetised values on defined ecosystem services are, to some extent, based on the idea that they are currently not being valued at their true worth (for example, Conservation International, 2009; Juniper, 2012). However, as well as there being numerous methodological problems involved in attempting to undertake a cost-benefit analysis of nature (see Wegner and Pascual, 2011), the idea of conceiving of nature in terms of marketable assets is very contentious, not least because it implies widespread commodification and privatisation. Although this process has been happening for some time, PES takes this into new realms by, not just privatising the material goods that can be taken from nature, but also privatising the functions and processes of nature.

Similarly, carbon trading projects, including 'cap and trade', 'REDD' (Reducing Emissions from Deforestation and Forest Degradation) and other associated market-based approaches intended to provide economic incentives for reducing emissions, also appear to be ineffective (see, for example, Lohmann, 2010). Instead of being sanctioned for failing to meet emissions targets, industrialised countries have been able to buy extra pollution permits (Coelho, 2012).

These market approaches are reflected in, and promoted by, the 'green economy' and 'green growth' agendas now being strongly pushed by international organisations such as UNEP (2011) and the OECD (2013). UNEP (2011) defines a green economy as one that achieves 'improved human well-being and social equity, while significantly reducing environmental risks and ecological scarcities', and claims that 'A green economy does not favour one political perspective over another. It is relevant to all economies, be they state or market-led' (UNEP, 2011, p 16). As such, the 'green economy' concept has been described as a 'floating signifier' (Jessop, 2012), that is, one that is amenable to a broad consensus. However, a market-based construction of this concept has come to dominate social, environmental and development policy and discourse, while redistributive or rights-based alternatives have been marginalised (Cook et al, 2012). This interpretation of the green economy promotes market mechanisms for the commodification and financialisation of nature, life and ecosystem services (UNEP, 2011). It emphasises the need for pricing mechanisms as an important way of reducing social and environmental externalities and invites the world to further intensify economic growth in order to reach sustainable development (UNEP, 2011, p 14). At times, the term is reduced to referring simply to the reduction of CO_2 emissions, meaning that nuclear energy can be part of a green economy. All the capitalist countries covered in this book are committed to this interpretation of the green economy.

Some social movement groups, particularly indigenous groups, have strongly criticised the 'green economy' and 'green growth' approaches because, they argue, they are premised on saving nature through commodifying it. They warn that although these approaches promise to eradicate poverty, they actually favour corporate interests and will create more environmental problems though their promotion of growth, risky technologies and the privatisation of land and nature. For example, at the Indigenous Peoples Global Conference on Rio+20 and Mother Earth, the following appeal was made:

> We urge all humanity to join with us in transforming the social structures, institutions and power relations that underpin our deprivation, oppression and exploitation ... We need to fundamentally reorient production and consumption based on human needs rather than for the boundless accumulation of profit for a few ... We demand that the United Nations, governments and corporations abandon false solutions to climate change, like large hydroelectric dams, genetically modified organisms including GMO trees, plantations, agro-fuels, 'clean' coal, nuclear power, natural gas, hydraulic

fracturing, nanotechnology, synthetic biology, bio-energy, biomass, biochar, geoengineering, carbon markets, Clean Development Mechanism and REDD+ that endanger the future and life as we know it. (From the Kari-Oca II declaration, 'Indigenous Peoples Global Conference on Rio+20 and Mother Earth', 17 June 2012)

Thus, market environmentalists insist that calls to change society, to consume less or to ban harmful activities are naïve or detrimental to the goal of a better world. Yet the technological fixes, dematerialisation and market-based mechanisms that they propose instead appear ineffective and/or positively harmful for the environment and likely to deter the advancement of all aspects of environmental justice.

However, the argument that capitalism is a cause of environmental injustice is based on the claim that it not only causes environmental damage, but also tends to polarise income and wealth inequalities, creates unemployment and underemployment and is prone to periodic crises that tend to be borne by the worst-off. The class divisions that occur in a capitalist society favour some lives and marginalise others, and benefits and costs are distributed according to purchasing power. There is no rational way to prioritise under a capitalist system, in which the market decides how commodities are allocated. Poor people do not obtain necessary goods because access to commodities is determined, not by desire or need, but by having sufficient money or credit to make purchases. At the same time, wealth is taken from the working class and siphoned off to elites, enabling vast concentrations of wealth. A system that produces inequality and depresses workers' wages ensures that many will not have access to even the basic necessities.

Though wealth is supposed to 'trickle down' under this system it is, in fact, being drawn up. Consequently, around 0.1% of the world population currently hold 50% of world income (Capgemini and Merrill Lynch Wealth Management, 2013) and 44 of the world's 100 largest economies are corporations (Keys and Malnight, 2012). Moreover, the situation appears to be worsening. In 2012, Oxfam released a new report stating that the income of the world's richest 1% had increased by 60% in the last 20 years. Furthermore, the world's 100 richest people earned enough in 2012 to end extreme poverty, worldwide, four times over (Oxfam, 2012). As Magdoff and Foster (2011) point out:

> There is a logical connection between capitalism's successes and its failures. The poverty and misery of a large mass of

the world's people is not an accident, some inadvertent by-product of the system, one that can be eliminated with a little tinkering here or there. The fabulous accumulation of wealth – as a direct consequence of the way capitalism works nationally and internationally – has simultaneously produced persistent hunger, malnutrition, health problems, lack of water, lack of sanitation, and general misery for a large portion of the people of the world. (Magdoff and Foster, 2011, p 83)

Furthermore, inequality increases as a result of the drive to expand the market as far as possible. Neoliberal government policies that have allowed the market into new areas through trade liberalisation agreements, privatisation, loans and 'structural adjustments' often strip low-income communities of their rights and resources. The North America Free Trade Agreement (NAFTA), for example, has meant that foreign multinational companies have the right to sue national governments if their environmental laws affect company profits (Newell, 2007).

In order to extend the market, poor countries have been encouraged to take out loans. A number of authors argue that repayment of debt is a significant factor in promoting destruction of the environment in the global South (for example, George, 1991; Bello, 1993; Gonzalez, 2001). The World Bank and the International Monetary Fund (IMF) often require export-led structural adjustment as a condition of loans. These pressures have resulted in unsustainable resource extraction, for example, the use of open-cast mining techniques and intensive deforestation, to produce export commodities. Increased production has meant declining prices for primary commodities, causing governments of the South to attempt to still further augment production by increasing extraction, creating further environmental damage and displacement of poor people.

Inequality is both socially and environmentally harmful. A study of the US found that more unequal states had several times more, and worse, pollution and weaker environmental laws, than more equal states (Boyce, 2001). More recently, Wilkinson and Pickett (2009), in the UK, found that consumption levels are higher in more unequal societies. They explain this in terms of 'emulative consumption' (Veblen, 1994 [1899]), where, in an unequal society, life becomes a battle for respect so that 'everyday life is an unremitting demonstration of the ability to pay'. The wealthy not only spur each other on in feats of over-consumption, but transform patterns of consumption all the way down the social hierarchy. Further investigating this idea, Dorling (2010) has shown that higher levels of inequality in a country tend to correlate with a greater consumption of meat, water and flights; as well as the production of more waste and a larger Ecological Footprint.

Therefore, capitalism's propensity to deepen inequality creates a barrier to achieving substantive and distributive environmental justice. With regard to procedural environmental justice, neoclassical economists would argue that the economic freedom of competitive capitalism and the ability to acquire private property are prerequisites of political freedom (for example, Hayek, 1944; Friedman, 1952). According to this view, capitalist societies are more free, open and transparent, and therefore more likely than socialist societies to be influenced by citizens pressing for environmental improvements.

However, though there appears to be freedom under capitalism, Critical Theorists would generally argue that democracy under capitalism is limited because there is a ruling class who work to control society in their own interests. The capitalist class has the most resources to spend on behalf of its interests and is able to subvert local and national democracy through funding anti-environmental movements and election candidates and forming powerful lobbies to shape government policies to protect its economic interests (Faber and O'Connor, 1993; Monbiot, 2001; Faber, 2008; Magdoff and Foster, 2011). For example, Monbiot documents numerous examples where big business has overruled parliamentary democracy in the UK and public provision 'has been deliberately tailored to meet corporate demands rather than public need' (Monbiot, 2001, p 4). Faber (2008) refers to the networks of powerful interest groups that undermine environmental progress as the 'polluter-industrial complex'. These are think-tanks, policy institutes, research centres, foundations, legal associations, political action committees, public relations firms and so on, that are 'committed to discrediting the environmental movement and to dismantling state programs and policies that promote environmental justice, protect public health, and safeguard the earth' (Faber, 2008, p 15). He describes how these groups, financed by corporate bodies, have dominated environmental debates in the US, appearing to express objective, factual, expert-based opinion, while working for particular economic interests. Similarly, in the UK, a classic example of this was the struggle to ban asbestos which was thwarted for many years by industry misinformation and concealment. The asbestos companies produced skewed epidemiological reports to promote their message that asbestos-related diseases disease are rare, that proper controls are in place and that any risky elements of asbestos are 'locked in' (McCulloch and Tweedale, 2008). Yet, the number of cumulative asbestos-induced deaths in the country had already reached about 77,000 by 2012, with another 55,000 predicted (Howie, 2012).

As a consequence of the power of these wealthy elites, a culture develops among political leaders in capitalist countries based on the assumption that, what benefits capitalist business, benefits the country as a whole (Magdoff and Foster, 2011). Therefore, in general, the state has played a very limited role in environmental protection, largely restricted to regulating pollution, with virtually no attempt to restrict the over-use of resources. Though trades unions do act as a balancing element, there is an overall democratic deficit in the capitalist workplace. Workers generally do not choose the technology they will work with, where their workplace will be located, how the production process will be organised, what they will produce, who their bosses are or what level of remuneration they will receive (except to the extent that they can take or leave the job in the first place). The media can also act as a counterweight to elite power, but the mainstream media in capitalist societies, though widely viewed as relatively free, present a limited range of views as a consequence of their close ties with corporations and the state (Chomsky, 1997). Therefore, only those that adhere to a limited spectrum of opinion are granted a significant voice within the mass communication networks (Chomsky, 1997; Bagdikian, 2004). When environmental problems are reported, it is usually in a way that is disconnected from the wider issues, and grassroots campaigns against environmental damage receive little coverage unless they have some entertainment value (Hofricher, 1993). This situation can only undermine procedural environmental justice.

Therefore, capitalism is problematic for environmental justice in terms of its substantive, distributive and procedural aspects. However, many would argue that capitalism cannot be the cause of environmental injustices, as severe environmental problems also occurred, and continue to occur, in communist and socialist systems, such as the former Soviet Union and China. Some consider that these problems occur because these systems are based on an environmentally damaging philosophy. It is evident that traditional socialist thought has tended to be suspicious of ideas of a natural order, within which humans should fit (Dobson, 2007); and socialists have been challenged by arguments about the limits to growth, alleging the wealthy will merely pull up the drawbridge, rather than consider the redistribution necessary to limit global growth. The transition to socialism has mainly been approached in terms of revolutionising the means of production and increasing productivity to meet basic needs, rather than aiming to achieve a balance between humanity and the rest of nature. On the other hand, many communists and socialists claim that socialism, though a diverse and contested philosophy, has always contained an ecological perspective (for example, Mellor, 2006) and that environmental problems in socialist societies have been exaggerated for ideological reasons.

Hence, there has been a great deal of debate as to the degree to which Marx was pro- or anti-ecological. There are three main positions on this: that Marx was deeply anti-ecological (for example, Victor Ferkiss); that he considered ecology in his work, though he eventually chose to take a 'Promethean' (pro-technological, anti-ecological) approach (for example, Robyn Eckersley); and that he was profoundly aware of ecological degradation and this formed part of his analysis of both capitalism and communism (for example, John Bellamy Foster). All are agreed, however, that Marx and his fellow socialists of the period wrote at a time when it was generally considered that nature must be 'mastered' and 'conquered', and that this is reflected in their work. When their writing is taken overall, though, at least Marx and Engels appear to have had deep ecological concerns, as has been well documented by Burkett (1999), Foster (2000; 2008) and Foster et al (2010). For example, Engels wrote about a society in which people would 'not only feel, but also know, their unity with nature' and criticised 'the senseless and antinatural idea of a contradiction between mind and matter, man and nature, soul and body ...' (Engels, 1940, p 293). Marx argued that nature's commodification under capitalism led to its 'practical degradation' (in Parsons, 1977, p 17). He considered that communism would enable the complete return of man to himself as a social being and that part of this would entail a resolution of the conflict between humans and nature. Marx never thought that ecological problems would develop in a socialist country, believing that alienation of humanity from nature derives from the alienation of people from one another.

There is some evidence to show that the overall environmental record of former socialist countries was no worse than that of capitalist states around the same time (for example, Manser, 1993; Dominick, 1998). Dominick's study of the period of division in Germany, for example, shows that the communist East was initially less environmentally damaging than the West, due to lower levels of consumerism, though eventually this pattern was reversed, in large part because of the desire to compete economically with the West. Similarly, several authors assert that it was the emulation of capitalist technology that led to the environmental problems associated with Soviet industry (for example, Faber and O'Connor, 1993; Levins, 2005). However, the socialist record, while no worse, was clearly no better than that of capitalism.

It seems that the Soviet Union succumbed to the productivism and its associated environmental destruction that characterised early 20th-century modernity in general (Edelstein, 2007; Foster, 2008). In other words, such countries were influenced by Damaging Hegemonic Environmental Discourses. Both 'communist' and 'capitalist' societies have been equally committed to these beliefs and values, as Porritt (1984) describes:

> Both are dedicated to industrial growth, to the expansion of the means of production, to a materialist ethic as the best means of meeting people's needs and to unimpeded technological development ... From a point of view of narrow scientific rationalism, both insist that the planet is there to be conquered, that big is self-evidently beautiful, and that what cannot be measured is of no importance. (Porritt, 1984, p 44)

Hence, both capitalism and DHEDs appear to be important factors that explain environmental degradation. Yet, although the above explanatory factors have been separated out for the purposes of analysis, it is clear that the actual situation will be multi-layered, with many factors reinforcing and interacting. It is also evident that some of the debate about causes becomes unclear because analysts are talking about different aspects of environmental justice. Table 3.1 shows the main areas of justice that the proposed cause refers to.

Table 3.1: Causes of different aspects of environmental injustice

Cause	Substantive	Distributive	Procedural
Discrimination		Yes	Yes
Market dynamics		Yes	
Lack of citizen power	Yes	Yes	Yes
Industrialisation	Yes		
Individual behaviour/life-style	Yes		
Culture	Yes		
Capitalism	Yes	Yes	Yes

It is apparent that only the explanations of EJ in terms of capitalism and a lack of citizen power apply to all three dimensions of EJ. However, no single causal factor seems to completely explain environmental injustice. Theories of discriminatory intent seem to ignore structural processes;

market dynamic studies seem to be inconclusive and superficial, in that they de-contextualise decision making; lack of economic, political and social power is clearly important, yet examples have been given where poor and powerless communities seem to attain justice in spite of this; industrialisation appears to have caused numerous environmental problems but, by itself, does not explain patterns of socio-spatial environmental inequality; individual life-style explanations focus on consumer behaviour but ignore the manipulation that drives this; culture, based on Damaging Hegemonic Environmental Discourses, is evidently problematic for EJ but we need to understand why these particular values are promoted by elites; and capitalism seems to be logically predisposed to cause environmental harm and social inequality, but environmental damage also seems to occur in socialist countries. Of course, the above explanations are not necessarily mutually exclusive or easy to disentangle. For example, a company could decide to produce synthetic products (industrialisation) and deliberately target a low-income area for the siting of the facility (discrimination): because it believes there is less likely to be an effective opposition (citizen power); as this will reduce the costs associated with delay and, thereby, enable it to be more competitive (capitalism). Yet, as the rest of this book will continue to discuss, it appears that capitalism, alongside Damaging Hegemonic Environmental Discourses, links all the other causal factors together and seems to underpin them. Therefore, having highlighted the possible explanations for environmental injustice, the following chapters will provide numerous real-life examples that support and challenge these theories and the policies that arise from them.

Note
[1] Degrowth is not normally concerned with population growth but, rather, with consumption patterns, since it is predicted that the global population will stabilise and, very likely, begin to decline before the end of the 21st-century (Lutz et al, 2001). In general, population growth is inversely related to poverty so that, when needs are met, especially the education of women, populations will decline anyway (Lappe et al, 1998). Without waste and excess, a population of 9 billion (the number at which the global population is likely to stabilise) can easily be supported on earth.

FOUR

'Killing yourself is no way to make a living': environmental justice in the United States

No discussion of how to achieve environmental justice would be complete without reference to the United States, the birthplace of the concept and what has become known as the 'environmental justice movement'. This chapter will critically assess the state of environmental justice in the United States, drawing on the relevant literature as well as my own observations and a number of semi-structured interviews carried out between 2008 and 2012.

The US is typologised here as the most capitalist of the seven case-study countries examined in this book, primarily because it has no recent experience of extensive public ownership of the means of production (see Figure 1.1). Profit-seeking enterprise and capital accumulation are the fundamental driving forces behind economic activity; and there are relatively low levels of government regulation and involvement in production decisions. Though the government does use some fiscal and monetary policies to counteract negative tendencies in the economy, and a range of policies to improve social and environmental well-being, this has been less prominent over recent decades than in the other countries featured in this book.

As the economic datasets in Appendix 2 show, the United States is the world's largest economy in terms of GDP. For some time it has been the world's largest manufacturer, producing around a fifth of global output, though some analysts consider that it has now been overtaken by China (for example, IHS Global Insight, 2011). Even so, the country is currently experiencing a severe economic downturn following the 2007–08 financial crisis, resulting in very high levels of unemployment.

In spite of, or perhaps because of, being a major capitalist economy, the US has led the way in terms of environmental justice discourse and activism. Although struggles for a better and more equal environment had existed around the world for some time, they had not been conceptualised as 'environmental justice' until, in the 1980s, black communities in the United States began to protest about hazardous and polluting industries being located predominantly in their neighbourhoods. Prior to this, there had been similar struggles in the US over indigenous land rights, public health and community empowerment. However, the specific beginning of the environmental justice movement is usually traced back to protests against plans to site a PCB landfill in predominantly African-American Shocco Township in Warren County, New York State. One of the activists who opposed the landfill, the Reverend Benjamin Chavis, coined the term 'environmental racism', making the link to the black civil rights movement. Several reports followed that provided further evidence of a significant correlation between the location of hazardous waste sites and the racial demographics of the county (Bullard, 1983; US GAO, 1983; UCC CRJ, 1987). For example, Bullard (1983) published a report which showed that in Houston, a city with a 25% black population at that time, six of the eight city-owned waste incinerators and three of the four landfills were sited in black neighbourhoods. Environmental justice activism and research then grew rapidly, culminating in the 1991 First National People of Color Environmental Leadership Summit, held in Washington, DC. This meeting, organised and attended by more than 650 grassroots and national leaders, adopted key environmental justice principles that included the right to freedom from ecological destruction; participation as equal partners at every level of decision making; a safe and healthy work environment; and the cessation of the production of all toxins, hazardous wastes and radioactive materials (First National People of Color, 1991).

Following this, environmental justice made a relatively quick ascent from grassroots to executive level. The United States Environmental Protection Agency (EPA) established the Office of Environmental Equity in 1992 (later to become the Office of Environmental Justice). In the same year, the Environmental Justice Act was introduced in Congress that would have placed a moratorium on the siting or permitting of new chemical facilities that release toxics that significantly impact on human health and well-being. However, this Act was not passed, then or since, despite numerous attempts to reintroduce it. Even so, in 1993 the EPA established the National Environmental Justice Advisory Council to give advice and make recommendations to the EPA. Following this, in 1994, the Clinton administration passed Executive Order 12898 on 'Federal Actions to Address Environmental Justice in Minority Populations and Low Income Populations'. This order instructed every national state department to develop an agency-wide environmental justice strategy and to ensure that any of its activities that substantially affect human health or the environment should be conducted in a way that does not discriminate on the basis of 'race, color or national origin' (Clinton, 1994, Sec. 2-2). Though the Order did not initially define EJ, the EPA later adopted the following definition:

> Environmental Justice is the fair treatment and meaningful involvement of all people regardless of race, color, national origin, or income with respect to the development, implementation, and enforcement of environmental laws, regulations, and policies. Fair treatment means that no group of people should bear a disproportionate share of the negative environmental consequences resulting from industrial, governmental and commercial operations or policies. Meaningful involvement means that: (1) people have an opportunity to participate in decisions about activities that may affect their environment and/or health; (2) the publics [*sic*] contribution can influence the regulatory agency's decision; (3) their concerns will be considered in the decision-making process; and (4) the decision makers seek out and facilitate the involvement of those potentially affected. (US EPA, 1998)

At this point, the United States was the most advanced country in the world with regard to specific guidance on the distributive aspects of environmental justice. The ability to conceptualise EJ and build a movement based on this seems to have occurred out of the historical context of a diverse array of social movements, including those organised for indigenous land rights, public health, community empowerment and black civil rights. For example, as a result of the civil rights struggles of the 1950s and 1960s, Title VI of the Civil Rights Act of 1964 was passed, which prohibited the state, or recipients of national state funds, from discriminating on the basis of race, colour or national origin (EJRC, 2012).

However, distributive environmental justice faced a major setback when George W. Bush became president, in 2001. During his administration, the Office of Environmental Justice lost some financial support and became less effective. There was also a significant setback as a result of a 2001 ruling by the US Supreme Court that ended the ability of private parties to sue on the grounds of disproportional impact alone, so that, henceforth, they would also have to establish that there had been intentional discrimination. As discussed in Chapter Three, this is very difficult to prove. Even so, the EJ legislative framework in the US remains strong. The next sections discuss the extent to which this has enabled the achievement of substantive, distributive and procedural environmental justice.

Substantive environmental justice in the United States

Pre-dating environmental justice activism, the mainstream environmental movement of the 1960s and 1970s had seen some success with the development of significant environmental policy and legislation. Most of the major US environmental law was passed at this time, including the National Environmental Policy Act 1970, one of the world's first-ever laws to establish a broad national framework for protecting the environment. These new regulations significantly reduced overall emissions so that, between 1980 and 2010, carbon monoxide was reduced by 71%; nitrogen oxides by 52%; sulphur dioxides by 69%; particulates by 83%; and lead by 98% (US EPA, 2012).

However, pollution and other environmental issues remain serious, and attempts to introduce further environmental legislation have been met by a continual backlash from businesses and the political Right, who have often perceived regulations as threatening their financial interests. This has resulted in frequent gridlock when attempts are made to progress new legislation, for example, in relation to limiting greenhouse gas emissions. As a result, regulation remains patchy and contains numerous loopholes. For example, the Clean Air Act 1963 (and its revised versions of 1970, 1977 and 1990) do not include ambient standards for all toxic chemicals; not all of the standards in the Safe Drinking Water Act 1974 (and amendments made in 1986, 1996 and 2005) are enforceable; and the Toxic Substances Control Act 1976 (TSCA) applies only to new chemicals, so that the vast majority of chemicals have never been tested. To a large extent, risk assessment and risk management have taken the place of elimination of risk.

In general, the US performs poorly on most international environmental rankings (see the environmental datasets in Appendix 2). The country is currently the largest per capita emitter of CO_2 and other greenhouse gases globally (IEA, 2012) and the seventh in terms of per capita energy consumption (US Energy Information Administration, 2012). One of the most controversial environmental issues in the US at the moment is 'fracking' (hydraulic fracturing), involving deep drilling and injecting large volumes of water and chemicals into the earth in order to collect natural gas. There has been a great deal of public concern about this as a result of scientific reports that have revealed the potential for earthquakes, as well as for chemical and gas contamination of local ground water and the surrounding air (for example, Brodsky and Lajoie, 2013; van der Elst et al, 2013).

Distributive environmental justice in the United States

The United States is a country with high levels of income inequality, as is evident from its Gini Coefficient, reported to stand at 0.36 (SWIID, 2011) or 0.40 (World Bank, 2011a) (see Appendix 2). As discussed in Chapter Three, this provides the basis for distributive environmental injustice. In the US, income level and other life chances are often linked to race and ethnicity. For example, more than 25% of the black and Latin American population are living in poverty, compared to less than 10% of the white population; black unemployment has generally been twice the level of white unemployment for as long as the data has been tracked; and, though black people make up only about 12% of the population, they make up 40% of the prison population (Shapiro et al, 2010; Sullivan et al, 2012). In the US, racism is still deeply ingrained in society, as one of the interviewees for this book explained:

> "There has been a history of racism, a devaluing of black American lives in the United States, under-valuing. There was a time when they thought that black people were less than human, three-fifths a person[1] ... and that has just been passed down, hasn't been removed from, it might have been removed from the legal documents, but it's not been removed from the culture, from the customs of the country. That's something that people continue to work at but it's going to take time. If you perpetuate something for a couple of hundred years, it's going to take time to get rid of it, at least from people's hearts and minds ... Some of the racism is very entrenched and persistent." (Interview, 18 May 2012, Brian Gilmore, Clinical Associate Professor, Michigan State University, College of Law)

There are innumerable studies and reports that confirm on-going distributive environmental injustice in the United States and evidence continues to mount, with black and minority ethnic and low-income groups continuing to bear greater environmental burdens than the society at large. In 2006, Mohai and Saha, using a new 'distance-based' methodology that counted the number of low-income and minority people within a fixed distance of a particular facility, found an even larger percentage of low-income and minority households to be living near hazardous waste sites than was previously thought. It is unsurprising, then, that the environmental justice activists and organisers I spoke to described a wide range of environmental problems affecting their communities, including toxic incinerators, landfills, mines, nuclear waste dumps, deforestation, privatisation of water and a lack of economic and community resources (for example, interview, 30 January 2013, Elizabeth Yeampierre, Chair, National Environmental Justice Advisory Council; interview, 1 February 2013, Yomi Noibi, Executive Director, ECO-Action; interview, 25 May 2012, Stuart Myiow, Secretary, Mohawk Traditional Council).

Distributive environmental injustice in the United States was particularly highlighted during Hurricane Katrina, where, because of racial disparities in transportation, healthcare, housing and employment, disproportionately large numbers of people of black and other minority ethnic background were affected (Pastor et al, 2006). These disparities, not only increased their likelihood of living in a flood-risk area, they also reduced their ability to be evacuated and made it more difficult for them to recover, as many had been unable to afford household or contents insurance (Pastor et al, 2006). Indigenous groups have also particularly been the victims of distributive environmental injustices in the United States, having had to contend with some of the worst pollution in the country (Taliman, 1992; LaDuke, 1999), which has severely affected their health outcomes (Dawson and Madsen, 2011). They have often been the recipients of landfills, incinerators and other waste facilities (see, for example, Angel, 1992; Gedicks, 1993) and various forms of 'radioactive colonialism', including the mining of uranium and the disposal of nuclear wastes on their land (Churchill and LaDuke, 1992).

Procedural environmental justice in the United States

Since the 1980s, the US environmental justice movement has insisted on participation in environmental decision-making processes, including access to information. The Freedom of Information Act 1966, was an important foundation for environmental justice claims in the United States, though numerous loopholes exist regarding what information may remain secret. For example, under the Toxic Substance and Control Act 1976, companies have been able to conceal the identities of chemicals when they submit health and safety data by claiming that this is 'confidential business information'. Though this is now beginning to change under the Obama administration, environmental justice groups are still frustrated by the lack of a right to know (for example, interview, 30 January, 2013, Joe Wasserman, Hartford Community Organizer, Connecticut Coalition for Environmental Justice). Even when information is available, it may not be accurate and can be biased towards those who have financial power, as a recent case regarding fracking illustrates. The University of Texas Energy Institute, in a major study reviewing incidents of possible contamination resulting from fracking, found no confirmed evidence for ground-water contamination from subsurface fracking operations (Groat et al, 2012). However, the Director of the Institute and principal investigator for the study, Dr Charles Groat, was at that time a board member of a natural gas exploration concern, the Plains Exploration and Production Company. He appears to have received $1.5 million in cash and stock awards from the company, but failed to disclose that information when the study was released. This conflict of interest obviously casts doubt on the study's findings. This is a classic example of the manoeuvrings of what Faber (2008) has described as the 'polluter-industrial' complex, as described earlier (see Chapter Three), highlighting how capitalism can undermine procedural justice.

The relative lack of resources available to environmental justice communities exacerbates their lack of power. For example, one of the groups I interviewed, the Connecticut Coalition for Environmental Justice (CCEJ), has been campaigning to close down a waste incinerator in Hartford that it says releases mercury, dioxin, nickel and many other toxins known to cause cancer, asthma, diabetes and neurological problems. CCEJ members believe that the incinerator emissions explain the very high childhood asthma rate (41%) in the town. CCEJ is also working on a national campaign for legislation to ban the most toxic chemicals in consumer goods. In both cases, the burden of proof falls on the group and it is expected to prove its concerns beyond doubt, despite having very limited resources (interview, 30 January 2013, Joe Wasserman, Hartford Community Organizer, Connecticut Coalition for Environmental Justice).

There is also an issue regarding EPA grants to environmental justice groups. These grants are potentially an effective tool for expanding the capacity of the community to play a role in environmental decision making. However, it is obviously more difficult for communities to contest decisions made by the very organisation that provides them with funds. Even so, the interviewees for this book did not consider that their aims and methods had been compromised by receiving funding from the EPA. For example, Eco-Action, a community-based organisation founded to confront environmental health threats, received a large grant from the EPA in 2009 to develop a partnership between residents, community organisations, municipal government, state agencies and local businesses that would assess environmental exposures and establish priorities for risk reduction. Its Executive Director told me:

> "The EPA has helped us with this project but I do not allow them to manipulate me. I know where they are coming from and they know where I am coming from … I would not let them stop me doing the right thing just because they are funding us. No! … They might try to move us in their own direction but we put our foot down and say this is our mission; we are not going to change it." (Interview, 1 February 2013, Yomi Noibi, Executive Director, ECO-Action)

Even so, in general, it appears that, with regard to public involvement in environmental decision making, the EPA has not embraced the grassroots environmental justice movement's demands for full democratic participation in decision making but has, rather, focused on data analysis, economic opportunity and managed public participation, in particular defining and managing the EJ community (Holifield, 2004). Hence, it has found ways to manage community involvement so as to improve public relations, mainly by allowing the public to submit recommendations (Foreman, 1998; Holifield, 2004). What has often happened, Holifield (2004) asserts, is that EJ communities have been brought into the fold of the project of neoliberalism by increasing trust in EPA decision making and undermining the possibility of protest. He asks:

> to what degree have EJ grants, EJ coordinators, and other resources for managed community involvement led – or failed to lead – community activists to forsake grassroots confrontational tactics 'outside the system' in favor of more collaborative approaches? (Holifield, 2004, p 296)

Holifield (2004) argues that the Clinton administration drew selectively from the broad, progressive agenda of the environmental justice movement, using only those elements that were compatible with neoliberalism. Clinton's Executive Order No. 12898 was implemented with a strong focus on establishing a scientifically verifiable 'EJ community' and managing communities that raised environmental justice allegations. Although the EPA's policy on environmental justice conceded that managers should treat as EJ cases those communities who 'self-identify' as such, it also stated that 'GIS demographics and low-income data *must be obtained* to make an *accurate* determination' of EJ status (US EPA, 1999, p 12; emphasis added). This contradiction has meant that, to this day, the EPA is still unclear about whether an EJ community can be designated on the basis of a spatially defined technical representation or through collective political representation (Holifield, 2012).

However, possibly because of the recognition and financial support they receive, the number of environmental justice organisations in the US continues to increase so that there are now probably more environmental justice organisations in the United States than in any other country in the world. These have been influential to some extent, in that there have been a number of achievements and successes for individual communities who have been able to 'see off' major polluters and shut down toxic incinerators and landfills (for example, see Pellow and Brulle, 2005; EJRC, 2012). One of the earliest of these successes was the environmental justice struggle against the Shintech Corporation in the late 1990s. This was focused on the lower Mississippi river industrial corridor in Louisiana, where over 125 companies, then and now, manufacture a range of chemical products, including fertilisers, paints and plastics. The area had been dubbed 'Cancer Alley' by environmentalists and local residents, as a result of the health effects of living near to these plants (Bullard, 1994a). In 1996, Shintech announced plans to build a polyvinyl chloride (PVC) facility in this area, specifically in Convent, a town with an 83% black population. This plant would add over 600,000 pounds of PVC waste contaminants to the air annually (Bullard and Johnson, 2000). PVC products and the chemicals used to create them are linked to cancers, reproductive disorders and impaired mental development (Belliveau and Lester, 2004). Local residents formed a grassroots environmental campaign and, together with the Tulane Environment Law Clinic, which gave free legal assistance, mounted the first major environmental justice court challenge. The battle between Shintech and Convent attracted international attention, as it was a test of the effectiveness of the new environmental justice legislation. After six months of intense organising and legal manoeuvring, residents of Convent and their allies convinced the EPA to place the permit on hold and, another year later, Shintech scrapped its plans to build the PVC plant before the court case was decided.

This was hailed as a major victory for environmental justice. However, Shintech went on to locate its factory in nearby Addis, 25 miles (40 kilometres) north of Convent and, shortly after, built another in nearby Plaquemine. This example illustrates the power of the EJ movement to halt local contamination, as well as its limitations in that industry can often merely relocate to another, perhaps less powerful, community.

Causes of environmental injustice in the United States

This chapter has described how the United States has been at the forefront of developing EJ concepts, policies, institutions and legislation. It has also given an overview of the serious and, in some respects, growing EJ problems. As Table A1.1 in Appendix 1 summarises, the country is weak on the substantive, distributive and procedural aspects of EJ, as well as on the intergenerational, inter-species and international dimensions. The main issues are excessive use of resources and production of waste; high levels of environmental inequities, based on pronounced social inequalities; and inadequate procedural justice frameworks and policies, which have often focused more on managing and controlling communities than on empowering them. Therefore, the US Environmental Justice Indicator score stands at -11.8 (see Table A1.1, Appendix 1). This means that the US performs the worst out of the seven case-study countries.

As the US has been so advanced in terms of developing EJ policy and practice, why has it not achieved a better level of environmental justice? It seems that US companies appear to have worked around the regulations, making use of loopholes in the law and relocating when necessary, thereby merely displacing the problem. The Shintech example illustrates the shortcomings of the environmental justice legislation, firstly, in that it places the burden of proof on communities and not on polluting industries and, secondly, in that it focuses mainly on distributional justice and not substantive justice, failing to develop pollution prevention as the main and overarching strategy. The First National People of Color Environmental Leadership Summit principles called for the prevention of pollution at the point of production, rather than mitigation after the fact, but industry's need for profit continues to be the paramount consideration.

Legislation has mainly focused on the management and mitigation of risk, the control of public resistance to environmental harms and cleaning up ecological damage after it occurs. The way that the government has worked with business to limit regulation and focus on controlling EJ communities seems to be a key reason for the lack of progress on environmental justice in the United States, despite the development of so much apparently progressive legislation and so many seemingly supportive institutional frameworks. Some interviewees were clear that their environmental problems were rooted in the market economy. For example, a Mohawk hereditary chief associated with the 'Longhouse tradition', which covers an area including Quebec, Canada as well as New York State in the US, stated:

> "Capitalism is a collective suicide because it destroys the land, and everyone participating in capitalism, thereby, is committing suicide because, when you destroy the land, you are destroying your home, and when you destroy your home, you destroy yourself. So the native people know that destroying the land is no way to make a living. Killing yourself is no way to make a living so there is nothing within capitalism that is a human practice. It's a subhuman practice that has enslaved the people into actually having no choice but to kill themselves." (Interview, 25 May 2012, Stuart Myiow, Secretary, Mohawk Traditional Council)

However, other environmental justice activists I spoke to emphasised racial discrimination or the powerlessness of low-income communities when explaining the reasons for environmental injustice in the US (for example, interview, 30 January 2013, Elizabeth Yeampierre, Chair, National Environmental Justice Advisory Council). Although capitalism has formed and contributed to environmental injustice in the United States, its pattern has been a racist one. Environmental injustices are part of a legacy of institutional racism against black and other minority ethnic communities, as one interviewee emphasised:

> "Environmental injustice in the United States started when indigenous people were put on reservations, on the worst land; when people lived in slave quarters; when nations, like Puerto Rico, were invaded; when land that could have been used for growing was used to locate polluting industry … Our experience is part of a legacy of abuse." (Interview, 30 January 2013, Elizabeth Yeampierre, Chair, National Environmental Justice Advisory Council)

Furthermore, black and other minority ethnic groups in the US have been encouraged or, in some cases, even forced, to accept Damaging

Hegemonic Environmental Discourses. For example, the historic cultural assimilation of indigenous people in the United States, between 1790 and 1920, attempted to transform indigenous culture, including environmental values such as the importance of reciprocal relationships between humans and nature (Hoxie, 1984). 'Americanisation' policies were used to ensure that indigenous people learned United States (European-American) customs and values, so that they could join the mainstream society. Traditional religious ceremonies were outlawed and 'residential schools' (boarding schools) were established that indigenous children had to attend. Here, they were forced to speak English, study 'relevant' subjects, attend church and leave their tribal traditions behind. Interviewees from the Mohawk community that I spoke to felt that this oppression was behind some of the ecological destruction they were now witnessing in their communities:

> "Because of religion and the government working to take our lands and destroy our people, they put a residential school system on our people and therefore the women did not have access to teach their children the values of the land and how to protect it and they took away our laws, our own laws to protect the land … so that right now we have to fight for the air quality, the water quality, the land quality and the animal rights because, look, for instance, all this cement all around us, a long time ago it wasn't like that. The cement, the asphalt – it's poison to the earth. Nothing can grow in it anymore … In the past it was just some roads, like maybe the main road … that was paved … but now people pave their driveway and they pave their whole yard because they want everything smooth, they don't want their cars dirty …" (Interview, 25 May 2012, Kawisente Carole McGregor, Bear Clan Female Chief, Tehanakarine)

They spoke of this in connection with their anger and sadness regarding the recent trend for indigenous people in North America to take up enterprises that contradict traditional values about respect for nature, such as renting out their green space for landfill, and accepting nuclear waste for storage.

We can, therefore, see evidence to support several of the theories regarding the causes of environmental justice here – environmental harms resulting from industrialisation; the location of toxic facilities in low-income areas in accordance with market dynamics; discrimination that devalues certain groups; powerlessness, with regard to some communities being less able to resist toxics in their communities; life-style, in terms of a pervasive consumerist existence; and culture, as carried in Damaging Hegemonic Environmental Discourses. However, the overwhelming reason for environmental injustice in the US appears to be the capitalist system, which enables and requires business and governments to join forces to ensure the continuance of profit-making production, regardless of the harm to human health. This appears to be the lynch-pin that connects these theoretical explanations for environmental injustice.

Though there are no signs that the US is ready to rethink its commitment to this system, there have been a number of notably positive policy developments in recent years which may begin to improve the environmental justice situation somewhat. Since 2010, the Obama administration has reinvigorated coordinated national action on environmental justice. Only three days after taking office, Obama appointed Lisa Jackson as the first African-American to head the EPA, and Jackson has now reconvened the national Interagency Working Group on Environmental Justice. Clinton's (1994) Executive Order has also now been revived, with 17 national agencies recently signing a statement that they agree to the framework, procedures and responsibilities of integrating environmental justice into all of their programmes, policies and activities (Memorandum of Understanding on Environmental Justice and Executive Order 12898). Furthermore, in 2011, Democrat Jessie Jackson Jnr introduced proposed legislation that would amend the Constitution of the United States to effectively establish a right to a clean, safe and sustainable environment in the country (H.J. Res 33) (Library of Congress, 2011 – see govtrack.US for an update of its progress). Moreover, in 2012 the Department of Health and Human Services (DHHS) issued a new draft Environmental Justice Strategy (US DHHS, 2012) for public comment that explicitly affirmed the social and environmental determinants of health, recognising the importance of clean air and water, healthy neighbourhoods, safe work places and healthy foods (Gracia and Koh, 2011).

However, the recession and austerity measures in the United States have clearly slowed down the progress of EJ, as other issues have come to the fore, as one interviewee for this book highlighted:

> "In recent years, say the last five years, the focus has just been on trying to exist … people have just been trying to get through the day because of unemployment, and the collapse of the financial markets impacted so many black people in the US … the unemployment rate shot up … In

some cities it is 40% amongst black youth. It's hard to focus on something like environmental justice when you have to think about just getting something to eat and maintain shelter over your head and not get sick ... People are just trying to keep their job, trying to get their bills paid during this recession ..." (Interview, 18 May 2012, Brian Gilmore, Clinical Associate Professor, Michigan State University, College of Law)

In this climate it may become even more difficult for disadvantaged communities to resist the pressure to accept toxics. The new efforts to increase environmental justice that are under way with the Obama regime appear to offer some hope, but it does not seem that real progress can be made until the United States addresses its extensive problems arising from the prevailing capitalist economy – inequality and the prioritisation of company profits.

Note

[1] This refers to an agreement between Southern and Northern states of the US reached during the Constitutional Convention of 1787. Only three-fifths of the slave population were counted for the purpose of taxation and representation in Congress. The North did not want slaves to be counted as part of the population at all, as it would increase the Congressional seats apportioned to the South, so the three-fifths compromise was agreed.

FIVE

'The world has been deceived': environmental justice in the Republic of Korea (South Korea)

The concept of environmental justice came relatively recently to the Republic of Korea (henceforth, South Korea), developing out of mainstream environmentalism, which began in the 1980s (Lee, 2009). Unlike environmentalism in Europe and the US, which initially focused on the preservation of ecosystems, however, South Korea's early environmentalism was concerned with the impact of pollution on human health. This initial recognition of the importance of the environment for humans made it easy to begin to think about environmental justice issues. In 1999, a landmark moment for environmental justice in South Korea occurred with the first Environmental Justice Forum, organised by the Citizens' Movement for Environmental Justice, now one of the largest and fastest-growing environmental organisations in the country. The Forum reported that rural regions frequently experienced environmental injustice in the form of a lack of sanitation and improved drinking water, as well as the increased siting of contaminating facilities in or near their communities. This chapter will outline the current substantive, distributional and procedural aspects of environmental justice in the South Korea. However, before proceeding further, some of the political and economic features of the country will be briefly outlined to set the context.

Since shortly after the Korean War, which divided the peninsula, South Korea has adopted a capitalist, and increasingly neoliberal, form of political economy. This particularly intensified when the country ratified the 1986 Uruguay Round of the General Agreement on Tariffs and Trade (GATT),[1] thereby adopting a free trade system. This meant reducing import tariffs and other forms of economic protectionism, a direction reinforced when South Korea underwent a 'structural adjustment' in 1998, which intensified privatisation and deregulation. From 2008, President Lee Myung-bak, a former CEO of car manufacturer Hyundai, continued to steer the country towards neoliberalism, as promised in his inaugural address, in which he stated:

We shall increase our effectiveness by abiding to the small-government, big-market principle. The jobs that are not meant for the government shall be privatised. Only then will we see investments and consumption increase once again. Corporations are the source of national wealth and the prime creator of jobs. All who wish must be allowed to start a business and build a factory without difficulty. We also need to create an environment where entrepreneurs can invest freely, and our companies can roam the world market with much excitement. Unnecessary regulations will be cast away or reformed as early as possible. Opening of the market to the foreign sector is an unavoidable mega-trend. Such an economy as ours, which depends so much on exports, should increase our national wealth through free trade regimes. (Lee Myung-bak, former South Korean President's inaugural address, 2008)

Lee Myung-bak's term of office ended in February 2013, when Park Geun-hye of the Saenuri Party became the first female president of the country. Park Geun-hye has more centrist leanings than Lee Myung-bak, but the party in power is the same (albeit with a new name) so that, in general, the policy direction seems unlikely to change. An essential aspect of the governing party's strategy has been an emphasis on economic growth, which has continued at a high rate of about 6% annually in recent years, much of it driven by exports (OECD, 2006) (see economic datasets in Appendix 2). The country is now the world's twelfth-largest economy, with energy-intensive industry and manufacturing accounting for more than a quarter of GDP (UNEP, 2010).

Substantive environmental justice in the Republic of Korea

Under Article 35 of the Constitution, all Korean citizens have the right to a healthy and pleasant environment. This right is supported by extensive environmental legislation, with the Framework Act on Environmental Policy (FAEP) forming the basis of the law.[2] An OECD (2006) review of the Republic of Korea's environmental performance considers that the country is making major progress in addressing air, water and waste problems, especially in urban areas. In particular, there have been major cuts in sulphur oxides and particulates; improvements in water and waste infrastructure, including recycling, incineration and sanitation; as well as advances in biodiversity protection.

However, despite these improvements, South Korea continues to face a number of serious environmental challenges. Primarily, as the environmental datasets in Appendix 2 illustrate, the country has a large Ecological Footprint, at 4.6 global hectares per person. This is mainly due to the country's very high resource use and levels of pollution, a consequence of the rapid industrialisation and urbanisation that has occurred since the 1980s. During this period, South Korea developed an energy dependency on imported fossil fuels so that it now imports 97% of its total energy requirements (UNEP, 2010). Rapid growth also put pressure on South Korea's water resources, leading to many problems with regard to water scarcity and the ambient quality of rivers, lakes and coastal waters (UNICEF/WHO, 2012). There are also problems associated with asbestos in building materials (Choi et al, 2010); pesticides and fertilisers (OECD, 2006); waste management; the destruction of sensitive ecosystems; over-fishing; and toxic leaks from US military bases (Green Korea United, 2008).

Furthermore, since liberalisation, food self-sufficiency has declined, from 70% in the 1980s to 26% in 2011 (Lee and Müller, 2012). The country is now very dependent on food imports and has become one of the world's biggest outsourcers of food production. Large tracts of land have been purchased to grow crops and bio-fuels, as attempted in the now infamous Daewoo Logistics–Madagascar deal of 2008. This 'land grab' particularly attracted attention because of its size (1.3 million hectares) and the ensuing riots and overthrow of the Madagascan government. Half of Madagascar's arable land, as well as some rainforests, were to be converted into palm and corn monocultures for South Korea's food and energy consumption, while much of the local population went hungry. Those already living on the land were never consulted or informed about this deal. In this, and similar land grabs, the government and private companies of South Korea worked together to try to secure lucrative business opportunities in overseas agricultural production. Hofman and Ho call this 'developmental outsourcing', that is, 'global off-shoring in which the state plays a key role in planning, intervention and regulation' (Hofman and Ho, 2012, p 37).

These various environmental problems have persisted even though, over the last two decades, there has been a great deal of policy focus on the issue. Successive South Korean presidents have been keen to portray themselves as environmental leaders, initiating policy in a top-down way through a series of dramatic visions and action plans. Initially, President Kim Young-sam, elected in 1993, pronounced that he would be the first of the country's leaders to improve the environment. A National Action Plan to implement Agenda 21 was formulated, though, in general, little changed as the country continued to pursue a growth-oriented development strategy. Following this, in 1997, President Kim Dae-jung set up a Presidential Commission on Sustainable Development (PCSD), which set national goals and policy direction for sustainable development in various sectors. Similarly, the subsequent President, Ro Mu-hyun, declared a 'National Vision for Sustainable Development' with the goal of continuing Korea's growth 'while maintaining balance between the economy, society and the environment' (in Chung and Hwang, 2006, p 2). A National Strategy for Sustainable Development (NSSD) was completed in 2006 following multi-stakeholder consultations, including with government departments, civil society organisations and businesses. Notably, the issue of equality was present within the original sustainability strategy, which explicitly stated that:

> Korea's 'compressed economic growth' caused the increase of social conflicts due to a concentration of wealth and lack of social welfare system such as employment, public health and welfare. This proves that social basis for sustainable development cannot be established without an equitable distribution of wealth. (NSSD, 2006, p 9)

Hence, at that time there was an emphasis on managing economic, social and environmental sectors in a comprehensive and integrated way. However, Ro Mu-hyun's successor, Lee Myung-bak, went on to propose his own grand vision for the country: 'Low-Carbon Green Growth' (LCGG). This, he announced, would be the new national development paradigm for the next 60 years (NRCS, 2012). As a result, a Presidential Committee on Green Growth was launched in 2008 and the previous Presidential Commission on Sustainable Development was disbanded. The Low-Carbon Green Growth strategy was to be implemented through a 'Green New Deal' project announced in 2009, where green growth was to be combined with job creation. Many governments around the world have, similarly, recently added environmental content to fiscal stimulus programmes in response to the recession. However, South Korea went further than any other country in this when it announced that 81% of public investment would go towards green initiatives, equivalent to 2.6% of GDP. The government has laid out three objectives for green growth: economic growth with minimal use of energy and resources; reduced CO_2 emissions and environmental pollution with the same energy and resource use; and new growth through research and development in green technologies, so as to achieve early dominance in international markets. The LCGG strategy is to be implemented mainly through incentives for companies to develop green technologies and products; public information/education to increase awareness of, and demand for, green products; and regulatory measures (particularly the reduction of greenhouse gas emissions from industry).

Though not required to reduce emissions under the Kyoto Protocol, due to its developing economy status at the time of the negotiations in 2009,[3] the government set a greenhouse gas reduction target of 30% by 2020, the most ambitious target so far of the Non-Annex I countries. In order to achieve this, a Target Management System was initiated that, after consultation with affected businesses, will be mandatory. This is a step ahead of the voluntary agreement system that has been set up in most other countries. The government will provide a great deal of financial assistance to enable the targeted companies to comply, subsiding up to 50% of the cost of installing energy-efficient and low-carbon facilities as well as offering loans and tax exemptions for the remaining costs. Carbon trading is also considered to be a pillar of the LCGG strategy. In 2012, the South Korean National Assembly passed a law to introduce a national carbon trading scheme by 2015, making it one of the first countries in the world to set up such a scheme. The UK Department of Energy and Climate Change worked with South Korea to help draft the legislation (House of Commons Energy and Climate Change Committee, 2012).

Innovation and new technology is the main emphasis of the green growth strategy, supported by billions of dollars of public finance (Ministry of Knowledge Economy, 2009). The strategy also includes various financial policies designed to mobilise public funds to use as credit for environmental businesses through public financial institutions, such as the Korea Development Bank and the Korea Credit Guarantee Fund. In addition, tax credits for small and medium-sized energy-saving companies and other financial incentives are available for different phases of environmental business development, including research and development, and commercialisation. Alongside some clearly beneficial technologies, such as photovoltaic panels, wind energy technology and Light-Emitting Diode (LED) appliances, the government also plans to develop the following, more questionable (if not highly damaging), technologies: fuel cells; carbon capture and storage; nuclear reactors; green cars; bio-technology; robot applications; nano fusion; and bio-pharmaceuticals (Ministry of Knowledge Economy, 2009; National

Science and Technology Council, 2009; Presidential Council for Future and Vision, 2009).

Rather than focus on reducing unnecessary demand, as would be consistent with the need to live within planetary boundaries, under the green growth strategy consumption is projected to increase by 32% over the next 20 years (PCGG, 2009). Though renewables are to be developed in a bid to develop an advantage in the world market for low-carbon technologies (Kang et al, 2012), up to 50% of the energy required to grow the economy will be provided by nuclear power (Sanders, 2010). This will mean that 12 additional nuclear power plants will need to be built, in addition to the existing 20 (Sanders, 2010).

Alongside this, the Korean Ministry of Education, Science and Technology is promoting 'green growth education', much of it focused on stimulating demand for green products and encouraging individual green behaviour patterns (see GGGI, 2011). To help develop the market for ecological products, the government has introduced a mandatory eco-friendly product procurement scheme for public institutions and provides incentives, as well as practical information, to encourage citizens to shop green. For example, commercial banks have been encouraged to give preferential rates to customers who purchase eco-products, with a specific credit card linked to their account (Kang et al, 2012). In addition, since 1992 the government has managed an eco-labelling system for consumer products. This includes various voluntary systems, where producers employ more or less verifiable measures that provide consumers with environmental information on the product, including its carbon footprint.

In 2010, the government helped to set up the Global Green Growth Institute (GGGI), which it now leads, dedicated to diffusing green growth around the world (GGGI, 2013). The underlying assumption, as outlined in its 'vision' is:

> the belief that economic growth and environmental sustainability are not merely compatible objectives; their integration is essential for the future of humankind. (GGGI, 2013, p 1)

Though the outcome of Korea's green growth policy is, as yet, uncertain, UNEP (2010) is now presenting the Republic of Korea as a model green growth nation. However, there is much opposition to 'green growth' from Korea's trade union and environmental justice community, including the Citizens' Movement for Environmental Justice; Green Korea United; the Korean Green Party (Plus); Federation of Korean Trade Unions; Korean Federation of Construction Industry Trade Unions; Korean Power Plant Industry Union; and the Korea Peasants League. These groups refer to the LCGG strategy as 'green wash', warning that the portrayal of this programme as a successful model by the international community, including UNEP, is based on a lack of understanding and knowledge of what is really happening in Korea. They have stated:

> The world has been deceived by the Korean government's new vision for 'Green Growth'. This Green Growth policy currently touted in Korea is no more than an economic development vision ... Large scale civil engineering projects and constructions, such as nuclear power plants, are driving the Korean environment into a catastrophe. (COP15 Korea NGOs Network, 2009)

Their criticisms include: the lack of focus on reducing energy use; the planned increase in nuclear power; the low renewable energy targets; the focus on developing an overseas food supply; the emphasis on road transport, as opposed to railways; the increased privatisation of resources, including water; the emphasis on projects that benefit developers at the expense of the environment; and the proposed deregulation of some environmental legislation (for example, interview, 21 January 2013, Heeseon Sim, Policy Officer, Citizens' Movement for Environmental Justice). The government's LCGG strategy has included the deregulation of factory sites and the lifting of green belt restrictions within the Seoul region to enable more growth and development. Furthermore, large-scale engineering projects have featured highly in the strategy. One of the most controversial of these is the 'Four Rivers Restoration Project'. This project was to dredge, dam and 'beautify' four major rivers, supposedly to increase the supply and quality of fresh water and prevent flooding and drought, as an adaptation to climate change. The project accounts for 36.8% of the budget for the government's Green New Deal, the highest share (Yun, 2010). Polls show that more than 70% of Korean citizens criticise the project on the grounds that it will kill the ecosystems of the four rivers and because the project has proceeded without respect for legal processes, including laws relating to environmental policy and Environmental Impact Assessments (Yun, 2010). For these reasons, in most of the interviews and informal conversations carried out with Korean citizens for this book, a great deal of concern was expressed regarding the project (for example, interview, 1 February 2013, Yujin Lee, Director of Policy Making

Committee, Korean Green Party Plus). The interviewees believe the government is carrying out these projects, not for the environment, but for the benefit of civil engineering and building contractors. The LCGG strategy will not even succeed in lowering carbon emissions, they argue, as South Korea's carbon footprint could increase with the resulting burst of construction.

Korean academics have also been critical of the LCGG strategy. For example, Yun (2010) argues that the government's proposed policies and projects are based on a distorted and narrowed concept of 'green', purely focusing on carbon emissions. Yun considers that this policy is being used to make the active pursuit of growth more palatable and to narrow the acceptability of environmental policies that are not combined with growth. This co-option of the green agenda has, to some extent, taken attention away from the domestic environmental movement and subsumed green under what amounts to a growth-biased discourse. This Damaging Hegemonic Discourse around growth is now, however, being widely challenged, even by high-level state executives:

> "Many of us are concerned about the Green Growth Strategy. I think, mostly, this strategy is to incentivise industry which produces environmental goods, for example, companies producing wind and solar power generators … It is not exactly an environmental policy, it is more a business strategy and, more controversially, it emphasises nuclear energy as an alternative energy to oil but the nuclear waste problem has not been solved in Korea so it will be a great problem if this strategy continues to be implemented." (Interview, 9 October 2012, Social Policy Executive, Government of the Republic of Korea)

Hence, it is a pivotal moment in South Korea in terms of the direction of its environmental policy, with significant tensions between those who support and oppose LCGG. Although it is too early to judge the longer-term outcomes of this policy, it has a number of concerning aspects, especially in that it promotes many risky and/or ineffective technologies and programmes.

Distributive environmental justice in the Republic of Korea

In the Republic of Korea, unlike in the United States, environmental justice claims are not made on the basis of race. Though there are now over one million migrants from parts of East and South-East Asia, and there is recognised discrimination, in particular towards people from North Korea (Kang, 2010), there is not the same history or extent of racial oppression as in the United States. In addition, migrants tend to be more dispersed than in some other countries, and so they are less likely to bear environmental burdens that others do not.

South Korea's main social divisions are based on income and class. Until the 1997 Asian financial crisis, the country maintained a relatively equal income distribution, but, since then, disparities have progressively increased. There has been extensive casualisation of employment in recent years, with the number of irregular workers, that is, workers without contracts, rising sharply since 1998 (OECD, 2012). Today, more than half of the workforce, or 17 million people, is considered to be irregular (that is, without contracts or with inadequate contracts), earning just 53% of the regular average wage (Jones and Urasawa, 2012). This casualisation has led to a decline in wages, overall, as well as to increased inequality. One of the main reasons for the casualisation of the workforce is cost cutting in order to maintain profitability and competitiveness. In a national survey, 32.1% of firms cited reducing costs as the most important reason for hiring non-regular workers (OECD, 2007). As Jones and Urasawa (2012, p 6) state,

> The widening income disparity reflects a number of structural changes ... Korea's international competitiveness and continued output growth depend on such structural changes, making it important for the authorities to facilitate, rather than hinder, such changes.

As well as receiving lower wages, non-regular workers also tend to have more precarious employment and less social security coverage (Jones and Yoo, 2012). Therefore, most poverty in South Korea is among the working poor (Koh, 2011).

This endemic social inequality, especially when combined with geographical segregation on the basis of income, has underpinned distributional environmental injustice. In South Korea, income groups tend to concentrate geographically, as in most other countries. This segregation on the basis of income is evident in Seoul, for example, in the immense difference between the neighbouring Guryong and Gangnam districts (see Figure 5.1). Guryong is a sprawling slum district of plywood and tarpaulin shacks where more than 2,000 people now live without proper sanitation or access to gas or electricity. On the other side of a six-lane motorway is opulent and glitzy Gangnam, now internationally famous as a result of the song 'Gangnam Style'.

Although, in 1989, a public rental housing programme was launched targeting low-income households, the gap in housing conditions between income classes is still large (Ha, 2010). There are now fewer squatter settlements, but many of their former residents continue

Figure 5.1: Guryong and Gangnam

Source: Mike Stulberg/Chincha (2013)

to live in difficult circumstances. Many households are living in accommodation that does not meet minimum standards for size and basic facilities. Furthermore, some of the former squatters now live in 'Jjogbang', whereby they rent a bed for a number of hours and then another person or persons rent the same bed for the remaining hours of the day (Ha, 2010). Housing and other development has also led to forced evictions for some low-income groups. This has particularly been an issue in Seoul, where, in the early 1980s, people living in self-made homes on the outskirts of the city were forced out in order to make way for high-rise apartments. People lost their lives during these eviction processes and, as a result, South Korea's evictions were highlighted as an example of the most brutal and inhuman in the world (Kim, 2010). Heeseon Sim, Policy Officer for the Citizens' Movement for Environmental Justice (interview, 21 January 2013), told me that these forced evictions of low-income groups continue, whilst landlords and developers still make excessive profits through redevelopment.

A number of academic studies have detailed other forms of disproportionate environmental burdens in South Korea, including: Park's (2001) analysis of the Seoul–Incheon Canal construction, which caused a loss of livelihood and farming for some low-income local residents; Jeon's (2003) study of the marginalisation of fishermen and farmers in the Saemangeum region, the location for the largest reclamation plant in Korea; Seo's (2001) work on development in the rural Yongin Area, where developers made excessive profits at the expense of local farmers; Han's (2001) study of urban landfill, showing a lack of procedural justice; Seo's (1991) analysis, showing a correlation between low-income areas and dust density; and Lee's (2009) study of the siting of a coal plant at Yeongheung Island against the wishes of local low-income groups. In Korea, distributive environmental justice also links to rural/urban location. Contaminating facilities are often located in rural areas, where people have lower incomes, even though they are predominantly providing services for urban communities (Lee, 2009).

Procedural Environmental Justice in the Republic of Korea

Procedural environmental justice depends on basic democratic rights and civil liberties. These appear to be assured in South Korea, with the constitution guaranteeing freedom of speech, freedom of the press and the right to free assembly and association for all citizens. In addition, since the Act on Disclosure of Information by Public Agencies 1998, citizens have been able to demand information held by public agencies (though with the exception of information pertaining to national security, trials in progress and personal information about individuals). Furthermore, under the provisions of the Environmental Impact Assessment Act 2009, there is a responsibility to hold environmental hearings and to announce these hearings and disclose relevant documents to the public, unless prohibited according to the exceptions listed above.

However, the degree to which these rights and freedoms are genuine has recently come under question. A UN Special Rapporteur for Human Rights reported that freedom of expression has diminished in South Korea since 2008 and that there have been an increasing number of cases where individuals who contradict the government's position are prosecuted and punished on the basis of domestic regulations that do not conform to international law (La Rue, 2010). The law allows prison sentences of up to seven years for praising or expressing sympathy with the North Korean regime, for example. Moreover, a new law, introduced in 2011, banned demonstrations in 'places of security and safety'. Most of the South Korean interviewees for this book expressed concern about civil liberties, including a high-level government officer who requested that his identity be anonymised. He stated:

> "People will get in trouble for saying what the government doesn't like ... In the past, especially in the 70s, the Security Service investigated people that were opposed to the President himself but, since the 1990s, the democratic process was firmly established ... but the current President exploits his authority illegally to prevent opposition opinion ..." (Interview, 9 October 2012, Senior Economist, Government of the Republic of Korea)

With regard to environmental decision-making processes, though Environmental Impact Assessments (EIAs) must be carried out prior to new developments, there are many loopholes in practice. For example, EIAs do not have to be announced in the mainstream media and there is no obligation on authorities to accept the results of the hearings. Many of the South Korean interviewees for this book considered that procedural environmental justice in the country is tokenistic, arguing that a limited range of people attend EIA hearings and that there is rarely a revision to the proposal as a result of the opinions expressed. For example, I was told:

"Now in Korea there are many environmental protests, especially about proposed nuclear plants, for example, in Samcheok and Yeongdeok and transmission lines from those plants ... The plants are located in areas were older people, marginalised people, farmers live ... There is supposed to be a hearing process but it doesn't really work. Sometimes, it is deceitful, as they only invite those who support the plant. Local people often do not know the hearings are going on. Then, the location of the plant is announced and local people are shocked ... The process is not really genuine; it does not take into account local opinion." (Interview, 1 February 2013, Yujin Lee, Director of Policy Making Committee, Korean Green Party Plus)

In spite of, or perhaps because of, these failings of the environmental decision-making processes, there is now a thriving EJ movement in Korea. As the number of environmental groups increases, larger umbrella organisations have developed to coordinate activities, including the Korean Federation for Environmental Movements, Green Korea United and the Citizens' Movement for Environmental Justice. Presently, their main campaigns are opposing the Four Rivers Restoration Project, resisting the further development of nuclear power and the construction of a naval base on Jeju Island, as well as supporting local groups who are opposed to the siting of toxic facilities in their communities (interview, 21 January 2013, Heeseon Sim, Policy Officer, Citizens' Movement for Environmental Justice). However, despite the proactivity of the campaign groups, their effectiveness is severely limited by government and corporate manipulation and repression.

Lee's 2009 study provides an in-depth illustration of the problems that can occur when citizens attempt to enact or demand their rights. In a study of the construction of a coal-fired power plant in Yeongheung (Figure 5.2), he pinpoints a number of procedural injustices. Firstly, prior to obtaining legal permission to start construction, the developers, KEPCO, had already purchased the site for the plant, indicating their confidence that permission would be granted despite any local opposition that might occur. Secondly, though there were some public meetings about the planned plant in the early stages, the company allowed only a few local residents who had seemed favourable to the plan to participate. These were the residents from whom it obtained written consent for the construction. Thirdly, when the formal EIA was conducted, it did not properly consult local people. There is a legal loophole in Korea that permits the developers to select the company that will carry out the EIA, and so the developers chose a company that was sympathetic to its proposal. Fourthly, when local residents realised what the environmental impacts of the proposed plant would be on local air and water, they began to publicly protest. The developers used carrots and sticks, in the form of compensation payments, to entice them to give up their opposition, alongside government repression, including arrest (Lee, 2009). These strategies undermined the campaign and opposition eventually died out. This lack of inclusive and participative environmental decision making exemplifies the lower steps of Arnstein's (1969) 'Ladder of Participation' (see Figure 2.1), from placation, at best, to manipulation, at worst.

Figure 5.2: The Yeongheung coal plant

Source: Hosuk Lee (2009)

Lee (2009) considers these combined manipulations and crack-downs to be common strategies used by government and private companies in South Korea to push through development programmes, in spite of the wishes of locals. Compensation payments are only ever for a tiny proportion of environmental costs, but they are sufficient to divide the community and undermine solidarity.

Speaking in general terms about the difficulties that exist for activists in South Korea, a political actor explained:

"There is sometimes a lot of violence at these protests ... Some people are hit by policemen and vigilantes hired by the companies ... People are also often fined for being at the construction site. It is a lot of pressure for them because they are really poor. Their entire life they had nothing to do with the police but now they have become criminals for protesting against these development plans ... Some of them continue to oppose but others give up because of the pressure ..." (Interview, 1 February 2013, Yujin Lee, Director of Policy Making Committee, Korean Green Party Plus)

Therefore, the apparent rights and freedoms in South Korea are sometimes little more than a façade. They are swept aside as the South Korean government, working hand-in-hand with private companies, rushes to deliver a particular growth-based vision of development.

Causes of environmental injustice in the Republic of Korea

In some ways, South Korea has made a substantial effort to address its environmental problems. A number of policies have been initiated that should contribute to environmental justice, including setting mandatory CO_2 emissions targets; investing heavily in environmental projects and programmes; issuing eco-friendly product procurement directives; and promoting green life-styles. However, there are continuing problems with regard to all three aspects of environmental justice. Substantive injustices include water pollution, inadequate housing, excessive use of natural resources and weak environmental legislation. Distributive injustice occurs on the basis of unequal income in a highly divided society, with poorer people often likely to lose out in development and regeneration projects. In terms of procedural justice, there are restrictions on freedom of expression and participatory environmental decision making is often tokenistic. Therefore, the Republic of Korea scores poorly on the Environmental Justice Indicator Framework developed for this book, with an overall rating of -9.6 (see Table A1.1 in Appendix 1).

The explanations for these injustices could be given in terms of 'market dynamics', with wealthier householders being able to avoid environmental harms; or life-style choices where, for example, citizens 'choose' the private car over public transport; or discrimination, as factories are located in rural areas where it is perceived locals will be less likely to complain; or lack of power, as poor communities can be divided by compensation pay-outs or the need for jobs. However, the themes of industrialisation, capitalism and culture seem the most pertinent to the South Korean experience of environmental injustice.

South Korea's rapid industrialisation has clearly put pressure on the environment. However, the government has encouraged this type of development, setting aside inconvenient environmental issues. State and business interests have worked together to push through development programmes, in spite of local environmental concerns. This point was also highlighted by the OECD during an environmental review of South Korea in 2006, when it noted 'a risk of environmental concerns being too often superseded by development interests in local decision-making' (OECD, 2006, p 17). The industrialisation and growth discourse of the South Korean government reflects the need for profit within an overarching capitalist political economy. That is not to say that useful development projects have not been undertaken, such as increasing sanitation coverage, but that some of the projects appear to be more about enabling profit and growth than about satisfying human needs (for example, the Four Rivers Restoration Project).

Furthermore, distributional environmental injustice in South Korea, underpinned by increasing inequalities, appears to be worsened by capitalist processes, in particular, the need to maintain competiveness in a global market. Intensified global competition has prompted businesses to reduce labour costs and pursue employment flexibility by hiring non-regular workers on much lower wages and with insecure contracts. As the Republic of Korea is being drawn further into the global market, its possibilities for environmental justice appear to become more remote. Global neoliberal capitalism puts the state at the service of the market and business interests. For example, during the 1986 Uruguay Round of the GATT negotiations and at subsequent meetings of the World Trade Organization, South Korea sought to reduce trade restrictions for its export-oriented industries, such as heavy manufacturing, electronics and textiles. However, in return, the country was required to end agricultural protectionism and, hence, largely lost its ability to produce local food, as it became flooded by products from abroad. This may have actually undermined the development of the poorer areas of the country.

South Korea has for some time prioritised growth and now it uses the discourse of green growth to head off any criticisms that growth is not viable when we are already living beyond the Earth's limits. It is a firmly embedded Damaging Hegemonic Environmental Discourse in South Korea, as is apparent in this interviewee's comment:

"Between environmental protection and economic growth, people will generally say that growth is more important ... People still want these large infrastructure projects ... It is quite rare that growth is questioned. Discussions about limits to growth are not active in Korea, even among scholars; I cannot say who is talking about the limits to growth. No one is thinking about it or debating it." (Interview, 1 February 2013, Yujin Lee, Director of Policy Making Committee, Korean Green Party Plus)

Yet, the high rate of growth has not evidently improved general well-being. The relative poverty rate in South Korea doubled between 1996 and 2008 during a period of very high growth (Jones and Yoo, 2012). Even the OECD has made a statement regarding the need for Korea to look beyond growth in its policies, stating:

While economic growth can help reduce income inequality and poverty, Korea's experience shows that achieving a high growth rate is not sufficient in itself to address inequality and poverty. (OECD, 2012, p 1)

Even looking beyond direct material needs, growth does not appear to have been successful in meeting psychological needs, either. Suicides have almost doubled over the last ten years so that the country now has the second-highest suicide rate in the world (Värnik, 2012).

Therefore, for all the South Korean government's apparent commitment to environmentalism, it still continues to promote growth and tries to convince us, through its Low Carbon Green Growth strategy, that the two are compatible. Hence, the country rates very poorly on the Environmental Justice Indicator Framework, both absolutely, and relative to the other six countries. Although it is still too early to completely understand the impacts of the policy, green growth as a national development paradigm does not seem to deliver environmental justice and appears unlikely to. The kinds of policies and programmes that have been implemented as part of the Low Carbon Green Growth strategy have generally been socially and environmentally harmful, suggesting that this policy approach could be disastrous if adopted on a global scale.

Notes

[1] The GATT (General Agreement on Tariffs and Trade) predated the WTO (World Trade Organisation) as a multilateral organisation regulating international trade. Both have emphasised reducing tariffs and other trade barriers.

[2] For a comprehensive overview of environmental law in the Republic of Korea, see Global Legal Group (2009).

[3] Korea is considered a 'Non-Annex I' country within the Kyoto Protocol and, therefore, is not required to set a legally binding reduction target under the Climate Convention.

SIX

'Regulation means bad': environmental justice in the United Kingdom

The UK is located towards the middle of the capitalist/socialist spectrum used in this book because it is a mixed economy and has seen various phases of more, and less, free market economics. Although capitalism has been the bedrock of the UK economy since the 19th century, in 1945 the election of the Labour Party saw the adoption of more socialist leaning nationalisations of major industries, the creation of the welfare state and Keynesian economic policies. These changes broadly survived until a dramatic swing in the opposition direction occurred when Margaret Thatcher, the leader of the Conservative Party, was elected Prime Minister in 1979. Her government began the re-establishment of monetarist policies, a reduction in the government's role in the economy, restrictions on the power of the trade unions and wide-scale privatisation of state-controlled firms, including the electricity, gas and water industries. There has not since been a reversal of these policies, despite 13 years of Labour government between 1997 and 2010. However, not all the gains of the 1945 period have been lost, particularly those in relation to social welfare. At the present time, the country is in the midst of a severe economic crisis and many low-income groups have been adversely affected by the current Conservative-Liberal Democrat Coalition government's austerity policies.

Environmental justice, as a concept, emerged in the UK in the late 1990s, mainly via the academic community, which became interested in the interrelationships between geographical space and conceptions of equity and justice. This interest developed such that, by 2011, after the US, the UK appeared to have the greatest number of published English language research studies on environmental justice in the world (Reed and George, 2011). Environmental justice has also, at times, been debated by government and by policy makers. However, the four nations that make up the UK have taken up the concept at different rates and with varying emphases. In Scotland, there is direct use of the term, while in England there is a tendency to refer to 'environmental equality' rather than 'environmental justice' (for example, Environment

Agency, 2012). Scotland has been far more advanced and proactive on EJ, overall, than the other nations. For example, in 2002, Scotland's First Minister, Jack McConnell, stated that social and environmental justice was to be a theme of his administration (McConnell, 2002). Following this, in 2005, Scotland's Strategy for Sustainable Development dedicated an entire chapter to EJ (Scottish Executive, 2005). The Welsh Assembly has also taken up the issue of environmental justice, but to a lesser extent (Welsh Assembly Government, 2009). However, in the North of Ireland, environmental justice has received comparatively little attention. Turner (2006) considers this to be partly due to a lack of resources, but also because, for some time, environmental issues played a relatively minor role in comparison to 'The Troubles'. In England, environmental justice was first highlighted as a government concern in the late 1990s, though the concept did not appear explicitly in policy documents until the 2004 and 2005 Sustainable Development Strategies (HMG, 2005). At around the same time, environmental factors began to be included in UK government indices of deprivation monitoring (ODPM, 2004) and the environmental justice agenda was taken up by the UK Sustainable Development Commission (SDC).

Overall, a far broader environmental justice agenda has emerged in the UK than in the US with regard to the range of issues, especially in that there is a greater emphasis on access to environmental 'goods' and fairness in procedural matters. There is also a wider focus in terms of social dimensions, which has included age, gender, disability and class, with race and ethnicity playing a relatively minor role compared to that in the US. Where race has been discussed, it is usually in relation to access to the countryside and a lack of inclusion of black and minority ethnic people in the UK environmental movement (for example, Agyeman, 2001; 2002). It is important to note, though, that there is a large overlap between BME and low-income groups in the UK, with around two-fifths of the BME population living in low-income households, twice the rate for white people (Parekh et al, 2010). Therefore, while the focus of most UK studies is on 'deprived communities', it is important to note that this will cover a large proportion of BME people.

It is also important to point out that research and policy on environmental justice in the UK is often found within work on 'social exclusion'. The term is used to denote how, because of their financial limitations as well as social attitudes, people on low incomes are excluded from various resources, institutions and practices that would enable them to enjoy a reasonable quality of life (Levitas et al, 2007). The concept embraces a broad set of dynamic and multidimensional indicators of poverty, including poor housing, low educational attainment, ill-health and associated environmental factors.

While successive UK governments, since the early 2000s, have acknowledged the need to address environmental justice, they have tended to be vague with regard to proposed concrete actions in terms of targets, priorities or funding streams. Though the last Labour government initiated several programmes, policies and strategies that promised to tackle social and environmental problems together (for example, Neighbourhood Renewal), there were major criticisms that these initiatives did not deliver on the ground (see for example, criticisms made by the Sustainable Development Commission, 2003). In general, UK governments have failed to incorporate environmental justice considerations as an intrinsic part of policy and decision-making processes and, since the Coalition government came to power in 2010, the issue has gradually disappeared from policy discourse, as will be discussed in the next sections.

Substantive environmental justice in the United Kingdom

A serious substantive environmental justice issue in the UK, as in the US, is the high per capita use of resources and production of waste, as evidenced by a large per capita Ecological Footprint (see environmental datasets in Appendix 2). However, in terms of local living environments, one of the most serious environmental issues is air pollution. In 2010, the Committee on the Medical Effects of Air Pollutants estimated that in the UK there had been more than 340,000 years of life lost, equivalent to 29,000 early deaths, over the previous year, due to anthropogenic PM air pollution (COMEAP, 2010).[1] The majority of this pollution comes in the form of toxic gases and particulates from car exhausts and diesel engines, including nitrogen dioxide (NO_2), PM10s and PM2.5s. The UK has consistently failed to meet European Commission (EC) targets and timetables to bring air quality to acceptable standards for health and, consequently, the EC has now launched infringement proceedings against the government.

Another important substantive justice issue in the UK, as in many other countries, is the ubiquitous use of synthetic chemicals in consumer products. Testing of household dust has revealed that the extensive use of these chemicals in household products is leading to complex contamination of the home across the UK (Santillo et al, 2003). The nature and extent of the threats presented by toxic chemicals in consumer products, are increasingly being recognised (UNEP, 2012) and EU efforts have been made to control them (or example, 2007 legislation on REACH – Registration, Evaluation, Authorisation and Restriction of Chemicals). However, this law will not be fully implemented until 2018 and, even then, it will determine the risk only for individual chemicals, though most impacts are multiple. Chemicals in food are also of concern. The UK Pesticides Campaign has been engaged in a long-running legal case with the UK government over the use of toxic pesticides, which is now before the European Court of Human Rights. The Campaign's voice is relatively weak, though, as the key organisation advising UK ministers on chemical safety, the Chemicals Regulation Directorate, receives approximately 60% of its funding (around £7 million per year) from the agrochemical industry (Georgina Downs (UK Pesticides Campaign), cited in Hickman, 2012). This is yet further indication of the influence of the 'polluter-industrial' complex.

Another important issue that relates to the high Ecological Footprint of the UK is that of waste. This is often portrayed as a problem of life-style or individual behaviour, though UK citizens often have limited choices about the amount of waste they create. For example, most items purchased come with excessive, unnecessary, and often unwanted, packaging. It is estimated that one quarter to one third of domestic waste is made up of packaging (The Open University, 2008; York City Council, 2012). Although a specific EU Waste Directive, introduced in the UK in 1997, requires packaging to be minimised and recyclable, it seems that implementation of the Directive in the UK has largely focused on the recycling aspect, rather than minimisation (INCPEN, 2012; Valpak, 2012). This emphasis appears to have had a negative impact, as people now feel that it is not necessary to reduce packaging if they are able to readily recycle (MORI, 2002). It would make more sense to require businesses to reduce their packaging, as 'zero waste' proponents advocate (for example, Edgerly and Borrelli, 2007), but, as one NGO explains, 'the problem is that packaging is driven by the desire to promote brands and make money' (Green Choices, 2012, p 1).

The present UK Coalition government has stated that it is committed to being 'the greenest government ever' (Cameron, 2010). There has been some progress in this regard, to the extent that the government has passed the world's first national Climate Change Act, committed to ambitious and legally binding carbon emissions targets, aiming to reduce emissions by 34% by 2020 (from 1990 levels). However, at the same time, the Coalition has undermined the chances of achieving this ambition through other changes to UK environmental law. The law pertaining to the environment in the UK is comprehensive, made up of a combination of public law, which sets environmental standards and authorises activities; criminal law, which defines environmental crime; international law; private law; property law; and EC law. The last of these is particularly important, providing the basis for 80% of current UK environmental law.[2] In 2012 the UK Environmental Law Association (ELA) expressed concerns that UK environmental legislation is too complex and lacks clarity and that, consequently, this limits access to justice (UK ELA, 2012). On the back of this, the Department for the Environment, Food and Rural Affairs (Defra) announced a number of 'Red Tape Challenge Environment Theme'[3] proposals to rationalise or 'refresh' environmental legislation. Although this may seem necessary, in view of the ELA report findings, there are concerns that these proposals are unhelpful and out of proportion; and that they will have a very negative environmental impact (for example, Carrington, 2012a). At the time of writing, there are plans to cut scores of environmental regulations, including some controls on asbestos and industrial air pollution, as well as some of the laws regarding the protection of wildlife and common lands.

The Coalition government had also intended to drastically cut down planning regulations, but was forced to back down on some aspects of this, in particular a default 'yes' to development. The resulting National Planning Policy Framework promises a 'presumption in favour of sustainable development' (DCLG, 2012, p 4). However, though couched in the language of sustainability, many of its concrete goals seem to fly in the face of achieving this. For example, with regard to 'sustainable transport' the document states that local authorities should 'support strategies for the growth of ports, airports or other major generators of travel demand in their areas' (DCLG, 2012, p 9).

In order to justify these cuts to environmental legislation, the changes are disingenuously framed in terms of being necessary to meet public demands for streamlining the law, and to meet the need for housing and jobs. Therefore, the 'Red Tape Challenge' is presented as being led by the public, even though, according to a *Guardian* analysis, 97% of the public responses to the consultation have demanded stronger protection, or no change, to environmental rules (Carrington, 2012b). Furthermore, the government now calls for a massive private sector house building programme to increase jobs and housing provision. To this end, it plans to reduce rules regarding the reasonable cleaning up of contaminated land because, according to the government, they create a burden for the housing industry (Carrington, 2012a). Whether or not the UK really needs more housing is, in any case, questionable. Although, in 2012, 34,080 households with children were accepted as homeless in the UK, this was often because they could no longer afford to pay the rent or mortgage for the house they had, not because there was nowhere for them to live (Shelter, 2013). In addition, there are currently 710,000 empty homes in the UK (Empty Homes Agency, 2012) and 1.6 million UK citizens have a second home (2011 UK Census). Hence, there are probably more than enough houses for everyone, if housing were organised according to need.

It seems more likely that these cuts to environmental legislation are an attempt to kick-start the faltering economy and support business interests. The government has explicitly asserted that eliminating these laws will save UK businesses £1bn (Paterson, 2013). The current Chancellor, George Osborne, has made clear that business interests will always trump environmental concerns, though he has framed this as an issue of jobs, stating:

> I am worried about the combined impact of the green policies adopted not just in Britain, but also by the European Union, on some of our heavy, energy-intensive industries. We are not going to save the planet by shutting down our steel mills, aluminium smelters and paper manufacturers. All we will be doing is exporting valuable jobs out of Britain. (Osborne, 2011)

Consequently, many critics are now worried about the current government's approach to environmental legislation and its implications. For example, Labour MP Joan Walley, Chair of the UK Environmental Audit Committee, stated:

> "the real concern now is the attitude that the current government has which seems to be equating regulation means bad ... If the government reduces the number of regulations, that sends a message about ... the importance of the environment ... we have somehow, almost imperceptibly moved from a situation whereby everyone was understanding what the greenest government ever should look like and should be to, almost, 'oh well, at a time of recession and at a time of austerity the last thing on our minds are these green issues'." (Interview, 25 October 2012, Joan Walley, MP, Chair of the UK Environmental Audit Committee)

This focus on business interests in environmental policy is also evident in the government's 'green economy' strategy which focuses on the market and states explicitly that '... decarbonising the economy provides major opportunities for UK businesses' (HMG, 2011: 4). Therefore, the Coalition government seems to be pursuing contradictory policies. On the one hand it is setting ambitious targets for reducing CO_2 emissions and, on the other, it is deregulating in order to satisfy business interests and increase economic growth.

Distributive environmental justice in the United Kingdom

In a report on inequality in the UK, Hills et al (2010) concluded:

> Inequalities in earnings and incomes are high in Britain, both compared with other industrialised countries, and compared with thirty years ago ... There remain deep-seated and systematic differences in economic outcomes between social groups across all of the dimensions we have examined – including between men and women, between different ethnic groups, between social class groups, between those living in disadvantaged and other areas, and between London and other parts of the country. (Hills et al, 2010, p 1)

Statistical surveys support this analysis, indicating a relatively high level of inequality in the UK, as evidenced by the Gini Coefficient, reported to be 0.34 (IFS, 2012) or 0.36 (World Bank, 2011a; SWIID, 2011) (see socioeconomic datasets in Appendix 2). One aspect of this is that there has been a long-term pattern of health inequalities on the basis of income, race and class (Marmot et al, 2010). For example, those in the most deprived UK neighbourhoods suffer, on average, 13.6 years more of poor health than those in the most affluent neighbourhoods (House of Commons Health Committee, 2009). Although the drivers of health inequalities are likely to be multi-factorial, it is increasingly being recognised in the UK that the local physical environment plays an important role in determining geographical differences in mortality and morbidity (for example, Marmot et al, 2010).

There has been a great deal of research that shows the extent of environmental disparities in the UK. In 2003, Walker et al carried out the first major national study in the UK on the relationship between environmental quality and social deprivation, finding that deprived communities suffer the worst air quality, live closest to polluting facilities and are more likely to be located in coastal flood-risk areas. Following this, numerous studies reported that low-income communities experience a disproportionate burden of environmental 'bads', such as pollution, toxic facilities and landfills, as well as a lack of access to environmental goods, including energy for heating and cooking, healthy food, transport and green space (for example, Boardman et al, 1999; McLaren et al, 1999; DETR, 2001; ESRC, 2001; FOE, 2001; Lucas et al, 2001; HMG, 2005). In 2004, the UK Sustainable Development Research Network reviewed the main body of UK literature on environmental inequities and concluded that 'Environmental injustice is a real and substantive problem within the UK' (Lucas et al, 2004), summarising that many of the UK's most deprived communities experience both poor local environmental quality and differential access to environmental goods; and that they are disproportionately exposed to cumulative environmental risks as well as being disproportionately vulnerable to those risks (Lucas et al, 2004).

Since these early days, the evidence of environmental disparities in the UK has accumulated, especially in relation to:

- air pollution (for example, Gouldson and Sullivan, 2007; Xie and Hou, 2010)
- transport (for example, Jephcote and Chen, 2012; Lucas and Currie, 2012)
- proximity to landfill sites (for example, Richardson et al, 2010b)
- flood risk (for example, Fielding, 2007; 2012; Walker and Burningham, 2011)
- food poverty (for example, Dowler and O'Connor, 2012)
- fuel poverty (for example, Fahmy et al, 2011)
- access to green space (for example, Mitchell and Popham, 2008)
- multiple inequitable burdens (for example, Fairburn et al, 2009; Pearce et al, 2010).

Although a few studies have also, directly or partly, contradicted the general pattern (for example, Smith et al, 2010; Mitchell and Norman, 2012), this work is still vastly outweighed by the studies that confirm social-spatial environmental inequities in the UK.

There have also been new studies on the disproportionate impacts of environmental policies relating to street-cleaning services (for example, Hastings, 2007); waste disposal (Bell and Sweeting, 2013); and energy (for example, Fahmy et al, 2011). These illustrate the triple injustice that occurs when social and environmental policy fails to join up. For example, UK energy policy has negative consequences for low-income

Figure 6.1: Overhead pylons in Lockleaze, Bristol

Source: Karen Bell (2008)

households. This is a major issue because fuel poverty contributes significantly to an average 30,000 excess winter deaths in the UK each year, as well as increased incidence of ill-health and demands on the National Health Service, particularly for young, older and disabled people (see, for example, Stockton and Campbell, 2011). It is shameful that the UK, as one of the wealthiest countries in the world, has such a high rate of fuel poverty, especially in comparison to most European countries, where the weather is far colder. The situation has worsened since 2003, as soaring gas and electricity prices have not been offset by rising incomes or energy-efficiency measures (DECC, 2011c; Hills, 2012). Hence, according to the most recent figures, more than four million UK households are now living in fuel poverty (DECC, 2011a). Yet, while household energy prices have increased by up to 9% annually, energy companies have continued to increase their profits (by as much as 27% in 2011–12) (Moulds, 2013).

Although there might seem to be an inherent tension between the need to reduce carbon emissions and to make cold homes warmer, it is important that these environmental improvements are achieved in a socially just way which does not increase fuel poverty, as the 'Hills Fuel Poverty Review' has highlighted (Hills, 2012). Therefore, we need to find synergistic policies that both alleviate fuel poverty and reduce carbon emissions. Yet, UK government programmes to reduce CO_2 emissions are currently funded by consumers via energy bills – that is, all customers pay a set amount on each unit of energy consumed. This has a greater impact on poorer people, whose energy bills make up a significant proportion of their household expenditure (Fahmy et al, 2011). Moreover, new policies, such as the 'Green Deal', the centrepiece of the Energy Act 2011 (DECC, 2011b; 2011c), rarely help fuel-poor households (Stockton and Campbell, 2011; Ekins and Lockwood, 2011). This policy includes finance arrangements to allow householders to pay for energy-efficiency measures through loans attached to their property, to be repaid through their electricity bills. However, critics argue that the fuel poor may be unable to access loans, or unwilling to take out loans because of 'debt aversion'. In addition, many live in rented properties and so cannot take part in these schemes, as they would not be able to make the necessary alterations to their homes.

Another UK energy policy, Feed-in Tariffs (FiTs) for energy generation from renewable sources, has been criticised on similar grounds. An obligation is imposed on regional or national utility companies to buy the energy derived from renewable sources. People who have enough income to invest in the equipment can install micro-generators and sell the excess electricity generated (although it will be some time before they can recoup their investment). FiTs, therefore, provide economic opportunities for wealthier people who can afford to invest in the new technology but the programme is funded through an additional levy on all consumers' bills. Consequently, there is injustice, not only with regard to costs falling disproportionately on low-income groups, whose energy costs make up a larger proportion of their financial outgoings, but there is also a lack of equal access to the potential benefits of this policy. These examples illustrate how environmental policy that does not consider equity issues can exacerbate distributive environmental injustice.

Although environmental inequities in the UK have been recognised by successive governments for almost a decade, there has been very little action to address the issue, and the action that has been taken has not been effective (ESRC, 2001; Lucas et al, 2003; 2004; Sustainable Development Commission, 2003; Blair and Evans, 2004). Furthermore, there have been few attempts to identify and monitor the distributional impacts of environmental policies. In the only forms of environmental appraisal that have legislative status in the UK – Environmental Impact Assessments, Strategic Environmental Assessments and Sustainability Appraisals – there is little or no consideration of distributional issues (Walker, 2007; 2010). However, until recently, there has been an

Environmental Equality Indicator among Defra's (2010) goals for sustainable development. Also, general UK equalities legislation has offered some protection against distributional environmental injustice. In particular, the Equality Bill 2010 saw the introduction, in 2011, of a Public Sector Equality Duty (Home Office, 2011), which introduced a duty on all public sector organisations in England, Scotland and Wales to take proactive steps to promote equality and to eliminate discrimination with regard to those categories covered by the Act (for example, on the basis of gender, race, disability and age). Part of this duty included carrying out Equality Impact Assessments to gauge the impact of policies and projects on disadvantaged groups. Since 2010, the Environment Agency has been asked to supply information to Defra in relation to this duty (Interview, 28 September 2012, Manager, Environment Agency). Though the duty does not cover social class or people on low incomes, it is a valued piece of legislation for other equalities groups. For example, a leading campaigner for environmental justice in the UK said on this point:

> "The Duty to promote equality has already had a big effect ... because it made our message become part of mainstream practice. That is very powerful and it will continue to help all people that are working on equality to advance ... Agendas are often eroded by all kinds of things, like if there is a shortage of money, one of the first things they cut are the things they think are fringe interests, not central to their core purpose, but with the Duty being there, equality does not entirely fall off the agenda." (Interview, 2 October 2012, Judy Ling Wong, Black Environment Network)

However, both Defra's Environmental Equality Indicator and mandatory Equality Impact Assessments are now under threat. All Defra's sustainability indicators are being revised, following a national consultation. However, the Environmental Equality Indicator disappeared from the list of indicators on the consultation web page, though we are now promised that a revised indicator will be '... developed after the main indicator set is published in July 2013' (Defra, 2013: 6). The main UK campaigning organisations for environmental justice, Capacity Global and the Black Environment Network, are working hard to get this reinstated, arguing that the Environmental Equality Indicator was one of the few things that the government had set up to help protect environmental justice. Again, these changes seem to be motivated by the desire to ensure that private sector interests are satisfied, as was evident when David Cameron, the Prime Minister, in a speech to the Confederation of British Industry, spoke of Equality Impact Assessments in dismissive terms, as part of the 'bureaucratic rubbish' that gets in the way of British business (Cameron, 2012).

With the current government, there appears to be a general change of emphasis, away from equality and towards growth, localism and voluntarism as solutions to environmental injustice. However, an Environment Agency manager who I interviewed for this book felt that the current government did not necessarily lack interest in distributional issues, but:

> "the current administration thinks about these things differently, in terms of localism, and their argument would be that, if it is important locally, then there is scope to do it. So these issues will still be being addressed if you are an area with lots of issues of deprivation ... What's changed is this central prescription of doing something about it ... I think, we don't corporately now emphasise the delivery of those social justice type issues." (Interview, 28 September 2012, Manager, Environment Agency)

Figure 6.2: Polluting factory in a low-income area of Glasgow

Source: Karen Bell (2013)

Therefore, despite there being well-documented environmental inequalities in the UK, what little protection exists now faces the axe.

Procedural environmental justice in the United Kingdom

Until the mid to late 1980s, the dominant official perception in the UK, as throughout Europe, was that the public had no role to play in techno-scientific debates, as problems were to be identified and solved by scientists and qualified experts (Felt et al, 2009). When the public were hostile towards scientific and technological developments, they were largely considered to be ignorant (as in the case of people protesting against nuclear power at that time). This view was referred to as the 'public deficit model' (Irwin and Wynne, 1996), and the solution to this was considered to be better public education. However, since then, participation in environmental decision making has increasingly been emphasised in UK policy making. Yet, as public engagement has increased, there have been more and louder critiques of how such processes work in practice (for example, Bickerstaff et al, 2010). Initiatives designed to include the public in decision making are organised in such a way that they often, paradoxically, deny the possibility of local views being articulated, let alone listened to and acted upon. This is particularly the case for disadvantaged communities (Evans and Percy, 1999). For example, one of the interviewees for this research, representing BME issues, complained of:

> "local authorities putting on consultations and putting out notices so late that there are only two people and they tick the box and say yes, we did have a consultation ... [but] the politicians have already decided what they want. The way the consultations are designed, the crucial questions are never asked. The balance between what the people want and the politicians, it's tipped towards those in positions of power ... it's much better than it used to be but it still continues ... Unless you feel that change will come if you speak up, you won't speak up because you'll think it is a waste of time." (Interview, 2 October 2012, Judy Ling Wong, Black Environment Network)

Concerns have been raised regarding whether the participation is genuine; whether those that do participate represent a broad spectrum of the public; and whether these participatory events are, in fact, no more than rituals designed to satisfy legal requirements (for example, Eames and Adebowale, 2002). There are, in particular, recognised problems around how statutory, commercial and voluntary agencies interact with local communities. For example, Lowndes et al (1998) report the anxieties of officers and members of local authorities with regard to greater public involvement. There is an attempt to galvanise people into a sense of responsibility for delivering targets set by government or local authorities, rather than responding to local concerns. Hence, local people in deprived communities have been engaged in prescribed ways, such as being expected to sit on organisational bodies like Neighbourhood Renewal steering groups (Dinham, 2005).

In my research for this book, as well as in previous studies I have carried out in deprived areas in the UK (for example, Bell, 2008), I have found that it does not seem to be the case that people living in deprived areas are unwilling or unable to effectively engage in the environmental decision-making process. Other studies also suggest that, in spite of inadequate participatory processes, there are high levels of sustained community involvement in disadvantaged areas, though people need to see results in order to sustain motivation (Burningham and Thrush, 2001; Brown, 2002; Dinham, 2005) and want to work on their own agendas, rather than those imposed on them (CDP, 1977). Rather, it appears that residents are keen to engage but the participation processes they encounter are not meaningful, accountable or empowering. For example, residents of Lockleaze, a low-income area of Bristol, spoke to me of their experience with regard to their local market and other initiatives that were part of the 'Neighbourhood Renewal' programme. They said:

> "The [Neighbourhood Renewal] meetings were gruelling. In the end I was so disgusted ... I left because I just thought there is nothing I can do about it. It's just making me unhappy and there's nothing I can do. I've got to find another way. I haven't found it yet." (Interview, 16 July 2007, unemployed resident of Lockleaze – low-income area of Bristol)

> "Local people are just disillusioned. They've been promised so much. They are disappointed. Disappointment is the main reason I don't go [to the Neighbourhood Renewal meetings] any more. I can't get anything done. I feel very

frustrated. My voice doesn't seem to carry any weight."
(Interview, 25 July 2007, retired resident of Lockleaze –
low-income area of Bristol)

The dismissive and disempowering way that this community was treated
is well illustrated with regard to the Lockleaze Community Market.
Because the estate had become virtually a 'food desert', with most of the
fresh food shops closing, residents campaigned, fundraised and planned
for over three years to set up what became a thriving local market for
the community (Figure 6.3). However, key local development workers
imposed their decisions on the community, changing the locations,
timings and funding strategy for the market, against the explicit wishes
of the traders and local people. Local knowledge was dismissed and
ignored, and eventually the professional workers decided to close the
market down (see Bell, 2008).

Figure 6.3: Lockleaze Community Market

Source: Karen Bell (2008)

There seemed to be little willingness on the part of local agencies
to shed or share power. Neighbourhood Renewal, and other local
partnerships, appeared to be less about enabling the community to
press for, or create, better services and more about legitimising council
decisions and managing the community.

Local consultation processes can be manipulated by promises of facilities or spending. For example, under Section 106 of the Town and Country Planning Act 1990, contributions can be sought from developers towards the costs of providing community and social infrastructure, the need for which has arisen as a result of a new development taking place. Hence, local development debates often focus on squabbles over the 'S 106 money', who will get it and what for, dividing the community and undermining solid opposition to the development project. Similar scenarios are likely to arise since the UK government announced that communities that accept shale gas drilling (fracking) in their locality will be compensated by up to £100,000, along with 1% of the revenues for each well fracked.

Low-income communities in the UK lack power in that they have difficulties in acquiring environmental information. Few would know how to find out what substances were being emitted from local facilities and their health effects. The Environment Agency makes some environmental data accessible at a local level through its 'What's in your backyard?' and 'Your right to know' web pages.[5] Through these pages the public can access maps of local facilities, but it is hard for untrained citizens to interpret the information given. The web pages inform the public as to whether the facility is deemed to be safe, but do not inform them about the controversies around safety limits or differential vulnerabilities.

The imbalance of power in environmental decision making could be partly addressed through the support of outside environmental agencies or links with environmental justice organisations. Though a few UK groups have been very active on EJ issues, in particular, Friends of the Earth; Capacity Global; the Black Environment Network; and the London Sustainability Exchange, in general, most mainstream environmental agencies in the UK do not pay attention to equalities issues and people in deprived areas rarely join environmental organisations because of their lack of local presence and an absence of accessible information (Burningham and Thrush, 2001). In general, the mainstream UK environmental movement is pursuing its aim of environmental protection with limited reference to equalities and using a narrow definition of the term 'environment', defined by and of relevance to white, middle-class people (Agyeman, 2001; 2002).

It is notable that there is no grassroots EJ movement to compare with the situation in the US (Bickerstaff and Agyeman, 2009). Consequently, in contrast to the US, environmental justice activists in the UK have not been able to impact as strongly on the regulatory or political environment and have tended to focus more on local issues. They are also impeded in that, in general, recent UK governments have tended to be resistant to policy advice or influence, as two managers at the Environment Agency, who wished to remain anonymous, explained to me. One explained that, in the past, there was a sense of being a co-creator of environmental policy, but this had now changed:

> "[Before], it was OK to actually lobby government, to publish position statement, respond publicly to consultations [but] ... we don't have policy advisors now ... They don't like quangos like us publicly saying what our position on things is." (Interview, 28 September 2012, Manager, Environment Agency)

Perhaps because of this apparent government desire to quieten potential dissent, in 2011 the Coalition government decided to abolish the Sustainable Development Commission, whose role it was to hold the government to account over environmental matters, ostensibly to make efficiency savings in order to reduce the fiscal deficit (SDC, 2010).

When these participatory means to achieve EJ break down, citizens and organisations theoretically have the possibility to contest environmental decisions via the courts. Under the Aarhus Convention, 1998 (Directive 2003/35/EC), all EU citizens have a right to do this. However, the Sullivan Report by the Working Group on Access to Environmental Justice (WGAEJ, 2008) found that the current law on costs in England and Wales is not in line with the Aarhus Convention's Article 9(4), requiring that remedies must be 'fair, equitable, timely and not prohibitively expensive'. Furthermore, in 2009, the Environmental Law Foundation (ELF) produced a report showing that, with regard to decisions affecting the local environment, those with less money routinely lose out to those with more. The research indicated the collapse of more than half of cases before they reach the courts, overwhelmingly because of cost. It concluded that 'This denial of access to environmental justice, particularly when the challenge is to a public body, seems shabby and mean spirited in a modern democracy' (ELF, 2009, p 23). An alliance known as CAJE (made up of Capacity Global, Friends of the Earth, the Royal Society for the Protection of Birds and WWF) complained to the European Commission about UK non-compliance with Aarhus, in particular with regard to the 'not prohibitively expensive' aspect. The EC has now referred the matter to the European Court of Justice (European Commission, 2011). This could ultimately result in large financial penalties for the UK.

Therefore, though the UK government now recognises the need for procedural environmental justice and has signed the Aarhus Convention, there are substantial inadequacies, particularly with regard to including disadvantaged groups in environmental decision making and fair processes.

Causes of environmental injustices in the United Kingdom

This chapter has briefly outlined a range of environmental injustices in the UK. Unsurprisingly, then, the UK achieves a fairly low Environmental Justice Indicator score of 1.9. In terms of substantive justice, though there is a generally adequate level of the basic services that we expect to find in a developed country, such as improved drinking water, there are problems in terms of high resource use and production of waste; unhealthy levels of air pollution; and exposure to ubiquitous toxic chemicals. Distributive injustice is built on the UK's high levels of income inequality and enduring racism. Clean air, transport, energy and safe living environments are not universally available and these environmental inequalities appear to link with socio-spatial disparities in health. Furthermore, environmental policy does not always take into account social effects, and this is likely to worsen if the planned removal of the Environmental Equality Indicator and Equality Impact Assessments goes ahead. Although more consideration is now given to making environmental decision making more inclusive, as in the US, the inclusion processes are often more about managing communities than empowering them. Furthermore, it is not easy for people to inform themselves about local environmental threats and, for many people, it is not affordable to pursue environmental claims through the courts.

Why does the UK have such an inadequate situation of environmental justice? Throughout the interviews with UK environmental policy makers, it was commonly suggested to me that environmental problems are a result of a lack of public interest, or even apathy. This is a classic 'individual behaviour/life-style' explanation for environmental injustice. For example, I was told:

> "I don't believe the public demands action on climate change ... on the whole, in the UK at least, the politicians have been ahead of the public in terms of action on climate change. That's not to say that there aren't strong movements, social movements, NGOs demanding action, but I think,

across the general public at large, there isn't, especially since the recession started, climate change and environment do not appear anywhere on anyone's top ten list ..." (Interview, 25 October 2012, Mark Kember, Chief Executive Officer, The Climate Group)

"The biggest tool of all will be informed public debate because no matter what economists or government ministers or the United Nations decide, there has to be buy-in from the general public and understanding that this is in all our best interests. Public opinion leverage is the one factor that is missing in any large-scale way." (Interview 25 October 2012, Joan Walley MP, Chair of the UK Environmental Audit Committee)

However, the interviews and conversations that I conducted with UK citizens, particularly with low-income groups, lead me to believe that, in general, people are concerned about the environment but feel that they are unable to take action because all their time and energy is taken up with work and dealing with immediate problems and responsibilities. Equally, they are not able to change their production or consumption patterns because they feel that they lack choices and that, if they did make the required change/sacrifice, it would not make any real difference. Interviewees were generally very aware of the limitations in terms of what they could achieve alone, as is evident in this comment:

"It is important that we do our bit, but what we do locally is really just a drop in the ocean. It is important but we've got to think bigger ... The Council could provide solar panels to everyone but spending money on wars abroad and Trident missiles means you can't do that." (Interview, 13 July 2007, hospital worker, resident of Lockleaze)

Though there are likely to be many explanatory factors for the UK's low EJI score, a better overall explanation would seem to be the demands of the market economy, which, as has already been discussed, has meant that the UK government is trying to resolve the EJ issues while maintaining business as usual. In addition, some of the problems seemed to be explained by Damaging Hegemonic Environmental Discourses, such as an unquestioning acceptance of the need for growth and a perceived zero-sum game between meeting humans needs and protecting the environment. The lack of mesh between environmental and social policies may go back to the way that people are trained in either 'natural science' or 'social science', so that work is then structured along these dividing lines. For example, a manager at the Environment Agency stated:

> "In general, the intellectual technical skills around social issues is not high in the wider Defra family. It is only recently that Defra have invested in social people, social researchers. Most officers in Defra, Natural England and the Environment Agency have a natural sciences background ... In general, I would characterise the situation by, in the Environmental Agency, environmental measures are most important, economic measures are increasingly important ... social measures are the poorer of the three ... our priority job is to do with the environment, other bits of government are to do with social and economic agendas, so you could argue, with our limited resources, we need to fix the environment because nobody else will ... I think that might be the view of some of the people at the top these days." (Interview, 28 September 2012, Manager, Environment Agency)

Hence, although the UK context for environmental justice has, at times, been positive, it is now deteriorating. Government policies now appear to be contradictory, setting strict carbon-reduction targets and emphasising sustainability, while, at the same time, deregulating planning and pushing a growth economy seemingly to comply with business interests. The public are conveniently condemned for a lack of interest in environmental matters, perhaps to absolve the political leadership of responsibility for creating effective policy. The UK government, in leading one of the richest countries in the world, would appear to have many more choices than do the governments of less wealthy countries. However, it appears that, as a capitalist state, it is constrained by the profit and growth imperatives and so is unable to effectively address UK environmental injustices.

Notes
[1] PM = particulate matter. PM10 = particulate matter of less than 10 microns in diameter.

[2] A good introduction to environmental law in the UK is Bell and McGillivray (2008).

[3] The 'Red-Tape Challenge' is a Coalition government drive, ostensibly devised to reduce unnecessary, outdated or ineffective legislation.

[4] Since the 1970s there has been an increasing amount of research suggesting that electric and magnetic fields affect human health and can cause childhood and adult leukaemia, miscarriage and depression (see www.emfields.org).

[5] 'What's in your backyard?' provides access to environmental data at a local level: www.environment-agency.gov.uk/homeandleisure/37793.aspx. 'Your right to know' is a public register of environmental permits and licences: www2.environment-agency.gov.uk/epr/.

SEVEN

'We have always been close to nature': environmental justice in Sweden

Sweden's internationally recognised welfare system and progressive environmental policies should enable a high level of environmental justice but, as will be explained, this has not occurred to the extent that might be expected. While public discourse is very focused on environmental challenges, especially climate change, 'environmental justice', as a concept, has not been widely or intensively debated by Swedish policy makers, researchers, NGOs or the public. In particular, the distributional aspect of promoting justice among different groups *within* national boundaries has not been emphasised in discussions regarding sustainability and is only rarely highlighted in political and planning discussions (Bradley et al, 2008; Bradley, 2009; Gunnarsson-Östling and Höjer, 2011). Hence, many of the people I spoke to in Sweden were unaware of the concept of environmental justice, and/or did not think it to be a major issue for the country. For example, the Executive Director of the Stockholm Environment Institute told me:

> "If you take the air pollution problem, for instance, it is a problem that you could arguably say is worse in cities, but within the cities themselves, it is not something that is worse in certain areas than others based on some social grouping ... One of the things that does come up, you could say there is a social dimension, is the fact that the people in lower income groups have more problems related to poor quality food ... That could be an issue, but it is not something that is really being discussed in Sweden. We don't have the classic poverty problem with lower income groups living in areas with much higher exposure to air pollution or water pollution ..." (Interview, 7 December 2012, Johan Kuylenstierna, Executive Director, Stockholm Environment Institute)

However, a few Swedish academics have focused on distributional and procedural environmental justice and many reports have been produced on the substantive aspects of EJ, as will be outlined in this chapter. The interviews and participant observations that I carried out in early 2013 will also add to this picture. First, though, I will briefly outline some of the contextual political and economic background.

Sweden has a mixed, though overwhelmingly capitalist, economy and has the eighth-highest per capita income in the world (IMF, 2012, data from 2011). The country is often considered to exemplify a caring form of capitalism, proving that a market economy does not inevitably destroy the environment or increase inequality. It is known for its strong public sector and redistributionist economic policies, most attributable to the pre-eminence of the left-wing Swedish Social Democratic Party, which has most often been in power over the last century.[1] Though some of these leftist policies are still in place (for example, there is still a redistributive income tax system), many of them have now been replaced with policies more typical of a traditional neoliberal capitalist state. For example, the country now has a comparatively low corporate tax rate; inheritance tax has been abolished; and electricity supply, telecommunications, postal services, healthcare and public transport have all largely been deregulated and wholly, or partially, privatised. Some of these reforms have occurred under the government of the centre-right Alliance for Sweden coalition of parties that have been in power since 2006, though others predate this, such as the abolition of inheritance tax (2005).

Sweden's wealth is, to some extent, the result of its small population, as well as its abundant natural resources, particularly metals, timber, uranium and hydropower. However, the level of wealth is also a product of Sweden's colonial history, including a Swedish slave trade that continued until 1847[2] (Eltis and Engerman, 2011). Currently, the Swedish economy is characterised by knowledge-based, export-oriented manufacturing, with the engineering sector accounting for 50% of exports, alongside telecommunications, cars and pharmaceuticals. The country has, historically, almost always maintained high rates of growth, as compared to other countries[3] (see economic datasets in Appendix 2 for current comparison). Even now, while many European countries are in economic crisis as a result of government austerity drives, Sweden maintains a growth rate of 1.4%. The Swedish government is keen to promote growth and considers that growth is compatible with the achievement of environmental and social goals (Sweden.SE, 2012).

Hence, because of this combination of its being a market-based economy, yet with a recent experience of strong state control of the economy and a relatively progressive welfare system, I have placed

Sweden in the middle of the capitalist/socialist spectrum (see Figure 1.1).

Substantive environmental justice in Sweden

In many ways, Sweden has been a global pioneer in environmentalism, being one of the first countries in the world to establish an Environmental Protection Agency, in 1967, and hosting the first UN Conference on the Environment, in 1972. It has adopted very ambitious targets to lower greenhouse gas emissions and has already managed to reduce them significantly (OECD, 2011a). Furthermore, the country ranks first in the EU in consumption of organic foods, recycling and the production of energy from renewable sources (Sweden.SE, 2012). The most important basis for environmental protection in Sweden is the 1999 Environmental Code (Ministry of the Environment, Sweden, 2000). This sets out 15 national environmental quality objectives, with a 16th added in 2005, to serve as guidance to government agencies as well as private actors. A full range of principles, policies and goals are covered by the Environmental Code, including:

- sustainable development
- the polluter pays principle
- the precautionary principle: 'the mere risk of damage or detriment involves an obligation to take the necessary measures to combat or prevent adverse health and environmental effects' (Ministry of the Environment, Sweden, 2000, p 11)
- the burden of proof: 'It is the operator who, in accordance with the burden of proof principle, must demonstrate that the cost of a protective measure is not justified from an environmental point of view or that it represents an unreasonable burden' (Ministry of the Environment, Sweden, 2000, p 10)
- the reasonableness principle: 'conditions associated with operations must be based on environmental considerations while not involving unreasonable expense' (Ministry of the Environment, Sweden, 2000, p 13)

Thus, Swedish environmental legislation and individual behaviour seem to support the achievement of substantive environmental justice. However, as the environmental datasets in Appendix 2 suggest, especially those that include resource use and waste production (for example, the Ecological Footprint and Happy Planet Index), the vision of Sweden as a social and environmental haven is not the whole story. Historically and currently, Sweden is, and continues to be, a serious polluter. During the 20th century its industry was dominated by mining, iron and steel smelting, paper and pulp milling and large-scale manufacturing, causing substantial local pollution of air and water. Though some of this industrial activity is now outsourced to the poorer countries of the world, there are still some significant environmental problems within Sweden itself. For example, air quality guidelines are constantly being exceeded in certain areas, particularly in parts of Stockholm that are especially close to roads with heavy traffic (City of Stockholm Environment and Health Administration, 2006). PM10s are believed to cause between 3,000 and 5,000 premature deaths annually in the country, corresponding to a reduction in average life span of 6 to 12 months (European Environment Agency, 2011). There is also a problem of contamination from high levels of pharmaceutical drugs in waste-water purification plants, surface water, drinking water and fish caught in the wild[4] (Fick et al, 2011). In addition, the Worldwide Fund for Nature (WWF) has recently criticised Sweden for harmful practices in relation to timber harvesting, with 2,000 forest-dwelling species now threatened (WWF, 2012b).

Also highly problematic, in terms of substantive environmental justice, is the fact that Sweden's economy is built on a number of environmentally harmful industries, with the top 20 largest companies registered in Sweden including:Volvo (cars, including SUVS), Ericsson (telecommunications), Vattenfall (electricity generation, mainly from fossil fuels, nuclear and hydropower), Svenska Cellulosa Akiebolaget (pulp and paper manufacture), Sandvik (tools, mining and construction), Hennes & Mauritz (H&M) (so-called 'fast fashion', that is, disposable fashion), IKEA (the world's third-largest consumer of wood) and Preem (oil refineries and petrol stations). The country consumes a substantial amount of electricity per capita, one of the highest rates in the world, with the majority (about 85%) of electricity derived from nuclear and hydroelectric power (Sweden.SE, 2012). Though Swedish citizens voted for a phasing out of nuclear power in a national referendum held in 1980, three nuclear power plants with a total of ten reactors remain. Moreover, in June 2010, the Swedish parliament decided to allow new nuclear power plants to be built once again (Sweden.SE, 2012).

Although the objectives of the 1999 Environmental Code were to be reached within one generation, that is, in the mid to late 2020s, a review of the objectives, carried out in 2008, found that ' the pace of the progress being made is not sufficient to achieve the environmental quality objectives by 2020' (Environmental Objectives Council, 2008, p 6). A more recent statement admitted that at least five of the objectives will not be met by the 2020 deadline (Sweden.SE 2012). Yet, despite not being able to meet its own environmental objectives, its large Ecological Footprint and the glaring irony of attempting to build a green economy on the manufacture of environmentally harmful products, Sweden somehow maintains its environmental credibility. It appears that Sweden's image of environmentalism is built on quite a narrow conception of the term, embedded in a rhetoric in which Swedish people are associated with a general notion of environmental responsibility in the form of tidiness, recycling and interest in nature (Bradley, 2009). Therefore, for example, the authorities fail to see the ironic inconsistency of greeting airline passengers arriving at Stockholm's Arlanda airport with sound recordings of Swedish birdsong. The following excerpt from an interview with a Swedish policy maker illustrates how the image of nature-loving Swedes obscures the more serious environmental harms:

> "As a nation we have a strong connection to the environment … We have always been close to nature. We are a very sparse population.[5] Even if you live in Stockholm, it only takes you 10 minutes in any direction to be out of town and in the forest. So nature is very close. There has also been a very strong perception of vacationing out of the city, so one out of every four has a country house … There's a very strong tradition of free time means out of the city." (Interview, 7 December 2012, Government Policy Director)

The fact that so many people in Sweden had a second home ('country house') was seen to be evidence of ability to connect with nature, rather than an environmental problem in terms of resource use. Hence, while second home ownership is one of the highest in the world, significantly increasing the country's Ecological Footprint, Sweden's environmental image remains virtually untainted. Therefore, Bradley et al (2008, p 72) rightly observe, 'what has been defined as environmentally-friendly behaviour appears to have been framed by Swedish middle-class norms and habits'.

As in the other capitalist countries discussed in this book, Swedish environmental policies and planning are characterised by a technical view of environmental issues, which provide opportunities for 'green growth' (Gunnarsson-Östling and Höjer, 2011). The dominant discourse is ecological modernisation, where technical solutions are paramount and economic growth is considered necessary for solving environmental problems. According to the Swedish Environmental

Protection Agency (SEPA), environmental policy is based on a 'shared societal view of the need for a small country with an open economy to be in the vanguard of economic modernisation' (Lönnroth, 2010, p 6). Interviewees for this book generally agreed that the desire for economic growth is a priority for most people in Sweden. For example, the Executive Director of the Stockholm Environment Institute commented:

> "Like anywhere else, if you ask the majority of politicians, if you ask the labour unions, if you ask the majority of the people, the clear priority is still development. We are like other European countries, arguing that we are much more focused on the environment but, particularly when there are economic problems in a country, immediately the focus will shift towards economic growth. I think we are no different there from anyone else, even though sometimes we try to pretend we are." (Interview, 7 December 2012, Johan Kuylenstierna, Executive Director, Stockholm Environment Institute)

Hence, the achievement of Sweden's environmental objectives may be limited by the commitment to growth, implying that production and consumption levels must continue to increase from current levels. The 'reasonableness principle' of the environmental code provides a get-out clause to ensure that business remains profitable and growth can be maintained. Because of this focus on technology to solve environmental problems within the context of continuing growth, there is less emphasis on ensuring that social policy supports environmental policy (and vice versa). For example, when reforms were made to Swedish education, children were no longer expected to enrol in the school that was physically closest to them, but parents could choose the school they wanted for their children, however far away. This reform caused increased travel and, thereby, increased pollution, as well as an increase in the amount of traffic in proximity to the schools; environmental impacts that had not been considered when developing the policy (Bradley et al, 2008).

Distributive environmental justice in Sweden

Sweden's reputation for high social development and low levels of inequality is borne out by a number of socioeconomic datasets, as Appendix 2 summarises. For example, Sweden ranks tenth globally in terms of human development (UNDP, 2011); first in gender equality (UNDP, 2011); and third in terms of income equality (World Bank, 2011a). The Gini Coefficient has been reported as 0.25 (World Bank, 2011a) and 0.22 (SWIID, 2011). Low levels of inequality are a result of a substantial welfare state and a progressive tax system brought in by a succession of Social Democratic governments. The country also still has the second-highest public social spending as a percentage of its GDP, out of all the OECD countries (OECD, 2011b). Furthermore, rents are determined locally via negotiation between representatives of landlords and tenants, with social housing rents acting as benchmarks. These policies should predict low levels of distributional injustice, since this aspect of EJ is built on inequality, as explained earlier.

However, Sweden's wealth is distributed much less equally than its income, with the richest 10% of the population reportedly owning 72% of the nation's wealth (Credit Suisse, 2010). The wealth Gini Coefficient of 0.85 is one of the highest in the developed world and higher than the European average (Credit Suisse, 2010). In addition, the country's levels of inequality and poverty have seen one of the biggest increases in the OECD over the last generation (OECD, 2011b). Furthermore, unemployment has been increasing and is now 8.8%, rising to 24.2% among young people (Statistics Sweden, 2012b). The escalating rates of poverty and inequality are, to some extent, a result of changes to welfare. Though some of the welfare state programmes have survived, from the 1980s on, Sweden began slowing the expansion of the welfare state and even rolled back some previous progressive reforms. Spending on welfare benefits such as pensions, unemployment and disability entitlements has fallen by almost a third from the early 1990s and services such as education, health and welfare have been partially privatised (Ginsburg and Rosenthal, 2006).

Moreover, income inequalities, as in many countries, have a racial dimension. Although it is often viewed as an ethnically homogenous nation, 19.6% of Sweden's population now consists of people with a migrant background, defined as born abroad or born in Sweden of two parents who were born abroad (Statistics Sweden, 2012a). Migrants from wealthier countries and native Swedes have a relatively higher income than do other migrants, especially those from poorer countries (Andersson and Nilsson, 2011). These low-income migrants are made up of refugees, labour migrants, family reunification migrants and asylum seekers who have come predominantly from Iran, Chile, Lebanon, Turkey, Western Asia, South-East Europe and Africa.

Some of the migrant interviewees for this book were very positive about how they had been treated in Sweden. For example, one said:

"It is not hard to live here. All the people are very kind ...
The environment is good. Sweden is the best for being clean.
Sweden's rules are good for people. We have free language
lessons, free education for children, free breakfast and lunch
at school for children, a bus pass for them. The government
help you to get a job ..." (Interview 11 February 2013,
South-East Asian migrant female at the Multi-Cultural
Centre, Fittja)

Indeed, there have been some recent improvements with regard to the
treatment of migrants and minorities, including a new Discrimination
Act that came into force in 2009. There has also been recent
recognition, since 2011, of Sweden's indigenous population, the Saami,
at the constitutional level.

Even so, there is much cause for concern regarding the degree of
racial discrimination in Sweden. Despite its liberal image, Sweden has
a long history of mistreatment of minorities. In the past there has been
forced sterilisation of Roma, mixed race, single parent, transgender
and other minority groups, a practice that, in the case of transgender
people, ended only recently, in 2012 (Law Library of Congress, 2013).
The more visible migrant groups have historically been assigned lower
status in Sweden and so have fared less well on a number of indicators
such as labour market participation, incomes and health (Socialstyrelsen,
2010; Igerud, 2011). In addition, it has recently come to light that
Swedish police have, for years, been keeping an illegal registry of all
Roma, including keeping information on children and those who
have never committed a crime (Statewatch, 2013). In a recent report,
the European Commission Against Racism and Intolerance (ECRI,
2012) criticised Sweden for the rise of xenophobic and Islamophobic
political parties; violent attacks on migrants; educational inequality;
labour market discrimination and 'De facto residential segregation ...
compounded by discrimination in the housing market that particularly
affects Roma, Muslims, Afro-Swedes and asylum seekers' (ECRI, 2012,
p 8). The report noted that Roma, who make up almost 1 in 20 of the
population, 'continue to face discrimination in all fields of daily life;
they continue to be marginalised and are particularly disadvantaged
socially and economically' (ECRI, 2012, p 8). In addition, it was noted
that problems relating to land rights and land use continue to have an
adverse effect on the Saami. It has been difficult for them to participate
in decision-making processes that affect them, including those regarding
mining projects that would threaten their traditional way of life. This

contributes to keeping them in a disadvantaged situation (ECRI, 2012, p 8).

Despite this racist context, in May 2013 the world was shocked when so-called 'race riots' broke out in the migrant areas of Sweden (Figure 7.1), sparked by the police shooting of a migrant man. There has not yet been thorough research into the cause of these riots, though it is not difficult to believe, as some have suggested (for example, Nordin, 2013), that they were the result of structural inequality and racism.

Figure 7.1: After the riots in Rinkeby, a Stockholm suburb

Source: Rikard Stadler/Demotix (2013)

The inequalities that exist in Sweden form the basis of socio-spatial segregation. Although mixed neighbourhoods have continuously been part of Swedish housing policy aims since the mid-1970s, there has been very limited success in this regard (Igerud, 2011). Non-European migrants still tend to live in areas separate from native Swedes and other migrant groups (Socialstyrelsen, 2010). To some extent this is due to discrimination in the housing market, resulting from landlords being less likely to let to migrants. However, there is also some evidence that self-segregation is a factor, including, but not only, the flight of native Swedes from visible migrants, that is, those who can be identified as migrants by their physical appearance (Socialstyrelsen, 2010). Residential segregation on the basis of ethnicity also reflects the relatively weak economic status of migrant households within the housing market, so that they are generally confined to the sector of the city where it is possible for them to afford rented accommodation.

In assessing distributive environmental justice, we particularly need to know whether inequality and segregation in Sweden results in related environmental disparities. A Swedish policy analyst I spoke to thought this was not the case, stating:

> "We have segregation problems, not in the same way that there are in some other European cities but, of course, we do have areas, particularly in Stockholm, but also in Goteborg and Malmö and other major cities where, in certain suburbs, 85% are of non-Swedish or non-European background. So that is segregation – there is no question about it ... but I wouldn't argue that they are more exposed to environmental problems. Actually the environmental conditions generally are quite good, [they live in areas] outside of the city ... there are green areas close by ... a lot of opportunities for recreation, close to lakes and so on. The problems there are more of a social and economic nature, rather than of an environmental nature. They have problems with low income and higher unemployment and so on. I am not saying that there are no problems, but they are not environmental." (Interview, 7 December 2012, Johan Kuylenstierna, Executive Director, Stockholm Environment Institute)

Indeed, Sweden's environmental policy appears to show a relatively strong awareness of the need to consider distributive issues. These aspects were incorporated into the first Swedish National Sustainable Development Strategy (NSDS) (NSDS, 1994), which discussed poverty reduction, public health, social cohesion, welfare, employment and education, as well as regional and community development.[6] Similarly, the current NSDS (2006) clearly recognises distributive issues, emphasising the importance of prioritising 'broad-based initiatives aimed at eliminating health and mortality discrepancies among various social and economic groups' (NSDS, 2006, p 22).

However, after interviewing residents in the low-income areas of Stockholm where a large proportion of migrants live, including Tensta, Rinkeby and Fittja, I found that there were some distributive issues. Although there was, apparently, good access to green space, as I had been informed, there were injustices in terms of housing, fuel and food. For example, people living in those areas told me that their houses were of poor quality as they had problems with asbestos and damp (for example, interview, 9 February 2013, female resident B, Tensta, Stockholm). In addition, they said that they had problems paying their energy bills (for example, interview, 10 February 2013, male resident, Tensta, Stockholm). Some also felt they did not have enough money to eat healthily. For example, one interviewee said:

> "If you want to eat healthy food you need a good economic situation. It's expensive to buy good stuff, not luxury food, just good food ... Everything is hard if you don't have money. Dumpster diving[7] is always a possibility, but it is getting hard to do now. The shops say it is stealing and they put fences around and lock up the skip to try to stop people doing it." (Interview, 8 February 2013, male resident A, Södermalm, Stockholm)

Distributive environmental justice in Sweden is a new area of academic interest, so there are few published studies on this, as yet. Those studies that exist report evidence of distributive injustice in terms of greater environmental burdens of pollution and traffic in lower-income communities (for example, Isaksson, 2001; Rönnbäck, 2005; Chaix et al, 2006; Bradley et al, 2008). Rönnbäck's (2005) research found that large roads in Stockholm were far more likely to be built in tunnels if the income of the affected residents was high, or the proportion of migrants in the area was low. This was confirmed in a later study by Bradley et al (2008), who analysed the plans for the location and design of new major roads in Stockholm in the 1990s (the 'Dennis Package'). In the affluent central parts of Stockholm, as well as the wealthy municipality of Ekerö, the roads were to be built in tunnels, paid for by a large national budget. Yet, in the north-western districts of Stockholm (Hjulsta, Tensta and Akalla), areas of higher unemployment, poverty and a higher proportion of migrants, the roads were to be built above ground (Bradley et al, 2008). In many cases, the new roads were to cut through local green spaces in the poorer districts. Part of the reason for the uneven distribution of benefits and burdens in the Dennis Package road plan was the different value given to the green spaces. In the wealthier areas, they were well-known as cultural heritage sites whereas, in the poorer areas, the green spaces that were valued by local people were considered to be of little worth.[8]

Although low-income Swedish people tend to carry the environmental burdens, wealthier Swedes create more pollution and environmental degradation. A Swedish Environmental Protection

Agency report (2007) found that 10% of the highest disposable income households in Sweden contribute more than three times as much to Sweden's CO_2 emissions as the least wealthy 10%. This is largely because wealthy households buy more goods and services, have larger homes, or second homes, and are more likely to own cars (SEPA, 2007). Many of the middle-class Swedes who conform to the pattern of tidiness, recycling and interest in nature, mentioned earlier, have some of the largest Ecological Footprints, per capita, in the world (Bradley et al, 2008). Their footprint is far greater than that of the low-income residents, who may not be particularly tidy, interested in nature or in recycling but, for economic reasons, do not own cars or large houses.

Yet, as in many of the countries looked at in this book, the illusion remains that poor people are responsible for environmental degradation. In a study comparing two areas of Stockholm, a low-income migrant area (Tensta) and a more affluent white area (Gamla Spånga), Bradley et al (2008) found that public strategies for environmental education for sustainable development in Stockholm were primarily directed towards the low-income migrant area. Tensta residents were encouraged to adopt 'eco-friendly life-styles' in the form of recycling, keeping the area tidy and using public transport and low-energy light bulbs, and so on, while the more affluent Gamla Spånga area, nearby, received very little communication in this respect. As the authors speculate, it may be that the policy focus is skewed towards low-income areas because local tidiness gets mixed up with perceptions of eco-efficient living. The wealthier area, Gamla Spånga was green, attractive and tidy, and so seemingly 'unproblematic', even though it is an area of high resource consumption.

Hence, there is evidence of intra-national distributive environmental injustice in Sweden, as well as international injustice in the form of environmental and social harm resulting from Sweden's excessive consumption and waste.

Procedural environmental justice in Sweden

In 2011, Sweden ranked fourth in the world in the Economist Intelligence Unit's 'Democracy Index' (EIU, 2011). We could, therefore, assume that Sweden would achieve a high level of procedural environmental justice and, to some extent, this appears to be the case. Public participation legislation, under the Planning and Building Act and the Environmental Code, requires that minimum levels of consultation be met, including the provision of public hearings and opportunities to send written comments. Consultations should be carried out in several rounds, should include all affected groups and there must be a right to appeal against the final decision. There are reports in the literature of meaningful involvement of citizens in consultations and environmental decision making. For example, research by Jonsson (2005) on citizens' advisory committees for water resource management in Rönneå found a positive public involvement process.

The character of Sweden's democracy is considered to be consensual and this is reflected in the overall approach to environmental politics, which are based on consensus building and the assumption that economic growth, social justice and environmental protection can sit easily together. Potential conflicts, controversies or power issues are generally not discussed (Bradley et al, 2008). Swedish industry has tended to cooperate with, rather than confront, government while assuring that its interests are preserved (Lönnroth, 2010). For example, when the government established the Environmental Protection Agency in 1967 and introduced the Environment Protection Act of 1969, industry representatives pushed for a focus on technology as the basis for environmental protection (Lönnroth, 2010). The government also allowed some compliance monitoring to be delegated to industry itself. A consensus also emerged with trade unions, who generally agreed that pollution control would occur as a result of new technology and modernisation. Hence, Sweden's democracy could be considered as 'post-political', focusing on the management of issues as technical problems, with limited overt conflict or confrontation. One of the interviewees for this book complained that:

> "The unions will not speak out because they have a very close relationship with industry. Most of them are not defending the rights of workers now, especially immigrant workers who are really exploited, working in conditions that break all the laws about working hours and health and safety." (Interview, 10 February 2013, community café volunteer, Stockholm)

As Fraser (1992) and Young (2002) would predict (see Chapter Two), this consensus is sometimes maintained through marginalising or excluding opposing voices with several studies showing limited, weak and tokenistic involvement of citizens in environmental decision making in Sweden. For example, Khan (2003), in a study of public involvement regarding the siting of wind turbines in two locations, found that, in spite of organising EIAs and public hearings, as required, 'no special effort was made in either case to facilitate access to information or support the participation of local residents' (p 12) and that 'the public was let into the process when strategic decisions had already been made' (p 1). Khan (2003) considers that, in general,

> Public consultation at the project level in Sweden implies a limited scope of participation. The public enters into the planning process at a relatively late stage, when a draft plan for the project already exists. Even if the draft plan is in a preliminary form and many issues are open to change, the basic outline of the plan has been decided, meaning that the debate is not about which issues to discuss, but about how they should be resolved. (Khan, 2003, p 9)

In a recent example of this kind of exclusion, a UK company, Beowulf Mines, which is planning to mine for iron ore in Saami customary grazing lands in Jokkmokk, Northern Sweden, falsely claimed the Saami communities were involved in the Environmental Impact Assessment (Saami Resources, 2013). Since the end of the last Ice Age, the Saami have herded reindeer and nurtured a philosophy of living in harmony with nature. However, the Saami areas in Sweden are currently experiencing an explosion in prospecting and mining that is preventing the local communities from carrying out their traditional reindeer herding activities. The EIA is currently being reviewed but, in the meantime, Beowulf mines is attempting to carry out test explosions on the land, and Swedish police are arresting Saami activists and supporters who try to prevent this (Saami Resources, 2013). The ability for the community to be heard is limited by the government's interest in jobs and development and the company's focus on profit, as a Saami community representative explained:

> "There is not much work in the Northern areas of Sweden; there's a lack of infrastructure so you can argue, if there is mining here, you have more power to survive and you have a lot more opportunities to get work. For those who are pro mining, they often use this kind of argument ... but that is only the half-truth. When you talk about mining in Northern Sweden, the majority who come to work, as we say, 'fly in, fly out'. They don't actually live at the mining site in the local community, they live somewhere else, so they don't contribute to the local community ... But for us, and those I represent, it is about the possibility to have a nomadic way of life in the future ... The reindeer, they

are programmed by biology to graze from the mountains to the coast and from the coast to the mountains and these are yearly movements and when you have mining on traditional grazing lands, you have a problem. We are depending on grazing pasture for our existence … I don't know if the mining companies have a picture of what reindeer herding is … We have talked to the Beowulf mining company. We have been to two AGMs. They try to listen but at the bitter end for the Chairman, he has to protect his stock-market value and those who have invested money. From their point of view, it doesn't matter if we sacrifice a few Saami for profit." (Interview, 24 September 2013, Jenny Wik Karlsson, Chief Lawyer at the Swedish Saami Association)

According to Swedish law, the comments and opinions of the public are not binding for decision makers. Therefore, the citizen is not guaranteed any influence, whatever their level of participation. This is the case in all the countries discussed in this book, corresponding to 'placation' or 'consultation' on the lower rungs of Arnstein's (1969) 'Ladder of Participation' (see Figure 2.1), since power holders reserve the right to judge the legitimacy of the advice given (see Chapter Two). The state agencies tend to view public participation in environmental decision making as inherently limited because scientific and technical knowledge is considered to be consistently superior to knowledge developed through lived experience. For example, a SEPA report states:

> Policy – and politics – generally depends on citizens' expressions of their personal experiences of implementation. Environmental policy is somewhat different, in the sense that it also has to be founded on a solid base of natural science and technology which, on the whole, is inaccessible to the population at large. Policy on the environment is therefore expert-driven to a larger extent than most other policy areas. (Lönnroth, 2010, p 7)

When such processes of consultation fail, a backup in terms of procedural justice is that citizens should be able to take their case to the judiciary. Like several of the other countries featured in this book, Sweden has a system of environmental courts. The environmental courts include technical experts, and decisions will be based on the legality of a decision and on the technical merits. Again, this limits justice for those who have knowledge or understanding that is not yet scientifically accepted or part of current legislation. However, though in most countries fees for bringing cases to Environmental Courts and Tribunals can be high and a barrier to access to justice (Pring and Pring, 2009), in Sweden there are no such fees and the loser does not normally pay the winner's costs. Even so, the costs of legal representatives and expert witnesses are not covered and these can be comparatively much greater.

An alternative or parallel course of action to achieve procedural environmental justice is to lobby or campaign, either in an ad hoc way or through an environmental NGO. There are a number of such environmental campaign organisations in Sweden, some more established and traditional, others more informal and grassroots. The more formal groups include Friends of the Earth Sweden and the Swedish Society for Nature Conservation (SSNC). Although these large groups are often seen as very influential, even they face challenges in terms of taking on powerful lobbies. For example, the Chair of the Swedish Society for Nature explained:

> "It is difficult to protect the environment when businesses start to mobilise from the opposite position, and also when there are issues relating to property rights, such as hunting, the setting aside of nature protection areas, stipulations in forestry regulations, stricter measures of biodiversity. In those cases, they might make a more principled debate that landowners are entitled to do what they want without anyone interfering ... They can sometimes portray the issue ... as city people want to oppose rural people but, for us, it is more about the general public versus the individual, so it is important to frame this in the right way to set the agenda." (Interview, 11 January 2013, Mikael Karlsson, President of the European Environmental Bureau and Chair of the SSNC)

The research interviews also indicated that there are disparities in procedural justice between different socioeconomic groups in Sweden, with low-income groups less likely to exert influence over environmental decision making than wealthier groups. For example, one interviewee stated:

> "Quite recently, they [the government] wanted to build a motorway over a lovely green island called Långholmen. A lot of people, especially middle-class people, were very upset

about this and they managed to stop it happening. When the right people make a fuss, basically people who do not look like me, people with high positions, when they say no we do not want a motorway here, the city and the government listen. That's the only way to get them to listen." (Interview, 10 February 2013, male resident, Fittja, Stockholm)

Therefore, Sweden exemplifies some positive aspects of procedural EJ, such as free access to legal services for environmental matters, and the right to inclusion in environmental decision making. However, in practice, the level of influence varies significantly as a result of an emphasis on a consensual, technical-managerial approach to environmental decision making that can silence and exclude less powerful groups.

Causes of environmental injustice in Sweden

In many ways, Sweden has been a global pioneer in environmental protection and it rates relatively highly in comparison to the other capitalist countries on the Environmental Justice Indicator Framework used in this book, with an overall EJI score of 2.8 (see Table A1.1 in Appendix 1). However, there are a number of enduring environmental justice issues, not least the high average per capita Ecological Footprint of the inhabitants. There are also on-going problems with regard to air pollution, water pollution and the use of nuclear energy. In terms of distributive EJ, there are also significant issues, exacerbated by centre-right governance eroding the relatively low levels of income inequality. In particular, those living on low incomes, often of black and other minority ethnic heritage, experience difficulties in accessing some environmental goods, such as food, good housing and fuel. The legislation seems progressive with regard to procedural EJ, yet in some cases, it is being implemented weakly so that the degree of public influence on environmental decision making varies significantly. In particular, the evidence suggests that information and opportunities to participate are not always timely and that powerful vested interests can dominate agendas.

That Sweden ranks more highly in terms of its EJI than the other capitalist countries covered in this book is probably because it prioritised environmental issues at an early stage and because it has provided social support to its citizens over a long period of time. In terms of the injustices that exist, in general, the causes appear to be a result of the government's basic and fundamental acceptance of high consumption and economic growth; increases in social inequality; a general lack of awareness and understanding of environmental justice; a lack of focus on the distributional impacts of policy among decision makers; and weakly implemented consultation procedures.

There is evidence of each of the theoretical causes of environmental injustice in the Swedish case –industrialisation, power dynamics, market mechanisms and discrimination, individual behaviour, capitalism and culture. Having been through its own process of industrialisation, Sweden is now shifting its industry to poorer countries that continue to manufacture the commodities required for domestic consumption. Power issues are also very relevant, in that middle-class groups appear to be more influential and there is no guaranteed influence as a result of participatory processes. Market dynamics occur when wealthier Swedish people are able to buy better houses in healthier and/or more pleasant locations. Discrimination has also been described here, including in relation to housing. Life-style is also important, with wealthier Swedes buying second homes and large cars (albeit to enable them to feel 'closer to nature'). Yet all these factors appear to link to capitalism, with its associated over-production; need to control communities who resist 'development' that is profitable to vested interests; tendency to concentrations of wealth and power; and marginalisation of vulnerable groups.

Ecological modernisation is now the dominant mode of addressing environmental issues in Sweden, in the hope that business will solve environmental problems through technical innovation; the service sector will become a more important element of the economy; and the public will adopt more eco-friendly life-styles. Yet, Sweden's economy is mainly built on the production of cars and disposable items of clothing, furniture and technology. The kind of eco-friendly life-styles that are promoted are those that do not threaten levels of consumption, such as recycling and not dropping litter. This continues to facilitate company profits and economic growth, both necessary for the maintenance of capitalism. Though the most negative impacts of capitalism are avoided through some redistributive policies, the overall policy orientation towards growth as a Damaging Hegemonic Environmental Discourse means that it has been difficult to achieve environmental justice. There is now a budding counter-hegemonic discourse in Sweden, however, as indicated in the following comment:

> "[Recently] … there's been a more open discussion about,
> that there might be other ways of development than just
> GDP … that development can contain more than just

economic aspects ... That comes from the fact that more and more people are arguing [that] one part of development is actually having more time available for your family and so on, not necessarily making more money ... The question is – what does development mean? For some people and the way it has been promoted ... development is having more stuff ... for others development may mean that you have more time to do other things." (Interview, 7 December, 2012, Johan Kuylenstierna, Executive Director, Stockholm Environment Institute)

However, it seems that any incipient paradigm shift away from DHEDs and capitalism is held back by fears that it may be counter-productive to make more radical demands. For example, I was told:

"I would say that, given the situation of environmental policy today, if you had half an hour with the Finance Minister of Sweden, would you convince him that GDP and growth is a bad idea or would you say that, according to neoclassical economics, setting the right price is essential, please do that, and he would say yes to the latter but no to the former. So we need to be pragmatic. We need to be there on the ideological debate, questioning the growth machine but, at the same time, we need to work according to some kind of ecological modernisation ideas that are really improving the situation today. We can't wait for the mental revolution, for the ideological revolution. We need to push down emissions on a daily basis, we need to stop the logging of natural forests every day and I don't think the Minister of Finance or the Ministry of Forestry will change their understanding of the economic model but every tree we can prevent from being cut down will be an environmental gain." (Interview, 11 January 2013, Mikael Karlsson, President of the European Environmental Bureau and Chair of the Swedish Society for Nature Conservation)

Therefore, although environmentalism has long been a focus of the policy agenda in Sweden, as with the other capitalist countries discussed in this book, this is increasingly being framed in terms of opportunities for green growth, market mechanisms and ecological modernisation. In a situation of rising inequality in the country, it is more important than ever that environmental justice research and theory informs the work of Swedish planners and policy makers. Though all the possible explanations for injustice seem to apply here, the main driver of environmental injustice appears to be the market system. Sweden's Environmental Justice Indicator score is higher than those of the other capitalist countries featured in this book because, until recently, Swedish governments have prioritised environmental and social protection. Even so, the government continues to relocate environmental problems to low-income periphery nations and to marginalised groups at home. Sweden's more nature-loving and caring form of capitalism is still evidently unable to achieve environmental justice.

Notes

[1] In only five national elections (1976, 1979, 1991, 2006 and 2010) have the centre-right parties won enough seats in Parliament to form a government.

[2] Sweden possessed overseas colonies in Africa, North America and the Caribbean from 1638 to 1663 and from 1784 to 1878. The areas colonised were very small compared to other empires, and Sweden lost most of the conquered territories during the 18th and 19th centuries.

[3] However, there have been some occasional drops in growth rates, including a record low of -3.9% in 2008.

[4] The science and activities concerning pharmaceuticals in the environment that affect human and other animal species is an emerging EJ issue. Every year, an estimated 100,000 tons of antibiotics are used around the world and the number of pharmaceuticals used in medicine continues to grow. These may affect a wide range of environmental organisms through their presence in drinking and surface water (Kümmerer, 2009).

[5] Sweden is very sparsely populated, having a total population of only just over 9.5 million, with about 85% of the population living in urban areas (Statistics Sweden, 2012a).

[6] The country's first Sustainable Development Strategy (SDS) was published in 1994 and this was revised as the National Sustainable Development Strategy (NSDS) in 2004 and 2006.

[7] Dumpster diving is the US term for the English word 'skipping' to denote the practice of searching through commercial or residential waste skips for discarded food or other needed items.

[8] In 1997, the entire Dennis Package was abandoned because of lack of agreement over a range of issues, though several of the above-ground roads were built later.

EIGHT

'The rich consume and the poor suffer the pollution': environmental justice in the People's Republic of China

China, as a nominally socialist country that is famously beset with serious environmental problems, appears to contradict the theory that it is capitalism that has produced the global ecological crisis. Some avoid this conclusion by arguing that China is now, or always has been, a capitalist country, so that there is no inconsistency. Whether or not this is the case is a contentious debate, attracting fiercely opposing views, but most would agree that China certainly no longer conforms to the standard socialist model. Following the revolution in 1949, the country initially pursued a typically socialist path but, since 1978, a series of economic reforms have introduced aspects of capitalism. For example, there has been an incremental introduction of private enterprise, including foreign direct investment, initially in Special Economic Zones, but now operating more extensively. The government has officially described the reformed system as a 'socialist market economy' and as 'socialism with Chinese characteristics'. Yet the country is now of major importance to global capitalism, being the largest exporter, and second-largest importer, of goods in the world. It has come to encompass an array of private, national, foreign, municipal and state-owned companies (and hybrids, such as joint ventures). Furthermore, state companies, both national and local, have increasingly taken on many of the characteristics of privately owned businesses, in terms of surplus value creation, appropriation and competition. In general, the boundaries between the state and the private sector have blurred, as one interviewee emphasised:

> "Since the Chinese Community Party announced that entrepreneurs would no longer be barred from joining, entrepreneurs began to be a dominant force in Chinese society. I think they are getting more and more powerful but, at the same time, we have no very clear division between government and entrepreneur. Businessmen and

officials have too close a relationship, they cooperate too much." (Interview, 9 November 2012, Lu Feng, Professor of Environmental Philosophy, Tsinghua University)

However, for the purposes of this book, I have placed China on the socialist side of the capitalist/socialist spectrum (see Figure 1.1) because, though the Chinese system contains capitalist relations of production, it still maintains a basic commitment to socialism, according to the current constitution and official statements. In addition, the state still appears to play a major role in economic enterprise and employment (Wang, 2010).

Until very recently, there were virtually no studies of environmental justice in China. Though this is now beginning to change, the published work, so far, mainly approaches the topic from a substantive, ethical or legal perspective, rather than investigating the distributional and procedural elements of EJ. In analysing this work, it is necessary to carefully consider its credibility, since environmental justice can be exaggerated or minimised for political reasons. There is no doubt that China faces severe environmental problems, particularly in that it is the world's top emitter of CO_2 (IEA, 2011), sulphur dioxide (SO_2) and nitrous oxide (NO_x) (Keeley and Yisheng, 2011)[1] and the largest global consumer of coal, hydroelectric power, metals, cement and fertiliser (Chinese Academy of Sciences, 2010). However, whilst the Chinese government and its supporters openly admit the severity of the problems, they tend to put this in the context of the efforts that are being made to remedy the situation (for example, MEP – China, 2009). Western analysts and media commentators, on the other hand, paint an almost entirely negative picture of environmental conditions in the country, with little or no mention of government successes in rectifying the situation (for example, Watts, 2012). In this chapter I have attempted to go beyond these crude divisions.

Substantive environmental justice in China

China has made some progress in addressing its environmental issues in recent years. There have been slight improvements to urban air quality, especially with regard to reductions in SO_2, PMs and NOx emissions (MEP - China, 1995–2009). Industrial waste water chemical oxygen demand (COD), one of the main indicators of water pollution, also fell significantly between 2001 and 2008 (Shen, 2006; MEP - China, 2009; Vennemo et al, 2009). In addition, access to improved sanitation in rural areas increased from 7% in 1990 to 46% in 2010 (WHO-UNICEF,

2006; World Bank, 2012c). There has also been a rapid reduction in the proportion of the urban population living in slums, from 37.3% in 2000 to 29.1% in 2009 (United Nations, 2012).[2] Furthermore, there have been a number of successful programmes to restore forests, lakes and grasslands (Yisheng, 2011). Moreover, public awareness of environmental issues is now greater than ever (Xiaomin, 2011).

Yet, despite these specific improvements, overall environmental conditions in the country have generally worsened over the last 30 years (Yisheng, 2011). The main challenge is pollution and its impacts on health, in particular, chronic respiratory and cardio-vascular disease and cancer, which have all increased steadily in both rural and urban areas during the recent period of industrialisation (Holdaway, 2011). Though there have been some improvements in urban air pollution, according to the World Bank (2007), only 1% of the urban population lives in a city with an annual average level of PM10 that is below the European Union's air quality standards.

Another major issue is water scarcity. Desertification has intensified threefold over the last 25 years, several major rivers have run dry and some lakes and wetlands have disappeared (Chinese Academy of Sciences, 2010). China's per capita fresh water supply is less than 2,000m3, similar to that of some tropical African countries (World Bank, 2011b). The depletion of deep groundwater is of particular and growing concern (World Bank, 2007) as replenishing this supply could take thousands of years. There is also a major issue with regard to drinking water quality, with 13% of the population still lacking access (World Bank, 2012c), despite significant improvements to the service and infrastructure in recent years (NBS, 1996–2011). Furthermore, the latest report published by the Chinese authorities assessing the national state of the environment (MEP – China, 2009) describes very high levels of COD (one of the main measures of water pollution) in national water sources. The report shows that 42% of river water is unfit for human contact and 34% of the water in China's major lakes is unsuitable for any use at all (MEP – China, 2009). Despite the advice to avoid polluted water, many people have no real alternative but to use it for drinking and cooking (Vennemo et al, 2009). Furthermore, about half of the water that is considered unfit for human contact (class IV) is still allowed for irrigation, so water pollutants still reach the population through the food chain (Vennemo et al, 2009). The impact of industrial waste water on fields and crops is substantial. In the case of rice, for instance, about half of the yield fails to meet Chinese standards of safety, having been found to contain significant amounts of mercury, cadmium and lead (World Bank, 2007). Although a causal link has not been established with the consumption of industrial waste water in China, it is notable that the rates of stomach and liver cancer are 50% higher in rural China than in the country's major cities (World Bank, 2007, citing China's Ministry of Health, 2004). There are also reports of 'cancer villages' – cancer clusters in rural areas where water and soil have been polluted by heavy metals or dioxins. These are particularly found along the Xiang River in South-East Hunan, where there are a number of chemical, metallurgical and mechanical industrial plants (Liu, 2010; Wang and Wang, 2011).

The government's programmes to address these environmental problems have primarily been regulatory, but also, to some extent, technical and economic. Environmental issues have moved rapidly up the policy agenda in recent years so that the country now has a relatively advanced environmental policy and legal framework, comparable to that of developed countries (Holdaway, 2011; Keeley and Yisheng, 2011; Xiaomin, 2011). The first environmental framework law, the Law on Environmental Protection, was passed in 1979 and later supplemented by a raft of specific legislation. Of all the laws passed by the National People's Congress, environmental legislation has been approved most rapidly and most often, amounting to about 20% of the total laws passed over the last 30 years (Wang and Wang, 2011). In addition, environmental courts have now been established and their numbers are steadily increasing (see Wang and Gao, 2010).

Yet, while there has been significant progress, these legal changes seem to have had limited success in reducing environmental problems. This seems to be because, as Wang and Wang (2011) point out, the first generation of so-called 'single-issue' environmental laws has tended to emphasise setting and meeting discharge restrictions, rather than removing the pollution source itself, as would be consistent with 'productive justice'. Furthermore, even within this narrow focus, pollution monitoring has remained rather limited, generally only carried out in relation to common industrial discharges and largely confined to major cities, key rivers and important waterways (Yisheng, 2011). There are also endemic problems with regard to enforcement, regulation and implementation (Keeley and Yisheng, 2011). In particular, central government policies and national laws are often not well enforced in local areas. Environmental Impact Assessment law is often violated (Wang, 2007b) and industries have been known to make agreements with local environmental officials to secure non-interference in their activities (Bernard et al, 2006). Van Rooij et al (2012) consider that such problems are facilitated by the capture of state regulatory institutions by business elites.

In addition to the regulatory approach to solving environmental problems, China has also emphasised innovation, science and technology. There is strong respect for technocrats, and these tend to occupy the most important jobs. Often the technological approaches have taken the form of large and ambitious engineering or biological projects. Some of these have been indisputably helpful, such as the widespread installation of electrostatic precipitators (air cleaners) and fabric filters in power plants and major industrial facilities (Vennemo et al, 2009). Others have not been as demonstrably effective, such as the huge 'Green Wall of China' project, an attempt to hold back the encroaching desert by planting a 2,800-mile forest. Still others, such as the South-North Water Diversion project, have generated as many problems as they seek to address (Keeley and Yisheng, 2011).

China has also used economic approaches to address its environmental problems. Most notably, the country has been at the forefront, internationally, of developing a Green GDP, a national accounting system that includes environmental costs and benefits and the use of natural resources (Wang et al, 2011). The United Nations, World Bank and OECD, among other global institutions, have all expressed interest in this initiative.

Therefore, though China continues to face severe environmental problems, it is attempting to address them by using a combination of standard and innovative methods. Though its problems are concerning, it is important to remember that China's per capita emissions of greenhouse gases and other compounds are much lower than those of many countries (see environmental datasets in Appendix 2). China has a population of 1,343 billion (CIA, 2011), equivalent to 22% of the world total, therefore emissions can be high while still being relatively low per capita. It is also important to bear in mind that a substantial amount of the environmental problems that China faces are a result of meeting consumer demand elsewhere, particularly in Europe and North America (see, for example, Davis and Caldeira, 2010).

Distributive environmental justice in China

Before the beginning of economic reforms, China was one of the most egalitarian countries in the world, in terms of incomes. Since then, inequalities have risen significantly, so that China's Gini Coefficient, estimated to be 0.33 in 1980 (Fan and Sun, 2008), had risen to 0.42 by 2005 (World Bank, 2011a). The introduction of a housing market has been a major driver of inequality in the country. In the past, the state allocated homes to its citizens but, in 1998, much of the country's urban residential housing stock was privatised. Now, most Chinese people buy their own homes, with official figures showing that home ownership is currently 89% in the cities. The government has tried to minimise the widening inequalities by reining in particular kinds of sales, such as multiple purchases by a single buyer. At the same time, it is building tens of millions of state-subsidised apartments to provide housing for Chinese citizens who can no longer afford to buy or rent privately.

Income difference is most striking between regions and between rural and urban communities (Ma, 2010; Zhang and Zou, 2012). In particular, inequality between the eastern coastal region and the rest of China has been on an upward trajectory since the 1980s (Fan and Sun, 2008). Various studies identify a variety of determinants that explain increased regional inequality, including regional development policies (for example, Special Economic Zones in coastal provinces); privatisation of national industry; fiscal decentralisation; and global market integration (Fan and Sun, 2008; Zhang and Zou, 2012). The government has implemented a number of programmes to reduce these regional inequalities, including the 1999 'Western Development Program' (the so-called 'Go West' policy), launched to boost the economic development of the 12 provinces in Western China. There is some evidence that these programmes have had some success (Fan and Sun, 2008).

A key question in assessing distributional environmental inequalities in any country is the issue of which socioeconomic lens to use. It is not always appropriate to directly use those environmental justice categories developed in the United States. Making correlations between ethnic group and environmental quality is difficult in China because the population is overwhelmingly made up of one ethnic group, the Han (91.5%).[3] Though there are 55 other ethnic groups, there may not be sufficient numbers of non-Han in an area to be able to make these socio-spatial correlations. Moreover, while low-status groups in the US have tended to be ethnic minority and low-income groups, in China, the low-status groups have been rural residents (Ma, 2010). Recently, many people originating from rural areas have moved to the cities, so that the urban share of the population increased by 46% between 1998 and 2008 (Xiaomin, 2011). These groups are referred to as 'rural migrants' and, though their income may change with relocation, their status does not (Ma, 2010).

Therefore, studies looking at distributional environmental justice in China in relation to the traditional categories of income and race have produced very mixed findings. Some studies suggest that China's poor are disproportionately affected by higher levels of particulate pollution (for example, World Bank, 2007; Balme, 2011) and a lack of safe water and sanitation facilities (Carlton et al, 2012). However, Brajer et al (2010) found that, though inequitable burdens of air pollution based on income increased in Chinese cities up until 2004, since then, overall clean-up efforts have diminished disparities. In another study, Ma (2010) reports that environmental harm is more likely to be associated with higher incomes, that is, affecting those who are engaged in well-paid industrial jobs. Holdaway (2011), similarly found that, rather than the poorest groups who tend to live in less developed areas being most impacted by pollution, it is mainly the middle-income and transitional areas that are most affected, including peri-urban and industrialising areas. There are also mixed findings with regard to a correlation between quality of environment and ethnicity. Ma (2010), focusing on Henan province and using a distance-based approach, finds no relationship between industrial pollution and ethnic group (though perhaps this is because there is little ethnic variation in that region). However, Balme (2011) argues that environmental burdens *do* fall disproportionately on minority ethnic groups, pointing to Yunnan province, where many of the dams constructed by the government over the past years have been located in minority ethnic areas.

These variations in findings regarding the importance of income and race in relation to environmental disparities may be explained, to some extent, by differences in the methodologies used; the environmental issues considered; and underlying political agendas, such as whether there is a desire to portray China in a favourable light or not. Most authors tend to agree, however, that the main divide, in terms of distributional environmental justice in China, is between the urban and rural populations (Ma, 2010; Balme, 2011; Carlton et al, 2012). For example, Ma (2010) found that rural residents suffer more from pollution and are less able to access environmental services than are urban dwellers, after other socioeconomic factors are accounted for. This study is supported by World Bank data (2012c) that shows that, while urban piped water coverage had reached 98% by 2010, rural coverage was still at only 79% (World Bank, 2012c). In the same year, access to improved sanitation was 68% in urban areas, but only 46% in rural areas (World Bank, 2012c). The interviewees for this book also agreed that the rural/urban consideration was the main distributive environmental justice division in the country (for example, interview, 1 November 2012, Dr Lei Xie, Specialist in Environmental Politics, University of Exeter).

In China, rural people have traditionally been a low-status social group. Various studies report that rural residents and rural migrants have often been described by Chinese media and urban dwellers as 'backward', 'unclean' and 'lacking in culture' (Hathaway, 2010). Other research on inequalities between rural and urban residents has shown there to be differentials in a number of conditions, including wages and living conditions (Wang, 2009); working hours (Du et al, 2006); education (Wei, 2007); and social security (Wei, 2007). In addition, rural migrants in urban areas experience disadvantage and discrimination in obtaining employment and in wage offers (Meng and Zhang, 2001). Therefore, environmental inequalities are an additional aspect of the general pattern of rural/urban inequality. Some of these problems seem to arise from the *Hukou* system, established in the 1950s in order to limit migration from rural areas to urban areas and, thereby, to prevent urban overcrowding and food shortages. Under this system, each Chinese citizen is designated either a rural or an urban registration status and is given access to a number of services (particularly housing, healthcare and schooling), restricted to the place where they are registered. It has been argued that the *Hukou* system has advantaged urban residents over rural residents in many ways, including access to subsidised food, urban employment, housing, healthcare, pensions, education, welfare programmes and cultural activities (Wu and Treiman, 2004; Liu, 2005). Thus, the *Hukou* system has been described as the most important determinant of advantage and disadvantage in China and a major factor contributing to the rural/urban divide (Ma, 2010).

The *Hukou* system appears to have particularly contributed to the relative disadvantage of rural migrant workers. Widening gaps between wealthier areas and the poorer areas since the 1980s have induced massive migration, in search of employment, from inland to coastal regions (for example, Fan, 2008). The *Hukou* system restricts rural migrants' access to some public services in order to dissuade them from settling permanently (Balme, 2011). They tend to move to polluted areas that lack urban facilities (for example, sanitation, improved water supply) where there are jobs and cheap accommodation, clustering in the immediate suburbs surrounding urban areas (Balme, 2011). A large proportion also live in their work place (JSB, 2006). Therefore, they are, generally, in a vulnerable and difficult position compared to non-migrants, whether urban or rural residents. Yet, though the *Hukou* system may be creating environmental injustices for many people, it could be argued that it is actually preventing worse environmental injustices that might arise from unlimited migration to the cities. Urban areas are already very strained in terms of their ability to provide adequate infrastructure and basic services to their populations and this situation would only worsen if there were no restrictions. Even so, because of the difficulties surrounding the *Hokou* system, there has been pressure from some groups to reform it and this is now a major debate in China. Reforms have already been initiated in some provinces and cities, though the system still remains in the large conurbations.

Apart from the difficulties arising from *the Hokou* system, other reasons for rural environmental disadvantage appear to be that polluting firms move to rural areas to take advantage of lower labour costs or less stringent environmental protection. For example, since 1998, new coal-fired power plant construction has been strictly prohibited in large and medium-sized cities and their immediate suburbs (MEP - China, 1998), thereby pushing companies to locate these facilities in rural areas. This makes sense in some respects because non-urban areas are less populated, but, in practice, it creates unhealthy environments for rural people living close to the plants. There are also some indications that China is copying the Western strategy of moving pollution sources out of city centres and building higher chimneys so that emissions are dispersed and diluted, removing the problem at a local level only (Vennemo et al, 2009). Therefore, when the urban environment improves, it is often because problems have actually gone elsewhere, to the peri-urban or rural area. Several interviewees described how China's environmental problems are highly mobile, generally moving from larger to smaller cities, from urban to rural areas and from more to less developed areas of the country (for example, interview, 11 January 2012, Sze Pang Cheung, Campaign Director, Greenpeace East Asia). This points, again, to the need for productive justice as a foundation for both substantive and distributional justice.

Procedural environmental justice in China

There are two main institutions of political participation in China – the NPC (National People's Congress), the legislative body; and the CPPCC (Chinese People's Political Consultative Conference), which acts as an oversight organisation. Both the NPC and the CPPCC are important for articulating and coordinating citizens' concerns (Xie, 2011). At the regional level, Local People's Congresses (LPCs) and their respective committees are authorised to adopt local regulations, provided these do not contradict national legislation. There are elections for local representatives to the LPC and these representatives, in turn, elect members to the Provincial People's Congress (which, subsequently, elects members to the National People's Congress). The Chinese Communist Party (CCP) acts as the ideological guide for the state. The extent and methods of influence the Party has on decision making is deeply controversial. Critics of China's democracy state that, as the CCP nominates candidates for all the major positions in the judiciary and legislative institutions, democracy is limited. Others, for example, Bell (2006), point out that candidates are selected on the basis of 'political meritocracy', that is, on their examination performance and prior work record. The Chinese academics, leaders and citizens who support this policy consider that such a system is fairer, as voters would tend to make candidate choices based on their own immediate interests, whereas selected candidates ensure a balance between individual interests and wider interests.

Focusing specifically on environmental decision making, there is now a general trend in China to expand the possibilities for public participation in policy making:

> "In the past, the government monopolised environmental management, but now, with changes in legislation, there is more scope for others to be involved in environmental policy making, including for the public." (Interview, 1 November 2012, Dr Lei Xie, Specialist in Chinese Environmental Politics, University of Exeter)

Over the past 20 years, among the hundreds of new environmental laws and regulations that have been passed, many have aimed to increase public participation in environmental decision making and improve public access to environmental information. The first of these was the Environmental Impact Assessment Act 2003, which makes explicit reference to public environmental rights and interests and states the importance of public participation in EIAs. Later, the Measures on Environmental Administrative Reconsideration Act 2008 enabled citizens to challenge Environmental Protection Agencies' policy decisions. As the public have gained greater awareness of their legal rights they are more frequently challenging the government on environmental matters, especially decisions made at a local level.

Recent years have also seen a transition towards greater transparency and information disclosure in the country. In 2008, China adopted 'Open Government Information Regulations', making it one of only 90 countries worldwide to have freedom of information legislation. In the same year, the Environmental Information Disclosure Decree of 2008 was announced, which meant that, henceforth, both Chinese and international companies must disclose environmental information within 30 days of a public request. As a result, environmental information is now readily available and this has enabled more public involvement in environmental governance. At the same time, there has been a broadening and diversification of information sources, with greater media autonomy from the state and increased numbers of people with internet access (Xie, 2011). Internet expansion has significantly aided the evolution of environmental activism and the emergence of social movements in China, providing an important way for groups to publicise their campaigns and achievements (Tao, 2011).

These legislative changes, especially increased access to information, have driven a 15-fold expansion of environmental litigation (Lubman, 2010). This litigation has been a powerful factor in ensuring the enforcement of environmental legislation, highlighting loopholes in the legislation, alerting higher levels of government to local problems, driving legal reforms and enabling environmental policy to develop 'from below', to some extent (Balme, 2011; Wang, 2011). There are now several legal aid centres that help pollution victims to make their case, for example, the Centre for Legal Assistance to Pollution Victims. In cases where health has been damaged by pollution, the burden of proof lies with the polluter, not the victim.

However, despite these advances, some analysts, for example, Wang and Wang (2011), argue that environmental legislation always emerges in a top-down fashion in China. They consider that legislation is unilaterally initiated by the government or the Party and that citizens are rarely given a real voice. One particular criticism of procedural environmental justice in China is the alleged lack of an independent and effective judiciary (for example, Palmer, 2006). It appears that many cases of environmental harms fail to come to court, or to obtain compensation when they do (Balme, 2011), and courts rarely recognise the evidence relating to health damages (Wang, 2007b). Furthermore, the cost of taking a case to court puts citizens at a decisive disadvantage to corporations, for whom the costs are often trivial in comparison to their potential company profits (Balme, 2011).

Xie (2011) considers that it is because of these limits to legislative processes that citizens are increasingly choosing to use direct action when their environmental interests are violated. Environmentalists have been active in China since the 1970s, acting as a loose network of scientists, NGOs and government officials (Yisheng, 2011). In the early days, Chinese grassroots environmental organisations were mostly engaged in environmental education and awareness raising, directed largely at the general public. The 'activism' was politically neutral and strategically non–confrontational, often consisting of organised tree planting, bird watching and rubbish collection (Tao, 2011). At first, these individuals and groups were marginalised and largely ignored, but they have since gained increasing recognition and are now beginning to have some significant influence on public discourse and legislation. In particular, since there have been greater possibilities for accessing information and influencing decision making, there has been an explosion in the number of new Environmental Non-Governmental Organizations (ENGOs) at both national and local level, so that there are now more than 3,000 registered and 2,000 unregistered groups (Balme, 2011; Xie, 2011). These ENGOs have been very effective in raising environmental awareness, monitoring environmental activities and participating in environmental decision making, even though they often lack resources, personnel, premises and funding (Yang, 2005; Xie, 2009). On a number of occasions they have substantially changed decisions, and even the course of environmental policy (Balme, 2011). For example, the actions of ENGOs were able to stop construction of 13 dams on the Nu River along a major seismic fault-line (Mertha, 2008).[4]

In general, Chinese ENGOs have exerted pressure on government and corporations in whatever ways were permissible within the institutional status quo, while generally aiming to be as politically neutral and tactically non-confrontational as possible (Tao, 2011). Through these methods, they have built alliances with enlightened and sympathetic government officials, the media, academics and national leaders through the National People's Congress and the Chinese People's Consultative Conference (Tao, 2011). As Tao explains, this choice to be politically neutral has made them more acceptable to the government than they might otherwise have been and they have been able to take advantage of competition between government agencies. Though, in theory, there is a balance of power between government agencies responsible for environmental protection and those focusing on economic development, in practice, 'the authority of the former has typically been trumped by that of the latter' (Tao, 2011, p 283). Consequently, politically marginalised environmental government agencies are happy to have the support of ENGOs.

Many international NGOs that have operated in China for a long time have begun to make the environment their dominant issue. In general, international NGOs in China are sharply divided, in terms of, both ideology, and choice of tactical approaches, with some having a positive disposition to the government and others being highly critical (Tao, 2011). For those that are critical, highlighting China's environmental problems is a powerful, and seemingly non-political, way to attack the government. For example, I was informed that:

"Environmental issues are not as sensitive as other issues, like human rights, and therefore there are a lot of people in China, and some of them are very influential, who pay a lot of attention to environmental issues because of an interest in social change ... They see the environment as less sensitive and something they can actually focus on and talk about." (Interview, 11 January 2012, Sze Pang Cheung, Campaign Director, Greenpeace East Asia)

Although the Chinese government has generally adopted a positive attitude towards ENGOs, it has not been completely at ease with them (Tao, 2011). In particular, the Chinese ENGOs that are receiving funds from other governments are sometimes regarded suspiciously and may be perceived, rightly or wrongly, as being foreign-directed enterprises (Economy, 2005). It may be that some are using environmentalism as a way of working for wider change, whether that be for progressive reasons or to undermine socialism in general, as the government fears.

However, while some use the environmental agenda to push for wider change, those with environmental concerns are, in some ways, becoming less political. Although environmental activism, including demonstrations, has increased dramatically in China since the mid-1990s (Lei, 2009), according to Lora-Wainright et al (2009) citizens have learned to become compliant about their campaigning goals, dropping their calls for less pollution and instead focusing on compensation payments. It appears that compensation comes to replace the original demands as a result of industries' sustained refusal to engage with their requests (Wainwright et al, 2009). The local industries they campaign against contribute significantly to local revenue through taxes and pollution fees as well as providing employment to local residents and incoming migrant workers. Therefore, some people, especially local leaders, welcome them.

As in the capitalist countries, there is evident inequality among social groups in terms of their ability to be heard on these issues (Van Rooij, 2010; Yang, 2010). In urban areas, it is commonly the social elites that confront the government on environmental issues (Xie, 2011). The growing middle class has legal knowledge and resources which it can bring to bear against government decisions. One well-known example of social elite resistance was the 2007 opposition to the proposed construction of a paraxylene (PX) petrochemical project in the Haicang district of Xiamen, near a residential area. Members of the Chinese People's Political Consultative Conference signed a motion to oppose the project and tens of thousands of local citizens took to the streets in protest. The concerned residents also gained support from a number of national media outlets (Wang, 2007a). In the face of this concerted opposition, the provincial government and the Xiamen city government eventually announced that the plant would not be built in Haicang (FON, 2007). However, two years later, the project was moved to the Gulei peninsula in Zhangzhou, about 30 miles to the west (Xie, 2011). Hence, procedural justice was achieved only at a local level and for elite groups, but the hazardous production could continue elsewhere. This highlights, again, the importance of productive justice.

Causes of environmental injustice in China

This chapter has described how new legislation and collective action have enabled significant improvements in environmental policy making in China over the last decade. However, we have also seen how, as in the United States and other countries, the impressive legal and institutional developments have, so far, failed to produce a reasonable level of environmental justice. As Table A1.1 in Appendix 1 summarises, China's Environmental Justice Indicator score comes to just 5.9. There are still on-going substantive environmental justice problems in relation to air, water and soil pollution, alongside high overall CO_2 emissions. In terms of distributive environmental justice, rural migrants seem to experience disproportionate environmental burdens, particularly when they move to peri-urban areas of cities, where they have fewer choices with regard to work and housing. In relation to procedural EJ, there have been many recent improvements in public participation, but it is elites that are most able to effectively engage in these processes. Their relative wealth means that they are not desperate for jobs and are less likely to be bought off with compensation payments.

Because China still exhibits elements of socialism, yet has only achieved a low EJI score, this would seem to discredit the theory that capitalism is a fundamental driver of environmental injustice. Industrialisation would seem to be a better explanation for the environmental injustices found, in China's case. It is clear that China is facing similar problems to those of other countries in their earlier stages of industrialisation but, because it is industrialising later, and more rapidly, the problems have been conflated (Yisheng, 2011). The country is unusually dependent on its manufacturing industry, such that the industrial share of GDP in China is almost twice that of India (Felipe et al, 2008). However, when China's environmental problems are ascribed to 'industrialisation', it is important to reflect on the processes that are compelling this. Much of the recent industrialisation is a result of

China's incorporation into the global market economy. China has been at the core of globalisation, developing international trade, welcoming trans-national corporations and encouraging foreign direct investment. Opening to foreign investment, despite the general perception that foreign companies have higher environmental standards, has increased socially and environmentally harmful production practices, including the violation of labour rights, the production of unsafe goods, and the infringement of environmental regulations (Globalization Monitor, 2010; 2012). For example, trans-national water companies, such as Veolia Water, the world's largest water company, are now making millions in profits, while polluting China's drinking water and imposing high tariff increases on China's citizens (Globalization Monitor, 2010; 2012).

A high proportion of the goods being manufactured in China are to feed capitalism's growth machine. Consequently, China's position as the 'factory of the world' has meant that it has 'borne the brunt of environmental costs, and taken the resulting blame' (Yisheng, 2011, p 20). As a former periphery nation, according to World Systems Theory (Wallerstein, 2004), China has sought to incorporate itself into the global economy so as to provide jobs and meet basic needs. Hence, local governments turn a blind eye to corporate environmental misconduct because the region depends on tax revenue from these same businesses. National government funding contributes only a small proportion towards the operating costs of local governments, who have to ensure local jobs and provide many public services, including education, public health and environmental protection. Consequently, many local governments succumb to offers made by private developers so as to help them address immediate problems, regardless of the environmental or health consequences, which may be felt much later. This situation is compounded by a cadre evaluation system that emphasises the level of industrial development as an indicator of the success or failure of local officials (Wang and Wang, 2011). Therefore, many in China now argue that environmental protection should be included in the criteria for evaluating the performance of all governmental officials (Yisheng, 2011). In some areas of the country, this has now begun to happen, for example, in the city of Nanchang (Xinhua News Agency, 2012).

Therefore, the main alternative explanation for the lack of environmental justice in China – industrialisation – appears to be driven and formed by capitalist economic processes. Though China is not officially a capitalist country, it has been unable to escape the dynamics of global capitalism. Though there were ecological crises before market reforms were introduced in China, for example, during the 'Great Leap Forward' and the Cultural Revolution (Shapiro, 2001), the current environmental crises are far more intense and damaging in the long term, with their possibly irreversible consequences.

The Chinese government has, for some time, recognised that it needs to overhaul its development model. In 1994, the State Council published its report on Agenda 21, admitting that China's model is resource and energy intensive and highly polluting and, therefore, unsustainable (State Council, 1994). Since then, there have been a number of other strategic statements, including statements on ecological modernisation (2002), the scientific outlook on development (2003) and resource and energy conservation (2004) (Yisheng, 2011). Yet, the government's dependence on exports has trapped it in the industrial model. Therefore, China is so immersed in capitalist processes that it is severely impeded in its ability to attain environmental justice.

Neoclassical economists in China argue that the solution is, therefore, to implement even more market policies to address these problems, framed as 'externalities' (Hou, 2012). However, others think that if the economic model is causing the problem, that model should be rejected in favour of reinvigorating socialism, which would better protect China's environment. For example, China's Deputy Minister of the Ministry of Environmental Protection, Pan Yue, has stated:

> 'Social justice' is a core concept of 'sustainable development' and also a core aim of socialism. So, in theory, socialism is more suited to the realisation of sustainable development than capitalism ... In China, pollution has been moved from East to West and from the city to the rural areas. The rich consume and the poor suffer the pollution. The economic and environmental inequalities caused by a flawed understanding of growth and political achievement, held by some officials, have gone against the basic aims of socialism and abandoned the achievements of Chinese socialism. (Pan Yue, 2006a)

While the use of market policies has clearly worsened environmental problems, Damaging Hegemonic Environmental Discourses have also had a powerful impact, creating positive associations with growth and consumerism (Yisheng, 2011). It is important to consider why these Damaging Hegemonic Environmental Discourses exist in a socialist society. Although it seems to be, in part, because they reflect values that are consistent with capitalism, it may also be because they replicate Western beliefs and values, disseminated through forms of cultural domination, as interviewee Lu Feng posited:

"I think that the whole modernisation ethic comes from the West … For more than a hundred years, this kind of ideology has been the dominant ideology in China. Today though the Communist Party refuse the democracy of the US, they think their lifestyle, industry, science and technology are more advanced than ours … I think that is absolutely wrong, I think the ancient Chinese civilisation has some advantages over the modern. It is much more sustainable than the modern industrial civilisation so I think that many people in China are wrong in their views about their lives, about happiness, about the meaning of human living." (Interview, 9 November 2012, Lu Feng, Professor of Environmental Philosophy, Tsinghua University)

The Damaging Hegemonic Discourse around growth has been very powerful in China. Alongside a desire for growth, a consumer mind-set has developed, influenced by advertising and the ability of global capital to penetrate Chinese markets. These pressures have meant that China has now become the world's second-largest market for luxury goods (Yisheng, 2011). Interviewee Lu Feng reflected:

"Since the market reforms in China, a majority of people have internalized the values and norms of a market-dominated economy. The media has encouraged people to try to make money and become rich … Before, people were not so greedy as today. Now people always try their best to make more money, to get more material wealth, cars, cell phones, washing machines. They try their best to improve the material conditions of living, but during Mao's time people did not behave like this. … Many people now think that they need more and more things and new things. For example, they change their cell phone every two or three years. They think new things are always better …" (Interview, 9 November 2012, Lu Feng, Professor of Environmental Philosophy, Tsinghua University)

Yet, these DHEDs also appear to have existed before the 1979 reforms. For example, Hou (2012) describes how, for some time, government and citizens generally believed that strong economic growth could solve all their problems. He emphasises that they strived to surpass the capitalist countries' economic growth, in order to show that socialism is better than capitalism. Even when it became apparent that growth was causing so many environmental problems, those who opposed it

> were accused of elitism or neglecting the on-going problem of poverty in China … Famously, growth-obsessed Government officials and developers attacked environmentalists by proclaiming that China's poor would rather die from inhaling pollutants than from starvation. (Yisheng, 2011)

Growth was seen as necessary in order to gain a higher standard of living for the people. In some ways, growth has been very positive for China. As Chinese GDP multiplied, per capita incomes increased almost tenfold (1978–2008) and the number of those in poverty fell from approximately 65% of the population to 10% (1981–2011) (Keeley and Yisheng, 2011). However, the environmental cost of this is now being widely recognised and, consequently, China's obsession with growth is finally beginning to shift. In 2006, Pan Yue stated that the extent of environmental damage is worse than portrayed, so that high GDP did not achieve what it set out to, even financially, because of the cost of cleaning up the resulting environmental disaster:

> While the central Government admits to some of the environmental degradation caused by rapid economic growth, the picture it paints is incomplete … more realistic estimates put environmental damage at 8–13 percent of China's GDP growth each year, which means that China has lost almost everything it has gained since the late 1970's due to pollution … (Pan Yue, 2006b: 1)

More recently, Pan Yue (2010) has spoken of the need to promote an 'ecological civilization', based on Chinese traditional culture, which emphasises harmony between humanity and nature. Following this, in 2011, the then Prime Minister, Wen Jiabao, announced that China is lowering its annual economic growth target, from 7.5% to 7%, partly to contain soaring prices but also because 'We absolutely must no longer sacrifice the environment for the sake of rapid growth' (Wen Jiabao, 2011). Though most of the Chinese population were captivated by the positive gains of growth, they are also now becoming much more aware of the environmental cost and it appears that

"China, arguably, is now experiencing the same kind of environmental awakening that existed in the developed countries three or four decades ago." (Interview, 11 January 2012, Sze Pang Cheung, Campaign Director, Greenpeace East Asia)

A number of Chinese academics now speak of the need to replace the current system with a new model of development (for example, Lu, 2011; Yisheng, 2011). These analysts argue for a move beyond sticking-plaster solutions that will deliver only a certain level of localised environmental improvement amid overall environmental deterioration, and highlight the need for a solution that replaces the existing model of economic development with a less ecologically destructive one. This view has been accompanied by a burst of academic interest in various forms of ecological Marxism, with 549 of the 598 articles that have ever been published on this in China having been written in the decade 2001–2011 (see Wang, 2012). Some now argue that this has awakened a new understanding and interpretation of socialism itself (Hou, 2012).

Around the world, many governments of low-income countries have admired China's growth performance and seen it as model that they could follow. However, though China has performed remarkably in economic terms, it has been at a high environmental cost and, ultimately therefore, at a high cost for human lives. China's achievements in terms of environmental justice have been hampered by capitalism and Damaging Hegemonic Environmental Discourses, but new values, or reinvigorated traditional values, now appear to be on the ascent. In particular, the ecological civilisation paradigm appears to be a viable new model of sustainable development that incorporates environmental justice. With two divergent pathways ahead – continued growth and environmental collapse, or the pursuit of an ecologically and socially balanced civilisation – many are now closely watching to see how development in China unfolds.

Notes

[1] Both SO_2 and NO_x cause acid rain, and nitrogen compounds cause eutrophication (Gruber and Galloway, 2008) and contribute to the formation of ground-level ozone, which is detrimental to human health (Aunan et al, 2000).

[2] These figures are published estimates of the actual proportion of people living in slums. This is measured by a proxy, represented by the urban population living in households with at least one of the following four characteristics:

(a) lack of access to improved water supply; (b) lack of access to improved sanitation; (c) overcrowding (three or more persons per room); and (d) dwellings made of non-durable material (United Nations, 2012).

[3] Other groups include Zhuang, Manchu, Hui, Miao, Uighur, Tujia, Yi, Mongol, Tibetan, Buyi, Dong, Yao and Korean (2000 census, quoted in CIA, 2011).

[4] These dams are controversial because they usually require communities to be relocated, affecting their living environment as well as their cultural heritage. They also have a profound impact on local eco-systems.

NINE

'Recuperating all that we have lost and forgotten': environmental justice in the Plurinational State of Bolivia (Bolivia)

Discussions of environmental justice in Bolivia tend not to focus on the siting of hazardous waste and processing facilities, as in the United States and Europe, but, rather, to emphasise issues such as access to land and water, the defence of traditional seeds, agricultural practices, infrastructure developments, the effects of resource extraction and international climate justice. While researchers and academics have not generally taken up the term,

> "Environmental justice is within the general discussions, the social movement meetings, the NGOs. There have been demands for compensation from people affected by industrial impacts but this is very marginal. People think more in terms of the right to consultation than about the health impacts of pollution." (Interview, 20 March 2013, Martin Vilela, International Relations representative of the Bolivian Platform on Climate Change)

This insistence on a right to consultation is, in part, an outcome of the current government's emphasis on citizen participation, empowerment and the 'decolonisation' of Bolivia in terms of politically and culturally undoing the pernicious effects of colonialism. After 500 years of colonial and neoliberal domination, in 2005, Bolivia took a radical change of direction when the MAS (Movimiento al Socialismo – Movement toward Socialism) secured electoral victory with Evo Morales as its leader. Since then, MAS has undertaken frequent electoral contests, including recall elections, and national referendums, all of which have been marked by high levels of voter turnout and endorsement of its policies. These large majorities have enabled the government to carry out the kind of radical reforms that were not possible for former Leftist presidents of the region, such as Salvador Allende of Chile.

The election of MAS was part of a wave of new Left-leaning governments coming to power across Latin America from the late 1990s, most now affiliated to the regional cooperation project, ALBA.[1] ALBA or 'The Bolivarian Alliance for the Peoples of Our America' is an organisation based on the idea of social, political and economic cooperation between the countries of Latin America and the Caribbean. It is rooted in a socialist approach and a vision of social welfare, mutual economic aid, the rights of indigenous peoples, social participation and fair and equitable distribution (ACN, 2009). Just at the time when the West had declared socialism to be dead, these ALBA-affiliated governments proposed a post-neoliberal development strategy embodied in the general concept of 'twenty-first century socialism'. There has been much speculation as to what this term means in practice. While it may mean nothing more than socialism that relates to modern conditions, some argue that it indicates a reappraisal and critique of past Leftist strategies and assumptions (for example, Harnecker, 2010), and others describe it as solely a more humanitarian form of capitalism (for example, Kennemore and Weeks, 2011).

The MAS position on socialism, indeed, appears complex. Evo Morales has called himself a 'Marxist-Leninist' (Pomeraniec and Stefanoni, 2009) and, on a number of occasions, has affirmed the need to reject capitalism. For example, in April 2008, at the UN Permanent Forum for Indigenous Affairs, he said that the international community should 'eradicate capitalism' and substitute it with 'communitarian socialism' if it hoped to save the planet (Morales Ayma, 2008). Yet, Vice-President Álvaro García Linera has spoken of the need to encourage 'Andean capitalism' as an integral part of Bolivia's economic policy, albeit as a temporary and transitory mechanism. Some of the changes that MAS has brought in have been described as 'revolutionary' (see Dunkerley, 2007), while others claim that they are only minimal reforms that ultimately enable the continuance of neoliberalism (for example, Webber, 2010; 2011). Hence, there is much debate about whether the MAS government is genuinely heading towards socialism, or giving way to an accommodation with neoliberalism. However, what is clear is that the Bolivian government, alongside the other new Leftist governments of Latin America, has embarked on a major programme to regain state control of the economy, effectively changing the economic model from a predominantly free market one to a mixed economy, with strong state management. In 2009, the new State Constitution described the model as a 'plural economy', based on, not just a combination of private and state, but also strong community, social and cooperative sectors.

The effort to gain greater state control over the economy is part of the decolonisation process, alongside eliminating racism and social injustice. This process was initiated with the official MAS development strategy – the National Development Plan (MPD, 2006) – and further embedded in Bolivian institutions and culture with a new constitution, approved by majority in a national vote, which refounded Bolivia as a plurinational, communitarian state. The preamble states:

> We're constructing a new State ... based on respect and equality for all, with principles of sovereignty, dignity, complementarity, solidarity, harmony and equality in the distribution and redistribution of social goods, where the quest for the common good predominates; with respect for economic, social, juridical, political and cultural plurality of the inhabitants of this earth; in collective coexistence with access to water, work, education, health, and housing for all. We will leave in the past the colonial, republican, and neoliberal State. (Gobierno de Bolivia, 2009)

The MAS rise to power was largely a reaction to neoliberal reforms that had been carried out as part of structural adjustment programmes imposed on the country as World Bank and IMF loan conditions. For two decades, Bolivia carried out all the classic political and economic reforms, including privatising state enterprises; opening the country to foreign capital; cutting social services; and eliminating import tariffs (see Kohl and Farthing, 2006; Postero, 2007). The resulting privatisations, drastic reductions in state spending, cheap imports and implementation of austerity measures resulted in mass unemployment and plummeting wages. This led to the massive popular resistance that swept MAS to power.

However, despite the progress made in terms of nationalising resources, MAS has been unable to alter the extractivist, primary export model of the colonial and neoliberal era that still characterises the Bolivian economy (Molero Simarro and Paz Antolin, 2012). Gudynas (2013, p 15) defines 'extractivism' as 'a form of extraction of natural resources on a large scale or with high intensity, of which at least 50% are for export, either as raw materials or those with a minimal degree of processing'. Hence, extractivism is not just the activity of resource extraction, but a development model in which society is organised on the basis of exploiting resources for export. The Bolivian economy remains extractivist because private multinational firms continue to extract the majority of the country's natural gas and minerals. However, the share of income from these industries that goes to the state has increased significantly under the MAS administration. This has enabled the government to introduce new programmes in health, education and social security and helped to reduce rates of extreme poverty (Kohl and Farthing, 2012), but it has not been sufficient to enable Bolivia to build a broader basis for income or employment (Wanderley, 2008; Gray Molina, 2010). The theme of extractivism will reoccur in the follow sections, focusing on specific aspects of environmental justice.

Substantive environmental justice in Bolivia

Until recently, environmental concerns received relatively little attention from Bolivian governments, and ecological considerations were usually subordinated to the goals of growth. Historically, Bolivia's extractive industries, especially silver, gold and tin mining, have caused numerous on-going environmental problems, including land degradation, deforestation, pollution and siltation of waterways, leaving vast regions desertified and communities sickened, impoverished or displaced[2] (Slunge and Jaldin, 2007; World Bank, 2008a; EPI, 2012a). As well as there being a minimal focus on environmental harms during the colonial and neoliberal eras, there was little attention given to the provision of environmental goods, such as improved water and sanitation services. As the environmental datasets in Appendix 2 show, these services are still generally inadequate. Currently, 29% of those living in rural areas do not have access to an improved water supply and 90% of rural residents do not have access to improved sanitation (UNICEF/ WHO, 2012). Consequently, infant mortality is high, particularly in rural areas, as a result of diarrhoea caused by contaminated water and inadequate sanitation. In 2006, up to 80% of diseases in the country were estimated to be carried by water (MPD, 2006). Furthermore, water scarcity is a growing problem in parts of the highlands, valleys and El Chaco; a problem that is being further aggravated by climate change (Slunge and Jaldin, 2007). In cities, air pollution is a serious problem, especially when combined with high altitudes (Slunge and Jaldin, 2007). The main sources are motor vehicles, industry (especially brick production, metal smelting and oil refining) and the burning of waste. Indoor air pollution is also an issue, with almost 80% of those living in rural areas using firewood and other solid fuels for cooking and for heating their homes (Sánchez-Triana et al, 2006). Therefore, the government is prioritising the provision of basic environmental services, while reducing pollution through regulatory means. Bolivia's Director General of Environment and Climate Change explained:

> "For the government, the environmental priorities are water and basic sanitation, as well as electricity and gas services ... these are the priorities to improve quality of life. We also focus on climate change ... and measures to prevent negative environmental impacts from mining and hydrocarbons, using environmental licences ..." (Interview, 25 March 2013, Francisco Salvatierra Iwanami, Director General of Environment and Climate Change, Bolivia Ministry of Environmental Protection)

Unlike many other countries, in Bolivia, most bottom-up environmental protests have been about control over resources, rather than the health effects of pollution. During the neoliberal era there were a series of influential popular uprisings known as 'resource wars'. The most well-known of these, the *guerra del agua* or 'water war' began in 1999 when the government decided to privatise the water in Cochabamba, granting a concession to Aguas de Tunari, a trans-national company. Upon taking over, the company, not only increased water rates by more than 200%, but claimed control of water all over the city, including that collected by people in their own water-butts and through neighbourhood-based water cooperatives. In a self-organised referendum, the population of Cochabamba overwhelmingly rejected the privatisation of the city's water services and a heterogeneous alliance of social movements began to mobilise to demand the renationalisation of the water (Olivera and Lewis, 2004; Albro, 2005). In 2000, protests erupted, roads were blocked and a general strike paralysed the city. After one demonstrator was killed by the military, resistance further intensified until the government was eventually forced to rescind the concession made to Aguas de Tunari. Emboldened by the success in Cochabamba, activists and intellectuals in other parts of Bolivia subsequently focused on their own local water privatisations, in La Paz and El Alto, until these were also rescinded. These resource-war protests were framed in opposition to high prices, and also as a rejection of the privatisation of Bolivia's natural resources in general, and their control by foreign interests.

As a result of this social movement pressure, MAS made its main electoral platform the nationalisation of natural resources. One of its first acts when it came to power was to begin to nationalise all aspects of the production and sale of hydrocarbons in the country. In 2006, Supreme Decree No. 28701 (the Nationalisation Decree) initiated this process, declaring that the state would regain control of gas and oil resources through ownership of 51% of the shares of the recovered companies (they had formerly been state owned, until capitalised in 1996). Shortly after this decree was announced, Evo Morales' approval rating in Bolivia shot up to 81% (World Public Opinion, 2006), confirming how important the issue of control over natural resources is to Bolivians. The companies holding concessions were given six months to renegotiate the terms of their contracts. The tax and royalties gained by the state as a result of the new contracts increased from an average 18% of profits to as much as 82% (Postero, 2010b).

The MAS government is now attempting to address the huge environmental challenges that the country faces, through an approach known as 'Vivir Bien' (Living Well), sometimes also referred to as 'Buen Vivir', 'Suma Qamaña' in Aymara, 'Sumaj Kawsay' in Quechua, or 'Ñande Reko' in Guaraní. Rooted in the worldview of Andean indigenous groups, the concept of 'Vivir Bien' describes a communal and ecologically balanced approach to addressing the environmental crises, while meeting human needs and achieving equality. It aspires to living in harmony with other human beings and nature in relationships of service and reciprocity; and subsumes all economic and social objectives to the protection of ecosystems, which are considered to be the foundation for the accomplishment of all social goals (Radcliffe, 2012). Importantly, Vivir Bien implies that we are part of a whole, so that we cannot live well if other humans do not, or at the expense of our environment. Vivir Bien inherently critiques some Damaging Hegemonic Environmental Discourses, in particular the accepted need for economic growth, the perceived separation of humans from nature and the modernist idea of infinite progress through technology, and moves towards the goal of meeting needs and satisfying rights. Under this ethos, the economy is based, not on the profit motive, but on respect and care for humans and the rest of nature in a spirit of solidarity. Therefore, Vivir Bien challenges, both capitalism and Damaging Hegemonic Environmental Discourses.

The Bolivian government is the first government in the world to fully embrace this philosophy. According to the new constitution, all development projects should now be evaluated through a lens of Vivir Bien. The approach was further strengthened with the passing of the 'Framework Law of Mother Earth and Integral Development for Living Well' in 2012. This national legislation establishes 11 new rights for nature, including: the right to life and to exist; the right to continue vital cycles and processes free from human alteration; the right to pure water and clean air; the right to balance; the right not to be polluted;

the right to not have cellular structures modified or genetically altered; and the right not be affected by mega-infrastructure and development projects that affect the balance of ecosystems.

In 2010, an international victory for Vivir Bien occurred when the United Nations voted unanimously to accept Bolivia's proposal to make access to water a human right. Another example of the implementation of the Vivir Bien approach is Bolivia's unique position on the world stage with regard to the issue of climate change. In this, Bolivia experiences intra-national environmental injustice. Though the country is one of the world's smallest contributors to climate change, it is already being severely impacted, experiencing rising temperatures, melting glaciers and more frequent extreme weather events, including floods, droughts, frosts and mudslides. For example, glaciers, major providers of fresh water, are retreating at an alarming rate. Those that lie below 5,000m are expected to disappear completely within 20 years, leading to severe water shortages that will affect agricultural production. The Bolivian government has taken a principled position in the United Nations climate change negotiations, pushing for a binding, ambitious and justice-based agreement. For example, in December 2009, at the UN Conference of the Parties in Copenhagen (COP15),[3] Bolivia advocated climate reparations from the global North to the South, and called for a 1C maximum limit on temperature increases. In the following year, in response to the perceived inadequacy of the COP15, Bolivia hosted the World Peoples' Summit on Climate Change and the Rights of Mother Earth in Cochabamba. The results of the Summit were collated into a document entitled the 'People's Agreement', which reiterated the need for a 1C limit on temperature rises and reaffirmed the demand for climate reparations. Specifically, it stated that, in order to redress developed countries' historical responsibility for climate change, they should give 6% of their respective GDPs to climate adaptation funds, to be managed by national governments at the United Nations, not the World Bank (Shultz, 2010). Following the Peoples' Summit, the Bolivian government was the only country to defend these positions at the COP16 in Cancún and, hence, not to sign the Cancún Accord.

As is the case with many who challenge Damaging Hegemonic Environmental Discourses, Bolivia is often portrayed as proudly, even defiantly, anti-modern, and against science and progress. Yet, appreciating and valuing traditional ways and knowledge does not mean that the Bolivian government is any of these. State-sponsored science and technology projects are increasingly prominent in Bolivia and much is being done to foster work in these fields, though with an emphasis on using local materials and methods and respecting indigenous or ancestral knowledge (Centellas, 2010). For example, traditional medicine, which is much less likely to have a negative environmental impact than allopathic medicine, is now being promoted by the state. The government is intent, not only on creating a national system of traditional medicine, but on ensuring that it has the same status as Western medicine (Johnson, 2010). This is enshrined in the new constitution, which declares: 'It is the responsibility of the state to promote and guarantee the respect, use, investigation, and practice of traditional medicine' (Article 42). A Vice Ministry of Traditional Medicine and Interculturality is being established and there are plans for academic programmes in the study and promotion of traditional medicine; mutual referrals between physicians and traditional medicine providers; and systems of regulation, certification and accreditation for traditional medicine (MSD, 2006). For this reason, coca is also promoted for its medicinal and cultural value (Farthing and Kohl, 2010). At the same time, nutritious indigenous crops that have fallen out of widespread popular consumption (for example, grains such as quinoa and amaranth) are being promoted (Johnson, 2010). These programmes are consistent with the widespread desire of Bolivians to reclaim their own resources and modes of knowledge production. Science is being used as a tool for Bolivian development on local terms, not as a sign that Bolivia is 'catching up' with developed nations (Centellas, 2010).

Because of the strong respect for environmental limits inherent in the Vivir Bien approach, we might expect that the policy would help to increase the likelihood of attaining substantive environmental justice. However, continued dependence on extractivism is a serious constraint to its effective implementation. Yet, ironically, attempts to move away from extractivism may cause more environmental destruction in Bolivia if, as planned, this is achieved through increasing the processing of raw materials. The government intends to develop value-added metal mining and to produce lithium batteries (used in electric cars). Consequently, Bolivian tin (for example, in Vinto), silver and lead (for example, in Karachipampa) and iron and steel (for example, in Mutún) smelters are now being reopened and lithium processing is being developed on the Uyuni salt flats.

Part of the reason why Vivir Bien has not yet enabled the country to move beyond extractivism is its relatively recent introduction to policy. Vivir Bien is not yet significantly developed as a concept or a practical programme. Without this work, it is open to a variety of interpretations. The interviews and discussions that I carried out in Bolivia in early 2013 indicate that, though most people in Bolivia are aware of the concept, they were not clear what it would mean in practice. For example, a government officer responsible for carrying out environmental consultations said:

> "If you ask me, I do not understand very well what Vivir Bien is. Vivir Bien, the Law of Mother Earth, that paradigm is really new and I have not had the opportunity to understand and ask questions … so it has to be socialised … I think it is a culture, it is not a simple law. For example, for me, Vivir Bien is very different to if you ask people from the country. I do not really understand it. We are not really working on Vivir Bien at the moment." (Interview, 27 March 2013, Senior Environmental Manager, Ministry of Public Works, Services and Housing)

Others had clearer conceptions, but with diverse emphases. For example, some focused on Vivir Bien as an element of the transition to socialism and liberation from external domination, as emphasised by a MAS representative who said:

> "For me, Vivir Bien, is our Andean cosmo-vision. We are a plurinational state so we are at this stage of finding our path to Vivir Bien. The path before was that of capitalism, that of the rich, now it is that of the people, to serve the people. Therefore, now our plurinational state is taking the path of the people. We are recuperating all that we have lost and forgotten …" (Interview, 4 April 2013, Leonida Zurita Vargas, Secretary of International Relations, MAS)

Others emphasised the right to basic services, as in the following comment:

> "Vivir Bien is to live in harmony, to achieve food sovereignty, value our products, our healthy food, to guarantee the right to water, electricity, basic services to all the population." (Interview, 8 April 2013, Juanita Ancieta Orellana, Executive Secretary of the National Confederation of Indigenous Women of Bolivia – Bartolina Sisa)

Still others felt that the new law of 'Mother Earth and Integral Development for Living Well' was not sufficiently strong with regard to environmental protection, indigenous rights to resist development or the direct and explicit rejection of capitalism (for example, interview,

20 March 2013, Martin Vilela, International Relations representative of the Bolivian Platform on Climate Change). Hence, though the law opens up debate and can be a useful tool for the social movements that seek to establish a different model of development, some argue that it should have been more explicit in its environmental and socialist commitments.

Distributive environmental justice in Bolivia

Bolivia experiences both race and income inequity (see socioeconomic dataset in Appendix 2). This is a pattern that has developed as a result of its colonial history, although a concerted effort is now being made to reduce both, with some apparent success. According to Bolivia's National Institute of Statistics, poverty levels fell from 60.6% in 2005 to 49.6% in 2010, with the greatest reduction occurring in rural areas (from 77.6% to 65.1%) (INE, Bolivia, 2013). Recent international figures back these findings, indicating that there has been a significant drop in absolute poverty rates (the proportion of those living on less than US$2 per day) from 60% in 2006 to 30% in 2011 (CIA, 2011). Also, illiteracy, which stood at approximately 14% in 2006, has now been eradicated (UNESCO, 2009). In addition, there has been a reduction in the proportion of the urban population living in slums (that is, dwellings that are overcrowded, made of non-durable material, or without access to improved water or sanitation services) (United Nations, 2012). Furthermore, there have been inroads into reducing inequality. According to government statistical data, the Gini Coefficient dropped from 0.62 in 2005 to 0.53 in 2009, the latest date for which there are figures (INE, Bolivia, 2013).

The main programmes for reducing poverty and inequality have been transfer payments targeting the most vulnerable groups, including an annual stipend for children who stay in primary school (Bono Juancito Pinto); a national pension and social security scheme (Renta Dignidad); a national health insurance programme for under-25s; a supplement for women who are pregnant or have young children (Bono Juana Azurduy); and long-term investments in health and education, particularly in rural areas (Interview, 8 April 2013, Magdalena Lázaro, General Secretary of the National Confederation of Indigenous Women of Bolivia – Bartolina Sisa). The MAS government has also approved annual increases in the national minimum wage of between 5% and 20% each year. In addition, redistribution of wealth has occurred through land reform. Lands that were not being used productively have been partially redistributed to the indigenous peasantry, though any radical transformation has been prevented by fierce opposition from the Bolivian oligarchy which controls the agricultural and industrial sectors in the East. Despite all these improvements, there is still much more to do, however, as the country remains the second-poorest in the Americas according to official reports (for example, UNDP, 2011).

The issue of race inequality is also a significant challenge to overcome. Of the 10.3 million people living in Bolivia, the vast majority identify themselves as indigenous, and nearly 62% are native speakers of an indigenous language (INE, 2003; World Bank, 2008b). Inequality between indigenous and white groups has a long history in Bolivia, resulting from a 500-year history of colonialism by external powers (Spain, Britain and the United States). Therefore, as explained earlier, one of the fundamental themes of the MAS administration is to 'decolonise' Bolivia in order to rid the country of its legacy of racism. MAS has, indeed, made impressive inroads into this, greatly increasing indigenous participation in decision making and legislating for the recognition of indigenous rights. The new constitution highlights the 'plurinational' nature of the Bolivian state, thereby recognising its 36 indigenous nations. It also specifies a number of indigenous rights, including those of self-government and self-determination, collective landownership, community involvement in the economy and the need for prior consultation on matters affecting indigenous people.

Even so, significant inequalities in Bolivia remain, despite attempts to overcome them in recent years. However, whether these inequalities translate into distributive environmental justice is not clear from the literature. While there has been substantial interest in Bolivia's legal developments with regard to environmental and social change, there appear to be no studies that specifically look at the socio-spatial patterns of distributional environmental justice within Bolivia, correlating ethnicity or income with environmental degradation. The data that would enable us to carry out such as analysis is not, to the best of my knowledge, presently collected. Yet, poverty and inequality obviously limit access to, and create disparities in access to, environmental goods that have to be paid for, such as food, housing and transport, and will prevent people from moving away from environmental hazards. Therefore, we can assume that, while poverty and inequality continues in Bolivia, distributive injustice will be found.

Procedural environmental justice in Bolivia

The MAS government places a strong focus on participatory democracy, which is to run alongside a representative system. Article 7 of the

2009 Constitution states that the democratic system is exercised both directly (that is, communal self-government) and via representation (that is, through the representative democratic system). It is considered that the involvement of social movements and local people is essential to the success of the MAS project, and popular mobilisation is encouraged to push through changes (Dangl, 2010). Hence, Bolivia's National Development Plan contains substantial mechanisms to improve participation in governance structures (Gobierno de Bolivia, 2006), as does the 2009 Constitution. For example, the Constitution requires prior consultation before any extractive industry begins work on indigenous or campesino land (Articles 30, 352 and 403). In addition, the Constitution protects freedom of expression, laying out an expansive right to communicate freely (Article 2), while also imposing a duty to communicate with 'truth and responsibility' (Article 107). A freedom of information Bill is also currently pending in the legislature. Furthermore, special 'Agricultural and Environmental Courts' have now been set up.

Many of the Bolivians I spoke to were pleased about the level and methods of consultation (for example, interview, 8 April 2013, Pablo Solares, Secretary for Cooperatives, Central Workers Union of Bolivia – COB). However, some of the social movement organisations (for example, the Indigenous Federation of Eastern Bolivia – CIDOB) maintain that the law on prior consent has not been implemented, pointing, for example, to the reopening of the Corocoro copper mine without an Environmental Impact Assessment. Furthermore, some of the environmental NGOs that I spoke to complained that they are now being marginalised in terms of their influence (interview, 26 March 2013, Ing. Gumercindo Benavidez Gutierrez, Executive Director, Multiple Services of Appropriate Technology - SEMTA).

The role of environmental NGOs in Bolivia is highly contentious. Government and public mistrust of environmental NGOs has arisen out of political tensions, whereby some of these organisations are seen as being allied to those forces that are attempting to bring down the government. MAS policies have met with substantial opposition from elites in Bolivia, who feel that their interests are threatened. In particular, the MAS government has faced significant resistance from the previously dominant, right-wing, white political classes of the Media Luna (Half Moon), the country's four Eastern departments of Santa Cruz, Tarija, Beni and Pando. These four Eastern departments have mobilised against the MAS throughout its term in office, promoting demands for regional autonomy to expand their control over the region's oil and gas and in order to resist transformative policies, such as land reform. They often build on elite racist sentiments to gather support (Gustafson, 2006) and have good access to the media to propagate their messages, as opposition groups largely control the media in Bolivia (Interview, 1 April 2013, Eddy Lopez, Journalist, Bolivian National Network of Environmental Journalists). Some consider that these groups, and the NGOs linked to them, are supported by the United States under its agenda of 'democracy promotion' (for example, Bigwood, 2008; Allard and Golinger, 2009). This view is shared by some members of the government. For example, Vice President, Álvaro García Linera, referring to tensions in Bolivia, has stated, 'Wherever there is conflict, if you dig a little, USAID or NGOs linked to USAID are at the heart of the problem' (in Paredes, 2010). Therefore, there is a level of animosity towards NGOs, particularly environmental NGOs, among Bolivian citizens. They feel that NGOs use environmentalism as a way to undermine the government and intervene without invitation. For example, one interviewee remarked:

> "Environmentalism is something of the NGOs. There are many – they are like a plague, financed by capitalist governments, working in their interests and manipulated by them. We don't trust them much. In the East of the country, where there is more opposition to the government, they are very strong. We feel used and manipulated by them. They are financed externally and work for their own agenda in our name but without our agreement." (Interview, 1 April 2013, Matilde Delgado Mamani, social movement activist, Cochabamba)

The politics surrounding the construction of a road through the Isiboro Ségure Indigenous Territory and National Park (TIPNIS) in the central lowlands of Bolivia[4] is of great illustrative value with regard to the internal conflicts around environmentalism in Bolivia. The international media have focused on these protests and the supposed hypocrisy of the government, in particular, Evo Morales, in wishing to build a road through a sensitive ecosystem. The government considered the road to be essential to connect the states of Beni and Cochabamba and to bring services to the people living in the TIPNIS region. Yet, international environmental NGOs, as well as less formal groups and local organisations, including the lowland indigenous federation, CIDOB, argued that the construction of the road would be ecologically and socially very damaging. Some groups on the Left accused the government of pursuing pro-capitalist development at the expense of the rights of indigenous people, considering the road to be mainly a means of facilitating hydrocarbon exploration and extraction. In some cases, the protesters and NGOs involved proposed that the area be designated as untouchable, that is, a sacred space, not to be altered.

However, far from the situation being that of indigenous people in opposition to the government, as the media tended to portray it, the TIPNIS situation was characterised by conflicts between the different social movements. When analysing environmental justice claims in Bolivia, it is important to remember that the indigenous communities of the country should not be viewed as one group with common values and opinions. In Bolivia, members of the indigenous population take very different positions with regard to a number of environmental and social issues. This is, in part, due to the history of their formation. Some groups, often supported by international NGOs, anthropologists and religious groups, have organised specifically around identity, ethnicity and culture, for example, CIDOB. Other groups have focused more on class or a critique of capitalism, for example, the predominately Aymara and Quechua highland campesinos, who have formed the Sole Union Confederation of Bolivian Campesino Workers of Bolivia (CSUTCB), the Union Confederation of Bolivian Colonisers (CSCB) and the National Federation of Bolivian Campesino Women – Bartolina Sisa (FNMCB-BS) (Postero, 2010a). Therefore, though CIDOB and other groups were opposed to the TIPNIS road, the main campesino groups (largely indigenous), leaders from the Central Workers Union of Bolivia (COB) and indigenous groups in the south of TIPNIS all came out in support of a road, highlighting the benefits that the road would bring in terms of access to basic services and ability to trade.

In October 2011, the government responded to the protests by passing Law 180, prohibiting the construction of a road through TIPNIS and designating it as untouchable. Even so, protests continued, on the grounds that an untouchable status would undermine the livelihood of some of the local people. Consequently, the government set up a consultation process regarding whether the road should be constructed through TIPNIS and if the area should be designated as untouchable. When the extended consultation process ended in December 2012, the result was that, of the 69 indigenous communities included, 54 agreed to support the road (6 could not be reached and 5 boycotted the process) (Supreme Electoral Tribunal – TSE, Bolivia, 2013). Many saw the process as a triumph for participatory democracy, while others continue to allege that the consultation was manipulated, for example, through linking the construction of the road to the promise of clinics and schools.

While the government was portrayed as 'developmentalist' and the indigenous protesters as focused on nature and the protection of their community and way of life, the reality was much more complex. Although superficially the issues seemed to be about whether the provision of services and economic development should override the maintenance of the traditional way of life of the local indigenous communities, this is in the context of a much larger question about how to meet the needs of some groups while respecting nature and the needs of others. This debate is necessary and positive, though it takes place in a context whereby such fissures within the progressive movements for change can be utilised by right-wing groups to further a return to neoliberalism (Fuentes, 2011). The Bolivian government has denounced the role of NGOs, USAID and the Santa Cruz opposition as fomenting the TIPNIS protests. It is difficult to tell the extent to which the opposition to the road was really about environmental issues or actually an attempt to undermine the government. There were differing views about this among those I spoke to, though most took the latter position. For example, I was told:

> "TIPNIS was a struggle mounted by the Right – indigenous people linked to NGOs that are working on environment issues but involved in projects such as carbon markets. But a large proportion of indigenous people want, not just roads, but healthcare, education … It was a theme that the opposition used to challenge Evo Morales. It was not an environmental issue, as it has been portrayed in other countries, it was a political issue. If it had been ecological, we would have supported the protests but it was not like that …" (Interview, 1 April 2013, Ramiro Saravia, founder, Red Tinku – Tinku Network)

The TIPNIS situation shows that the government has followed the popular will, and shown a willingness to consult and enter into dialogue. In this example, and others, the MAS administration tries to steer a course between environmentalism and developmentalism, which it considers to be the essence of Vivir Bien. It also appears that the government has learned much from this situation. When I spoke to managers who are responsible for organising planning and development, they all said how important it was to consult so as to avoid some of the problems that had occurred in the past (for example, interview, 27 March 2013, Ing. René Nestor Bascopé Cañipa, Environmental Manager, Transport Sector, Vice Ministry of Transport). I participated in one of these consultations regarding the proposed cable car development for La Paz and found the outreach and engagement processes to be impressive (fieldwork notes, 27 March 2013 – see Figure 9.1).

Figure 9.1: Consultation on new cable car public transit system for La Paz

Source: Karen Bell (2013)

The causes of environmental injustice in Bolivia

If the theory embodied in this book is correct, that environmental justice can be achieved through building an alternative economic system that is not based on capitalist processes and through developing a culture that promotes ecologically sustainable environmental values, then Bolivia should have a positive general situation of environmental justice. The EJI Framework (see Table A1.1 in Appendix 1) shows that Bolivia does compare well to the other countries featured in this book, with an overall score of 7.6. This relatively favourable outcome is mainly because of stronger scoring on the procedural justice indicators, as well as a small per capita Ecological Footprint. However, the score is still low in absolute terms. Some would argue that the reason for this is that Evo Morales and the MAS government, despite their rhetoric, are still dedicated to an environmentally and socially harmful industrialised development process. For example, one interviewee commented:

"There is a discourse from the government which gives an international impression but, in Bolivia, they are continuing with these practices that cause environmental and social problems ... The government maintains the discourse of Vivir Bien but takes the road of industrialisation ... We have high levels of poverty so we have to change but we are questioning that this is based on extractivism that will have high social and environmental costs ..." (Interview, 20 March 2013, Martin Vilela, International Relations representative of the Bolivian Platform on Climate Change)

Evo Morales' election campaign for his second term promised an 'industrial leap forward', alongside the physical integration of the country. However this is because, in general, social movements in Bolivia have asked for more, not less, of this kind of development (Fuentes, 2011). For many, decolonisation can be accomplished only through industrialisation accompanied by redistribution. Therefore, in the MAS strongholds of El Alto and Potosi, protesters have tended to march for access to basic services, for more factories and for roads. In order to provide these services and facilities, the government currently has to depend on its extractivist base. This is part of a wider pattern in which, according to Dependency Theory (Frank, 1967) and World Systems Theory (Wallerstein, 2004), the global economy has long been structured around the mass extraction of resources in the periphery nations of Latin America, Africa and Asia for consumption in Europe and the United States. However, MAS emphasises the difference between extraction that contributes to welfare and that which fills the pockets of foreign corporate executives. Even so, in Bolivia resources generate conflicts between social movements because, while taxes from natural resource exploitation go to boost national or sub-national budgets, the environmental and social costs are felt at the point of extraction.

It is proving difficult to make a definitive break from neoliberalism, so capitalist relations of production are still the dominant mode of economic activity in Bolivia. Consequently, many on the left, in Bolivia and beyond, are frustrated by the pace of change. The unions, represented by the COB, often complain that Evo Morales is too reformist, for example, when he renegotiates contracts with oil companies, rather than completely nationalising these enterprises. Yet, Bolivia's method of change appears to be based on Gramsci's 'war of position' with the Left incrementally occupying spaces in the public sphere (Bilbao, 2008; Geddes, 2010). This slow process of change can be frustrating for some orthodox Marxists who speak of the need to 'smash the state' and expropriate the banks, large agricultural estates and monopoly industry (for example, Woods, 2008). Yet, it is evident that some tensions are still to be worked through. While many Bolivians consider development to be the material and financial precondition for achieving the goals of Vivir Bien, others argue that development is the cause of the denial of the rights of Mother Earth and, consequently, that Vivir Bien can only be achieved by taking a different path, away from the classical notions of development, and putting the environment first. As García Linera et al (2010) have pointed out, these tensions are a necessary part of the process of change. MAS has been in power for only six years and it is not fair to expect it to correct the legacy of almost 500 years of colonial and neoliberal rule in such a short time. The government of Bolivia, as with countries throughout the global South, is implicated in, and constrained by, myriad regional and global economic forces that make environmental justice a difficult proposition.

Even so, Bolivia is, perhaps, the most promising country in terms of the policies that are in place for achieving environmental justice. This is largely due to its more favourable procedural justice approach as well as the predominance of counter-hegemonic environmental discourses. Vivir Bien is replacing the dominant vision of humans above nature with that of humans as part of nature, promising a way of achieving a society that is both ecologically sustainable and socially just. If Bolivia, in spite of the pressures upon it, can find a way to achieve the goals it has set, then it may provide a viable alternative model of development, rooted in environmental justice.

Notes
[1] ALBA was set up in 2004 by the Venezuelan and Cuban governments as an alternative to the trade liberalisation and free trade agreements, such as CAFTA and FTAA. There are now eight member states – Cuba, Venezuela, Bolivia, Dominica, Antigua and Barbuda, Ecuador and Saint Vincent and the Grenadines (Honduras withdrew following the 2009 coup) (Muhr, 2013).

[2] Modern open-pit mining techniques cause extensive environmental harm, since they often demolish and pulverise mountains, and soak the ore in cyanide solutions. These techniques leave entire mountain ranges devastated, create enormous toxic 'tailings reservoirs' and produce acid drainage that contaminates entire river systems. Some minerals require the use of liquid mercury to separate them from the ground ore, leading to mercury poisoning in the local area.

[3] The COP meets annually to assess progress in relation to the United Nations Framework Convention on Climate Change. This is an international environmental treaty that was agreed at the UN Conference on Environment and Development, held in Rio in 1992. There are 195 'parties', that is, signatory countries.

[4] Isiboro Sécure became a national park in 1965 and was later designated to be combined indigenous territory and national park in 1990.

TEN

'Socialism creates a better opportunity': environmental justice in Cuba

In 2006, Cuba earned international recognition as the only country in the world to have achieved sustainable development (WWF, 2006). This was based on the country's relatively high indicators for social development, in conjunction with a small per capita Ecological Footprint. Sustainable development is not the same as environmental justice (Dobson, 1998), though, with its distributional and procedural dimensions. There have not been any previous studies that specifically look at environmental justice in Cuba,[1] but there has been a great deal of research that is relevant, examining Cuba's natural environment, legislative framework, environmental policy, decision-making processes and social structures. These studies are outlined and analysed in this chapter, alongside my own primary research interviews and field experiences. Somewhat more space in this book has been given to examining Cuba because it seems necessary to explain in more depth its unusual environmental justice outcomes, as will be evident.

It is important to note, though, that discussions on environmental and social issues in Cuba are deeply controversial. Hence, although the WWF (2006) found Cuba to be the only country in the world to have achieved sustainable development, Cuban exile academics have for some time described it as a country that is environmentally and socially in ruins (for example, Diaz-Briquets and Pérez-López, 2000). In particular, the English-language literature on Cuba is dominated by the writings of academics, described by their opponents as 'Cubanologists', who, it is alleged, have:

> Under an academic mantle and with pretended scientific objectivity ... led the ideological and political struggle against socialism and Cuba. (Rodriguez, 1983: 7)

Relevant tenets of 'Cubanology' are that Fidel Castro, and now Raúl, dominate decision making, that there is a lack of democracy, that civil society is repressed and that there is on-going economic mismanagement. Therefore, supporters of the revolution complain of a 'concerted campaign of disinformation' against the country (Saney, 2004, p 5). It is not just those who generally oppose socialism that have taken this position. Criticism has also come from the Left, with some Marxists viewing Cuba as 'Stalinist' and 'state-capitalist', rather than socialist (for example, Gonzalez, 1992, p 85). However, Cubanology is part of a particular political context whereby, since the revolution in 1959, Cuba has been the recipient of relentless US efforts to overthrow the government. The most widely known aspect of this is the 'blockade'[2] which the United States has maintained against Cuba since 1963, prohibiting commercial business with the island. The blockade was further reinforced in 1992 with the 'Torricelli Law', and again in 1996, with the 'Helms-Burton Act'. The 1992 Law prohibits foreign-based subsidiaries of US companies from trading with Cuba, travel to Cuba by US citizens and family remittances to Cuba. Under the 1996 Act, any non-US company that deals economically with Cuba can be subjected to legal action. As well as using the blockade and disinformation tactics to try to destabilise the Cuban system, the US has also used proactive sponsorship of opposition groups and a campaign of aggression, including sabotage, terrorism, an invasion, attempted assassinations of the leadership, biological attacks and hotel bombings (Saney, 2004; Kapcia, 2008). The situation amounts to an undeclared war (Ludlum, 2008) and, consequently, many Cubans and supporters of the regime are reluctant to admit any government failings that could be used as justification for further attacks. Therefore, it has been argued that, with regard to Cuba, there are few reliable sources and 'as a result, the scholar operates in a research universe of partial fact and educated inference' (Crawford, 2004, p 4). Despite these difficulties, I have endeavoured to outline a range of perspectives in this chapter so as to present as accurate as possible an assessment of environmental justice in Cuba.

First, however, it is useful to outline the relevant political and economic features of the Cuban system. Cuba is a self-proclaimed socialist country and the main ideological force in the country is the Communist Party (Partido Comunista de Cuba, PCC),[3] which, according to the Cuban Constitution, is:

> the highest guiding force of the society and the State, which organises and guides common efforts toward the goal of constructing socialism and the advance towards a communist society. (Constitution of the Republic of Cuba (1992), Article 5)

From the early days of the revolution, the US blockade pushed Cuba towards an economic dependency on the Soviet Union and the Eastern European 'Community for Economic Cooperation' (COMECON). Consequently, after COMECON collapsed in 1989 and the blockade tightened, the country faced an economic disaster, with its GDP falling by more than 48% (Diaz-Briquets and Perez-Lopez, 1995). In Cuba, this era was referred to as the 'Special Period in Peacetime', implying the need for measures that would normally apply during war, in order to cushion the effect of the crisis on the population. Although a high standard of free universal healthcare and education was maintained and social programmes to sustain public welfare were stepped up (Barbeira et al, 2004), some shortages could not be avoided. Because of its history of colonialism, Cuba was still dependent on external trade and, therefore, needed to pursue hard currency in order to buy material necessities. The country, therefore, had to begin to interact with the capitalist world. Following extensive consultation with the population, it was decided to use some market-based policies, a path that has been referred to as an attempt to 'use capitalism to save socialism' (Taylor, 2009, p 4). These policies included the development of tourism; legalisation of the dollar; individual self-employment; joint ventures with foreign capital; intensification of natural resource extraction for export (especially nickel); and increases in the availability and promotion of consumer goods in order to capture dollars sent as remittances (Dello Buono, 1995; Mesa-Lago, 2005; Raby, 2006). Since then, there have been a number of swings toward and away from market policies over time, in the somewhat experimental style in which Cuba makes policy (Yaffe, 2009). In 2011, there was another wave of intensive change following a lengthy nationwide consultation process in the lead-up to the Cuban Communist Party's 6th Congress. Wide-scale changes were agreed, including mass redeployment of state workers to cooperatives, more opportunities for self-employment, the phasing out of the food rationing system and the introduction of the private purchase and sale of cars and houses. This policy context is important for understanding the following sections, which look at the substantive, distributive and procedural aspects of EJ in Cuba.

Substantive environmental justice in Cuba

Historically, Cuba has suffered hundreds of years of environmental degradation as a result of intensive exploitation of minerals and other natural resources, lack of environmental legislation, exhaustive export commodity production and poor agricultural practices (see Diaz-

Briquets and Pérez-López, 2000; Houck, 2003; Maldonado, 2003; Whittle and Rey Santos, 2006). These problems began under colonial rule, first by Spain and then by the United States, during which time the main concern was rapid exploitation of natural resources (Fernández, 2002; Funes Monzote, 2008). Even after the 1959 revolution, the degradation intensified when the country embraced the so-called 'green revolution', an era of intensive, industrialised agriculture and heavy use of chemical fertilisers and pesticides[4] (Gonzalez, 2003). In Cuba, as in much of the world, these practices resulted in extensive water pollution, soil erosion and loss of natural areas (Diaz-Briquets and Pérez-López, 1993; Gonzalez, 2003).

However, in 1992, following the Rio Earth Summit, the government initiated a series of reforms aimed at redressing past environmental harms and minimising future degradation. This included establishing a new and powerful Ministry of Science, Technology and Environment (CITMA); publishing the country's first environmental programme – 'The National Environmental Strategy'; and passing new framework environmental legislation, Law 81, 'The Law of the Environment'. The new law established the basis of an enforcement system that includes emissions monitoring, inspections, civil and criminal penalties, as well as opportunities for private citizens to seek environmental justice through the courts. The most important general principles of Law 81, from an environmental justice perspective, are that it establishes:

- the right to a healthy environment (Article 4(a))
- the precautionary principle
- the right to environmental information (Article 4(e))
- the right to be consulted on environmental actions and decisions (Article 4(k))
- the necessity for community participation to achieve effective environmental decision making (Article 4(m))
- the right to access to administrative and judicial bodies to demand compliance with the law (Article 4(l)).

These legislative reforms were accompanied by practical measures that made a dramatic difference to Cuban daily life. For example, industrialised agriculture, featuring large-scale irrigation schemes and considerable inputs of chemicals, was rejected in favour of organic food production (Rosset and Benjamin, 1995; Levins, 2005). Cuba also moved away from a transportation system that was dependent on oil and turned to renewable energy sources and energy conservation (Guevara-Stone, 2009). In addition, reforestation schemes were stepped up and systems were established to ensure managed protection of ecologically, socially, historically and culturally important areas.

It is frequently alleged (for example, Diaz-Briquets and Pérez-López, 1995) that the environmental improvements made in the 1990s were not born of any genuine environmental commitment on the part of the government but were, rather, an improvised emergency response to the 'Special Period'. However, I do not believe this to be the case, as Cuba could have chosen other options, such as IMF-style cuts to basic services, in response to the crisis. Moreover, the environmental changes were consistent with on-going developments and debates in the country. For example, there were a number of environmental programmes already in place, going back to the 1960s (Levins, 2005), and the pre-existing environmental law (Law 33, passed in 1981) had been widely considered to be pioneering for the region (Whittle and Rey Santos, 2006). The relative weight accorded to environmental concerns in Cuba in the first decades after the revolution reflected the dominant thinking globally, though there were fierce debates between ecologists and those who advocated 'modernisation'. Levins argues that it is socialism that enabled the ecologists to eventually win the debate in Cuba because 'Nobody was pushing pesticides or mechanization to make a profit ... Socialism made ecological choices more likely' (Levins, 2005, p 14).

However, in spite of this progressive legislation and policy, environmental quality in Cuba is mixed. On the positive side, as Appendix 2 shows, Cuba performs well on most international environmental datasets. This was reflected in the fieldwork, in that many of the people I interviewed, or spoke to informally, said they were happy with their local environment and proud of the country's achievements in this respect. The most widely appreciated aspects included the provision of low-cost (or, sometimes, free) housing, food, public transport and utilities; successful energy-efficiency programmes; care of the population during hurricanes; urban agriculture initiatives; recently improved public transport; and new improvements to workplace safety (for example, interview, 4 February 2009, Resident A, Holguín). The 'Revolución Energética' (Energy Revolution), which began in 2006, is a particularly good example of an environmental policy that increases environmental justice by benefitting those on low incomes. This initiative endeavoured to save energy and use more sustainable sources. The programme included replacing older household appliances with more efficient and safer equipment, supplied free or at low cost to the entire population. Another important state programme that has furthered environmental justice is the development of environmental social work brigades.[5] The government took marginalised youth who were not in education or employment and paid them to attend university for a year to become social workers who would serve the poor communities they had come from, helping to identify and solve communal problems. Part of this work involved helping to implement the 'Energy Revolution', as well as supporting their communities to identify, investigate and address local environmental concerns (interview, 10 February 2009; Director of Social Work, Holguín).

Similarly, Cuba's transport policy also both improves the environment and increases social justice. The number of private cars is kept in check by the state's car ownership policy, whereby people cannot purchase cars just because they have the money to buy them. All cars are assigned according to the needs and responsibility that the person has and there is no encouragement to perceive cars as an individual item for consumption (though this policy is set to change as a result of the national consultations of 2011, where the majority of the population said that they wanted to legalise the private sale of cars). In general, the government tries to discourage the idea that cars are individual items for consumption. They are considered to be a resource to be shared, so there is an expectation that people with cars offer lifts to other people (fieldwork notes, 18 December 2008, informal conversation with Ministry of Basic Industry employee). At busy road junctions on the edge of some major towns, 'amarillos' (yellow people) are employed to facilitate the car sharing. There is also now considerable investment in public transport and, in addition, planning policies have reduced the need for travel. Mixed-use developments are encouraged so that, where new housing is constructed, enough new facilities and jobs are provided locally. Furthermore, financial support enables people to exchange their job for one closer to their home, if they wish (Enoch et al, 2004; Taylor, 2009).

Among the positive comments that I heard about the environment in Cuba, there were also a number of complaints, however. These were in regard to inadequate sanitation; unreliable water supply; river and air pollution; deficient waste-collection services; damaged streets; and insufficient housing (for example, interview, 27 December 2008, Resident A, San Miguel del Padrón, Havana). This fits with a previous government survey that reported extensive soil erosion, deforestation, inland and coastal water pollution, loss of biodiversity and poor sanitation (CITMA, 1997). Some of this environmental harm has been committed by individuals. For example, during the 'Special Period', deforestation, illegal hunting and fishing, illegal trade in wild species, habitat destruction and illegal dumping increased

(CITMA, 1992). However, the most severe environmental destruction has resulted from major projects and industries owned by the state or international companies (Maal-Bared, 2006). This has usually been in relation to tourism and industrial production. In particular, there have been reports of serious pollution from the expanding nickel industry (for example, Chavez, 2008). Even so, the annual average exposure level of urban residents in Cuba to the main air pollutant (PM10) is within the air quality guidelines given by the WHO (World Bank, 2010). Most developed and developing countries are not within these limits (World Bank, 2010). However, because air pollution tends to be concentrated locally, in specific areas, it is likely that some local PM10 levels would go above this.

River pollution also seemed to be a major issue in Cuba. Despite legislation to prevent water pollution, high levels of industrial as well as agricultural and urban wastes are dumped into the sea and rivers annually (see Aguirre and Portela, 2000). Although there has been less use of chemical fertilisers, pesticides and herbicides over the last decade, continuing high levels of water pollution were confirmed by several individuals and agencies in the research interviews (for example, interview, 11 March 2009, Delegate, *Poder Popular*, Cojimar).

There also seemed to be a general problem in Cuba regarding waste collection, but particularly in rural areas, with only 8% of rural residents receiving a waste-collection service (although all urban residents receive a service) (ONE, 2008). The underlying issue seemed to be a shortage of transport to collect the waste. In general, recycling seems to be an ad hoc affair, though there have been intermittent attempts to try to establish services (interview, 20 January 2009, Armando Fernández-Soriano, Coordinator of the Network of Political Ecology in Latin America and the Caribbean and Editor, Ilé – Annual of Ecology, Culture and Society). Despite these issues, there is very little waste in Cuba because most people seem to repair their belongings, buy second hand and, generally, not over-consume. Many of the mini-dumps in Havana have been cleaned up in the last ten years as a result of the government policy to allow unused land to be developed for small-holdings (Decree/Law 259) (Figure 10.1). Tens of thousands of acres of plots that were previously health hazards have now been cleaned up and leased, rent and tax free, to small farmers on a usufruct basis (interview, 9 January 2009, Worker A, Organopónico, Centro Habana).

With regard to the built environment, before the revolution, most poor people lived in shanty towns or forms of housing in multiple occupation (*solares, cuarterias, cuidadelas, pasajes* and *accesorieas*) with divided rooms and shared facilities (Taylor, 2009). The revolutionaries

Figure 10.1: Urban agriculture in Moa, Holguín

Source: Karen Bell (2009)

set out to ensure security of accommodation and, within the first three months, the government stopped evictions, reduced rents by 30–50% and drastically reduced utility costs. Later, it was mandated that rents could not exceed 10% of a family's income. The worst shanty towns were cleared and new houses were built through self-help programmes. The residents of these dwellings were made outright owners. There was a belief that home ownership would strengthen neighbourhoods, increasing attachment and social cohesion, so that, by the late 1990s, more than 85% of Cuban homes were owner-occupied. Residents now pay little or nothing for their houses, except for maintenance and repairs. The Urban Reform Law (1960) emphasises that housing is not a commodity but a basic human right and, correspondingly, the Cuban constitution asserts that the state 'works to achieve that no family be left without a comfortable place to live' (Article 9 (c)). However, housing construction came to a standstill for years as a result of the 'Special Period' shortages (Saney, 2004) and now, though there is no homelessness in Cuba, there is overcrowding, with the latest official figures reporting a housing shortage of 500,000 (ONE, 2002), mostly in the cities. Many of the people I interviewed in Cuba said the main problem in the country was the quality and quantity of the housing. Until 2011, it was illegal to buy and sell housing for profit, though residents had the right to exchange homes (*se permuta*). However, this policy was also changed as a result of the 2011 consultation, where the majority of the population expressed their wish to buy and sell their homes. Despite these housing problems, other aspects of the built environment were highly rated by those I spoke to. The parks, play areas, public open spaces, community centres, libraries, clinics, day centres and schools are of high quality and within easy reach of most people. Green space is generally easily accessible and well maintained and each school normally has its own fields and gardens, including vegetable plots.

With regard to access to food, all Cubans are ensured a basic amount of food through the ration programme, introduced in 1962. Each person has a '*libreta*', or notebook, assigned to them that entitles them to about one-third to one-half of their monthly nutrition at heavily subsidised prices (at the cost of the equivalent of about £1.50 a month). Many people also receive state-subsidised food through workers' kitchens, schools and hospitals, as well as dining rooms for disabled and older people (fieldwork notes, 4 January 2009, visit to state dining room, Cayo Hueso). All these programmes contribute to food security and, in addition, the government regulates the price of food so that it can be purchased with less than 20% of salaries. However, one previous study shows that food is the biggest expenditure for the Cuban household, using up to 30–50% of salaries, though this is usually to increase food choices, rather than to improve nutrition (Taylor, 2009). The ration system is another policy that is now being phased out as a result of the 2011 national consultation. However, free and subsidised meals will continue to be available through health centres, social services and schools. Workers' canteens, which had been closed in some parts of the country during 2009, will be reopened (Galeano, 2010).

With regard to another substantive environmental justice issue, care for the population during hurricanes, Cuba is renowned for its efforts. In 2008, the country was hit by three devastating hurricanes, Gustav, Ike and Paloma, but, because the government had taken precautionary measures, moving a quarter of a million people to safe shelter, only seven people died, whereas 700 were killed on the neighbouring island of Haiti. Similarly, in 2005, only two people died in Cuba directly as a result of Katrina, while in the US, at least 1,330 died (Davis et al, 2007).

Therefore, substantive environmental justice in Cuba is very mixed. The government's environmental experts that I spoke to recognised that there was no cause for complacency and were keenly aware of the work to be done (for example, interview, 15 January 2009, Dr Orlando Rey Santos, Director, CITMA). However, although there are clearly serious problems in particular areas, if we compare Cuba with other countries, it does seem to be doing relatively well in terms of substantive environmental justice. As the environmental datasets in Appendix 2 show, Cuba generally emits less CO_2 and other greenhouse gases, as well as performing better overall, than the other countries featured in this book. So, though substantive environmental justice in Cuba is seriously deficient for some people, it seems to be relatively good, when compared with other nations. Moreover, Cuba has to live with its own pollution because, unlike the high income capitalist countries, it is not exporting its waste to other parts of the world.

Cuba's positive substantive EJ situation may, however, be beginning to change. In 2010, Cuba slipped just out of the sustainable category, according to the WWF (2010). Cuba also dropped from 9th place in the Environmental Performance Index global rankings for 2010 to 50th in 2012, largely due to changes in air and water pollution, as well as coastal area protection. These changes appear to have occurred in conjunction with an increase in GDP and foreign direct investment (King, 2012). Furthermore, changes to food rationing, the introduction of a housing market and increases in the number of private cars may further undermine Cuba's level of substantive environmental justice in the future.

Distributive environmental justice in Cuba

Cuba puts great emphasis on achieving social equality, and uses macro-economic and social policies based on universality and equitable access to achieve this. This includes measures to reduce wage inequality; keep prices for goods and services low; assure equal and affordable access to essential food and consumer goods through the *libreta* ration-book system; and extend social security, welfare, sports and cultural activities to the entire population for free, or at very low cost. The introduction of these measures, in particular the *libreta*, has had the greatest benefit for the poor, while limiting the excesses of the rich, to some extent.

However, inequality began to increase in the 1990s as a result of 'concessions to capitalism', discussed earlier, that were brought in to survive the 'Special Period' (Hamilton, 2002; Mesa-Lago, 2006; Blue, 2007; Morris, 2008). In this context, inequality emerged between those who had access to dollars and those who did not, as well as between those who were employed in the informal sector and those who worked in the formal economy (Morris, 2008). The dollar-based sector of the economy covers the tourist sector, foreign businesses in joint ventures and some state enterprises that work in export markets. The literature on Cuba describes significant inequality between those who have access to hard currency (now CUCs, rather than dollars)[6] and those who do not, often depending on their links with tourism or overseas contacts (Hamilton, 2002; Morris, 2008). Although a few of the people I spoke to in Cuba, formally or informally, said they did not consider there to be any major income inequality, most confirmed a notable difference between those who have their own businesses and receive income from abroad and those who work for the state and receive their income in national currency (pesos or CUPs). The dual currency is often blamed for inequality, but it is not the currency itself that is the source of wealth, but simply that the CUC earners tend to have a much higher income.

As in many countries, some of the variation in income inequality has a racial dimension. For example, the increase in self-employment, implying access to resources that can be drawn on for the initial investment, discriminated against black people, who were less likely to have relatives abroad able to supply these start-up funds (Blue, 2007). However, though it seems that the economic changes since the early 1990s have increased inequality, several analysts agree that this difference is now beginning to narrow (for example, Morris, 2008). According to one recent estimate, the Gini Coefficient for Cuba is now 0.30 (Vision of Humanity, 2013).[7] Moreover, once the value of subsidised housing, utilities and food, as well as free services, is factored in, the actual inequalities are much lower. The existence of strong social security networks maintains a basic standard of living for all and, in 2005, there was an across-the-board rise in wages and retirement pensions (Ludlum, 2009). The government is also attempting to address the income differences by increasing peso salaries and working towards a single currency. Moreover, as the socioeconomic datasets in Appendix 2 indicate, Cuba maintains very high levels of human development, especially considering it is only a middle-income country (World Bank classification).

Distributive environmental injustice in capitalist societies is built upon residential segregation. This classic pattern of spatial segregation found in capitalist countries also existed in Cuba before the revolution. The poor were generally concentrated in shanty towns around the cities or in areas of older housing that could be divided up into units of multiple occupation. This produced differentiated elite white areas and poor areas of mixed blacks and whites (Taylor, 2009). Most analysts consider that this situation was greatly alleviated by the general programmes designed to reduce poverty, as outlined earlier, as well as a number of specific housing laws and policies (Oliveras and Núñez, 2001; Coyula and Hamberg, 2003; Sawyer, 2006; Taylor, 2009). These included redistributing housing vacated by the wealthy who had fled to the US, as well as the Law of Low Rents (1959) and the Law of Urban Reform (1960), which made housing affordable (or free) in any area of the city or country. Most importantly, the lack of a legal land or housing market, while allowing mobility through housing 'swaps', largely prevented segregation according to income. However, as Oliveras and Núñez (2001) point out, though these policies have significantly mitigated against segregation, four decades have proved insufficient to completely turn around a 400-year-old development pattern. In addition, though some poor people were relocated into the houses vacated by the rich after the revolution, there was no formal programme to diversify the residential areas. It might, then, be assumed that, to some extent, those who were wealthier before the revolution still inhabit the same areas. Therefore, although there are no areas officially recognised as poor, there are some districts where the population, though heterogeneous, is more likely to contain people on lower incomes (Ramirez, 2005).

Two studies that focus on neighbourhoods in the various zones of Havana assert a marked difference in quality between the areas (Mesa-Lago, 2002; Taylor, 2009). Taylor explains this as a result of the emphasis on rural development that occurred during the early stages of the revolution, leaving some of the blighted areas of the city to decay. This focus was considered necessary, at the time, to rebalance the huge differences between urban and rural standards of living that had developed before the revolution and to prevent mass migration to the cities (Taylor, 2009). My own experience affirmed the disparities in environmental quality between areas. It seemed that there was a considerable variation in environments between different areas of the cities, as well as different regions of the country. The main differences in environmental quality in Cuba appeared to be within cities, as well as between the east and west of the country and between urban and rural areas. However, it is not possible to say that one location would be generally better than another, since each seemed to display elements of both environmental 'goods' and environmental 'bads'. For example, air quality was better in rural areas, though waste collection and water services were poorer; while sanitation and water services were better in urban areas, yet pollution levels were higher.

Moreover, there was no basis for these environmental inequalities to be linked to social categories. I was frequently told that people in Cuba do not live in separate communities according to their income level, social status or race, as they might in capitalist countries. People said that their work colleagues, though they were all earning the same, and had the same job status, lived in diverse areas, with different levels of environmental quality (for example, 15 January 2009, Dr Reynaldo Jiménez Guethón, Director, FLACSO). My fieldwork impressions confirmed this, as there seemed to be a distinct lack of the separate communities based on income level, social status or race that are so easily recognisable in capitalist countries. However, it was not possible to verify these findings quantitatively, as socio-spatial data at a micro-level is not currently published for Cuba. Thus, though there was evidence of social inequalities, there did not appear to be geographical segregation based on income or race and there was no evidence of a pattern of distributive environmental justice in Cuba.

Procedural environmental justice in Cuba

In the West, Cuba is generally portrayed as having few, if any, of the ingredients of procedural justice – open, honest and inclusive decision-making processes; consistent application of rules; access to information; freedom of expression; or democratic institutions and systems. There is a common depiction by the Western media that Cuba is authoritarian, to the point of being 'a dictatorship'. In particular, Cuba has been criticised for the 'single party system' and the dominating role of the Communist Party (PCC) (for example, Lievesley, 2004). Even those who acknowledge and praise Cuba's participatory decision making seem to go on to assert that it is ultimately the PCC that determines policy. This occurs, it is alleged, through its control of the National Assembly and interference in administrative affairs (Houck, 2000; Lievesley, 2004). Lievesley (2004), for example, maintains that government officials look to the local PCC to cut through bureaucratic bottlenecks. Similarly, Houck (2000) asserts that the PCC is called upon to resolve interdepartmental conflicts so that disputes are 'resolved in an informal, Godfather-like fashion by the Secretary ...' (Houck, 2000, p 12). The over-representation of PCC members in positions of power is often represented as a manipulation of the system to ensure that those with political loyalty have power.

However, many have argued that, while Cuba's own system of democracy is very different to that in the West, it is as effective, and possibly more so (for example, Cole, 1998; August, 1999; Roman, 2003; Saney, 2004; Raby, 2006; Hernandez, 2008; Kapcia, 2008). These analysts argue that, though Cuba does not correspond to the capitalist model of democracy, characterised by multi-party elections, it practises an alternative direct popular democracy, featuring participatory decision making, election of representative delegates, a vibrant civil society, accountable and responsive government and an emphasis on equality and justice. Whereas capitalist notions of democracy stress competition and rivalry, Cuba's democracy emphasises consensus and consultation. Therefore, multi-party elections were widely rejected following the revolution, as they were associated with past experiences of corruption, division and United States manipulation. Roman (2003) argues that, because unity and consensus is a key component of Cuban ideals of democracy, unanimous votes in representative bodies are not evidence of control (by the PCC or Fidel/Raúl and so on) but, rather, indicate legitimate consensus worked out in lengthy discussion.

Although the main ideological force in Cuba is the Communist Party (*Partido Comunista de Cuba*, PCC), it has no legislative authority. Even so, it would seem that one dominant ideology would not be conducive to procedural justice, as it could limit discussion and marginalise those with opposing views. However, most people I spoke to in Cuba did not criticise the PCC in this respect, saying that it reflected the views of the citizens, since it was made up of the ordinary people. For example, I was told:

> "The Party can't ignore the people because the Party is the people. They are not devils or angels but are people, like me." (Interview, 28 December 2008, Resident A, Cayo Hueso, Centro Habana)

People also said that there are a diversity of views within the PCC; and that, in any case, a unified Party was the only way to prevent attempts to undermine the revolution by external forces. This assertion that there are a diversity of views in the PCC confirms the findings of other Cuba analysts, such as Saney (2004). The PCC can be seen as an organisation that works to identify the position of its members and then influence policy with a united voice. I did not find any evidence to imply that it dominates in any forceful or disempowering way. Since the 1990s, the Party Congresses have always been preceded by nationwide debate on policy, as in the recent case. There are, and have been, widely differing points of view raised within the Party, with different factions, for example, arguing for and against the use of market mechanisms. In addition, in some respects, the PCC has less power than other organisations, as it does not have the power to propose legislation (Saney, 2004), whereas the mass organisations, *Poder Popular* and groups of citizens do have this right (so long as supported by a minimum 10,000 of the population). Furthermore, the PCC is legally prohibited from nominating delegates to the Assemblies or participating in the elections. Many of the people I spoke to were adamant that the Communist Party had no administrative function. For example, I was told:

> "The Communist Party does not go saying things all over the place. They are more ideological. They do not run the country. The country is run by a government. It is very different ... the Party is technically not in power." (Interview, 16 October 2008, Environmental Educator, Antonio Nuñez Jímenez Foundation for Nature and Humanity).

Legislative power is exercised through the National Assembly of Popular Power (Asamblea Nacional del Poder Popular), assisted by Provincial and Municipal Assemblies made up of locally elected delegates. The National Assembly is the paramount state institution, in terms of representing the will of the people and passing legislation. Elections to the Assembly take place every five years. Candidates do not have to belong to the PCC and 34% of National Assembly delegates are currently not members of the Party. The Assembly members – 'Diputados' – elect the Council of State. The President of the Council of State is the Head of State and Government. Proposed laws are drafted by the National Assembly's permanent Commissions (working groups), which focus on various social and economic themes. These Commissions are made up of representatives of different political, social and cultural sectors of the population.

The Constitution provides for independent courts and judges (Article 122). However, it explicitly subordinates them to the National Assembly and to the Council of State (Articles 75, 121 and 122). Because of the complex relationship between the state and the judiciary, it is difficult to be clear about how much the judiciary can review the legality of government actions if it has carried out an environmentally damaging activity. According to the law, citizens can take the state or private companies to court over an environmental issue. Previous reports state that citizens rarely do this, however (Whittle and Rey Santos, 2006), and this was confirmed in the fieldwork interviews (for example, interview, 16 October 2008, Environmental Educator, Antonio Nuñez Jímenez Foundation for Nature and Humanity). The interviewees suggested that this could be because people are generally unaware of this right or of how to go about exerting it and/or because there is "not a culture of using this mechanism" in Cuba (interview, 15 January 2009 Dr Orlando Rey Santos, Director, CITMA). It was also suggested that people do not need to resort to the courts because the current procedures already ensure justice (interview, 9 February 2009, Environmental Specialist,

CITMA, Holguín). Even so, as one interviewee argued, the judicial route would be more accessible if there was a programme of education regarding the environmental legislation (interview, 16 October 2008, Environmental Educator, Antonio Nuñez Jímenez Foundation for Nature and Humanity). Cuba's judicial system is free for Cuban citizens but this may be tokenistic if there is insufficient independence from government and people are not aware of how to use the process.

Proposal for serious reforms of general government policy are circulated widely and discussed extensively in local branches of mass organisations, schools, workplaces and universities before being put to referendum or before opinion is channelled into National Assembly debates (Cole, 1998; Raby, 2006). Consultation via mass organisations is a fundamental part of Cuban democracy, as the nationwide consultation leading up to the 6th Party Congress in 2011 illustrates. A document on 'Draft Guidelines for Economic and Social Policy' was circulated and debated for three months beforehand, through meetings in workplaces, communities, mass organisations and Communist Party branches. Close to 9 million people participated, out of a voting population of 10.5 million (though some may have attended more than one meeting) and over half a million contributions were made. The final result was that the consultation endorsed the ideological premise that only socialism is able to overcome the country's difficulties and preserve the conquests of the Revolution, though it proposed some major changes, as has been discussed. Ludlum notes:

> Only 32 percent of the original 291 Guidelines survived unchanged, and 36 new ones were added. After the Congress the Guidelines were republished showing the original and revised contents, and explaining every change and how many opinions had informed it ... Most changes were advocated by just a few hundred Cubans' 'opinions', but a 'top fifteen' can be extracted that were supported by over 6000. These bear witness to the debate's genuine nature and political character. (Ludlum, 2011, p 1)

The first-ranked item (54,979 opinions) added the crucial word 'gradual' to the proposal to abolish the ration book that supplies food at subsidised prices. The sixth most popular item (13,816 opinions) was to permit the private sale of cars. Furthermore, the population expressed a wish to end the dual currency situation. Other agreed changes included a two-term limit on senior leadership roles, a greater economic role for the non-state sector and the legalisation of private sales of houses.

With regard to procedural justice in relation to environmental matters, there is a vast network of institutions and organisations that play a part in influencing environmental decisions in Cuba. As well as the legislative, executive and judicial bodies, the mass organisations, the Communist Party and environmental activist organisations, all participate. When I asked people how they would try to change an environmental situation or make a complaint about the environment, they almost always said that they would do this by approaching their *Poder Popular* delegate. The system of *Poder Popular* (Popular Power) is based on the *'mandat imperatif'* (or the 'instructed delegate model'), as developed by Rousseau and the Paris Commune. The central idea is that representatives should be truly accountable and responsive to their constituents, attempting to resolve all matters presented to them. The people I spoke to generally had great faith in their delegate as a representative, finding them to be reliable, hard working and trustworthy. This confidence may be a result of the accountability of the system, in that an ineffective delegate would quickly lose their job, as a *Poder Popular* delegate explained:

> "We meet with those that choose us four times a year. People are very demanding at these meetings. They can revoke us at any moment, and they do. We are not sacked by the National Assembly or anyone else, but by the people who elect us. They can do it whenever they want. They can say he's not what we thought, we made a mistake and that's it." (Interview, 26 February 2009, Delegate, Poder Popular, Habana del Este)

The vertical system of interaction between different levels of *Poder Popular* allows the government to have a close understanding of what is important to citizens and this seems to be what drives the agenda:

> "The most important part of the whole is if the government understands that it is important for the people ... At the moment income is very low and this is important to resolve ... they [the people] would be willing to have a better environment but the real possibility is very small as it is not something that people are currently saying much about. It depends on what the government considers a priority for the people." (Interview, 21 January 2009, Dr Juan Llanes-Regueiro, Director, CEMA – Centre for the Study of the Environment, University of Havana)

Here, the interviewee was using the term 'environment' in the restricted meaning of ecology, not the wider meaning that includes living and working conditions, about which Cubans are very vocal. The people I spoke to generally felt that they had been able to make their opinion known about environmental concerns, though the matter was not necessarily resolved in their favour, especially if additional resources were required. When this occurred many accepted the response, but some continued to raise issues. However, there are some limitations on the forms of resistance that Cubans are prepared to utilise. Street protest, for example, though not illegal, is not seen as an effective strategy, as explained by an environmental campaigner:

> "It will not be efficient [to protest] and it can be manipulated by dissidents and outside sources, because there is a huge magnifying glass on Cuba and it can be misinterpreted … For us, it does not make sense to chain yourselves to trees and things like that …" (Interview, 16 October 2008, Environmental Educator, Antonio Nuñez Jímenez Foundation for Nature and Humanity)

Some consider that the lack of street protest reflects the authoritarianism of the state. It is difficult to know if there is any truth in this, but I am convinced that some of the taken-for-granted assumptions about Cuba's supposedly repressive state are based on minimal evidence. For example, the World Prison Population List of 2009 stated that Cuba had the fifth-highest prison population rate in the world (Walmsley, 2009). However, when I wrote to the researcher who came up with this figure regarding his methodology, he replied:

> I used an old method, I invented in Eastern Europe far back in time, when prison figures were state secrets. I suggested some figures … and then, in private conversations, suggested that this was the figure. Body language gave often the answer. Sometimes I did this during lectures. I suggested some figures I felt pretty sure were too high, and also some I knew were too low, – they got uneasy, angry or head shaking over my naiveté, until I launched what I thought was the correct one, – then often met with a satisfied mumble. But no one had been a traitor and revealed the secret. In Cuba, my estimate is from a very respected person close to power. But the figures are old now … (E-mail reply, anonymised, 14 February 2010)

Though the subsequent data for the World Prison Population List states that there is no data available for Cuba (possibly as a result of a complaint that I made that the figure for Cuba appeared to be based on a guess), this figure continues to be reproduced in many major international comparisons of levels of state repression (for example, Vision of Humanity, 2013).

Similarly, contrary to those who claim that workers in Cuba are not free to make demands because there is no 'right to strike', there is, in fact, no legislation covering strikes, to prohibit or allow them (Ludlum, 2009), though trade unions can close down the workplace if the conditions are such that an imminent workplace accident is foreseen. Workers and union officials have exercised this right, for example, where there was not the necessary protective equipment (Interview, 4 March 2009, Elio Valerino Santiesteban, Head of Social Labour, CTC – National Trade Union Council). It is, however, alleged that in Cuba people complain only to the extent that it is 'acceptable to the Party, the establishment and the institutions of communism in Cuba' (Freedom House, 2008, p 9). In general, even those who are broadly sympathetic to the revolutionary project have argued that much more popular power is needed (for example, Lievesley, 2004). Cuba expert Anthony Kapcia (2008), however, contends that if people are not actively working against the revolution, or breaking the law, there are no limitations to speech or activities. Even so, he acknowledges that working against the revolution has been defined more narrowly at times when Cuba has been more threatened or when popular morale was at a low ebb. Although some expressive outlets, such as the media, have been more controlled, it is generally recognised that other arenas, such as academia and the arts, have enjoyed relative freedom and autonomy (see, for example, Hernandez, 2008; López-Vigil, 2008).

Even with regard to the media, there is much more variety and vibrancy than many outside of Cuba realise. According to official figures, there are currently 723 written news and journal publications (406 print and 317 digital), 88 radio stations, four national TV channels (two devoted to educational programming), 16 regional TV stations and an international TV channel (Instituto Cubano de Radio y Televisión, 2010). Although the state prohibits the private ownership of newspapers, the various newspapers that exist are operated by the different social organisations: the Communist Party, the CTC, the FEU (student association), and so on. Though this is a restriction on the press, it ensures that popular organisations have a voice and that the wealthy do not have disproportionate influence. Some interviewees for this book regarded the media as a means to protest, stating that they write letters to the press to complain about environmental issues (for example, interview, 22 December 2008, Community Development Worker, CFV – Félix Varela Centre). These kinds of complaints were taken very seriously, as explained by this *Poder Popular* delegate:

> "Look how people complain in the papers. The press is very strong. We always check the papers to see what has come out. They will mention people by name, the people that haven't done their job properly. We don't like them to say negative things about us ..." (Interview, 26 February 2009, Delegate, Poder Popular, Habana del Este)

However, though I saw articles and websites operating from Cuba that were quite critical of policies (for example, CubaNet), this did not seem to be reflected in the mainstream media, which seemed to be relentlessly positive. This confirms several authors who claim that, though there is a certain amount of liberal debate, the media does not reflect certain public grievances (for example, Hernandez, 2008; Kapcia, 2008). The external hostility towards Cuba increases fears that too much public criticism could pave the way for the restoration of capitalism. Therefore, the function of the media in Cuba is less that of a body with which to challenge state power and more of an organ for 'education and politicisation within a besieged revolutionary process' (Kapcia, 2008, p 148). Media restrictions are often exaggerated for political purposes, however. For example, so called 'internet restrictions', such as denial of access to internet facilities or blocking of web pages, are a result of outside interference, as services are generally limited by the blockade and not by the Cuban government (Ministry of Foreign Affairs, 2008; Pearson, 2010).[8] Many Cubans have access to e-mail through schools, workplaces and post offices, though the island does not have enough bandwidth to allow universal access (Ministry of Foreign Affairs, 2008). One interviewee commented:

> "There are pages that are denied access. Pornography, for example. But criticism from Miami is not denied. I read it every day. Everyone does. Nothing has happened to me." (Interview, 15 January 2009, Dr Reynaldo Jiménez Guethón, Director, FLACSO – Latin American School of Social Sciences)

During the informal conversations and interviews I carried out in Cuba people had a number of ways that they found out about their local environment: through *Poder Popular*, the media, the mass organisations, informal contacts, CITMA, other relevant ministries, health and safety representatives at work, the internet, the library and even their local GPs. Though some environmental information is published in Cuba, the more detailed and specific information was not readily available, however. Even so, information can be obtained upon request, as indicated by this comment from an environmental activist:

> "There are many factories upstream and a lot of the pollution from them goes into the rivers that pass through the protected area ... In our proposal [to make improvements to the protected area] we have listed all the names of the pollutants ... CITMA passed this information to us ... they gave us all the information and also the permission to use the information in the presentations ... The only thing that we really have in abundance in Cuba is knowledge. We don't hide what we know, nor do the institutions." (Interview, 6 March 2009, Representative, Abra del Rio, Environmental Project, Cojimar)

Several authors assert that freedom of expression is evident from the history of the revolutionary project, as Cuba has undergone frequent periods of reassessment (for example, Saney, 2004; Kapcia, 2008; Yaffe, 2009). Debates have focused on many issues, including fundamental matters, such as whether it was necessary to go through a capitalist phase, allowing market mechanisms and wage incentives; or whether to move faster towards socialism, replacing material incentives with moral ones. 'Losers' in the debates are rarely expelled or marginalised from the institutions they are involved in (Kapcia, 2008). The revolution, therefore, rather than being doctrinaire, has been characterised by an experimental approach; a willingness to correct mistakes and respond to demands for change; and a contested and evolving body of values and beliefs (Saney, 2004; Kapcia, 2008; Yaffe, 2009). Though the state has both instigated and constrained critical discourses, much of this containment effort has been related to the fact that Cuba has had to operate in an international situation where the dominant world power is intent on its destruction, leading to a consequent siege mentality.

The fieldwork interviews and conversations revealed numerous situations that demonstrated that citizens were able to freely express their demands and that the environmental decision-making processes worked well for citizens. Of particular interest are the Integrated Neighbourhood Transformation Workshops (Talleres de Transformación

Integral del Barrio – TTIB) that have been running since 1988. These are interdisciplinary projects involving architects, sociologists, engineers and social workers who usually live in the target areas. The TTIBs were designed to integrate social and physical planning and to pilot a new model of neighbourhood development where people are encouraged to find their own solutions and participate in decision making (interview, 31 December 2008, Director, TTIB – Barrio Principe, Plaza de la Revolución). These workshops have been globally recognised for their progressive work and as examples of best practice in terms of a participatory approach to neighbourhood regeneration. For example, the Transformation Workshop in La Güinera, Havana, was named as one of the most successful community development projects in the world (UN Habitat, 1996).

I visited two of the Havana-based Talleres. One was in Cayo Hueso, Habana Centro and the other in Principe, Plaza de la Revolución. The Cayo Heuso workshop, one of the first to be set up, had carried out extensive research on the buildings, infrastructure, green spaces and amenities in the area, identifying a number of social, economic and environmental issues. Like the other TTIBs, it did not have a project budget, though the state provides staff salaries, offices and work facilities. Even so, it had managed to improve housing, schools, health provision, lighting, waste disposal and streets in its area. The Cayo Hueso Taller now has three community centres, which serve as places where people can socialise as well as share their suggestions for the neighbourhood. Unlike disadvantaged areas in the UK, where I have sometimes had to pay more than £25 an hour to hire a community room, the TTIB centres can be used cost free by any local person, on a first-come, first-served basis.

In terms of actual changes that had occurred as the result of community input, I was told about reductions in the amount of polluting emissions from production plants as a result of citizen and worker complaints in Guanabo, Matanzas, the Bay of Havana and Holguín. I was also given examples of development proposals that had been abandoned or relocated as a result of public pressure, for example, a dam in Baracoa, and a micro-energy generator in Regla, Havana (for example, interview, 20 January 2009, Armando Fernández-Soriano, Coordinator of the Network of Political Ecology in Latin America and the Caribbean and Editor, Ilé – Annual of Ecology, Culture and Society).

However, there was also contradictory evidence, with numerous examples of a lack of citizen power. For example, leaking water pipes that had not been fixed, despite local people complaining for more than 30 years (interview, 27 December 2008, Resident C, San Miguel

Figure 10.2: Integrated Neighbourhood Transformation Workshop, Principe Barrio, Havana

Source: Karen Bell (2009)

del Padrón); on-going air pollution from a local hospital (interview, 28 December 2008, Resident B, Cayo Hueso, Centro Habana); and oil exploration projects begun without prior consultation (interview, 10 March 2009, Protected Area Team, Habana del Este). I was also told that the compulsory requirements to organise public hearings and other consultations were sometimes bypassed. An environmental NGO worker, for instance, said:

> "When the electrical generation was decentralised all over the country, they tried to proceed very, very fast and sometimes they did not follow the protocol with the Environmental Impact Assessment and the licence … It can be when there is an interest of the central government things happen very fast and sometimes they push and jump some of the stages. Then after, when the problem happens, they realise they have to be corrective because they didn't think enough of the environmental consequences." (Interview, 16 October 2008, Environmental Educator, Antonio Nuñez Jímenez Foundation for Nature and Humanity).

Another example of a procedural environmental justice failure concerns transgenic production. Despite the government commitment to the precautionary principle, GMOs (genetically modified organisms) have recently been released into the atmosphere for the first time in Cuba. In April 2010, without prior public consultation, scientists at the Center for Genetic Engineering and Biotechnology began 'field tests' with a corn transgenic. Field tests are probably an irreversible step because of the danger of cross-contamination through pollen drift[9] and, therefore, not to be undertaken lightly. Agro-ecologists in Cuba are now opposing the cultivation of this crop and asking for a moratorium until there has been a public debate on the issue (interview, 16 October 2010, Fernando Funes Monzote, Professor of Agro-Ecology, University of Matanzas).

Therefore, procedural environmental justice in Cuba was strong in terms of the network of organisations involved, the legislation and the participatory culture, but there were some deficiencies in terms of discouragement of protest, a lack of easily available information and inconsistencies, or omissions, with regard to consultation processes.

Causes of environmental injustice in Cuba

According to the criteria established for this study, Cuba has the most favourable Environmental Justice Indicator score of the seven countries investigated, by far, with an overall rating of 20.8 (see Table A1.1 in Appendix 1). Positive achievements in terms of substantive environmental justice occur as a result of a basic commitment, at all levels of society (though not necessarily all sections), to environmental and social protection and improvement, with a distinct focus on meeting human needs. This is backed up by a generally favourable overall policy and legislative framework. In addition to this, effective, and often innovative, programmes were enabled by an experimental and correctable approach and a collective spirit that facilitates sharing and community-based mobilisation to address environmental problems. However, though these positive policies and commitments deliver a relatively good level of general provision, there were numerous examples of unmet needs, both subjectively experienced and quantitatively measured; most notably a lack of improved water supply; local air pollution; insufficient and deteriorating housing; and inadequate sanitation and waste-collection services. Overall, Cuba was not strong on substantive environmental justice according to the criteria laid down in this study.

However, there was a generally much better situation of distributive environmental justice in Cuba. Policies that ensure universal and equitable provision have limited extremes of social and environmental inequality. In particular, affordable housing, utilities and public transport, as well as food rationing and limits to car ownership, are exemplary in this regard, though some of these policies are now being dropped. There were some spatial disparities in environments but, because people tend to live in mixed communities, there was little possibility for this to translate into socio-spatial environmental disparities based on race and income. Therefore, the key to distributional environmental justice in Cuba appeared to be the lack of a housing and land market, which prevented social segregation from developing.

There was a mixed picture in terms of procedural justice. The vast and penetrating network of community organisations enabled considerable community involvement and the quality of the educational system supported an informed and empowered citizenry. The bottom-up/top-down power structure also seemed to aid procedural justice, in that people were able to press for change via the system of tiered representation but, at the same time, those elected to higher levels could exercise the necessary control to balance competing demands. However, though there were clearly numerous ways for citizens to become involved in decision making, this did not always lead to influence. In particular, there were barriers and limits to accessing information and to political expression.

Some of the 'Cubanologist' literature explains Cuba's more recent environmental problems as a result of mismanagement and a lack of environmental commitment on the part of the government (for example, Diaz-Briquets and Pérez-López, 2000; Chavez, 2008). However, in general terms, my research found that the main factors that seemed to cause environmental injustice in Cuba were: economic shortages; external threats; Damaging Hegemonic Environmental Discourses; market-based policies; and a history of colonialism. All of these factors seemed to be driven, or exacerbated, by capitalism. Some of the alternative explanations for environmental injustice – discrimination, market dynamics, a lack of citizen power and industrialisation – also seemed to increase environmental injustice in Cuba, though these could also be linked to capitalism. For example, industrialisation explains some pollution but was connected to the need for hard currency. However, within this pattern lies more complex and paradoxical detail. Cuba has intra-national environmental justice problems, as a result both of being isolated from capitalism (for example, economic difficulties) and of being engaged with capitalism (for example, intense exploitation of primary resources). Similarly, the country has intra-national environmental justice successes, as a result of being detached from the global capitalist economy (developing greater self-sufficiency, inventiveness and alternative values), as well as through its opportunities to trade with capitalist countries (acquiring hard currency that could be used for environmental and social improvements). However, on balance, I would argue that environmental justice in Cuba seemed to be more undermined, rather than bolstered, by capitalism, because of the inequality and poverty that market influences, both historic and current, have fostered.

To begin with, colonialism in Cuba permanently altered the island economically, environmentally and socially, orientating the country toward primary export production, stifling indigenous industry and tying Cuba to a dependency on external trade (Fernández, 2002; Funes Monzote, 2008; Kapcia, 2008). Further, the economic crisis (which would almost certainly not have happened were it not for the context of both the blockade and the history of colonialism) led to the initiation of a number of policies, generally associated with capitalism. These measures, especially tourism, self-employment and the intensive exploitation of natural resources, have had a negative influence on Cuba's environment and society. For example, consumerism has increased as certain foods and experiences enjoyed by tourists have come to symbolise the good life and people come to gain status and identity from material, rather than social, achievements (Taylor, 2009). This may be linked to the increases in inequality that have accompanied the market reforms, as there is now mounting evidence that inequality drives higher consumerism (Wilkinson and Pickett, 2009; Dorling, 2010). Consumerism also promotes individualism and the notion that problems can be solved individually, rather than socially, thereby contradicting the philosophical basis of the revolution. This is, perhaps, the reason for the population now choosing to allow a market for houses and cars. Several interviewees were concerned about an apparent loss of socialist values. This was captured, for example, in the following comment:

> "When I was small, I saw life was different ... Parents gave what they could to their children. There were no dual currency or CUC shops. You could buy a lot. You did not have to think about brands of clothes. Now kids want a new rucksack every school year, otherwise they feel ashamed. Before I went with a jute rucksack and put on whatever clothes there were ... Now Cubans just want to see what

they can get ... I did not eat Chicklets or have jeans. I was very happy. People did not want to leave ... We have lost the love ..." (interview, 2 January 2009, Social Worker, Habana Vieja)

Some of the interviewees said they thought the younger people were taking the gains of the revolution for granted, now setting their sights on material goals, in place of social ones:

"We have achieved a lot and it is easy to take things for granted and just think about what you don't have. Young people here don't value what they have – the free education and the healthcare. They want more. My son complains we are poor and he wants an MP3 player because other kids have got them." (Informal conversation, Cojimar, fieldwork notes, 6 March 2009)

The government, while asserting that revolutionary ideology would protect the Cuban people from the problems associated with tourism, at first tried to isolate tourists from locals to prevent these problems. However, this did not work well and caused resentment, so that these policies had to be reversed (see Espino, 2008).

In addition, the blockade (which could hit hard as a result of the dependency on external markets), has affected the country in terms of the availability and cost of technology, as well as a general shortage of resources (Interview, 28 January 2009, Dr Allan Pierra-Conde, Director, ISMM – Higher Institute of Mining and Metallurgy, Moa). For example, problems with water supply have been linked to a shortage of replacement parts for the distribution network, originally built using US components (AAWH, 1997). The resulting lack of resources has also reduced the capacity of CITMA to carry out monitoring, to replace and modify polluting facilities and to adopt consistent standards. It seems that CITMA's enforcement authority is limited to the extent that there are still not extensive environmental standards. For example, many sugar factories, power plants and other ageing industrial facilities, built prior to Law 81, are not covered by environmental legislation. It was feared that strictly applying new standards to these plants might mean having to suspend operations, which could paralyse important industries critical to Cuba's economy and social welfare programmes. Therefore, CITMA has adopted a policy of applying environmental standards on a case-by-case basis, as explained by CITMA's Director of the Environment:

> "The new industry, since 1990, complies with international standards and norms ... but the old industries, say, the cement factory in Camaguey, do emit pollution ... The chimneys are very old ... If we close the factory it will improve the environment. But the state can't afford that. They don't want to close the factory because it is a source of income and because it is the workplace. Every case is particular and there are many factors involved – political, economic, environmental – and they all have to be balanced ... If you apply strict environmental standards today you would have a list where you would have to close 60 or 70 factories now but if you closed these factories it would be a problem for us. It is complicated." (Interview, 15 January 2009, Dr Orlando Rey Santos, Director, Directorate of Environmental Policy, CITMA)

Another important factor underpinning environmental injustice in Cuba is culture; more specifically, the influence of Damaging Hegemonic Environmental Discourses. As well as the increased consumerism, already described, there are social currents in Cuba that maintain a strong commitment to an industrialised, highly technological form of growth. This can most clearly be observed with regard to Cuba's bio-tech industry and the development of transgenics. I was told that the government was pursuing this path:

> "because of the industrial mentality in the whole world and the blind trust in the objectivity of science in Cuba and the wider world. They want to insert a gene without thinking of the consequences that it could bring. They think it would be an easy solution to the problem of food production ... Everywhere there are different mentalities – progressive, backward, atomistic, holistic – these are paradigms that conflict in modern societies and Cuba is no different ... the technocrats in Cuba think the same as those in England ... Profit is the motive in the capitalist countries but, in Cuba, it is the concern of the state to feed the people ... but it is an atomistic technology that sees the world in a simple way ... The idea that man can dominate nature is an anthropocentric vision of the environment that does

not respect the natural cycles and this has consequences."
(Interview, 16 October 2010, Fernando Funes-Monzote,
Professor of Agro-Ecology, University of Matanzas)

However, Cuba, though influenced by these values, has been able to
disregard them when necessary. So, for example, during the 'Special
Period', machines were often replaced by manual labour and oxen
took the place of tractors. Though production was slower, farmers
and workers noticed that productivity often increased. For example, a
Cuban farmer explained,

> before, you could only fit two cycles into the rainy season.
> For more than a month each year we couldn't prepare the
> land because the tractors got stuck in the mud. But an ox
> doesn't have that problem. You plough the day after it rains
> or even while it's raining if you want. (In Rosset, 1997,
> p 158)

Therefore, while a Damaging Hegemonic Environmental Discourse
would be that oxen are 'backward', in Cuba they were recognised as
sometimes being 'advanced'. Similarly, natural medicine is researched
and utilised on a par with allopathic medicine and citizens can choose
the healing path they take, with all forms of treatment respected equally
and offered without cost. At the same time, all Cuban GPs are trained
in environmental issues and how health is affected by the environment,
so that Cubans appear to have a much greater understanding of, and
interest in, environmental impacts on health (Fieldwork notes, visit to
Natural Medicine Clinic, Havana, 6 March 2009).

Finally, the US blockade seems to have conditioned and limited Cuba's
possibilities to achieve procedural justice. Many of the restrictions can
be related to the international context whereby the dominant world
power has been determined to destroy Cuba (Lievesley, 2004; Kapcia,
2008). This has created a sense of siege, and justified a war footing and
control of expression and political action (Kapcia, 2008). Kapcia states
that it is possible to correlate the amount of control with 'the level of
threat posed or perceived' (Kapcia, 2008, p 133), so that moments of
greater external pressure are associated with greater expectations for
the population to conform.

Much of this aggression towards Cuba may be because the country
has modelled an alternative to capitalism. Whether or not this is the
case, it generally seems that, even in socialist Cuba, internal and external
capitalist processes undermine its efforts to achieve environmental

justice. This seems to reinforce the idea that capitalism is a fundamental factor that should not be ignored in any analysis of environmental justice. However, as Cuba's Director of the Environment emphasised, any economic system, socialist or otherwise, needs to be driven by an environmental ethos:

> "It does not mean that, with socialism, the environment automatically improves. For example, what happened in Europe, with the countries of Eastern Europe, there were a thousand disasters. That is to say socialism creates a better opportunity but this opportunity has to be built upon and materialised but I think yes, that socialism is an advantage ... But I emphasise, it is not automatic, you have to try to create a socialist system where the environmental agenda is driven well, otherwise you will still have environmental problems. Nothing is given, it has to be achieved." (Interview, 15 January 2009, Dr Orlando Rey Santos, Director, Directorate of Environmental Policy, CITMA)

Over the last 20 years the environment has been a priority in Cuba. However, some of the changes that the population now wish to implement, in particular the ending of the food rationing system, the sale of private cars and, most importantly, the introduction of a housing market, all threaten to undermine Cuba's environmental justice achievements. Though Cuba has, so far, used market policies in a pragmatic way, retreating from them when necessary, it will probably not be easy to reverse the latest changes. However, whichever direction Cuba eventually takes, the country is currently a living reminder that there are radically different ways that we could organise our world.

Notes

[1] There is just one study on environmental justice in Cuba, but this focuses on inequality in access to the beaches and ecological reserves between Cuban citizens and tourists (Crawford, 2004), rather than disparities among citizens, which is the focus of this book.

[2] Following other authors, such as Lievesley (2004), I use the word 'blockade' rather than 'embargo' because the US does not just refuse to trade with Cuba but actively intervenes in Cuba's relations with other countries.

[3] This does not mean that there are no other political parties. Cuba's constitution was amended in 1992 to allow the formation of other parties

and there are now several, including: Partido Democrata Cristiano de Cuba (Christian Democratic Party of Cuba), www.pdc-cuba.org/; Partido Solidaridad Democratica (Democratic Solidarity Party), www.pasode. org/; Partido Social Revolucionario Democratico Cubano (Cuban Social Revolutionary Democratic Party), www.psrdc.org/.

[4] The projects within the green revolution spread technologies that had already existed, but had not been widely used outside of industrialised nations, including pesticides and synthetic fertilisers.

[5] 'Social workers' in Cuba perform a function broadly similar to community development workers in the UK.

[6] In 2004, Cuba ceased using the US dollar as an official currency so that now Cubans who receive monetary remittances from family members living abroad must trade-in their dollars for Cuban convertible pesos (CUC), set slightly higher than a one-for-one equivalency with the US dollar. CUCs can be used to buy consumer goods and services that are not supplemented by the state. They were intended to be a step towards a single currency. The traditional currency is the Cuban peso, with which Cubans are paid their state salaries.

[7] The World Bank and the UNDP do not publish Gini Coefficient data on Cuba.

[8] Cuba's internet connection comes via satellite from faraway countries, such as Italy and Canada, making it expensive and slow, and the US blockade prevents Cuba from obtaining a better service through underwater cable. There is an optical-fibre connection between Cancun and Miami that passes 32 kilometres from Havana, but the US denies Cuba access to it (Ministry of Foreign Affairs (Cuba), 2008; Pearson, 2010).

[9] Once released from the anthers into the atmosphere, pollen grains can travel as far as half a mile with a 15 mph wind in a couple of minutes (Nielsen, 2003).

ELEVEN

Achieving environmental justice

In all the seven countries featured in this book, there were numerous people inventively and determinedly striving to achieve environmental justice. This has resulted in a number of notable outcomes. The United States has been in the forefront of conceptualising environmental justice, as well as developing relevant institutional frameworks and legislation; the Republic of Korea has been a model in terms of setting mandatory emissions targets, investing highly in environmental strategies and programmes and promoting eco-friendly products and green life-styles; the UK has set ambitious greenhouse gas reduction targets; Sweden has for many years been a global leader in developing progressive environmental legislation; China's new environmental laws, collective action and public participation in environmental decision making have enabled significant improvements in environmental policy making over the last decade; Bolivia proposes the harmonious concept of 'Vivir Bien' and is one of the first nations in the world to legislate for the rights of nature through the new 'Law of Mother Earth'; and, in Cuba, tiered political representation, the prioritisation of equality and programmes that simultaneously meet both social and environmental need, all favour environmental justice. These successes provide much cause for hope but, despite all these positive initiatives, it is apparent that environmental justice is still generally lacking across the board. Out of a possible Environmental Justice Indicator score of 45, the highest score achieved in the countries analysed was only 20.8, in Cuba.

With regard to substantive environmental justice, in all seven countries a myriad of unmet environmental needs were apparent, from a lack of clean air to deficient sanitation and water services. Similarly, in relation to distributive environmental justice, there was a generally disappointing overall picture, with a range of environmental inequities built on pronounced social inequalities. Clean air; affordable public transport; sufficient energy for cooking and heating; and safe living and working environments were less available to low-status and/or low-income groups in almost all of the countries examined. Cuba was the only country where there did not seem to be evidence of socio-spatial environmental disparities based on race, income or status, primarily, it seems, because there has been, until now, no housing market and so people generally live in mixed communities. There were also across-the-board deficiencies with regard to procedural environmental justice. In all the countries, to a greater or lesser extent, procedural justice frameworks and policies often focused more on managing and controlling communities than on empowering them. It was not easy for people to inform themselves about local environmental threats and, even where people had the right of access to information, it was not made available to them in a timely way. Furthermore, in most of the countries it was not easy to pursue environmental claims through the courts because of the prohibitive costs. In both the capitalist and the socialist countries (except Cuba), community resistance was sometimes undermined by offers of compensation payments and local leaders often ignored community wishes when they clashed with corporate or elite interests. In all the countries, though there were often official channels set up for citizens to become involved in environmental decision making, such opportunities did not always enable actual influence. To some extent, the low EJI scores may be a reflection of the relative newness of environmental justice as a concept in that, in some countries, it has only recently begun to be recognised, let alone acted upon. However, it also appears to be that, in most cases, the piecemeal reforms that have taken place have failed to address the core issues that drive environmental injustice. Therefore, as stated from the outset, it is vitally important to be clear about the fundamental causes of the problem.

The causes of the environmental injustices

Despite all the countries falling decidedly short of achieving complete environmental justice, there was a significant difference between the EJI scores of the various countries. The results from the Environmental Justice Indicator Framework suggest that, at least for the countries examined in this book, the more capitalist leaning the countries were, the less they had achieved environmental justice (see Figure 11.1). In particular, Cuba is relatively advanced, largely because the country scores much higher on distributional justice and much lower on the Ecological Footprint than the other countries do.

It is important to be cautious when interpreting these scores, however. Many of the indicators used to achieve this numerical summary are not readily quantifiable, and there are too few cases to be able to make a generalisation regarding a fixed relationship between the extent of capitalism and the attainment of environmental justice. There may also be other causal explanations for the pattern; for example, the scores can also, to some extent, be related to income levels (with the US, Korea, the UK and Sweden all being high-income countries; while China and Cuba are upper middle income and Bolivia is lower middle income). Therefore, the graph should be considered only as an illustrative summary of the material collected. It would be interesting to further develop the EJI Framework, establishing precise numerical values and weightings for each indicator. Further research could be carried out using proxy indicators for the degree of socialism/capitalism (for example, percentage of workers employed in the public sector) and comparing these with proxy indicators for the other factors discussed in this book (for example, industrialisation or citizen power).

Figure 11.1: Environmental Justice Indicator scores in seven countries

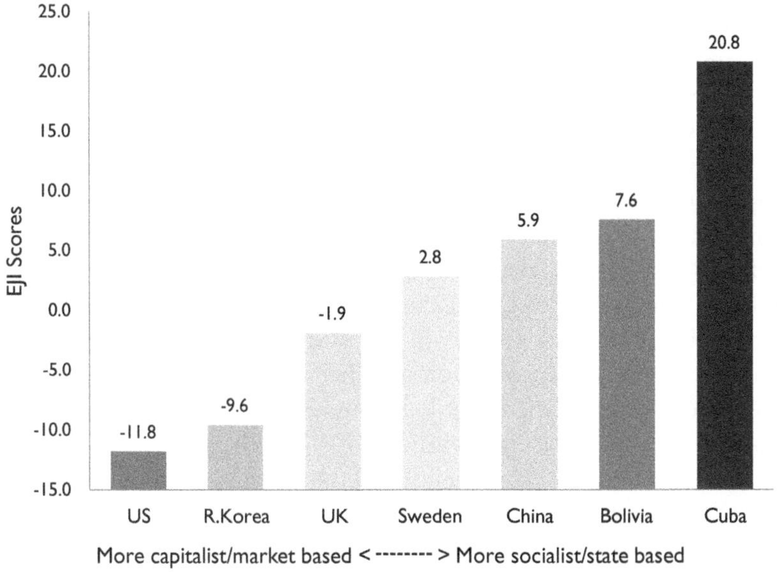

More capitalist/market based < -------- > More socialist/state based

The relationship between capitalism and the attainment of EJ suggested in Figure 11.1 should, however, be considered in the context of the other evidence and theory about the relationship between capitalism and environmental injustice that has been presented in this book. The background literature outlined in Chapter Three describes and explains the link between capitalism and environmental injustice. In particular, it is evident that a market economy requires profit and growth, so that these priorities come to dominate decision making at the expense of ecological and social concerns. Therefore, environmental reforms currently remain limited, being allowed a marginal existence only insofar as they do not interfere with the priorities necessary to maintain the health of the economic system. Consequently, environmental justice legislation, implementation and enforcement, where it exists, has mainly focused on the management of risk and the control of public resistance to environmental harms, rather than on eliminating harmful production and consumption altogether. The responses to determined protests about toxic facilities in the examples given in this book were often to relocate the hazard, rather than to shut it down. Capitalist processes also tend to exacerbate inequality, a strong foundation for distributional environmental injustice. In addition, they enable the disproportionate influence of business elites, which contributes to procedural environmental injustice. Worst still, the capitalist governments of the countries discussed in this book appear to be looking at the environmental crises as business opportunities. They are promoting profitable but ineffective and/or risky environmental solutions, such as carbon trading, geo-engineering, payments for ecosystems services and nuclear power, all of which could be devastating in terms of ecological and human health.

Where the socialist countries examined in this book rated poorly with regard to a particular environmental justice indicator, it appeared that this was, to a large extent, a consequence of the introduction of capitalist reforms (for example, the intensification of industrial production with China's opening up to global capitalism, resulting in reduced air and water quality); and/or a legacy, in terms of environmental destruction and social inequality, of prior neoliberal or colonial periods (for example, Bolivia's lack of endogenous development, resulting in a continuing need for extractivism).

Therefore, in both the capitalist and the socialist countries, it seems to be capitalist processes that have most prevented the attainment of environmental justice. However, it would be simplistic to assert that capitalist processes are the only cause of environmental injustice, as the case studies all provide evidence to support the theories that explain environmental injustice in terms of other factors, including discrimination, market dynamics, a lack of citizen power, industrialisation, individual behaviour and culture. Hence, the case studies included examples of less favourable treatment towards low-status groups (discrimination); of wealthier householders being able to avoid environmental harms by choosing to buy or rent property in less polluted areas (market dynamics); of environmental decision making not sufficiently involving or guaranteeing influence to those affected (a lack of citizen power); of environmental considerations being put aside on the grounds of the need for industry, in the hope it will bring income, development and jobs (industrialisation); of individuals over-consuming by 'choosing' to follow fashions in clothes, household items and gadgets (individual behaviour); and of the societal prevalence and reinforcement of growth-oriented and modernist beliefs embedded in Damaging Hegemonic Environmental Discourses (culture).

However, these other causal factors appear to be driven and exacerbated, if not entirely underpinned, by local and global capitalist processes. Many of these factors persist because they are convenient for, or perpetuated by, capitalism. For example, capitalism relies upon *discrimination* so that marginalised groups can carry the burden of its negative costs without excessive mainstream concern; it requires *industrialisation* so that production can increase while overall labour costs are cut, whether at home or farther afield; it relies upon a *lack of citizen power* so that economic decisions can be made on the basis of extracting the greatest profit, without regard for citizen concerns; it incorporates *market dynamics* that enable the concentration of wealth and power; it invokes *individual behaviour* or life-style choices that are based on high levels of consumption; and, finally, capitalism requires and promotes a compatible *culture* carried in Damaging Hegemonic Environmental Discourses, such as the unquestioning acceptance of growth, so that excessive production and consumption can continue, unfettered, in the face of impending environmental disaster. Because these factors are convenient for and integral to capitalism, they are unlikely to be severely challenged by the powerful elites that benefit from the system.

But, even if capitalism could be eliminated, would these other factors still create environmental injustices? There is not the space to develop a discussion on this for all the proposed causative factors, but it seems most useful to consider this in relation to the last factor, culture, as carried in Damaging Hegemonic Environmental Discourses. The case studies in this book show that, even within socialist systems, many people accept the prevailing DHEDs. For example, it is a rarely questioned assumption that growth is necessary for social progress. Growth has become a yardstick by which governments are measured, and high economic growth rates, whatever their long-term consequences, were applauded in all the countries looked at in this book. The result of this is that mainstream environmental policy encourages citizens to make only individual behavioural or life-style choices that do not threaten levels of consumption, such as recycling, not dropping litter or engaging in eco-friendly purchasing; rather than urging citizens to cease the consumption (and production) of unnecessary and/or toxic commodities altogether. Because this occurs in all the countries, this suggests that Damaging Hegemonic Environmental Discourses exist, and can be perpetuated, with or without capitalism. Yet, none of the countries was completely free of capitalism, so it could be argued that DHEDs may be just another symptom of capitalist processes. Classical Marxism would predict that dialectical changes to the functioning of the economy of a society would determine its social superstructures (including culture). Therefore, an end to capitalism would imply the end of DHEDs. However, because we now live in a globalised world, any national attempt to throw off capitalism would still be influenced by external values and beliefs. Because DHEDs are now so deeply embedded in global culture, like racist and sexist discourses, they would probably not magically disappear with a new political economic system. We would still be constrained by DHEDs that have developed historically, through particular interpretations of Western philosophies; those that are convenient for the continuance and expansion of capitalism. Though capitalism enables DHEDs, and benefits from them, they also appear to have a self-reinforcing momentum of their own.

However, though DHEDs were apparent in all the countries examined in this book, they were more strongly promoted and less contested in the more capitalist contexts. For example, the belief in the necessity for economic growth changed dramatically in China following the reforms of 1978, as people came to embrace consumerism and to define progress in terms of GDP. DHEDs are also more often challenged under socialist societies, through counter-hegemonic environmental discourses. For example, in Cuba, perhaps because business interests do not have sufficient power to obscure this awareness, the link between environments and human health appears to be widely understood and accepted. As Chapter Ten outlined, in Cuba, GPs receive training in environmental impacts on health and take an interest in their patients' living environments. Conversely, in the UK, there is a great deal of resistance to making this connection. For example, a recent UK report by the Royal College of Obstetricians and Gynaecologists (RCOG, 2013), while not explicitly saying that exposure to chemicals can harm a developing foetus, highlighted the hundreds of chemicals that pregnant women are exposed to through food packaging, medicines and cosmetics and advised avoidance as a precautionary measure. The response was widespread derision in the UK media and accusations that the Royal College of Obstetricians and Gynaecologists was irresponsibly provoking anxiety. Therefore, though DHEDs can survive without the support of capitalism, they may be easier to resist in less capitalist societies.

Hence a number of factors support or undermine the achievement of environmental justice, but a capitalist economy appears to be one of the most influential of these. Capitalism interacts in complex ways with these other factors, shaping them in particular ways, as is evident with regard to Damaging Hegemonic Environmental Discourses which, while having their own momentum, are nurtured and fuelled when they are convenient for capitalism. It may be that eliminating capitalism is a necessary condition for environmental justice, but not a sufficient condition, as these other factors also need to be specifically addressed.

Policy implications

If capitalist processes underlie and exacerbate environmental injustice, this would imply the need for countries to transform or reject these processes. It would suggest that environmental justice cannot be achieved through market mechanisms but, rather, through collective democratic control over the economy, where the needs of society and the environment are prioritised and labour and resources are redeployed to these ends. Yet a number of environmental and social justice advocates do not urge the demolition and rebuilding of whole economies but, rather, the reform and improvement of existing institutions (for example, Daly and Farley, 2004; Porritt, 2005; Boyle and Simms, 2009; Wilkinson and Pickett, 2009). Capitalism does come in many variants and, as the case studies show, some forms of capitalism are certainly less environmentally or socially damaging than others. Therefore, it is important to consider the possibility of the, perhaps easier, task of working to reform capitalism, minimising its negative impacts in order to achieve environmental justice. Even without setting out to dismantle capitalism, some of the policies already being successfully implemented in the countries discussed in this book, both capitalist and socialist, that appear to support environmental justice might be viable options for other nations (see Table 11.1).

The actors that might engage in transferring these policies include supra-national governmental institutions, elected national officials, political parties, civil servants, policy experts, think-tanks, NGOs, activists and social/environmental movements. However, policy transfer between countries is far from straightforward and not always successful. There are many issues to consider regarding whether these policies could, should and would be taken up in other nations. In particular, policy transfer does not always work because its success relies very much upon its original context and because there may be high levels of ideological resistance to implementing policies that appear to have

Table 11.1: Policies that could advance environmental justice

Country where implemented	Policies and practices that could enhance environmental justice
US	EJ legislation; EJ institutional framework; National Environmental Justice Advisory Council; EJ Strategy; funding for EJ organisations (but without expectations of controlling them)
Republic of Korea	Ecological subsidies; promotion of ecological consumer goods; eco-labelling.
UK	High greenhouse gas emissions reduction targets; minimum wage (though set very low); equality impact assessments (though under threat); equality indicator in sustainable development targets (also under threat); welfare provision (some also under threat)
Sweden	Progressive income taxation; free access to environmental courts; awareness of social issues in sustainable development policy; 49% of energy provided by renewables; rents determined locally via negotiation between representatives of landlords and tenants; welfare provision (some now under threat)
China	Green GDP accounting system; ecological taxes (though can be regressive in allowing the rich to carry on polluting); introduction of employee performance evaluation on the basis of advancing environmental protection; in litigation, the burden of proof lies with the polluter, not the victim
Bolivia	Policy framework based on living well in harmony with nature; promotion of natural medicine and traditional knowledge; water, resources and infrastructure under control of government and citizens
Cuba	Free education, healthcare and welfare provision; affordable housing in all geographical areas; free or low-cost public transport; free use of community meeting rooms; 'Transformation Workshop' style community development projects; participatory legislative system; training for GPs in natural medicine and environmental effects on health; environmental community workers; accessible government officers; restricted car ownership and use (now being partially phased out); mass consultations before any significant environmental reforms (not always implemented); free access to legal services with regard to environmental issues; local organic urban food production; nationalised public transport and utilities; local employment; rents capped to affordable levels in all geographical areas; vacant housing nationalised; lack of housing market (though this is now being reversed); relatively equal public sector wages

come from a country that is pursuing a completely different political and economic path (Dolowitz and Marsh, 2000). It would be difficult to try to implement socialist policies within a capitalism system; for example, eliminating housing markets or legislating for relatively equal public sector pay. Such proposals would clearly threaten, and be resisted by, corporate and elite interests, those that Faber (2008) describes as the 'polluter-industrial complex'. However, the capitalist/ socialist spectrum that I have used for this book suggests that there is much intermingling of policy, especially around the middle of the spectrum. Furthermore, the case studies show that some of the socialist-style policies and programmes implemented within capitalist countries, such as income transfers, do mitigate some environmental injustices. Even so, the data collected for this book, as summarised by the EJI scores, indicates that these programmes do not go far enough. A balance is always struck between that which is necessary to minimise environmental and social harms and that which is necessary for the maintenance of the capitalist economy. Yet, what may be required for the achievement of environmental justice is nothing less than a root and branch transformation of the economic system and the Damaging Hegemonic Environmental Discourses.

Whether capitalism should be reformed or replaced depends on whether it is particular modifiable aspects that are problematic, or whether everything about the system is so enmeshed that it must be rejected altogether. The main aspects of capitalism that seem to underlie the causes of environmental injustice described in this book are the *concentration of wealth and power* in the core capitalist countries (resulting in economic shortages and a lack of national autonomy at the periphery); the political and economic pressure to *incorporate into the world market*; the *commodification of resources* as a means to gain the hard currency that permits participation in the global market; *the need for growth* in the form of ever-increasing production and consumption (leading to the promotion of DHEDs such as consumerism, individualism, modernity and narrow environmental framing); *competition* (resulting in greater internal and external inequalities); *the profit motive* (driving competition and commodification); and *the irrationality of market forces* that are driven by profitability, rather than by human well-being and ecological considerations. It is difficult to envision how these components could be addressed without threatening the system itself. All these aspects are considered necessary for the successful maintenance of capitalism, so that any attempt to include policies that might challenge them would be resisted by those who have a vested interest in the preservation of the current system.

Even the nominally socialist countries discussed in this book are struggling to implement socialist policies because of the pressures imposed by a global capitalist context. Observation of the capitalist forces acting on, for example, Cuba might lead us to the theory that socialism in individual countries is not possible, especially in an under-developed country, as Trotsky predicted (2010 [1929]).[1] As Saney argues, Cuba faces a similar situation to that of many low-income countries:

> The problems that beset Cuba, on one level, reflect the incomplete material and cultural transformation of the society. The on-going and determined transformation of the society, with its twists and turns, was halted by events and factors external to and beyond the island's control. In short, the locus of the crisis is exogenous, leading to the unavoidable implementation of measures that erode the national project of social justice based on the extension of equality and equity. Cuba is caught in the international cauldron that has trapped the South. (Saney, 2004, p 121)

Consequently, while it is possible to make some advances towards environmental justice within a national setting, it seems that the ultimate elimination of the problem can occur only on the global scale. Therefore, some analysts assert that socialist countries could avoid market pressures and the potential collapse of socialism in their countries by spreading the revolution to other countries (for example, Martin, 2009). To some extent, this does seem to be already occurring in Latin America, with a 'pink tide' of left-leaning and socialist governments now gaining power in many Latin American states. In particular, the regional integration project ALBA seems to present a path out of these problems for Cuba and Bolivia, offering solidarity, exchange of resources, a socialist value base, support for ecological priorities and an alternative trading system (Muhr, 2013).

Hence to achieve environmental justice, it may be necessary to thoroughly dismantle capitalist processes. However, in most market-based economies, such as the UK and the US, there is a general reluctance to consider a move away from capitalism. Opponents of such a radical change usually cite one or more of the following reasons for persisting with capitalism. Firstly, if we attempt to break with capitalism, we would be going against 'selfish' human nature so that a more egalitarian, communal set-up would inevitably fail. Secondly, a dramatic shift is unrealistic and unattainable because capitalism is natural, inevitable or too powerful to challenge head-on. Thirdly, the struggle to overthrow capitalism would take our focus away from the more immediate and urgent issues, such as averting the environmental crises. Finally, it is argued, capitalism may not be perfect but it is the 'least-worst' option available for society and the environment.

The argument that a transformation away from capitalism and towards a more equal, sharing and less materialistic society would be contrary to human nature is exemplified in the following comment from a UK interviewee:

> "It is all very well to say we will overthrow capitalism but if we don't deal with what may or may not be basic human desires ... I mean, if you look at what's happened in China, I think the Chinese government has opened up to market forces partly because it realises that it's a great way to drive material wealth, but also because people want it, access to consumer goods and whatever it is people want to buy so ... people want creature comforts ... I don't think you'll find a period, either during capitalism or pre-capitalism, where people haven't wanted more in excess of what they have at the moment ... It's wrong to assume that if you get rid of capitalism you will get rid of all these problems." (Interview, 25 October 2012, Mark Kember, Chief Executive Officer, The Climate Group)

Here, it is assumed that 'human nature' drives people's appetite for consumer goods. However, consumerism, like other behaviours that are convenient for capitalism and deemed to be integral to our biological nature, is not an innate propensity. New research shows that consumerist thoughts and actions can be switched on or off according to the surrounding situation (Bauer et al, 2012). At present, the surrounding situation in most countries tends to unremittingly promote and reward consumerism. Most of the governments of the countries featured in this book (except Bolivia and Cuba) are explicitly keen to boost domestic consumption, and their citizens, particularly the young, are being relentlessly targeted by global corporations. Consumer desire is constantly being stoked. The acquisitive traits that result are then pronounced to be 'human nature', thereby making it impossible to think about organising society on any other basis. Furthermore, research has shown that consumerism is not aligned with our natural desire for well-being, as it is associated with degrees of emotional distress. Irrespective of personality, when a situation is set up to activate a consumer mind-set, people experience negative emotions so that, 'Merely viewing desirable consumer goods resulted in increases in materialistic concerns and led to heightened negative affect and reduced social involvement' (Bauer et al, 2012, p 517).

Similarly, biological evidence, based on the work of Darwin, is used to argue that we are inherently too selfish and competitive to be able to live in sharing societies. However, when Darwin adopted the term 'survival of the fittest' from Herbert Spencer, the concept of 'fittest' at that time meant 'most adapted to the environment'. Darwin was not referring to a need to out-compete our human rivals but, rather, explaining that it is the organisms that are most adapted to their environments that tend to survive. Often collaboration is the best survival tactic. Studies of small babies show that, though we have the natural ability to be selfish, we are also naturally cooperative and altruistic (see Rifkin, 2010, for an overview of this research). There is now growing psychological evidence to suggest that people intuitively prefer to share, rather than to act selfishly (for example, Rand et al, 2012). It appears that our main drive is to belong, so that much of our apparently selfish behaviour, including consumerism, is driven by this need. As Polyani stated, a human being:

> does not act so as to safeguard his individual interest in the possession of material goods; he acts so as to safeguard his social standing, his social claims, his social assets. He values material goods only in so far as they serve this end. (Polyani, 1944, p 46)

This may also help to explain why consumption levels appear to be higher in more unequal societies (Wilkinson and Pickett, 2009; Dorling, 2010), since inequality undermines that sense of belonging. It divides people from each other as they come to live in such vastly different subjective life worlds and objective life conditions.

The second argument for persevering with capitalism, that it is a natural and inevitable system or too powerful to dislodge, is very pervasive. As several authors have pointed out, it appears easier for us to imagine and persuade the public of a climatic Armageddon than that there could be an end to capitalism (for example, Swyngedouw, 2007). Yet, capitalism is no more 'natural' than any other system of human organisation that has existed over time. In fact, it is non-capitalist societies that have been the way humans have generally tended to organise for most of our history. The recent financial crisis has demonstrated how fragile the free market system really is, and, as the rise of anti-capitalist social movements and 21st-century socialist governments illustrates, capitalism has certainly not triumphed for eternity, as we were led to believe in the 'end of history' thesis (Fukuyama, 1992). Several analysts, for example, Žižek (2011), now argue that global capitalism is fast approaching its terminal crisis. So we should be considering, not so much if capitalism will end, but when, and how.

Global surveys of social values suggest that there are a whole raft of beliefs and values now simmering in human consciousness that would support radical social change. For example, a recent survey shows that the top 10 values of people living in the UK (in order of priority) are: caring, family, honesty, humour/fun, friendship, fairness, compassion, independence, respect and trust. However, the values that they perceive to be dominant in the country are: bureaucracy, crime and violence, uncertainty, corruption, blame, wasted resources, media influence, conflict, aggression, drug abuse and apathy (Barrett and Clothier, 2013). Therefore, it would appear that UK citizens are living in a society that does not reflect their values or meet their needs. This dissonant situation would suggest a strong possibility for change.

The third argument, that a struggle to overthrow capitalism would take our focus away from the more immediate issues, in particular, the environmental crises, is illustrated in the following comment:

> "I think you could make a strong argument that capitalism itself is inimical to a sustainable planet. However, I don't think we have time to overthrow capitalism before we deal with climate change and I also don't think confusing the two issues is particularly helpful. We can deal with at least some of the short-term things we need to do on environmental issues, including climate change, within the capitalist system." (Interview, 25 October 2012, Mark Kember, Chief Executive Officer, The Climate Group)

This concern over the urgency of our situation is understandable because, as discussed in Chapter One, environmental tipping-points are probably going to occur about 20 years from now at current rates of change. This short time period means that we must, indeed, take immediate action. Therefore, we should do all that we can within capitalism to avert the catastrophes that are on the horizon and to reduce those that are now already upon all those who are currently ill or dying as a result of inadequate environments. However, because it seems that capitalism is a fundamental element in driving these crises, as the evidence in this book suggests, the most effective action will be that which is framed in terms of the larger goal of reorientating our economic and political system.

The last argument for persisting with capitalism is based on the fear of what would replace it. Although this book has examined socialism as an alternative because there are no national-level alternatives at present, there are really numerous options. It is difficult to recommend socialism because it is often seen to be an old idea that has been defeated or, certainly, that is in retreat. Though this is not the case, as Cuba and Bolivia illustrate, for many in the West, socialism has an image problem. Some would argue that socialism's 'image problem' is deserved, because they feel very disappointed by the results of actually existing socialism. Yet, I think this is often based on a misunderstanding of the external pressures upon these countries and the extent to which such pressures have limited what they would, otherwise, have achieved. Levins eloquently urges us to have a little more patience because:

> Socialism is not a thing but a process, the process by which the working classes of the city and countryside and their allies seize the reins of society to satisfy their shared needs. Through a telescope, we get a glimpse of the world-historic significance of the first efforts to replace not only capitalism but also all class society by a more generous, just, and sustainable way of life. That is, we are trying to overcome a 10,000 year detour ... This is more important in looking at the first century of socialist innovation than how well these revolutionaries do it, the particular decisions and those unexpected changes that surprisingly occur, and even the enormous difficulties and deficiencies of this effort ... Socialism is a complex path, zigzagging and contradictory because the participants have different interests, respond in different ways to the events along the way, differ in knowledge and goals, in urgency and long term perspectives. (Levins, 2010)

As the examples of China, Bolivia and Cuba show, the environmental agenda has often been used to attack socialist governments, sometimes without good reason. There have clearly been mistakes but I consider that, if mistakes are followed by real learning and a genuine determination never to repeat them, then there is no cause for continuing condemnation or stubborn mistrust. The interviews conducted for this book indicate how far socialists have come in terms of acknowledging past mistakes. It is evident that many are now deeply committed to pursuing an ecological path and, in all the socialist countries, there were voices that advocated a new model of socialist development. For example, that of China's Deputy Minister of the Environment, who pledged to work for a new ecological civilisation and acknowledged that the costs of growth had outweighed the benefits, humbly admitting that 'China has lost almost everything it has gained since the late 1970s due to pollution … ' (Pan Yue, 2006b).

Globally, many socialists are now reappraising their own philosophy and beginning to incorporate a more respectful attitude to the environment (Dobson, 2007). At the same time, some environmentalists are coming to realise that environmentalism and socialism can be mutually reinforcing. Recognition of the planet's boundaries has strengthened the case for socialism because limited resources mean that there is a need to share more so that no one misses out. However, some socialists still need to reassess their assumptions and practices in order for this mutualism to reach its potential. As Cuba's Environmental Director pointed out, socialism needs to be driven by an environmentalist ethic. At the same time, there is much work to do to convince environmentalists that ecological problems are best resolved through redistribution, rather than technical, managerial or market-based measures. This is the agenda promoted by eco-socialists (for example, Mellor, 2006; Wall, 2010).

Although socialism could be a viable alternative to capitalism, in my opinion, it is not really possible to decide exactly what the new social and political model should be from where we now stand. This should, instead, be worked out in the course of the debates that will be necessary as we begin the necessary transformation. There are a range of other possible forms of political and economic systems, including many varieties of existing and potential forms of socialism; participatory economics (Parecon) (participatory decision making to guide the allocation of resources); retaining a market economy but with democratic workers' control of the workplace; communism ('to each according to their need'); or anarchist/libertarian communism, involving the abolition of the state, common ownership of the means of production and decision making by direct and/or consensus democracy. A post-capitalist world is up to us to imagine and invent.

Challenging Damaging Hegemonic Environmental Discourses

To achieve environmental justice, then, it appears necessary to dismantle the capitalist system, but we also need to challenge Damaging Hegemonic Environmental Discourses. One of the most effective ways to do this is to convince people of the veracity of counter-hegemonic discourses, in particular that:

1. Degrowth is desirable, necessary, important and inevitable.
2. Human and environmental well-being must be addressed holistically.

Both of these ideas are now beginning to gain traction, not only through the counter-hegemonic discourses of Vivir-Bien, ecological civilisation, degrowth and eco-socialism, but also through wider academic and policy research in the fields of ecological economics, critical geography and environmental sociology. For example, ecological economists are working on different ways of measuring human progress, as alternatives to GDP. As well as China's work on a Green GDP (see Chapter Eight), other alternatives that have been developed include the Index of Sustainable Economic Welfare and the Genuine Progress Indicator, which, rather than simply adding together all expenditures, are balanced by such factors as income distribution and the costs of pollution. In addition, ecological economists have produced the Happy Planet Index, where Cuba has come out in 6th (2006), 7th (2009) and 12th (2012) places in the three global surveys carried out so far (NEF, 2012).

Caring for humans and the environment holistically is also an idea that is beginning to gain ground, contradicting the DHEDs that see social and environmental issues as separate and competing. I have emphasised this as particularly important because the examples in this book have shown how often environmental injustices are justified on the grounds that they supposedly meet human needs, usually for jobs, housing, food or consumer goods. Yet, all these needs can be met, and better provided for, without harming the environment and actually enhancing it. For example, with regard to the need for jobs, more people could be employed in providing vital services that address our most urgent environmental and social problems, such as counselling people who are distressed; providing better home-care services; visiting people who are lonely or ill; re-establishing youth and community services; teaching school students in smaller classes; providing natural health services; growing local organic food; providing water and sanitation services for everyone who needs them, using appropriate technology;

making goods by hand using local, natural products; providing efficient, reliable and affordable (or free) public transport; mending items that are currently thrown away; shifting to renewable energy;[2] organising more efficient processes to save energy; cleaning up the ecological mess and so on. None of these jobs would increase environmental burdens and most would reduce them. Ecological processes are often more labour intensive (using human labour, rather than machines; for example, employing people to wash up cups, rather than manufacturing plastic throw-away versions). Therefore, there is no real jobs-versus-environment dilemma. Freed from the imperatives of profit-making capitalism, we could begin to employ people in socially necessary work and begin the huge task of actually addressing the shameful levels of global unmet need. Once we are freed from capitalism, we can also begin to make rational decisions about 'production-side environmentalism', that is, what is produced, rather than 'consumption-side environmentalism', what is consumed. Consumer choice has a minimum impact, whereas changes in production can have an enormous impact on every aspect of the environment. It is important, though, to be wary of some 'green jobs' discourse, since what is being advocated is not necessarily decent employment, in terms of working conditions or pay (UNEP, 2008). Some, so-called, 'green' jobs are often not even particularly good for the environment (UNEP, 2008). There are, of course, many issues to consider if we wish to revolutionise work in this way, but debates should now be under way with workers and their trade unions as to how these changes could practically happen.

Ideally, these jobs must be delinked from profitability. A global redistribution of wealth, within and between nations, could enable a basic income to be provided for all, regardless of whether their work is profitable or not. This should be provided as well as, and not instead of, welfare services. A global redistribution of wealth would mean, for example, that Bolivia could fund its social programmes and reduce rates of extreme poverty without unsustainable levels of extractivism. Redistribution is a vital component of environmental justice, anyway, not only for reducing inequality but also for decreasing unnecessary consumption. As the Worldwatch Institute has recently concluded, environmental sustainability is ultimately impossible without social equity (Renner, 2012). Responding to the Bolivian government's call for the countries of the global North to pay their ecological debt could be the starting-point for the necessary inter- and intra-national redistribution of wealth.

Therefore, it is important that challenging DHEDs happens alongside a challenge to capitalism and not instead of it. Many of Cuba's successful environmental programmes and policies are now being proposed by degrowth proponents for their own countries. These degrowth advocates have been inspired by how Cuba managed to sustain, and even improve, many aspects of well-being throughout the 'Special Period', when it was in a state of involuntary degrowth (as illustrated by the documentary *Power of Community*, Morgan, 2006), and how it continues to meet many human needs with a relatively low GDP. However, these enthusiasts ignore the political and economic context, so they do not specifically argue for the rejection of capitalism (Bell, 2010). Yet, as Bookchin argues, to take growth out of its proper social context of capitalism is to distort the problem:

> Perhaps the most obvious of our systemic problems is uncontrollable growth ... It's not enough, however, to blame our environmental problems on the obsession with growth. A system of deeply entrenched structures – of which growth is merely a surface manifestation – makes up our society ... Unless growth is traced to its basic source – competition in a grow-or-die market society – the demand for controlling growth is meaningless as well as unattainable. We can no more arrest growth while leaving the market intact than we can arrest egoism while leaving rivalry intact. (Bookchin, 1989, p 21)

It is difficult to imagine how degrowth, under capitalism, would work in terms of achieving environmental justice, since, when growth ceases or slows down within capitalist economies, unemployment and poverty generally increase. For example, in the US, between 1949 and 2008, unemployment increased every year, except in the 13 years when the GDP grew at greater than 5% (Magdoff and Foster, 2011). Therefore, several analysts argue that transitioning to a zero or degrowth economy under capitalism cannot be done in an equitable way (for example, Harvey, 2010; Magdoff and Foster, 2011). As Magdoff and Foster (2011, p 42) state:

> No-growth capitalism is an oxymoron: when growth ceases, the system is in a state of crisis with considerable suffering for the working class.

Consequently, degrowth would achieve environmental justice only if it were carried out hand in hand with extensive redistribution of income and wealth on a national and global level, something that is very unlikely to occur under capitalism.

Wrenching humanity free of the strictures of DHEDs and capitalism will require that people be informed and willing to think independently. Of course, we need more than changes of opinion but we would expect that, when a majority of the population have a different set of beliefs and values, those more in line with the achievement of environmental justice, this will lead to changes in policy. When an issue is perceived to be a priority for the public, it has to be on the agenda of elected officials. The need for a change in the dominant discourses can be considered as a need for paradigmatic change. As Meadows et al (1992) point out in their analysis of leverage points for social and environmental change, a shift at the paradigm level changes everything. Kuhn (1962) argued that paradigm change can best occur when a wide variety of individuals systematically point out the deficiencies of the 'old' paradigm while others proactively model a new one. The policies based on eco-civilisation, Vivir Bien and degrowth philosophies, which aim at changing economic practices to achieve a greater quality of life, provide some models for paradigmatic change and their ideas can open up debate throughout the world. Lu (2011) calls for a 'gradual revolution' that would begin with

> changes in prevailing values and beliefs, which often require leadership by intellectual and other social elites, which are then translated gradually into transformations of social institutions, modes of production and lifestyles ... It is necessary to remain hopeful, for revolutions or paradigm shifts often take place quietly and unexpectedly, when it is seemingly not possible to discern signs of impending social change ... (Lu, 2011, p 224)

However, no matter how quietly this paradigm shift occurs, it will eventually involve confronting the vested interests who maintain these DHEDs, that is, the many careers, reputations, resources and infrastructures that are dependent on the maintenance of beliefs that help to perpetuate the status quo. So far, there appears to be a reluctance to challenge, perhaps because many of us have something to lose if we stand up to these interests. As Foster (2010) reminds us, getting ahead in a career, whether academic, administrative or political, 'all too often involves self-censorship, a narrow focus on the relatively inconsequential, and leaving the big stuff – in terms of social change – off the table' (Foster et al, 2010, p 22). There are few who are brave enough, or in a sufficiently comfortable position, to propose the radical changes that appear necessary.

How to achieve change

Though it is hard to make a difference as an individual, social history shows us that dramatic and progressive social change has occurred when people organise together to make demands and work together to achieve them. This requires hope, a belief that we can make a difference and an inspiring and mobilising vision. Though there may seem little reason to be hopeful when we view all the problems that lie before us, the history of social change shows us that many ideas that seemed entirely hopeless at one time eventually do become the mainstream – from the banning of asbestos in the UK in 1999 after a 40-year struggle by victims, their families and their unions (McCulloch and Tweedale, 2008), to the election of a black president of the USA in 2008 and the more recent acceptance of same-sex marriage in 15 countries of the world. Achieving environmental justice is possible, because the problems discussed in this book have come about as the result of human activity and therefore, as humans, we can decide to stop these activities. Though this may be difficult, it will be much easier than living with the consequences of carrying on in the same way.

Though I do not think we have to decide the final model of our new ecological civilisation now, it is important to be clear about the values and standards that we are aiming for, even if these should change along the way. The Environmental Justice Indicator Framework used in this book is based on a vision that incorporates satisfying basic needs, as well as achieving well-being, equality, participatory democracy and ecological balance. For me, it is important that all these elements are seen to be part of environmentalism and environmental justice. A vision should encompass all that we really want. So when the UN announces that it aims to halve world hunger, we should, like Fidel Castro, ask "what about the other half?" (Graziano da Silva, 2013). Environmentalists can sometimes appear callous, especially in times of recession, as we talk of degrowth and consuming less, as if we do not care about jobs or meeting the needs of those who have the least. It is important that we show that we do care and that we have better ways of addressing those needs; ways that will achieve much greater human happiness and well-being for all. We have to paint a more compelling picture of the good life in an environmentally and socially just society and develop policies that will bring this vision about. We need to explain that what we propose may mean less unnecessary individual material consumption, but it will mean far better, more affordable (perhaps free) public goods, including health services, parks, libraries, schools, nurseries, transit systems, cultural activities, care services, food, housing and environmental services. Though people may have fewer gadgets and luxuries, they will have greater security, better relationships, more time and less stress. Environmental justice is the ideal framing for such thought and activity, linking environmental improvement to wider social and structural issues.

As Martínez-Alier (2010) suggests, environmental justice, eco-socialism, degrowth and other progressive social and environmental movements could draw strength from each other, to become a central force for change. For some, this might mean broadening their agendas to consolidate a stronger and larger progressive coalition with more universal appeal (Harvey, 1996). Alliances must be built between trade unionists, community groups, environmental justice movements and mainstream environmental organisations to work towards a better, healthier and safer workplace and society for all. To build these movements, it will be important to inform people about how the environment is affecting our health now; how little time we have to create a society that is ecologically and socially healthy and balanced; and the kind of organisations that concerned individuals can most effectively join. People are much influenced by social movement campaigns. Brulle et al (2012), examining a range of factors that could account for changes in levels of environmental concern in the US (in this case, about climate change), found that social movement advocacy was as important as elite cues (that is, government-level debates and statements) in influencing opinion, and more important than media coverage and public access to scientific information.

A number of left-leaning authors now argue that, rather than building social movements to confront power head-on, we should build a post-capitalist society through creating the alternatives that we can, now, within the system (for example, Holloway, 2002; 2010; Gibson-Graham, 2006). Such analysts assert that smaller, local practices and changes will provide the steps toward actual change. Gibson-Graham (1996; 2006), for example, argue that, by focusing so much on defeating capitalism, we inflate and exaggerate its power. They consider that arguing that we need an anti-capitalist reaction on a massive scale to dislodge the system can be a recipe for despair and resignation because the revolution does not seem very likely and is always tomorrow. Holloway (2002; 2010) takes a similar approach, arguing that alternatives to capitalism do not require confrontation with the state but can develop in autonomous social spaces. Holloway (2010) uses the metaphor of cracks in walls and sheets of ice, which may start as small chinks but can gradually widen, often unnoticed. Enough cracks will converge, naturally and inevitably, until the system shatters. In order to overthrow capitalism we must seek out or create these cracks, deepen them and aid their convergence. These authors have sought to give voice and recognition to anti-capitalist manifestations in the here and now, suggesting that capitalism is quietly being swept aside, anyway. Their position is that another world is, not only possible, but already in existence.

Though we ultimately need bold and ambitious responses, taking whatever small steps we can now is not at odds with working towards wider change, so long as we do not find all our time and energy used up in trying to lead an ethical life within a dubious system, rather than dismantling that system itself. Or involve ourselves in relatively minor matters that do not reflect the significance and scale of the crises that we now face. However, it may be that such attempts to create alternatives today come to wither under the pressures of capitalism. As Harvey argues in his critique of anti-capitalist utopian projects (Harvey, 2000), we can run from capitalism but we cannot hide. If our attempts to build alternatives outside capitalism fail, this can lead to resignation and despair. I, personally, subscribe more to the 'take power to change the world' than to the 'change the world by not taking power' approach, but perhaps we need both. As this book shows, there are many routes to achieving environmental justice but we must, with an open mind, debate which actions are really effective, and always be alert to the possibility of self-delusion with regard to the usefulness of our acts. What is probably best is to work at both levels, at the levels of major change and minor change. In the process of working for the less dramatic changes, we may bring about overall change and, in the process of working for major change, we can have some minor victories. Activities and campaigns for incremental change may eventually bring down the capitalist system anyway, as people become more aware of what is necessary and what is hindering progress.

However, whatever path we take to achieve environmental justice – challenging power head-on or building alternatives now – it is important for EJ supporters to be active. This might be difficult, as many activists have faced repeated defeats and state repression. Others have never been activists but have somehow come to feel that they have no power to effect change in the world. There is not the space to fully consider the reasons for the so-called 'apathy' that now seems to prevail in many countries. However, I would like to encourage people to work on themselves to resolve any traumas and disappointments that have left them with a sense of disempowerment and suggest Emotional

Freedom Technique and Percussive Suggestion Technique (for example, as explained by Beer and Roberts, 2013) as some excellent free self-help techniques. Campaigning for environmental justice can be very personally satisfying. Researchers have found that political activists generally live a happier and more fulfilling life than the average person (Klar and Kasser, 2009). We do not need everyone to participate in this struggle but we need the majority. If the majority became active and informed on environmental justice issues, then we could certainly avoid the crises that we are heading for, even within the short, 20-year window of opportunity that we have.

Final

This book has attempted to contribute to an evidence base to inform strategic and policy direction. Though I have looked at particular cases in unique situations, I wished to relate the work to the development of a theory around capitalism as a fundamental cause of environmental injustice. I have proposed that the elimination of capitalism is probably necessary in order to achieve environmental justice but is insufficient without also counteracting Damaging Hegemonic Environmental Discourses. From an academic point of view, I hope this theoretical position will be used for examining other cases and that the Environmental Justice Indicator Framework can be developed as a tool for evaluating policy. On a practical level, I hope that activists will consider the role of capitalism and DHEDs when attempting to understand the roots of environmental injustice and develop their campaigns correspondingly.

The current environmental, social and economic crises present a major challenge to capital, as well as being a new opportunity for its expansion through ever more extensive processes of commodification and monetisation. Those who wish to maintain the capitalist system are presenting aspects of these crises, such as the need to address climate change or to eradicate poverty, as separate issues. Therefore, social and environmental policy agendas have become increasingly technocratic, managerial and individualistic. We are focusing on reducing harm at the micro level when we should be widening our agenda and challenging a desperately unsustainable and deeply unfair economic system. By expanding this agenda, we can simultaneously achieve the equity, democracy and sustainability that are inherent in the idea of environmental justice. A healthy environment for all is achievable if we begin that radical transformation now.

Notes

[1] Trotsky stated:'The socialist revolution begins on the national arena, it unfolds on the international arena, and is completed on the world arena. Thus, the socialist revolution becomes a permanent revolution in a newer and broader sense of the word; it attains completion, only in the final victory of the new society on our entire planet ... The world division of labour, the dependence of Soviet industry upon foreign technology, the dependence of the productive forces of the advanced countries of Europe upon Asiatic raw materials, etc., etc., make the construction of an independent socialist society in any single country in the world impossible' (2010 [1929], p 5).

[2] A shift to renewable energy and energy efficiency would create up to four times as many jobs as investing in oil (Pollin et al, 2009).

Appendix I

Table A1.1: The Environmental Justice Indicator Framework for seven countries

Indicator	US	R. Korea	UK	Sweden	China	Bolivia	Cuba
Substantive							
Universal access to sanitation	Y	Y	Y	Y	N	N	N
Universal access to adequate waste disposal	Y	Y	Y	Y	N	N	N
Universal access to safe drinking water	Y	N	Y	Y	N	N	N
Universal access to adequate and sufficient food and nutrition	M	N	M	Y	N	N	Y
Universal access to clean air	M	N	M	M	N	N	N
Universal access to adequate and safe transport	M	M	M	Y	M	N	M
Universal access to green space for recreation and leisure	M	M	Y	Y	M	M	Y
Universal access to sufficient energy for cooking and heating	M	M	M	Y	M	N	Y
Adequate housing for all	M	N	M	M	M	N	N
Safe working and living environments for all	M	N	M	M	N	N	N
Universal protection from environmental disruptions (such as hurricanes, flooding)	M	N	M	Y	M	N	Y
Universal protection from potentially hazardous substances – harmful chemicals, GMOs, radiation, EMFs	N	N	N	N	N	N	N
Distributive							
Equal access to sanitation	Y	Y	Y	Y	N	N	Y
Equal access to adequate waste disposal	Y	N	Y	Y	N	N	N
Equal access to safe drinking water	Y	N	Y	Y	N	N	Y
Equal access to adequate and sufficient food and nutrition	N	N	N	N	M	N	Y
Equal access to clean air	N	N	N	N	M	N	Y
Equal access to adequate and safe transport	N	M	N	Y	M	N	N
Equal access to green space for recreation and leisure	N	N	N	M	M	N	Y
Equal access to sufficient energy for cooking and heating	N	N	N	Y	M	N	Y
Equally adequate housing for all	N	N	N	N	M	N	Y
Equally safe working and living environments for all	N	N	N	N	M	N	Y

Indicator	US	R. Korea	UK	Sweden	China	Bolivia	Cuba
Equal protection from environmental disruptions (such as hurricanes, flooding)	N	M	N	Y	M	Y	Y
Equal protection from potentially hazardous substances – harmful chemicals, GMOs, radiation, EMFs	N	N	N	N	N	N	Y
Procedural							
All parties that were affected by environmental decisions were invited to contribute to the decision-making process	N	N	N	Y	M	Y	M
All participants in the environmental decision-making process were treated with equal respect and value	N	N	N	M	M	Y	M
All environmental decisions were made publicly	M	N	M	M	M	Y	Y
All parties had access to sufficient resources to enable them to participate on an equal footing	N	N	N	N	N	N	M
The environmental decision-making process was open to all questions and alternatives	N	N	N	N	N	M	M
All affected had an equal right and an equal chance to express their point of view	N	N	N	M	M	Y	M
The relevant rules and procedures were applied consistently, with regard to different people and at different times	M	N	M	N	M	Y	M
All those affected received accurate and accessible information – timely, honest, easy to understand, digestible and easily available	N	N	N	M	M	Y	M
Those affected had control of the outcome of decisions (ideally, proportional to how much they would be affected)	N	N	N	N	M	M	Y
A fair outcome resulted from the process, in terms of substantial and distributional environmental justice	M	M	M	M	M	M	M
There was authentic, accessible and honest communication	M	N	M	M	M	Y	Y
There was a lack of external coercion	M	N	M	M	M	Y	Y
Those affected were included in all stages of decision making	N	N	N	N	M	Y	Y
All parties were accountable – that is, responsible to answer for their actions and decisions and to remedy them if necessary	M	N	M	M	M	Y	Y
Consensus decision making was carried out, whenever this was practical	N	N	N	N	N	Y	Y

Indicator	US	R. Korea	UK	Sweden	China	Bolivia	Cuba
Decision making was deliberative, that is, free from any authority of prior norms or requirements	M	N	M	N	N	M	N
Sufficient skills and personal resources have been available for those affected to participate on an equal basis	N	N	N	N	N	N	M
Use of a strong precautionary principle	N	N	N	M	N	Y	N
Freedom of association	Y	Y	Y	Y	M	Y	M
Right to peaceful protest	Y	Y	Y	Y	M	Y	M
Free access to legal redress	N	N	N	Y	M	N	Y
Scores (Y=1; M=.5; N=0)							
Mainly Yes	8	5	9	18	0	15	22
Mixed	7.5	3	7	6.5	14	2.5	6
Mainly No	0	0	0	0	0	0	0
Total indicators (Y=1; M=.5; N=0)	15.5	8	16	24.5	14	17.5	28
International, intergenerational, inter-species							
The above criteria have not been met through undermining the environmental justice of other species, nations and generations, that is, subtract Ecological Footprint, weighted ×3.8	27.3	17.6	17.9	21.7	8.1	9.9	7.2
Total Environmental Justice Indicators	-11.8	-9.6	-1.9	2.8	5.9	7.6	20.8

Note:
Y = Yes, the country generally achieves this;
M = Mixed;
N = No, the country generally does not achieve this.

Source: Bell (2012), based on triangulated quantitative and qualitative secondary data analysis, interviews with local experts and citizens, and participant observations.

Appendix 2
Datasets

Table A2.1: International economic datasets

Economic Dataset	US	R. Korea	UK	Sweden	China	Bolivia	Cuba
GDP, 2010 (millions of US$)[a]	14,447,100	1,014,369	2,253,552	458,725	5,739,358	19,640	64,220
GDP, 2010, global ranking[a]	1st	15th	6th	22nd	2nd	100th	63rd
Growth rate of GDP, 2010[b]	1.83	3.88	1.20	3.11	8.07	3.07	3.75
Growth rate of GDP, 2010[c]	2.17	6.23	1.55	6.5	10.45	3.77	0.89
GDP, 2010 (PPP)[d]	15,075,675	1,554,124	2,287,865	384,661	11,299,987	50,944	No data
GDP per capita, 2010 (millions of US$)[e]	46545.9	21052.17	36326.76	48906.21	4354.035	1977.915	5704.425

Notes:

[a] GDP at current prices in US dollars. Source: United Nations Statistical Division (2012), http://unstats.un.org/unsd/snaama/dnllist.asp, accessed 18 November 2012.

[b] Growth rate of GDP/breakdown at constant 2005 prices in per cent (final consumption expenditure). Source: United Nations Statistical Division (2012), http://unstats.un.org/unsd/snaama/dnllist.asp, accessed 18 November 2012.

[c] Growth rate of GDP/breakdown at constant 2005 prices in per cent (total value added). Source: United Nations Statistical Division (2012), http://unstats.un.org/unsd/snaama/dnllist.asp accessed 19 November 2012.

[d] GDP (PPP), IMF World Economic Outlook Database (October 2012), http://www.imf.org/external/pubs/ft/weo/2012/02/weodata/index.aspx, accessed 20 November 2012.

[e] Per capita GDP at current prices in US dollars. Source: United Nations Statistical Division (2012), http://unstats.un.org/unsd/snaama/dnllist.asp accessed 19 November 2012.

Table A2.2: International environmental datasets

Environmental dataset	US	R.Korea	UK	Sweden	China	Bolivia	Cuba
Ecological Footprint[a]	7.19	4.62	4.71	5.71	2.13	2.61	1.9
Happy Planet Index[b]	37.3	43.8	47.9	46.2	44.7	43.6	56.2
Happy Planet Index, global ranking (of 151 countries)[b]	105th	63rd	41st	52nd	60th	64th	12th
Non-CO_2 greenhouse gases per capita[c]	3.7	1.2	1.8	2.1	1.5	4.9	1.4
CO_2 emissions per capita[c]	17.3	10.6	8.5	5.3	5.2	1.3	2.8
Environmental Performance Index 2012, score[d]	56.6	57.2	68.8.	68.8.	42.2	54.6	56.5
Environmental Performance Index, 2012, global ranking (of 132 countries)[e]	49th	43rd	9th	9th	116th	62nd	50th
Depth of Hunger Index[f]	110	130	100	130	250	240	120
Percentage of population with access to improved water[g]							
urban	100	100	100	100	98	96	96
rural	94	88	100	100	85	71	89
national	99	98	100	100	91	88	94
Percentage of population with access to improved sanitation[g]							
urban	100	100	100	100	74	35	94
rural	99	100	100	100	56	10	81
national	100	100	100	100	64	27	91
Percentage of population with access to electricity, 2009[h]	100	100	100	100	99.4	77.5	97

Notes:

[a] Ecological footprint in average global hectares per person, 2008 data (WWF, 2012a).

[b] NEF (2012)

[c] UNDP (2011a)

[d] EPI (2012a)

[e] EPI (2012b)

[f] Kilocalories per person per day, based on 2008 data (World Bank, 2012a).

[g] UNICEF/WHO (2012)

[h] World Bank (2012b)

Table A2.3: International socioeconomic datasets

Socioeconomic dataset	US	R. Korea	UK	Sweden	China	Bolivia	Cuba
Human Development Index (HDI), 2011[a]	0.91	0.897	0.863	0.904	0.687	0.663	0.776
HDI, 2011, global ranking (of 187 countries)[a]	4th	15th	28th	10th	101st	108th	51st
Non-Income HDI, 2011[a]	0.931	0.945	0.879	0.94	0.725	0.742	0.904
Life expectancy at birth, 2011[a]	78.5	80.6	80.2	81.4	73.5	66.6	79.1
Gender Inequality Index, 2011[a]	0.299	0.111	0.209	0.049	0.209	0.476	0.337
Gender inequality, 2011, global ranking (of 187 countries)[a]	47th	11th	34th	1st	35th	88th	58th
Inequality, 2011 (Income Gini Coefficient)[b]	0.40	0.32	0.36	0.25	0.42	0.56	0.30[c]
	(2000 data)	(1998 data)	(1999 data)	(2000 data)	(2005 data)	(2008 data)	(2009 data)
Inequality, 2011, global ranking (of 160 countries)[b]	95th lowest	28th lowest	60th lowest	3rd lowest	102nd lowest	151st lowest	No data
Inequality, 2011 (Income Gini Coefficient) – standardised[d]	0.36	0.31	0.36	0.22	0.40	0.53	0.30
	(2010 data)	(2010 data)	(2010 data)	(2010 data)	(2005 data)	(2007 data)	(1978 data)

Notes:

[a] UNDP (2011a).

[b] World Bank (2011a).

[c] Vision of Humanity (2013).

[d] Solt (2011).

Appendix 3
Construction of the Environmental Justice Indicator Framework

In general, any list of EJ indicators will be subject to a number of limitations and assumptions. Ideally, this study should have used a comprehensive list of all possible environmental risks and gains, drawing on full datasets, reliably collected from each country. However, this would require the national and local collection of much more detailed data than is presently being collected or collated in any nation-state. Therefore, this book can provide only a very approximate overview of the situation in the countries covered. The EJI framework serves more as a snapshot summary of the apparent successes and failures of a country in its achievement of important aspects of EJ.

To establish the procedural, distributive and substantive indicators, I initially searched for other EJI frameworks, but none was based on the wide definition I considered necessary. However, the United States EPA framework for environmental justice was a useful resource (US EPA, 2004), as was work in the UK by Wheeler (2004). To establish the criteria for substantive and distributional justice, I have particularly focused on anthropogenic (caused by humans) environmental factors. Where 'naturally occurring' environmental phenomena are mentioned, it is in the context of what humans have done to prevent or exacerbate them. This focus is because the equity implications of human-sourced environmental problems are the most relevant to questions of justice, in terms of who benefits and who carries the burden for activities that impact on the environment.

To develop the indicators regarding substantive and distributional justice, a review and appraisal of health-relevant dimensions of physical environmental deprivation was conducted to select both health-detrimental (air pollution, lack of sanitation) and health-beneficial (safe housing, green space) dimensions. I also drew on previous work on composite measures of environmental deprivation (for example, Richardson et al, 2010a). In addition, I drew on secondary data from a number of international datasets (see Appendix 2).

There are many complex issues to resolve when assessing the health impacts of a single environmental indicator and this is even more problematic when considering the entirety of environmental quality in a geographical area. Investigating cumulative (over time) or multiple (different substance) impacts is very difficult. Although potential health hazards can be drawn up from the many lists of environmental hazards in existence (such as the Basel Convention, 1990; World Bank, 1999), this is a much-contested and still under-researched area, causing numerous practical problems, as agencies that have collated these lists testify (for example, UNEP, 2002). In addition, it is, ideally, important to assess not only the impact of environmental practices on health, but also the vulnerability of those affected, and the reversibility of the harm done.

It would be a very complex matter to assemble a list of standards and impact conditions on every aspect of the environment and recipient population. Therefore, I have focused on very simple substantive justice criteria that derive from widely accepted evidence of direct environmental impacts on health at a local level. Thus, I have not included ozone depletion or loss of species, for example.

I wanted to take into account subjective experience and so I did not attempt to 'objectively' operationalise each criterion, for example, to determine exact standards for 'adequate housing', 'clean air', 'treated with equal value', 'consensus decision-making' and so on. Instead, I relied on people's subjective satisfaction levels. For example, though I could not measure the calorific content of diets, I asked people if they thought they ate enough food and of sufficient quality, as part of questions relating to their satisfaction with the environment. This is not entirely unproblematic, as oppression is sometimes internalised so that some marginalised individuals or groups might say that they do not mind, or even that they like, an unhealthy local environment because they are used to it or because they feel defensive about their neighbourhood. Also, individuals may not understand the health impacts of poor quality environments or feel the effects of an unhealthy environment until many years later.

The EJI score for each country could have been calculated by weighting the relative importance of each indicator for the overall concept of EJ. However, because of the complexity of this with regard to cumulative, spatial and temporal variations, and the lack of consistent evidence with which to make this assessment, in terms of certainty about health impacts, this was not pursued. My approach has simplified the process to deciding whether the criteria were generally met or not. If the country generally appeared to meet the criteria, it was give a +1 point. If the situation was very mixed, a 0.5 score was given. No negative points were given at this stage. However, the Ecological Footprint for the country (weighted by ×3.8) was then subtracted from the total to give the EJI score for the country.[1] I felt this to be necessary to reflect the relative importance of the Ecological Footprint.

Note

[1] The weighting of ×3.8 enabled a possible score of 45, equivalent to the 45 points possible for the combined substantive, distributional and procedural EJ indicators. The highest Ecological Footprint in the world that year was 11.7 (in Qatar), so it was necessary to multiply all the scores by 3.8 so that the possible scores could reach 45.

References

AAWH (American Association of World Health) (1997) *The Denial of Food and Medicine: The Impact of the US Embargo on Health and Nutrition in Cuba*, Washington, DC: AAWH.

Acción Ecológica (2008) 'La Deuda Ecológica', www.accionecologica. org/.

ACN (Cuban News Agency) (2009) 'The ALBA Summit: New Goals of Social Justice', *The 10th Summit of the Bolivarian Alliance for the Americas (ALBA)*.

Adeola, F. (1994) 'Environmental Hazards, Health, and Racial Inequity in Hazardous Waste Distribution', *Environment and Behavior*, vol 26, no 1, pp 99-126.

Aguirre, B. and Portela, A, (2000) 'Environmental Degradation and Vulnerability in Cuba', *Natural Hazards Review,* vol 1, no 3, pp 171-9.

Agyeman, J. (2001) 'Ethnic Minorities in Britain: Short Change, Systematic Indifference and Sustainable Development', *Journal of Environmental Policy and Planning*, vol 3, no 1, pp 15-30.

Agyeman, J. (2002) 'Constructing Environmental (In)Justice: Transatlantic Tales', *Environmental Politics*, vol 11, no 3, pp 31-53.

Agyeman, J. and Evans, B. (2004) '"Just Sustainability": The Emerging Discourse of Environmental Justice in Britain?', *Geographical Journal*, vol 170, no 2, pp 155-64.

Albert, M. (2003) *Parecon: Life After Capitalism*, London: Verso.

Albro, R. (2005) 'The Water is Ours, Carajo!: Deep citizenship in Bolivia's Water War', in J. Nash (ed) *Social Movements: An Anthropological Reader*, Oxford and Cambridge: Basil Blackwell, pp 249-71.

Allard, J.-G. and Golinger, E. (2009) *La Agresión Permanente*, Caracas: Ministerio del Poder Poder Popular Para la Comunicación y la Información.

Andersen, Z.J. et al (2012) 'Diabetes Incidence and Long-Term Exposure to Air Pollution: A Cohort Study', *Diabetes Care*, vol 35, no 1, pp 92-8.

Andersson, H.E. and Nilsson, S. (2011) 'Asylum Seekers and Undocumented Migrants: Increased Social Rights in Sweden', *International Migration*, vol 49, no 4, pp 167-88.

Angel, B. (1992) *The Toxic Threat to Indian lands: A Greenpeace Report*, San Francisco: Greenpeace.

Arnstein, S.R. (1969) 'A Ladder of Citizen Participation', *Journal of the American Planning Association*, vol 35, no 4, pp 216-24.

Aunan, K. et al (2000) 'Surface Ozone in China and Its Possible Impact on Agricultural Crop Yields', *Ambio*, vol 29, no 6, pp 294–301.

Azomahou, T. and Van Phu, N. (2001) *Economic Growth and CO2 Emissions: A Nonparametric Approach*, Leuven, Belgium: Universite´ Catholique Louvain.

Bagdikian, B. (2004) *The New Media Monopoly*, Boston, MA: Beacon Press.

Bailey, C. et al (1993) 'Environmental Politics in Alabama's Blackbelt', in R.D Bullard (ed) *Confronting Environmental Racism: Voices from the Grassroots*, Boston, MA: South End Press, pp 107-22.

Balme, R. (2011) 'The Politics of Environmental Justice in China', *APSA 2011 Annual Meeting Paper.*

Barbeira, L. et al (2004) 'The End of Egalitarianism? Economic Inequality and the Future of Social Policy in Cuba', in J. Dominguez, O.E. Perez Villanueva and L. Barberia (eds) *The Cuban Economy at the Start of the Twenty-First Century*, Cambridge, MA: Harvard University, David Rockefeller Center for Latin American Studies.

Barnett, A.G. et al (2006) 'The Effects of Air Pollution on Hospitalizations for Cardiovascular Disease in Elderly People in Australian and New Zealand Cities', *Environmental Health Perspectives*, vol 114, no 7, pp 1018-23

Barrett, R. and Clothier, P. (2013) *The United Kingdom Values Survey: Increasing Happiness by Understanding What People Value*, Bury, Lancs: Barrett Values Centre.

Barrett, S. and Graddy, K. (2000) 'Freedom, Growth, and the Environment', *Environment and Development Economics*, vol 5, no 4, pp 433-56.

Bernardini, O. and Galli, R. (1993) 'Dematerialization: Long-term Trends in the Intensity of Use of Materials and Energy', *Futures*, vol 25, no 4, pp 431-48.

Bauer, M.A. et al (2012) 'Cuing Consumerism: Situational Materialism Undermines Personal and Social Well-Being', *Psychological Science*, vol 23, no 5, pp 517-23.

Beck, U. (1992) *Risk Society: Towards a New Modernity*, London: Sage.

Beck, U. (1995) *Ecological Politics in an Age of Risk*, Cambridge: Polity.

Beck, U. (1999) *World Risk Society*, Oxford: Polity.

Been, V. (1994) 'Locally Undesirable Land Uses in Minority Neighbourhoods: Disproportionate Siting or Market Dynamics?', *Yale Law Journal*, vol 103, no 6, pp 1383-22.

Beer, S. and Roberts, E. (2013) *Step by Step Tapping: The Amazing Self-help Technique to Heal Mind and Body*, London: Gaia.

Bell, D.A. (2006) 'Beyond Liberal Democracy, Political Thinking for an East Asian Context', *China Perspectives*, no 68, November–December, http://chinaperspectives.revues.org/3183

Bell, K. (2008) 'Achieving Environmental Justice in the United Kingdom: A Case Study of Lockleaze', *Environmental Justice*, vol 1, no 4, pp 203-10.

Bell, K. (2010) 'Environmental Justice: Lessons from Cuba', PhD thesis, School for Policy Studies, University of Bristol.

Bell, K. and Sweeting, D. (2013) 'Waste Collection as an Environmental Justice Issue: A Case Study of a Neighbourhood in Bristol, UK' in M.J. Zapata and M. Hall (eds) *Organising Waste in the City*, Bristol: Policy Press.

Bell, S. and McGillivray, D. (2008) *Environmental Law*, Oxford: Oxford University Press.

Belliveau, M. and Lester, S. (2004) 'PVC. Bad News Comes in 3s', Falls Church, VA: Centre for Health, Environment and Justice.

Bello, W. (1993) 'Global Economic Counterrevolution: The Dynamics of Impoverishment and Marginalization' in R. Hofricher (ed) *Toxic Struggles: The Theory and Practice of Environmental Justice*, Philadelphia, PA: New Society Publishers.

Benhabib, S. (1992) 'Models of Public Space' in C. Calhoun (ed) *Habermas and the Public Sphere*, Cambridge, MA: MIT Press, pp 73-96.

Bernard, M. et al (2006) 'Environmental Law in China', *Natural Resources Defense Council Website*, www.nrdc.org/international/ochinalaw.asp

Berry, G.R. (2003) 'Organizing Against Multinational Corporate Power in Cancer Alley: The Activist Community as Primary Stakeholder', *Organization and Environment*, vol 16, no 1, pp 3-33.

Bickerstaff, K. and Agyeman, J. (2009) 'Assembling Justice Spaces: The Scalar Politics of Environmental Justice in North-east England', *Antipode*, vol 41, no 4, pp 781-806.

Bickerstaff, K. et al (2010) 'Locating Scientific Citizenship: The Institutional Contexts and Cultures of Public Engagement', *Science, Technology and Human Values*, vol 35, no 4, pp 474-500.

Bies, R.J. and Moag, J.S. (1986) 'Interactional Justice: Communications Criteria of Fairness', *Research on Negotiation in Organizations*, vol 1, pp 43–55.

Bigwood, J. (2008) 'New discoveries reveal US intervention in Bolivia', *Upside Down World*, 14 October 2008, http://upsidedownworld.org/main/content/view/1522/1/.

Bilbao, L. (2008) *Venezuela in Revolution: Renaissance of Socialism*, Buenos Aires: Ediciones Le Monde Diplomatique.

Blair, F. and Evans, B. (2004) *Seeing the Bigger Picture: Delivering Local Sustainable Development*, York: Joseph Rowntree Foundation.

Blue, S.A. (2007) 'The Erosion of Racial Equality in the Context of Cuba's Dual Economy', *Latin American Politics and Society*, vol 49, no 3, pp 35-68.

Boardman, B. et al (1999) *Equity and the Environment: Guidelines for Green and Socially Just Government*, London: Catalyst Trust and Friends of the Earth (FoE).

Bookchin, M. (1989) 'Death of a Small Planet', *The Progressive*, no 53, pp 19–23,

Boyce, J.K. (2001) 'Power Inequalities and the Political Economy of Environmental Protection', Conference on Inequality, Collective Action, and Environmental Sustainability, Santa Fe Institute, Department of Economics and Political Economy Research Institute, University of Massachusetts, Amherst.

Boyle, D. and Simms, A. (2009) *The New Economics – A Bigger Picture*, London: Earthscan Publications.

Bradley, K. (2009) 'Just Environments: Politicising Sustainable Urban Development', School of Architecture and Built Environment, PhD thesis, Stockholm: KTH Royal Institute of Technology.

Bradley, K. et al (2008) 'Exploring Environmental Justice in Sweden – How to improve planning for environmental sustainability and social equity in an "eco-friendly" context', *Projections – MIT Journal of Planning*, vol 8, pp 68-81.

Brajer, V. et al (2010) 'Adjusting Chinese income inequality for environmental equity', *Environment and Development Economics*, vol 15, no 3, pp 341-62.

Brawn, E. et al (2013) 'The Other Care Crisis: Making Social Care Funding Work for Disabled Adults in England', London: Scope, Mencap, National Autistic Society, Sense, Leonard Cheshire Disability.

Brodsky, E.E. and Lajoie, L.J. (2013) 'Anthropogenic Seismicity Rates and Operational Parameters at the Salton Sea Geothermal Field', *Science*, vol 341, no 6145, pp 543-46.

Brown, A.P. (2002) 'Community Involvement: Findings from Working for Communities', *Development Department Research Programme Research*, Findings No 137, Scottish Executive Research Unit.

Brulle, R. et al (2012) 'Shifting Public Opinion on Climate Change: An Empirical Assessment of Factors Influencing Concern Over Climate Change in the US, 2002–2010', *Climatic Change*, vol 114, no 2, pp 169-88.

Bryant, B. and Mohai, P. (eds) (1992) *Race and the Incidence of Environmental Hazards: A Time for Discourse*, Boulder, CO: Westview Press.,

Buckingham, S. and Kulcur, R. (2009) 'Gendered Geographies of Environmental Justice', *Antipode*, vol 41, no 4, pp 659,

Bullard, R.D. (1983) 'Solid Waste Sites and the Black Houston Community', *Sociological Enquiry*, vol 53, no 2-3, pp 273–88.

Bullard, R.D. (1990) *Dumping in Dixie: Race, Class, and Environmental Quality*, Boulder, CO: Westview Press.

Bullard, R.D. (1992) 'Environmental Blackmail in Minority Communities', in B. Bryant and P. Mohai (eds) *Race and the Incidence of Environmental Hazards: A Time for Discourse*, Boulder, CO: Westview Press.

Bullard, R.D. (1993) *Confronting Environmental Racism: Voices from the Grassroots*, Boston, MA: South End Press.

Bullard, R.D. (1994a) *Dumping in Dixie: Race, Class and Environmental Quality*, Boulder, CO: Westview Press.

Bullard, R.D. (1994b) 'The Legacy of American Apartheid and Environmental Racism', *St John's Journal of Legal Commentary*, vol 9, no 2, pp 445-74.

Bullard, R.D. and Johnson, G.S. (2000) 'Environmental Justice: Grassroots Activism and Its Impact on Public Policy Decision Making', *Journal of Social Issues*, vol 56, no 3, pp 555-78.

Bullard, R. et al (2007) *Toxic Wastes and Race at Twenty, 1987–2007*, Cleveland, OH: United Church of Christ Justice and Witness Ministries.

Bunker, S.G. (2003) 'Matter, Space, Energy, and Political Economy: The Amazon in the World System', *Journal of World-Systems Research*, vol 9, no 2, pp 219-58.

Burkett, P. (1999) *Marx and Nature*, New York: St Martin's Press.

Burningham, K. and Thrush, D. (2001) *Rainforests are a Long Way from Here: The Environmental Concerns of Disadvantaged Groups*, York: YPS for the Joseph Rowntree Foundation.

Cameron, D. (2010) Speech to DECC, 14 May.

Cameron, D. (2012) Speech to Confederation of British Industry Annual Conference. 20 November.

Capacity Global (2007) 'The Aarhus Convention: Resource Centre Article', London: Capacity Global.

Capgemini and Merrill Lynch Wealth Management (2013) 'World Wealth Report', www.capgemini.com/thought-leadership/world-wealth-report-2013-from-capgemini-and-rbc-wealth-management

Carlton, E.J. et al (2012) 'Regional Disparities in the Burden of Disease Attributable to Unsafe Water and Poor Sanitation in China', *Bulletin of the World Health Organisation*, vol 90, pp 578–87.

Carrington, D. (2012a) 'Environmental Regulations Set to be Slashed', *The Guardian*, London, 16 March.

Carrington, D. (2012b) 'Slashing of Environment "Red Tape" is Far From Over', *The Guardian*, London, 19 March.

CDP (Community Development Project) (1977) *Gilding the Ghetto: The State and the Poverty Experiments*, London: CDP.

Centellas, K.M. (2010) 'The Localism of Bolivian Science Tradition, Policy, and Projects', *Latin American Perspectives*, vol 37, no 3, pp 160-75.

Center, J. (1996) 'Waste Management and Risk Assessment: Environmental Discrimination through Regulation', *Urban Geography*, vol 17, pp 400-18.

Chaix, B. et al (2006) 'Children's Exposure to Nitrogen Dioxide in Sweden: Investigating Environmental Injustice in an Egalitarian Country', *Journal of Epidemiology and Community Health*, vol 60, no 3, pp 234-41.

Chavez, J.C. (2008) 'Nickel Industry Contaminating Cuban Coasts'. *El Nuevo Herald* in miningandcommunities.org, 7 August.

Chinese Academy of Sciences (2010) *China Sustainable Development Strategy Report*, Beijing: Sustainable Development Strategy Study Group.

Choi, B. (1999) *Marxist Theory of Environmental Justice*, Symposium for Social Justice and Environmental Justice, Seoul National University.

Choi, S., et al (2010) 'Asbestos-containing Materials and Airborne Asbestos Levels in Industrial Buildings in Korea', *Journal of University of Occupational and Environmental Health*, vol 32, no 1, pp 31-43.

Chomsky, N. (1997) 'What Makes Mainstream Media Mainstream?', *Z Magazine*, www.chomsky.info/articles/199710--.htm

Chung, D.Y.-K. and Hwang, D.K. (2006) *The Korean National Strategy for Sustainable Development: A Background Report*, Chung nam, Korea: Department of International Economics, Sunmoon University.

Churchill, W. and LaDuke, W. (1992) 'Native America: The Political Economy of Radioactive Colonialism', in *The State of Native America: Genocide, Colonization and Resistance*, Boston, MA: South End Press.

CIA (Central Intelligence Agency) (2011) *Factbook, 2011*, https://www.cia.gov/library/publications/the-world-factbook/geos/bl.html.

CITMA (Ministry of Science Environment and Technology) (1992) La Habana, Cuba: Academia de Ciencias de Cuba, in Maal-Bared, R. (2006) 'Comparing Environmental Issues in Cuba Before and After the Special Period: Balancing Sustainable Development and Survival', *Environment International*, vol 32, no 3, pp 349-58.

CITMA (1997) *National Environmental Strategy*, La Habana, Cuba: CITMA.

City of Stockholm Environment and Health Administration (2006) *Air in Stockholm: Annual Report 2005*, Stockholm: City of Stockholm Environment and Health Administration.

Clinton, W.J. (1994) 'Executive Order: Federal Actions to Address Environmental Justice in Minority Populations and Low-Income Populations', Washington, DC: White House.

Coelho, R. (2012) 'Green is the Colour of Money: The EU ETS Failure as a Model for the 'Green Economy', *Carbon Trade Watch,* Barcelona: Carbon Trade Watch.

Cole, K. (1998) *Cuba: From Revolution to Development*, London: Pinter.

COMEAP (Committee on the Medical Effects of Air Pollutants) (2010) *The Mortality Effects of Long-Term Exposure to Particulate Air Pollution in the UK*, London: COMEAP.

Commoner, B. (1972) *The Closing Circle: Nature, Man, and Technology*, London: Jonathan Cape.

Conservation International (2009) 'Nature Provides: Ecosystem Services and Their Benefits to Humankind', www.conservation.org

Constitution of the Republic of Cuba (1992) http://www.cubanet. org/ref/dis/const_92_e.htm

Cooke, B. and Kothari, U. (2001) *Participation: The New Tyranny?*, London: Zed Books.

Cook, S., Smith, K. et al (2012) 'Green Economy or Green Society? Contestation and Policies for a Fair Transition', Occasional paper 10: Social Dimensions of Green Economy and Sustainable Development, United Nations Research Institute for Social Development.

COP15 Korea NGOs Network (2009) 'Korea's Green Growth = Extraordinary "Green Wash"', http://green-korea.tistory.com/101

Cox, R. (1996) *Approaches to World Order*, Cambridge: Cambridge University Press.

Coyula, M. and Hamberg, J. (2003) Understanding Slums: The Case of Havana, Cuba, in *The Challenge of the Slums: Global Report on Human Settlements 2003*, United Nations Human Settlements Programme (UN-HABITAT), David Rockefeller Center for Latin American Studies (DRCLAS), Harvard University.

Crawford, C. (2004) 'Environmental Justice in Cuba: Capital Needs, Developing a Tourist Infrastructure, and Liberty of Access to Natural Resources', Working Paper No 04-10, October, Andrew Young School of Policy Studies, Georgia State University.

Crédit Suisse (2010) *Global Wealth Databook*, https://www.credit-suisse.com/news/doc/credit_suisse_global_wealth_databook.pdf

Crenshaw, K. (1994) 'Mapping the Margins: Intersectionality, Identity Politics, and Violence Against Women of Color', in M.A Fineman and R. Mykitiuk (eds) *The Public Nature of Private Violence*, New York: Routledge, pp 93-118.

Cutter, S. (1995) 'Race, Class and Environmental Justice', *Progress in Human Geography*, vol 19, no 1, pp 107-18.

Daly, H. E. (1977) *Steady-State Economics. The Economics of Biophysical Equilibrium and Moral Growth*, San Francisco, CA: W.H. Freeman and Company.

Daly, H.E. and Farley, J. (2004) *Ecological Economics: Principles and Applications*, Washington, DC: Island Press.

Dangl, B. (2010) *Dancing with Dynamite: Social Movements and States in Latin America*, Oakland, CA: AK Press.

Davis, L.E. et al (2007) *Hurricane Katrina: Lessons for Army Planning and Operations*, US: Arroyo Centre, Rand Corporation.

Davis, S.J. and Caldeira, K. (2010) 'Consumption-Based Accounting of CO_2 Emissions', *The Proceedings of the National Academy of Sciences of the United States of America*, Washington, DC: PNAS.

Dawson, S.E. and Madsen, G.E. (2011) 'Psychosocial and Health Impacts of Uranium Mining and Milling on Navajo Lands', *Health Physics*, vol 101, no 5, pp 618-25.

DCLG (Department for Communities and Local Government) (2012) *Department for Communities and Local Government National Planning Policy Framework*, London: DCLG.

Deaton, A. (2008) 'Income, Health, and Well-Being around the World: Evidence from the Gallup World Poll', *Journal of Economic Perspectives*, vol 22, no 2, pp 53-72.

Debbané, A. and Keil, R. (2004) 'Multiple Disconnections: Environmental Justice and Urban Water in Canada and South Africa', *Space and Polity,* vol 8, no 2, pp 209-225.

Defra (Department for Environment, Food and Rural Affairs) (2010) 'Sustainable Development: List of Indicators: Indicator 60 – Environmental Equality', http://archive.defra.gov.uk/sustainable/government/progress/national/60.htm

Defra (Department for Environment, Food and Rural Affairs) (2013) 'Consultation on new Sustainable Development Indicators: Government response', London: Defra.

Dello Buono, R.A. (1995) 'An Introduction to Cuba in the Special Period', *Facultad Latino Americana de Ciencias Sociales Programa Cuba in Carta Cuba: Interdisciplinary Reflections on Development and Society*, La Habana, Cuba: Universidad De La Habana.

DETR (Department of the Environment, Transport and the Regions) (2001) *Road Accident Involvement of Children from Ethnic Minorities*, London: The Stationery Office.

de Vries, S. (2001) *Nature and Health: The Importance of Green Space In The Urban Living Environment*, Proceeding Green Spaces of the Symposium, 'Open Space Functions Under Urban Pressure', Ghent: 19–21 September 2001.

de Vries, S. et al (2003) 'Natural Environments – Healthy Environments? An Exploratory Analysis of the Relationship Between Greenspace and Health', *Environmental and Planning A*, vol 35, no 10, pp 1717–31.

Diaz-Briquets, S. and Pérez-López, J.F. (1993) 'Water, Development, and Environment in Cuba: A First Look', *Cuba in Transition,* vol 3, Proceedings of the Third Annual Meeting of the Association for the Study of the Cuban Economy (ASCE), Florida International University, Miami, 12–14 August.

Diaz-Briquets, S. and Pérez-López, J.F. (1995) 'The Special Period and the Environment', *Cuba in Transition, ASCE,* Vol. 5, Miami: Florida International University, pp 281–92.

Diaz-Briquets, S. and Pérez-López, J.F. (2000) *Conquering Nature: The Environmental Legacy of Socialism in Cuba*, Pittsburgh, PA: University of Pittsburgh Press.

Dietz, S. (2000) *Does an Environmental Kuznets Curve Exist for Biodiversity?*, Zurich: Institut fur Wirtschaftsforschung.

Dinham, A. (2005) 'Empowered or Over-Powered? The Real Experiences of Local Participation in the UK's New Deal For Communities', *Community Development Journal*, vol 40, no 3, pp 301-12.

Dobson, A. (1998) *Justice and the Environment: Conceptions of Environmental Sustainability and Dimensions of Social Justice*, Oxford: Oxford University Press.

Dobson, A. (2003) *Citizenship and the Environment*, Oxford: Oxford University Press.

Dobson, A. (2007) *Green Political Thought*, London/New York: Routledge.

Dolowitz, D. and Marsh, D. (2000) 'Learning from Abroad: The Role of Policy Transfer in Contemporary Policy-Making', *Governance*, vol 13, no 1, pp 5-24.

Dominick, R. (1998) 'Capitalism, Communism, and Environmental Protection – Lessons from the German Experience', *Environmental History*, vol 3, no 3, pp 311-32.

Dorling, D. (2010) 'The Economics of Inequality and the Natural Environment', http://sasi.group.shef.ac.uk/presentations/crete/

Dowler, E.A. and O'Connor, D. (2012) 'Rights-Based Approaches to Addressing Food Poverty and Food Insecurity in Ireland and UK', *Social Science and Medicine*, vol 74, no 1, pp 44–51.

Doyal, L. and Gough, I. (1991) *A Theory of Human Need*, London: Macmillan.

Dryzek, J. (1990) *Discursive Democracy: Politics, Policy and Political Sciences*, Cambridge: Cambridge University Press.

Du, Y. et al (2006) 'Impact of the Guest Worker System on Poverty and Wellbeing of Migrants Workers in Urban China', unpublished paper, Canberra: Australia National University.

Du, Y. and Parsons, J. (2009) 'Update on the Cost of Nuclear Power', Center for Energy and Environmental Policy Research (CEEPR) No 09-004, Cambridge, MA: CEEPR.

Duchin, F. (1998) *Structural Economics: Measuring Change in Technology, Lifestyles and the Environment*, Washington, DC: Island Press.

Dunkerley, J. (2007) 'Evo Morales, the "Two Bolivias" and the Third Bolivian Revolution', *Journal of Latin American Studies*, vol 38, no 1, pp 133-66.

Dworkin, R. (1993) 'Integrity', in M. Fisk (ed) *Justice*, Atlantic Highlands: Humanities Press.

Eames, M. and Adebowale, M. (eds) (2002) *Sustainable Development and Social Inclusion: Towards an Integrated Approach to Research*, York: Joseph Rowntree Foundation/YPS.

Easterlin, R.A. (2013) 'Happiness, Growth and Public Policy', *Economic Inquiry*, vol 51, no 1, pp 1–15.

Economy, E. (2005) *The River Runs Black,* Ithaca, NY: Cornell University Press.

ECRI (European Commission against Racism and Intolerance) (2012) *ECRI Report on Sweden*, Strasbourg: Council of Europe.

Edelstein, M.R. (2007) *Cultures of Contamination; Legacies of Pollution in Russia and the US*, Research in Social Problems and Public Policy vol 14, New York, NY: Elsevier.

Edgerly, J. and Borrelli, D. (2007) *Moving Toward Zero: From Waste Management to Resource Recovery School*, Montpelier, VT: Toxics Action Center.

EIU (Economist Intelligence Unit) (2011) 'Democracy Index', London: The Economist.

EJRC (2012) 'Environmental Justice Resource Center, Environmental Justice Timeline – Milestones', www.ejrc.cau.edu/summit2/percent20EJTimeline.pdf

Ekins, P. and Lockwood, M. (2011) *Tackling Fuel Poverty During the Transition to a Low-Carbon Economy*, York: Joseph Rowntree Foundation.

ELF (Environmental Law Foundation) (2009) *Cost Barriers to Environmental Justice*, London: ELF.

Eltis, D. and Engerman, S.L. (2011) *The Cambridge World History of Slavery: Volume 3, AD 1420 – AD 1804*, Cambridge: Cambridge University Press.

Enoch, M. et al (2004) 'The Effect of Economic Restrictions on Transport Practices in Cuba', *Transport Policy*, vol 11, no 1, pp 67–76.

Environmental Audit Committee (2010) 'Air Quality', www.publications.parliament.uk/pa/cm200910/cmselect/cmenvaud/229/22908.htm

Environmental Objectives Council (2008) 'Sweden's Environmental Objectives – No Time to Lose', Stockholm: EOC.

EPI (Environmental Performance Index) (2012a) 'Environmental Performance Index Summary Report'(based on 2010 data), www.epi.yale.edu

EPI (Environmental Performance Index) (2012b) 'Country rankings:Bolivia', New Haven, CT: Yale University.

Escobar, A. (1996) 'Constructing Nature: Elements for a Post Industrial Political Ecology', in R. Peet and M. Watts (eds) *Liberation Ecologies: Environment, Development, Social Movements*, London and New York: Routledge, pp 46-68.

Esping-Andersen, G (1990) *The Three Worlds of Welfare Capitalism*, Princeton, NJ: Princeton University Press.

Espino, M.D. (2008) 'International Tourism in Cuba: An Update', *Cuba in Transition*, vol 18, Papers and Proceedings of the Eighteenth Annual Meeting of the Association for the Study of the Cuban Economy (ASCE), Miami, Florida, 5–7 August 2008.

ESRC (Economic and Social Research Council) (2001) 'Environmental Justice: Rights and Means to a Healthy Environment for All', ESRC Global Environmental Change Programme, Special Briefing No 7, University of Sussex.

ETC (Action Group on Erosion, Technology and Concentration) (2010) 'Geopiracy: The Case Against Geoengineering', www. etcgroup.org/sites/www.etcgroup.org/files/publication/pdf_file/ ETC_geopiracy_4web.pdf

European Commission (2011) 'EC takes UK to Court on Cost of Environment Cases', *European Commission News,* 6 April.

European Environment Agency (2011) 'Air Pollution: Sweden', www. eea.europa.eu/soer/countries/se/soertopic_view?topic=air%20 pollution

Evans, B. and Percy, S. (1999) 'The Opportunities and Challenges for Local Environmental Policy and Action in the UK', in S. Buckingham-Hatfield and S. Percy (eds) *Constructing Local Environmental Agendas: People, Places and Participation,* London: Routledge.

Faber, D. (ed) (1998) *The Struggle for Ecological Democracy: Environmental Justice Movements in the United States,* New York: The Guilford Press.

Faber, D. (2008) *Capitalizing on Environmental Injustice: The Polluter-Industrial Complex in the Age of Globalization,* Lanham, MD: Rowman and Littlefield.

Faber, D. and O'Connor, J. (1993) 'Capitalism and the Crisis of Environmentalism', in R. Hofrichter (ed) *Toxic Struggles: The Theory and Practice of Environmental Justice,* Gabriola Island, BC: New Society Publishers.

Fahmy, E. et al (2011) 'Distributional Impact of UK Climate Change Policy: Interim Report', *JRF Programme Paper: Climate Change and Social Justice,* York: Joseph Rowntree Foundation.

Fairbrother, M. (2012) 'Rich People, Poor People, and Environmental Concern: Evidence across Nations and Time', *European Sociological Review,* vol 29, no 5, pp 910-22.

Fairburn, J. et al (2009) 'Environmental Justice in South Yorkshire: Locating Social Deprivation and Poor Environments Using Multiple Indicators', *Local Environment,* vol 14, no 2, pp 139-54.

Fan, C. (2008) *China on the Move: Migration, the State, and the Household,* New York: Routledge.

Fan, C. and Sun, M. (2008) 'Regional Inequality in China, 1978–2006', *Eurasian Geography and Economics,* vol 49, no 1, pp 1-20.

FAO (2013) 'Hunger Portal', Food and Agriculture Organisation of the United Nations, www.fao.org/hunger/en/

Farthing, L. and Kohl, B. (2010) 'Social Control: Bolivia's New Approach to Coca Reduction', *Latin American Perspectives,* vol 37, no 4, pp 197-213.

Felipe, J. et al (2008) 'The Diverging Patterns of Profitability. Investment and growth of China and India, during 1980–2003', *World Development*, vol 36, no 5, pp 741–9.

Felt, U. et al (2009) 'Science and Governance: Taking European Knowledge-society Seriously', Report of the Expert Group on Science and Governance to the Science, Economy and Society Directorate, Luxembourg: Directorate-General for Research, European Commission Office for Official Publications of the European Communities.

Ferlay, J. et al (2008) 'Cancer Incidence and Mortality Worldwide: IARC CancerBase No. 10', Lyon, France: International Agency for Research on Cancer.

Fernández, S.J. (2002) *Encumbered Cuba: Capital Markets and Revolt, 1878–1895*, Gainesville: University Press of Florida.

Fick, J. et al (2011) 'Results from the Swedish National Screening Programme 2010: Subreport 3', Pharmaceuticals, Stockholm, Sweden: IVL Swedish Environmental Research Institute Ltd.

Fielding, J. (2007) 'Environmental Injustice or Just the Lie of the Land: An Investigation of the Socio-Economic Class of Those at Risk from Flooding in England and Wales', *Sociological Research Online*, vol 12, no 4.

Fielding, J.L. (2012) 'Inequalities in Exposure and Awareness of Flood Risk in England and Wales', *Disasters*, vol 36, no 3, pp 477-94.

First National People of Color (1991) *Principles of Environmental Justice*, Washington, DC: First Nation People of Color Environmental Leadership Summit.

Fitzpatrick, T. (ed) (2011) *Understanding the Environment and Social Policy*, Bristol: Policy Press.

Fitzpatrick, T. (ed) (2014) *International Handbook on Social Policy and the Environment*, Cheltenham: Edward Elgar.

FOE (Friends of the Earth) (2001) *Pollution and Poverty - Breaking the Link,* London: Friends of the Earth.

FON (Friends of Nature) (2007) *Environmental Green Book*, Beijing: Friends of Nature.

Foreman, C. (1998) *The Promise and Peril of Environmental Justice*, Washington, DC: Brookings Institution Press.

Foresight (2011) *The Future of Food and Farming*, London: Government Office for Science.

Fosset, M. and Warren, W. (2005) 'Overlooked Implications of Ethnic Preferences for Residential Segregation in Agent-Based Models', *Urban Studies*, vol 42, no 11, pp 1893-917.

Foster, J.B. (2000) *Marx's Ecology*, New York: Monthly Review Press.

Foster, J.B. (2008) *Ecology and the Transition from Capitalism to Socialism*, New York: Monthly Review Press.

Foster, J.B. (2010) *Ecology against Capitalism*, New York: Monthly Review Press.

Foster, J.B. et al (2010) *The Ecological Rift: Capitalisms War on the Earth*, New York: Monthly Review Press.

Frank, A. (1967) *Capitalism and Underdevelopment in Latin America*, New York: Monthly Review Press.

Franzen, A. and Meyer, R. (2010) 'Environmental Attitudes in Cross-National Perspective: A Multilevel Analysis of the ISSP 1993 and 2000', *European Sociological Review*, vol 26, no 2, pp 219-34.

Fraser, N. (1992) 'Rethinking the Public Sphere: A Contribution to the Critique of Actually Existing Democracy', in C. Calhoun (ed) *Habermas and the Public Sphere*, Cambridge, MA: MIT Press, pp 109-42.

Freedom House (2008) *Change in Cuba: How Citizens View Their Country's Future*, Special Report, Washington, DC: Freedom House.

Friedl, B. and Getzner, M. (2003) 'Determinants of CO_2 Emissions in a Small Open Economy', *Ecological Economics*, vol 45, no 1, pp 133-48.

Friedman, M. (1952) *Capitalism and Freedom*, Chicago, IL: University of Chicago Press.

Freudenburg, W.R. and Gramling, R. (2011) *Blowout in the Gulf: The BP Oil Spill Disaster and the Future of Energy in America*, Cambridge, MA: The MIT Press.

Fuentes, F. (2011) 'Bolivia: Development Before Environment?', *Links: International Journal of Socialist Renewal*, http://links.org.au/node/2483

Fukuyama, F. (1992) *The End of History and the Last Man*, New York: Free Press.

Funes Monzote, R. (2008) *From Rainforest to Cane Field in Cuba: An Environmental History since 1492*, Chapel Hill, NC: The University of North Carolina Press.

Galeano, J. (2010) Régimen Cubano Eliminará Tarjeta de Racionamiento, La Prensa.com.ni, Managua, Nicaragua, 10 November 2010, http://m.laprensa.com.ni/internacionales/43177.

Galeotti, M. al (2006) 'Reassessing the Environmental Kuznets Curve for CO_2 Emissions: A Robustness Exercise', *Ecological Economics*, vol 57, no 2, pp 156-63.

Garcia Linera, Á. et al (eds) (2010) *El Estado. Campo de Lucha. La Muela del Diablo*, La Paz: CLACSO, Comuna.

Geddes, M. (2010) 'The Bolivian Road to Socialism', *Red Pepper*, September.

Gedicks, A. (1993) *The New Resource Wars: Native and Environmental Struggles Against Multinational Corporations*, Boston, MA: South End Press.

George, S. (1991) *The Debt Boomerang: How Third World Debt Harms Us All*, London: Macmillan.

Georgescu-Roegen, N. (1971) *The Entropy Law and the Economic Process*, Cambridge: Harvard University Press.

GGGI (Global Green Growth Institute) (2011) *Green Growth in Motion: Sharing Korean Experience*, Seoul, Korea: GGGI.

GGGI (2013) Overview, GGGI, http://gggi.org/about-gggi/organizational/organizational-overview/

Gibson-Graham, J.K. (1996) *The End of Capitalism (As We Knew It): A Feminist Critique of Political Economy*, Oxford: Blackwell.

Gibson-Graham, J.K. (2006) *Postcapitalist Politics*, Minneapolis: University of Minnesota Press.

Gill, S. (1993) *Gramsci, Historical Materialism and International Relations*, Cambridge: Cambridge University Press.

Ginsburg, H.L. and Rosenthal, M.G. (2006) 'The Ups and Downs of the Swedish Welfare State: General Trends', Benefits and Caregiving, New Politics, vol 11, no 1, pp 70-78.

Global Footprint Network (2012) www.footprintnetwork.org/en/index.php/GFN/

Global Legal Group (2009) 'Korea', in *The International Comparative Legal Guide to Environment Law 2009*, pp 274-80.

Globalization Monitor (2010) 'Complicity, Campaigns, Collaboration and Corruption: Strategies and Responses to European Corporations and Lobbyists in China', www.globalmon.org.hk/sites/default/files/attachment/0519lobbying-report1.pdf

Globalization Monitor (2012) 'Report on the Malpractices and Social and Environmental Abuses of European Companies Investing in China', www.globalmon.org.hk/content/report-malpractices-and-social-and-environmental-abuses-european-companies-investing-china

Gobierno de Bolivia (2006) *Plan Nacional de Desarrollo (National Development Plan)*, La Paz: Government of Bolivia.

Gobierno de Bolivia (2009) *República del Bolivia, Constitución de 2009 (Constitution of 2009)*, La Paz: Bolivia.

Gobierno de Bolivia (2012) 'Framework Law of Mother Earth and Integral Development for Living Well', from www.lexivox.org/norms/BO-L-N300.xhtml.

Goldtooth,T.B.K. (1995) 'Indigenous Nations: Summary of Sovereignty and It's Implications for Environmental Protection', in B. Bryant (ed) *Environmental Justice: Issues, Policies and Solutions*, Washington, DC: Island Press.

Gonzalez, C. (2003) 'Seasons of Resistance: Sustainable Agriculture and Food Security in Cuba', *Tulane Environmental Law Journal 16*, vol 16 (Special Issue: Environmental Law and Sustainable Development in 21st Century Cuba), pp 685-732.

Gonzalez, C.G. (2001) 'Beyond Eco-Imperialism: An Environmental Justice Critique of Free Trade', *University of Denver Law Review*, vol 78, pp 981-90.

Gonzalez, M. (1992) 'Can Castro survive?', *International Socialism* (London), Spring–Summer, pp 83-123.

Gore, A. (2000) *Earth in the Balance: Ecology and the Human Spirit*, Boston, MA: Houghton Mifflin.

Gough, I. (1994) 'Economic Institutions and the Satisfaction of Human Needs', *Journal of Economic Issues*, vol 28, no 1, pp 25-66.

Gough, I. (2011) *Climate Change, Double Injustice and Social Policy: A Case Study of the United Kingdom*, Geneva: UNRISD.

Gough, I. (2013) 'Carbon Mitigation Policies, Distributional Dilemmas and Social Policies', *Journal of Social Policy*, vol 42, no 2, pp 191-213.

Gould, K. et al (1996) *Local Environmental Struggles: Citizen Activism in the Treadmill of Production*, Cambridge: Cambridge University Press.

Gouldson, A. and Sullivan, R. (2007) 'Corporate Environmentalism: Tracing the Links Between Policies and Performance Using Corporate Reports And Public Registers', *Business Strategy and the Environment*, vol 16, no 1, pp 1–11.

Gracia, J.N. and Koh, H.K. (2011) 'Promoting Environmental Justice', *American Journal of Public Health*, vol 101, no S1, pp S14–S16.

Grandjean, P. (2013) *Only One Chance: How Environmental Pollution Impairs Brain Development – and How to Protect the Brains of the Next Generation*, New York: Oxford University Press.

Grant, W.B. (2009) 'Air Pollution in Relation to U.S. Cancer Mortality Rates: An Ecological Study; Likely Role of Carbonaceous Aerosols and Polycyclic Aromatic Hydrocarbons', *Anticancer Research*, vol 29, no 9, pp 3537-45.

Gray Molina, G. (2010) 'The Challenge of Progressive Change under Evo Morales', in K. Weyland et al (eds) *Leftist Governments in Latin America: Successes and Shortcomings*, Cambridge: Cambridge University Press, pp 57-76.

Graziano da Silva, J. (2013) Director-General of the United Nations Organization for Food and Agriculture (FAO), Congratulatory letter to Fidel Castro, 6 May, Prensa Latina.

Green Choices (2012) 'Packaging', www.greenchoices.org/green-living/food-drink/packaging

Green Korea United (2008) 'Environmental Problems Related to Military Activities', Submission to UNEP Asia-Pacific meeting, CSO Report from Republic of Korea.

Greenberg, J. (1993) 'The Social Side of Fairness: Interpersonal and Informational Classes of Organizational Justice', in R. Cropanzano (ed) *Justice in the Workplace: Approaching Fairness in Human Resource Management*, Hillsdale, NJ: Erlbaum, pp 79-103.

Groat, C.G. et al (2012) 'Fact-Based Regulation for Environmental Protection in Shale Gas Development', University of Texas, Energy Institute.

Grossman, G. and Krueger, A. (1995) 'Economic Growth and the Environment', *Quarterly Journal of Economics*, vol 110, no 2, pp 353-77.

Grossman, R. and Daneker, G. (1977) 'Jobs and Energy, Washington, DC: Environmentalists for Full Employment', in K.S. Shrader-Frechette (1991) *Risk and Rationality: Philosophical Foundations for Populist Reforms*, Berkeley, CA: University of California Press.

Gruber, N. and Galloway, J.N. (2008) 'An Earth-System Perspective of the Global Nitrogen Cycle', *Nature*, vol 451, no 7176, pp 293-6.

Gudynas, E. (2013) 'Extracciones, Extractivismos, y Extrahecciones: Un Marco Conceptual Sobre La Apropiación de Recursos Naturales', Observatorio del Desarrollo/CLAES, Centro Latinoamericano de Ecología Social, February, gudynas-apropiacionextractivismoextraheccionesoded2013

Guevara-Stone, L. (2009) 'La Revolucion Energetica: Cuba's Energy Revolution', *Renewable Energy World Magazine*, vol 12, www.renewableenergyworld.com/rea/news/article/2009/04/

Gunnarsson-Östling, U. and Höjer, M. (2011) 'Scenario Planning for Sustainability in Stockholm, Sweden: Environmental Justice Considerations', *International Journal of Urban and Regional Research*, vol 35, no 5, pp 1048-67.

Gustafson, B. (2006) 'Spectacles of Autonomy and Crisis; or, What Bulls and Beauty Queens Have to Do with Regionalism in Eastern Bolivia', *Journal of Latin American Anthropology*, vol 11, no 2, pp 351-80.

Ha, S.-K. (2010) 'Housing, Social Capital and Community Development in Seoul', *Cities*, vol 27, Supplement 1, pp S35-S42.

Habermas, J. (1984) *The Theory of Communicative Action, Volume 1, Reason and the Rationalization of Society*, Boston, MA: Beacon Press.

Hahnel, R. (2004) 'Protecting the Environment in a Participatory Economy', *Synthesis/Regeneration Online*, vol 34.

Hahnel, R. (2005) *Economic Justice and Democracy: From Competition to Cooperation*, Abingdon: Routledge.

Hamilton, D. (2002) 'Whither Cuban Socialism? The Changing Political Economy of the Cuban Revolution', *Latin American Perspectives*, vol 29, no 3, pp 18-39.

Hamilton, J.T. (1995) 'Testing for Environmental Racism: Prejudice, Profits, Political Power?', *Journal of Policy Analysis and Management*, vol 14, no 1, pp 107-32.

Hammersley, M. (1992) *What's Wrong with Ethnography?*, London: Routledge.

Han, M. (2001) *Reclamation of the Metropolitan Area and Environmental Justice*. Environmental Justice Forum in H. Lee (2009) The Political Ecology of Environmental Justice: Environmental Struggle and Injustice in the Yeongheung Island Coal Plant Controversy, PhD thesis, Florida: College of Social Sciences, Florida State University.

Hardin, G. (1968) 'The Tragedy of the Commons', *Science*, vol 162, no 3859, pp 1243-8.

Harnecker, M. (2010) 'Latin America and Twenty-First-Century Socialism: Inventing to Avoid Mistakes', *Monthly Review*, vol 62, no 3, pp 3-83.

Harvey, D. (1996) *Justice, Nature and the Geography of Difference*, London: Blackwell.

Harvey, D. (2000) *Spaces of Hope,* Edinburgh: University of Edinburgh Press.

Harvey, D. (2003) *The New Imperialism*, Oxford: Oxford University Press.

Harvey, D. (2006) *Spaces of Global Capitalism*, London/New York: Verso.

Harvey, D. (2010) *The Enigma of Capital, and the Crises of Capitalism*, New York: Oxford University Press.

Harvey, D. (2011) 'Nice Day for a Revolution', *Independent*, 29 April.

Hastings, A. (2007) 'Territorial Justice and Neighbourhood Environmental Services: A Comparison of Provision to Deprived and Better-off Neighbourhoods in the UK', *Environment and Planning C: Government and Policy*, vol 25, no 6, pp 896-917.

Hathaway, M. (2010) 'The Emergence of Indigeneity: Public Intellectuals and an Indigenous Space in Southwest China', *Cultural Anthropology*, vol 25, no 2, pp 301-33.

Hawken, P. et al (1999) *Natural Capitalism*, Snowmass, CO: Rocky Mountain Institute.

Hawkins, T.R. et al (2013) 'Comparative Environmental Life Cycle Assessment of Conventional and Electric Vehicles', *Journal of Industrial Ecology*, vol 17, no 1, pp 53–64.

Hayek, F.A. (1933) *Monetary Theory and the Trade Cycle*, London: Jonathan Cape.

Hayek, F.A. (1944) *The Road to Serfdom*, Chicago: University of Chicago Press.

Hayek, F.A. (1976) *Law, Legislation and Liberty, Vol 2*, London: Routledge.

Hernandez, R. (2008) 'On Cuban Democracy: Cuba and the Democratic Culture', in P. Brenner et al, *A Contemporary Cuba Reader: Reinventing the Revolution*, Plymouth: Rowman and Littlefield, pp 74-9.

Heynen, N.C. (2003) 'The Scalar Production of Injustice Within the Urban Forest', *Antipode*, vol 35, no 5, pp 980-98.

Hickman, L. (2010) 'James Lovelock on the Value of Sceptics and Why Copenhagen was Doomed', *Guardian*, 29 March.

Hickman, L. (2012) 'What is the Legacy of Rachel Carson's Silent Spring?', *Guardian,* 27 September.

Hills, J. (2012) *Getting the Measure of Fuel Poverty: Final Report of the Fuel Poverty Review*, CASE report 72, London: London School of Economics and Department for Energy and Climate Change.

Hills, J.A. et al (2010) *An Anatomy of Economic Inequality in the UK – Summary*, CASE report 60, London: London School of Economics and Political Science.

Hofman, I. and Ho, P. (2012) 'China's "Developmental Outsourcing": A Critical Examination of Chinese Global "Land Grabs" Discourse', *Journal of Peasant Studies*, vol 39, no 1, pp 1-48.

HMG (2005) *Securing the Future: Delivering UK Sustainable Development Strategy,* London: HM Government.

HMG (2011) *Enabling the Transition to a Green Economy: Government and Business Working Together,* London: HM Government.

Hofricher, R. (ed) (1993) *Toxic Struggles: The Theory and Practice of Environmental Justice*, Philadelphia, PA: New Society Publishers.

Holdaway, J. (2011) 'Environmental Justice, Health and Well-being; Reflections on the Chinese Experience', Research Seminar, 7 April 2011, UEA London, UK.

Holifield, R. (2004) 'Neoliberalism and Environmental Justice in the United States Environmental Protection Agency: Translating Policy into Managerial Practice in Hazardous Waste Remediation', *Geoforum*, vol 35, no 3, pp 285-97.

Holifield, R. (2012) 'The Elusive "Environmental Justice Community"': The Problem of Translating Places into Standardized Objects of Governance', Presentation to the Association of American Geographers Annual Meeting, New York, 24–28 February 2012.

Holloway, J. (2002) *Change the World without Taking Power*, London: Pluto Press.

Holloway, J. (2010) *Crack Capitalism*, London: Pluto Press.

Home Office (2011) *Equality Act 2010: Public Sector Equality Duty What Do I Need To Know? A Quick Start Guide for Public Sector Organisations*, London: Government Equalities Office.

House of Commons Energy and Climate Change Committee (2012) 'The EU Emissions Trading System: Tenth Report of Session 2010–12', London: The Stationery Office.

House of Commons Health Committee (2009) 'Health inequalities', London: The Stationery Office.

Hou, Y. (2012) 'Socialism and Ecological Crises: A View from China', *Journal of Sustainable Development*, vol 5, no 4, pp 126-31.

Houck, O.A. (2000) 'Environmental Law in Cuba', *Journal of Land Use and Environmental Law*, vol 16, no 1, pp 1-81.

Houck, O.A. (2003) 'Thinking about Tomorrow: Cuba's "Alternative Model" for Sustainable Development', *Tulane Environmental Law Journal*, vol 16, Special Issue: Environmental Law and Sustainable Development in 21st Century Cuba, pp 521-32.

Howie, R. (2012) 'Asbestos – Consequences of Inspectorate Failures', Presentation at Occupational Hygiene Conference 2012, Cardiff, BOHS, Chartered Society for Occupational Health Protection, Robin Howie Associates.

Hoxie, F.E. (1984) *A Final Promise: The Campaign to Assimilate the Indians, 1880– 1920*, Cambridge: Cambridge University Press.

IEA (International Energy Agency) (2011) *Emissions from Fuel Combustion 2011 – Highlights*, Paris, IEA.

IEA (2012) *Key World Energy Statistics*, Paris: IEA.

IEA (2013) *Energy Poverty*, Paris: IEA.

IFS (Institute for Fiscal Studies) (2012) *Living Standards, Poverty and Inequality in the UK: 2012*, London: IFS.

Igerud, M. (2011) 'Ethnic Congregation as a Segregation Factor in Göteborg, Sweden – A Study of Residential Ethnic Segregation Amongst Affluent and Poorer Immigrants', Göteborg: Department of Human and Economic Geography, Göteborg University.

IHS Global Insight (2011) 'China Passes the US as Largest Manufacturer', http://247wallst.com/2011/03/14/china-passes-the-us-as-largest-manufacturer/#ixzz2JSh4NqD8

ILO (International Labour Organization) (2013) 'Safety and Health at Work', www.ilo.org/global/topics/safety-and-health-at-work/lang--en/index.htm

IMF (International Monetary Fund) (2012) 'World Economic Outlook Database', www.imf.org/external/pubs/ft/weo/2012/02/weodata/index.aspx

INCPEN (Industrial Council for Packaging and the Environment) (2012) 'Legislation: Packaging and the Environment', www.incpen.org/displayarticle.asp?a=11&c=2

INE Bolivia (Instituto Nacional de Estadística. National Statistics Office) (2003) La Paz, INE (Instituto Nacional de Estadisticas de Bolivia/UMPA).

INE Bolivia (2013) La Paz 'Social Statistics', www.ine.gob.bo

Inglehart, R. (1990) *Culture Shift in Advanced Industrial Society*, Princeton, NJ: Princeton University Press.

Instituto Cubano de Radio y Televisión (2010) www.tvcubana.icrt.cu/noticias/el-instituto-cubano-de-radio-ytelevision-icrt/

Irwin, A. and Wynne, B. (1996) *Misunderstanding Science? The Public Reconstruction of Science and Technology*, Cambridge: Cambridge University Press.

Isaksson, K. (2001) 'The Future Traffic System? The Exercise of Power in Conflicts about Space and the Environment in the Traffic Issues of the Dennis Package', PhD thesis, Linköping Studies in Arts and Science, Linköping.

Jackson, T. (2009) *Prosperity without Growth: Economics for a Finite Planet*, London: Earthscan.

James, O.W. (2008) *The Selfish Capitalist*, London: Vermillion.

Jeon, J.K. (2003) 'The Saemangeum Reclamation Project and Circumstance-Alteration Principle under the Public Water-surface Reclamation Act', *Research on Environmental Laws*, vol 25, pp 81-99.

Jephcote, C. and Chen, H. (2012) 'Environmental Injustices of Children's Exposure to Air Pollution from Road-Transport within the Model British Multicultural City of Leicester 2000–09', *Science of the Total Environment*, vol 414, pp 140-51.

Jessop, B. (2004) 'Hollowing Out the "Nation-State" and Multi-Level Governance', in P. Kennett (ed) *A Handbook of Comparative Social Policy*, Cheltenham: Edward Elgar.

Jessop, B. (2012) 'Economic and Ecological Crises: Green New Deals and No-Growth Economies', *Development: Greening the Economy*, vol 55, no 1, pp 17-24.

Jevons, W.S. (1866) *The Coal Question: An Inquiry Concerning the Progress of the Nation, and the Probable Exhaustion of Our Coal-Mines*, London: Macmillan and Co.

Johnson, B.B. (2010) 'Decolonization and Its Paradoxes: The (Re) envisioning of Health Policy in Bolivia', *Latin American Perspectives*, vol 37, no 3, pp 139-59.

Johnson, M. et al (2005) 'Public opinion and dynamic representation in the American States: The Case of Environmental Attitudes', *Social Science Quarterly*, vol 86, pp 87-108.

Jones, R.E. and Dunlap, R.E. (1992) 'The Social Bases of Environmental Concern: Have They Changed Over Time?', *Rural Sociology*, vol 57, no 1, pp 28-47.

Jones, R.S. and Urasawa, S. (2012) *Promoting Social Cohesion in Korea*, OECD Economics Department Working Papers, No 963, Paris: OECD Publishing.

Jones, R.S. and Yoo, B. (2012) *Achieving the 'Low Carbon, Green Growth' Vision in Korea*, OECD Economics Department Working Papers, No 964, Paris: OECD Publishing.

Jonsson, A. (2005) 'Public Participation in Water Resource Management: Stakeholder Voices on Degree, Scale, Potential, and Methods for Future Water Management', *AMBIO: A Journal of the Human Environment*, vol 34, no 7, pp 495-500.

JSB (Jiangsu Statistical Bureau) (2006) *Survey Report on the Living Status of Rural Migrant Workers in Houzhou*, Jiangsu: JSB.

Juniper, T. (2012) 'We Must Put a Price on Nature if we are Going to Save it', 10 August, www.guardian.co.uk/environment/2012/aug/10/nature-economic-value-campaign

Kaatsch, P. (2010) 'Epidemiology of childhood cancer', *Cancer Treatment Reviews*, vol 36, no 4, pp 277-85.

Kang, D.M. (2010) *Towards Social Integration of the Korean Peninsula: Resolving Discrimination Against North Korean Defectors in South Korean Society*, Seoul: Seoul Yongsei University.

Kang, S. et al (2012) *Korea's Low-Carbon Green Growth Strategy*, Paris: OECD Development Centre.

Kann, M.E. (1986) 'Environmental Democracy in the United States', in S. Kamieniecki, R. Obrien and M. Clarke (eds) *Controversies in Environmental Policy*, Albany, NY: SUNY Press, pp 252-74.

Kapcia, A. (2008) *Cuba in Revolution: A History since the Fifties*, London: Reaktion Books.

Kari-Oca II declaration, 'Indigenous Peoples Global Conference on Rio+20 and Mother Earth', 17 June 2012, Museu da República in Rio de Janeiro, Brazil.

Keeley, J. and Yisheng, Z. (2011) *Green China: Chinese Insights on Environment and Development*, London: International Institute for Environment and Development.

Kennemore, A. and Weeks, G. (2011) 'Twenty-First Century Socialism? The Elusive Search for a Post-Neoliberal Development Model in Bolivia and Ecuador', *Bulletin of Latin American Research*, vol 30, no 3, pp 267-81.

Kennet, P. (2001) *Comparative Social Policy: Theory and Research*, Buckingham: Open University Press.

Kettunen, J. et al (2007) 'Associations of Fine and Ultrafine Particulate Air Pollution With Stroke Mortality in an Area of Low Air Pollution Levels', *Stroke*, vol 38, pp 918-22.

Keys, T. and Malnight, T. (2012) *Corporate Clout: The Influence of the World's Largest 100 Economic Entities*, www.globaltrends.com: Global Trends.

Khan, J. (2003) 'Wind Power Planning In Three Swedish Municipalities', *Journal of Environmental Planning and Management*, vol 46, no 4, pp 563-81.

Kim, C. et al (2010) 'Ambient Particulate Matter as a Risk Factor for Suicide', *American Journal of Psychiatry*, vol 167, no 9, pp 1100-07.

Kim, S.-H. (2010) 'Issues of squatters and eviction in Seoul: From the perspectives of the dual roles of the state', *City, Culture and Society*, vol 1, no 3, pp 135-43.

Kincheloe, J. and McLaren, P. (1994) 'Rethinking Critical Theory and Qualitative Research', in N. Denzin and Y. Lincoln (ed) *Handbook of Qualitative Research*, California: Sage.

King, D.M. (2012) 'Cuban Sustainability: The Effects of Economic Isolation on Agriculture and Energy', Paper presentation for the Western Political Science Association, Portland, OR, 24 March 2012.

Kiniyalocts, M. (2000) *Environmental Justice: Avoiding the Difficulty of Proving Discriminatory Intent in Hazardous Waste Siting Decisions*, North America Series, L.T. Center, University of Wisconsin-Madison.

Klar, M. and Kasser, T. (2009) 'Some Benefits of Being an Activist: Measuring Activism and Its Role in Psychological Well-Being', *Political Psychology*, vol 30, no 5, pp 755-77.

Knox, G. (2005) 'Childhood Cancers and Atmospheric Carcinogens', *Journal of Epidemiological Community Health*, vol 59, pp 101-5.

Knox, G. (2008) 'Atmospheric Pollutants and Mortalities in English Local Authority Areas', *Journal of Epidemiological Community Health*, vol 62, pp 442-7.

Koh, Y. (2011) *Social Safety Net in Korea: From Welfare to Workfare*, Seoul, Korea: Development Institute.

Kohl, B. and Farthing, L. (2006) *Impasse in Bolivia: Neoliberal Hegemony and Popular Resistance*, London: Zed.

Kohl, B. and Farthing, L. (2012) 'Material Constraints to Popular Imaginaries: The Extractive Economy and Resource Nationalism in Bolivia', *Political Geography*, vol 31, no 4, pp 225-35.

Kovel, J. (2002) *The Enemy of Nature: The End of Capitalism or the End of the World*, London: Zed Books.

Kratch, K. (1995) 'Special Report on Environmental Justice: Grassroots Reach the Whitehouse Lawn', *Environmental Solutions*, vol 8, no 5, pp 68-77.

Kuhn, T. (1962) *The Structure of Scientific Revolutions*, Chicago: University of Chicago Press.

Kumar, P. and Aggarwal, S.C. (2003) 'Does an Environmental Kuznets Curve Exist for Changing Land Use? Empirical Evidence from Major States of India', *International Journal of Sustainable Development*, vol 6, pp 231-45.

Kümmerer, K. (2009) 'The Presence of Pharmaceuticals in The Environment Due to Human Use – Present Knowledge and Future Challenges', *Journal of Environmental Management*, vol 90, no 8, pp 2354-66.

La Rue, F. (2010) Full text of the press statement delivered by the UN Special Rapporteur on the promotion and protection of the right to freedom of opinion and expression, after the conclusion of his visit to the Republic of Korea. Seoul http://www2.ohchr.org/english/issues/opinion/docs/ROK-Pressstatement17052010.pdf

LaDuke, W. (1999) *All Our Relations: Native Struggles for Land Rights and Life*, Boston, MA: South End Press.

Lake, R.W. (1993) 'Rethinking NIMBY', *Journal of the American Planning Association*, vol 59, no 1, pp 87-93.

Lake, R.W. and Disch, L. (1992) 'Structural Constraints and Pluralist Contradictions in Hazardous Waste Regulation', *Environment and Planning A*, vol 24, no 5, pp 663-81.

Lakes, T. et al (2013) 'Development of an Environmental Justice Index to Determine Socio-Economic Disparities of Noise Pollution and Green Space in Residential Areas in Berlin', *Journal of Environmental Planning and Management* (ahead-of-print), pp 1-19, www.tandfonline.com/doi/abs/10.1080/09640568.2012.755461

Lambert, T. and Boerner, C. (1997) 'Environmental Inequality: Economic Causes, Economic Solutions', *Yale Journal on Regulation*, vol 14, no 1, pp 195-234.

Lappé, F.M. et al (1998) *World Hunger: 12 Myths*, New York: Grove Press.

Lash, S. and Urry, J. (1987) *The End of Organized Capitalism*, Cambridge: Polity Press.

Latour, B. (2004) *Politics of Nature*, Cambridge, MA: Harvard University Press.

Law Library of Congress (2013) 'Sweden: Amended Transgender Law Now in Force', 11 January: LOC.

Le Grand, J. (2012) *Government Paternalism: Nanny State or Helpful Friend?*, 40 Years of Policy and Politics Conference 2012, University of Bristol.

Lee, H. (2009) 'The Political Ecology of Environmental Justice: Environmental Struggle and Injustice in the Yeongheung Island Coal Plant Controversy', PhD thesis, Florida: College of Social Sciences, Florida State University.

Lee, S.-K. and Müller, A.R. (2012) 'The Republic of Korean External Strategy Qualms: Analysis of Korean Overseas Agricultural Investment within the Global Food System', *International Conference on Global Land Grabbing II*, Ithaca, NY: Department of Development Sociology, Cornell University, Land Deals Politics Initiative (LDPI).

Lei, X. (2009) 'China's Environmental Activism in the Age of Globalization', Working Paper CUTP/006, London: City University.

Leonard, A. (2010) *The Story of Stuff*, London: Constable,

Leventhal, G.S. (1980) 'What Should be Done with Equity Theory? New Approaches to the Study of Fairness in Social Relationships', in K. Gergen, M. Greenberg and R. Willis (eds) *Social Exchange: Advances in Theory and Research*, New York: Plenum, pp 27-55.

Levins, R. (2005) 'How Cuba is Going Ecological', *Capitalism Nature Socialism*, vol 16, no 3, pp 7-25.

Levins, R. (2010) 'How to Visit a Socialist Country', *Monthly Review*, vol 11, April.

Levitas, R. et al (2007) *The Multi-dimensional Analysis of Social Exclusion*, London: Cabinet Office Social Exclusion Task Force.

Library of Congress (2011) Bill Summary & Status 112th Congress (2011–2012), H.J.RES.33, http://thomas.loc.gov/cgi-bin/bdquery/D?d112:9:./temp/~bddahA

Lievesley, G. (2004) *The Cuban Revolution: Past, Present and Future Perspectives*, Basingstoke: Palgrave Macmillan.

Liu, L. (2010) 'Made in China: Cancer Villages', *Environment: Science and Policy for Sustainable Development*, vol 52, no 2, pp 8-21.

Liu, Z. (2005) 'Institution and Inequality: The Hukou System in China', *Journal of Comparative Economics*, vol 33, no 1, pp 133-57.

Lohmann, L. (2010) 'Uncertainty Markets and Carbon Markets: Variations on Polanyian Themes', *New Political Economy*, vol 15, no 2, pp 225-54.

Lönnroth, M. (2010) 'The Organisation of Environmental Policy in Sweden: A Historical Perspective', Report 6404, Stockholm: Swedish EPA.

López Vigil, M. (2009) 'The Cuban Media' in P. Brenner et al, *A Contemporary Cuba Reader: Reinventing the Revolution*, Plymouth: Rowman and Littlefield, pp 386-93.

Lora-Wainwright, A. et al (2012) 'Learning to Live with Pollution: The Making of Environmental Subjects in a Chinese Industrialized Village', *The China Journal*, no 68, pp 106-24.

Low, N. and Gleeson, B. (1998) *Justice, Society and Nature: An Exploration of Political Ecology*, London: Routledge.

Lowndes, V. et al (1998) *Enhancing Public Participation in Local Government*, London: DETR.

Lu, F. (2011) 'Ecological Values and Capitalism', in J. Keeley and Z. Yisheng (eds) *Green China: Chinese Insights on Environment and Development*, London: International Institute for Environment and Development.

Lubman, S. (2010) 'Strengthening Enforcement of China's Environmental Protection Laws, China Real Time Report', *Wall Street Journal*, 22 March.

Lucas, K. and Currie, G. (2012) 'Developing Socially Inclusive Transportation Policy: Transferring the United Kingdom Policy Approach to the State of Victoria?', *Transportation*, vol 39, no 1, pp 151-73.

Lucas, K. et al (2001) 'Transport, the Environment and Social Exclusion. Environment and Equity Concerns about Transport', Findings Ref 721, York: Joseph Rowntree Foundation.

Lucas K. et al (2003) *What's in a Name? Local Agenda 21, Community Planning and Neighbourhood Renewal*, York: Joseph Rowntree Foundation.

Lucas. K. et al (2004) *Environment and Social Justice: Rapid Research and Evidence Review*, SDRN, London: Policy Studies Institute.

Ludlum, S. (2008) 'Cuba in the Post-Bipolar World', Undergraduate course handout, University of Sheffield.

Ludlum, S. (2009) 'Cuban Labour at 50: What About the Workers?', *Bulletin of Latin American Research*, vol 28, no 4, pp 542-57.

Ludlum, S. (2011) 'Restructuring the Revolution', *Cuba Si*, 26 July, www.cuba-solidarity.org.uk/cubasi_article.asp?ArticleID=151

Lutz, W. et al (2001) 'The End of World Population Growth', *Nature*, vol 412, pp 543-45.

Ma, C. (2010) 'Who Bears the Environmental Burden in China – An Analysis of the Distribution of Industrial Pollution Sources?', *Ecological Economics*, vol 69, no 9, pp 1869-76.

Maal-Bared, R. (2006) 'Comparing Environmental Issues in Cuba Before and After the Special Period: Balancing Sustainable Development and Survival', *Environment International*, vol 32, pp 349–58.

Maas, J. et al (2009) 'Morbidity is Related to a Green Living Environment', *Journal of Epidemiology and Community Health*, vol 63, pp 967-73.

Maas, J. et al (2006) 'Green Space, Urbanity, and Health: How Strong is the Relation?' *Journal of Epidemiology and Community Health*, vol 60, no 7, pp 587-92.

Macmillan Cancer Support (2013) 'Cancer Mortality Trends: 1992–2020', http://www.macmillan.org.uk/Documents/AboutUs/Newsroom/Mortality-trends-2013-executive-summary-FINAL.pdf

Magdoff, F. and Foster, J.B. (2011) *What Every Environmentalist Needs to Know About Capitalism*, New York: Monthly Review Press.

Maldonado, A. (2003) 'Cuba's Environment: Today and Tomorrow – An Action Plan', *Cuba in Transition 13. Papers and Proceedings of the Thirteenth Annual Meeting of the Association for the Study of the Cuban Economy*, Silver Spring, MD: ASCE.

Mansbridge, J. (1990) *Beyond Adversary Democracy*, New York: Basic Books.

Mansbridge, J. (1992) 'A Deliberative Theory of Interest Representation', in M.P Petracca (ed) *The Politics of Interests: Interest Groups Transformed*, Boulder, CO: Westview Press.

Manser, R. (1993) *Failed Transitions: The Eastern European Economy and Environment Since the Fall of Communism*, New York: The New Press.

Marable, M. (1983) *How Capitalism Underdeveloped Black America*, Boulder, CO: Westview Press.

Marmot, M. et al (2010) *Fair Society, Healthy Lives: A Strategic Review of Health Inequalities in England Post-2010*, London: UCL.

Martin, J. (2009) 'Cuba 50 Years Later – Where is the Revolution Going?', www.marxist.com/cuba-50-years-later-part-two.htm

Martinez-Alier, J. (2003) *Environmentalism of the Poor*, Basingstoke: Edward Elgar.

Martinez-Alier, J. (2010) 'Environmental Justice and Economic Degrowth: An Alliance between Two Movements', Coimbra, 20–22 October 2010, ICTA, Barcelona: Universitat Autònoma de Barcelona.

Martinez-Zarzoso, I. and Bengochea-Morancho, A. (2004) 'Pooled Mean Group Estimation for an Environmental Kuznets Curve for CO_2', *Economics Letters*, vol 82, pp 121-6.

Marx, K. (1969) [1875] *Critique of the Gotha Programme*, Moscow; Progress Publishers.

Max-Neef, M. (1995) 'Economic Growth and Quality of Life: A Threshold Hypothesis', *Ecological Economics*, vol 15, no 2, pp 115-18.

McAdam, D. et al (1996) *Comparative Perspectives on Social Movements*, Cambridge: Cambridge University Press.

McConnell, J. (2002) Speech on the Scottish Executive's environmental policy, Dynamic Earth, Edinburgh, 18 February.

McCulloch, J. and Tweedale, G. (2008) *Defending the Indefensible – The Global Asbestos Industry and its Fight for Survival*, Oxford: Oxford University Press.

McLaren, D. et al (1999) 'Pollution Injustice: The Geographic Relation Between Household Income and Polluting Factories', London: Friends of the Earth.

Meadows, D.H. et al (1972) *The Limits to Growth*, New York: Universe Books.

Melamed, C.R. et al (2011) 'Jobs, Growth and Poverty: What Do We Know, What Don't We Know, What Should We Know?', *ODI Background Notes*, May.

Mellor, M. (2006) 'Socialism', in A. Dobson and R. Eckersley (eds) *Political Theory and the Ecological Challenge*, Cambridge: Cambridge University Press.

Meng, X. and Zhang, J. (2001) 'The Two-Tier Labor Market in China – Occupational Segregation and Wage Differentials between Urban Residents and Rural Migrants in Shanghai', *Journal of Comparative Economics*, vol 29, no 3, pp 485-504.

MEP - China (Ministry of Environmental Protection, China) (1995–2009) 'State of Environment – Various Years', MEP.

MEP - China (1998) 'Official Reply of the State Council Concerning Acid Rain Control Zone and Sulfur Dioxide Pollution Control Zone', MEP.

MEP - China (2009) 'State of Environment 2009', MEP.

Mertha, A.C. (2008) *China's Water Warriors: Citizen Action and Policy Change*, Ithaca, NY: Cornell University Press.

Mesa-Lago, C. (2002) 'Growing Economic and Social Disparities in Cuba: Impact and Recommendations for Change', The Cuba Transition Project, Institute for Cuban and Cuban-American Studies (ICCAS), University of Miami.

Mesa-Lago, C. (2005) 'The Cuban Economy Today: Salvation or Damnation', The Cuba Transition Project, Institute for Cuban and Cuban-American Studies, University of Miami.

Mesa-Lago, C. (2006) 'Assessing Cuba's Economy Current and Future Capacity to Provide Social Justice', Presentation to Canadian Foundation for the Americas on 'Government and Social Justice in Cuba', Ottawa, June.

Meyer, A. (2000) *Contraction and Convergence: The Global Solution to Climate Change*, Cambridge: Green Books.

Ministry of Foreign Affairs (2008) *National Report by the Republic of Cuba to the Universal Periodic Review of the Human Rights Council*, Geneva: HRC.

Ministry of Knowledge Economy (2009) *Strategic Road Map to Develop Green Energy Industry*, Seoul, Korea: Ministry of Knowledge Economy.

Ministry of the Environment, Sweden (2000) *The Swedish Environmental Code*, Stockholm: Ministry of the Environment.

Mitchell, G. and Norman, P. (2012) 'Longitudinal Environmental Justice Analysis: Co-Evolution of Environmental Quality and Deprivation in England, 1960–2007', *Geoforum*, vol 43, no 1, pp 44-57.

Mitchell, R. and Popham, F. (2008) 'Effect of Exposure to Natural Environment on Health Inequalities: An Observational Population Study', *Lancet*, vol 372, no 9650, pp 1655-60.

Mohai, P. and Saha, R. (2006) 'Reassessing racial and socioeconomic disparities in environmental justice research', *Demography* vol 43, no 2, pp 383-99.

Mol, A.P.J. (1995) *The Refinement of Production: Ecological Modernization Theory and the Dutch Chemical Industry*, Utrecht: Jan van Arkel/ International Books.

Mol, A.P.J. (2003) *Globalization and Environmental Reform: The Ecological Modernization of the Global Economy*, Cambridge, MA: The MIT Press.

Molero Simarro, R. and Paz Antolin, M.J. (2012) 'Development Strategy of the MAS in Bolivia: Characterization and an Early Assessment', *Development and Change*, vol 43, no 2, pp 531-56.

Monbiot, G. (2001) *Captive State: The Corporate Takeover of Britain*, London: Pan.

Moore, M. (2009) 'Capitalism: A Love Story', USA: Paramount Vantage.

Morales Ayma, E. (2008) Statement by H.E. Evo Morales Ayma, President of the Republic of Bolivia. 7th Session Permanent Forum on Indigenous Issues, New York: United Nations Permanent Forum on Indigenous Issues.

Morgan, F. (2006) *The Power of Community: How Cuba Survived Peak Oil*, Yellow Springs, OH: Arthur Morgan Institute for Community Solutions.

MORI (2002) *Public Attitudes Towards Recycling and Waste Management, Quantitative and Qualitative Review*, London: The Strategy Unit, Cabinet Office.

Morris, E. (2008) *Poverty and Inequality in Cuba Today: The Policy Challenge*, Presentation at the International Institute for the Study of Cuba, London Metropolitan University, October.

Moulds, J. (2013) 'UK Energy Companies: Profits, Customers and Price Hikes', *Guardian*, 22 May.

MPD (Ministerio de Planificación del Desarrollo) (2006) *Plan nacional de desarrollo: Bolivia digna, soberana, productiva y democrática para 'Vivir Bien'*, La Paz: Ministry of Planning and Development.

MSD (Ministerio de Salud y Deportes) (2006) *Plan Estratégico: Medicina Tradicional y Salud Intercultural, 2006–2010*, La Paz: MSD.

Muhr, T. (ed) (2013) *Counter-Globalization and Socialism in the 21st Century: The Bolivarian Alliance for the Peoples of Our America*, London: Routledge.

Naess, O. et al (2007) 'Relation between Concentration of Air Pollution and Cause-Specific Mortality: Four-Year Exposures to Nitrogen Dioxide and Particulate Matter Pollutants in 470 Neighborhoods in Oslo, Norway', *American Journal of Epidemiology*, vol 165, pp 435-43.

Næss, P. and Høyer, K.G. (2009) 'The Emperor's Green Clothes: Growth, Decoupling, and Capitalism', *Capitalism Nature Socialism*, vol 20, no 3, pp 74-95.

Nammo (2012) 'We have Improved our Lead-Free Ammunition', www.nammo.com/News/We-have-improved-our-lead-free-ammunition-/

National Commission on the BP Deepwater Horizon Oil Spill and Offshore Drilling (2011) 'Deep Water: The Gulf Oil Disaster and the Future of Offshore Drilling', www.oilspillcommission.gov/final-report

National Science and Technology Council (2009) *Master Plan for Green Energy*, Seoul, Korea: National Science and Technology Council.

NBS (National Bureau of Statistics – China) (1996–2011) *Chinese National Statistical Yearbook*, Beijing: China Statistics Press.

NEF (New Economics Foundation) (2012) *Happy Planet Index – 2006; 2009; 2012*, London: NEF.

Newell, P. (2005) 'Race, Class and the Global Politics of Environmental Inequality', *Global Environmental Politics*, vol 5, no 3, pp 70-94.

Newell, P. (2007) 'Trade and Environmental Justice in Latin America', *New Political Economy*, vol 12, no 2, pp 237–59.

Nielsen, B. (2003) 'Tassel Emergence and Pollen Shed', Purdue University, Dept of Agronomy.

Nordin, A. (2013) 'The Pyres of Spring', *OpenDemocracy.Net*, www.opendemocracy.net/cities-in-conflict.

Nozick, R. (1974) *Anarchy, State and Utopia*, New York: Basic Books.

NRCS (2012) Abstracts of NRCS Green Growth Research 2011, Seoul: National Research Council for Economics, Humanities and Social Sciences.

NSDS (1994) *National Sustainable Development Strategy*, Stockholm: Ministry of the Environment.

NSDS (2006) *National Sustainable Development Strategy*, Stockholm: Ministry of the Environment.

NSSD (2006) *National Strategy for Sustainable Development of the Republic of Korea 2006–2010*, Seoul: Presidential Commission on Sustainable Development.

Oakes, J. et al (1996) 'A Longitutinal Analysis of Environmental Equity in Communities with Hazard and Waste Facilities', *Social Science Quarterly*, vol 25, no 2, pp 125-48.

O'Connor, J. (1998) *Natural Causes*, New York: Guilford Press.

ODPM (Office of the Deputy Prime Minister) (2004) *The English Indices of Deprivation* (revised), London: ODPM.

OECD (2006) *Environmental Performance Reviews: Korea*, Paris: OECD.

OECD (2007) OECD *Economic Survey of Korea*, Paris: OECD.

OECD (2011a) *Economic Surveys, Sweden, 2011*, Paris: OECD.

OECD (2011b) OECD *Social Indicators Key Findings*: Sweden, Paris: OECD.

OECD (2012) 'Economic Survey of Korea 2012', OECD Publishing, Overview, www.oecd.org/korea/economicsurveyofkorea2012.htm

OECD (2013) *Putting Green Growth at the Heart of Development: A Summary for Policy Makers*, Paris: OECD.

Olivera, O. and Lewis, T. (2004) *Cochabamba! Water War in Bolivia*, Boston, MA: South End Press.

Oliveras, R. and Ricardo Núñez, R. (2001) 'There will be Reason to Keep Balance: Urban Segregation in Havana: Policies, Instruments and Results', Paper presented at the International Seminar on Segregation in the City, Lincoln Institute of Land Policy, Cambridge, MA, 26-28 July 2001.

ONE (2002; 2008) *Statistical Yearbook of Cuba*, Havana: Office of National Statistics, Cuba, www.one.cu

Osborne, G. (2011) *Autumn Statement*, https://www.gov.uk/ government/news/autumn-statement-2011--3

Oxfam (2012) *The Cost of Inequality: How Wealth and Income Extremes Hurt Us All*, London: Oxfam.

Pacala, S. (2007) 'Equitable Solutions to Greenhouse Warming: On the Distribution of Wealth, Emissions and Responsibility Within and Between Nations', International Institute for Applied Systems Analysis Global Development Conference, Vienna, Austria, http://www.iiasa. ac.at/iiasa35/docs/speakers/speech/ppts/pacala.pdf

Palmer, M. (2006) 'Controlling the State: Mediation in Administrative Litigation in the People's Republic of China: Law, Finance, and Security', *Transnational Law and Contemporary Problems*, vol 16, pp 165-87.

Pan Yue (2006a) Interview with Zhou Jigang: 'The Rich Consume and the Poor Suffer the Pollution', *China Dialogue,* 27 October.

Pan Yue (2006b) 'China's green debt', Project Syndicate, 28 November.

Pan Yue (2010) 'Finding a Way to Civilization with Wisdom of the East', in S. Liao (ed) *Environmental Remedies: Sheri Liao's Talks with Eastern & Western Thinkers*, Beijing: Sanchen Press.

Parekh, P. et al (2010) *Monitoring Poverty and Social Exclusion*, York: Joseph Rowntree Foundation.

Paredes, I. (2010) 'Sectors Demand Proof against USAID and Challenge Evo to Expel Them', *La Razón*, 23 June.

Park, K. (2001) 'Seoul-Incheon Canal Construction and Environmental Injustice', *Environmental Justice Forum,* in Lee, H. (2009) *The Political Ecology of Environmental Justice: Environmental Struggle and Injustice in the Yeongheung Island Coal Plant Controversy,* Florida: College of Social Sciences, Florida State University.

Parr, A. (2009) *Hijacking Sustainability*, Cambridge, MA: MIT Press.

Parsons, H. (1977) *Marx and Engels on Ecology*, Westport, CT: Greenwood Press.

Pastille Consortium (2002) 'Indicators into Action – Local Sustainability Indicator Sets in their Context', London: London School of Economics and Political Science.

Pastor, J. et al (2001) 'Which Came First? Toxic Facilities, Minority Move-in, and Environmental Justice', *Journal of Urban Affairs*, vol 21, pp 1-21.

Pastor, M. et al (2006) *In the Wake of the Storm: Environment, Disaster, and Race after Katrina*, New York: Russell Sage Foundation.

Paterson, O. (2013) Environment Secretary, Owen Paterson, speech to Federation of Small Businesses National Conference in Leicester, 22 March.

PCGG (Presidential Committee on Green Growth) (2009) *Comprehensive Strategy for Development and Commercialization of Core Green Technologies*, Seoul, Korea: PCGG.

Pearce, J.R. et al (2010) 'Environmental Justice and Health: The Implications of The Socio-Spatial Distribution of Multiple Environmental Deprivation for Health Inequalities in the United Kingdom', *Transactions of the Institute of British Geographers*, vol 35, no 4, pp 522-39.

Pearson, T. (2010) 'Venezuela Helps Cuba Overcome US-Imposed Internet Restrictions', Venezuelanalysis.com

Pellegriti, G. et al (2013) 'Worldwide Increasing Incidence of Thyroid Cancer: Update on Epidemiology and Risk Factors', *Journal of Cancer Epidemiology*, vol 2013, Article ID 965212, 10 pages.

Pellow, D.N. (2002) *Garbage Wars: The Struggle for Environmental Justice in Chicago*, Cambridge, MA: MIT Press.

Pellow, D.N. (2007) *Resisting Global Toxics: Transnational Movements for Environmental Justice*, Cambridge, MA and London: MIT Press.

Pellow, D. and Brulle, R. (eds) (2005) *Power, Justice and the Environment: A Critical Appraisal of the Environmental Justice Movement*, Cambridge, MA: MIT Press.

Pepper, D. (2010) 'On Contemporary Eco-socialism', in Q. Huan (ed) *Eco-socialism as Politics: Rebuilding the Basis of Our Modern Civilisation*, Dordrecht: Springer, pp 33-44.

Pollin, R. et al (2009) 'The Economic Benefits of Investing in Clean Energy: How the Economic Stimulus Program and New Legislation Can Boost US Economic Growth And Employment', Amherst, MA: PERI – Political Economy Research Institute, University of Massachusetts.

Polanyi, K. (1944) *The Great Transformation*, Boston, Beacon Press.

Pomeraniec, H. and Stefanoni, P. (2009) 'I also am Marxist-Leninist So Are they Going to Expel me from the Organisation of American States?', Clarin.com: http://edant.clarin.com/diario/2009/04/28/elmundo/i-01907188.htm.

Pope, C.A. et al (1995) 'Health Effects of Particulate Air Pollution: Time for Reassessment', *Environmental Health Perspectives*, vol 103, no 5, pp 472-80.

Pops, G.M. and Pavlak, T.J. (1991) *The Case for Justice: Strengthening Decision-Making and Policy in Public Administration*, San Francisco: CA, Jossey-Bass.

Porritt, J. (1984) *Seeing Green*, Oxford: Blackwell.

Porritt, J. (2005, revised 2007) *Capitalism: as if the World Matters*, London: Earthscan.

Postero, N. (2010a) 'Morales's MAS Government Building Indigenous Popular Hegemony in Bolivia', *Latin American Perspectives*, vol 37, no 3, pp 18-34.

Postero, N. (2010b) 'The Struggle to Create a Radical Democracy in Bolivia', *Latin American Research Review*, vol 45, pp 59-78.

Postero, N.G. (2007) *Now we are Citizens: Indigenous Politics in Post-Multicultural Bolivia*, Stanford, CA: Stanford University Press.

Presidential Council for Future and Vision (2009) 'Master Plan for 17 New Growth Engines', Seoul, Korea: Presidential Council for Future and Vision.

Pring, G. and Pring, C. (2009) 'Creating and Improving Environmental Courts and Tribunals, Greening Justice', Washington, DC: World The Access Initiative/World Resources Institute.

Prys, M. (2004) 'The Contested Concept of Hegemony: Using Conceptual Analysis as a Tool for Clarification', Paper presented at the 45th Annual Convention of the International Studies Association in Montréal (17–20 March 2004).

Raaschou-Nielsen, O. et al (2013) 'Long-term Exposure to Traffic-Related Air Pollution and Diabetes-Associated Mortality: A Cohort Study', *Diabetologia*, vol 56, no 1, pp 36-46.

Raby, D.L. (2006) *Democracy and Revolution: Latin America and Socialism Today*, London: Pluto Press.

Radcliffe, S.A. (2012) 'Development for a Postneoliberal Era? Sumak Kawsay, Living Well and the Limits to Decolonisation in Ecuador', *Geoforum*, vol 43, no 2, pp 240-9.

Ramirez, R. (2005) 'State and Civil Society in the Barrios of Havana, Cuba: The Case of Pogolotti', *Environment and Urbanization*, vol 17, no 147, pp 147-70.

Rand, D.G. et al (2012) 'Spontaneous Giving and Calculated Greed', *Nature*, vol 489, no 7416, pp 427-30.

Ranft, U. et al (2009) 'Long-term Exposure to Traffic-Related Particulate Matter Impairs Cognitive Function in the Elderly', *Environmental Research*, vol 109, no 8, pp 1004-11.

Rathzel, N. and Uzzell, D. (2011) 'Trade Unions and Climate Change: The Jobs Versus Environment Dilemma', *Global Environmental Change - Human and Policy Dimensions*, vol 21, no 4, pp 1215-23.

Rawls, J. (1971) *A Theory of Justice*, Cambridge, MA: Harvard University Press.

RCOG (Royal College of Obstetricians and Gynaecologists) (2013) 'Chemical Exposures During Pregnancy: Dealing with Potential, but Unproven, Risks to Child Health', *Scientific Impact Paper No 37*, www.rcog.org.uk/files/rcog-corp/5.6.13ChemicalExposures.pdf

Reed, M.G. and George, C. (2011) 'Where in the World is Environmental Justice?', *Progress in Human Geography*, vol 35, no 6, pp 835-42.

Rifkin, J. (2010) *The Empathic Civilization: The Race to Global Consciousness in a World in Crisis,* New York: Jeremy P. Tarcher/Putnam.

Renner, M. (2012) 'Making the Green Economy Work for Everybody', in Worldwatch Institute, *State of the World 2012: Moving Toward Sustainable Prosperity*, http://blogs.worldwatch.org/sustainableprosperity/wp-content/uploads/2012/04/SOW12_chap_1.pdf

Richardson, E.A. et al (2010a) 'Developing Summary Measures of Health-Related Multiple Physical Environmental Deprivation for Epidemiological Research', *Environment and Planning A*, vol 42, no 7, pp 650-68.

Richardson, E.A. et al (2010b) 'The Mechanism Behind Environmental Inequality in Scotland: Which Came First, the Deprivation or the Landfill?', *Environment and Planning A*, vol 42, no 1, pp 223-40.

Rockström, J. et al (2009) 'A Safe Operating Space for Humanity', *Nature*, vol 461, no 7263, pp 472-475.

Rodríguez, J.L. (1983) 'La llamada Cubanología y el Desarrollo Económico de Cuba' *Temas de Economia Mundial* (no 7) referred to in Mesa-Lago, C. (1992) 'Three Decades of Studies on the Cuban Revolution: Progress, Problems, and the Future', in Damián J. Fernández (ed) Cuban Studies Since the Revolution Gainesville, University Press of Florida, pp 9-44.

Roman, P. (2003) *People's Power: Cuba's Experience with Representative Government*, Oxford: Rowman and Littlefield.

Rönnbäck, K. (2005) *Structural Discrimination when Building Roads*, Stockholm: Vänsterpartiet.

Rosset, P. (1997) *The Greening of Cuba*, Buffalo, NY: Black Rose Books.

Rosset, P. and Benjamin, M. (1995) *The Greening of the Revolution: Cuba's Experiment with Organic Agriculture*, Australia: Ocean Press.

Rumberger, R.W. (1984) 'High Technology and Job Loss', *Technology in Society*, vol 6, no 4, pp 263-84.

Saami Resources (2013) 'Saami Resources: Fighting for Self-Determination, Not Foreign Mineral Exploitation', http://saamiresources.org/

Samoli, E. et al. (2006) 'Short-Term Effects of Nitrogen Dioxide on Mortality: An Analysis Within the APHEA Project', *European Respiratory Journal*, vol 27, pp 1129-38.

Sánchez-Triana, E. et al (2006) 'Environmental Degradation', in Vicente Fretes Cibils, M. Giugale and C. Luff (eds) *Bolivia: Public Policy Options for the Well-being of All*. Washington, DC: The World Bank, pp 421-36.

Sandel, M. (1982) *Liberalism and the Limits of Justice*, Cambridge: Cambridge University Press.

Sanders, C. (2010) 'Korea: Environmental Problems and Solutions', *Asia-Pacific Business and Technology Report*, 1 February, 2010.

Saney, I. (2004) *Cuba: A Revolution in Motion*, London: Zed Books.

Santillo, D. et al (2003) 'Consuming Chemicals: Hazardous Chemicals in House Dust as an Indicator of Chemical Exposure in the Home: Part I — UK', Greenpeace Research Laboratories Technical Note 01/2003, Exeter: Greenpeace.

Sawyer, M.Q. (2006) *Racial Politics in Post-Revolutionary Cuba*, Cambridge, MA: Cambridge University Press.

Scandrett, E. (2007) 'Environmental Justice in Scotland: Policy, Pedagogy and Praxis', *Environmental Research letters*, http://iopscience.iop.org/1748-9326/2/4/045002

Schlosberg, D. (2004) 'Reconceiving Environmental Justice: Global Movements and Political Theories', *Environmental Politics*, vol 13, no 3, pp 517-40.

Schlosberg, D. (2007) *Defining Environmental Justice: Theories, Movements, and Nature*, New York: Oxford University Press.

Schnaiberg, A. (1980) *The Environment: From Surplus to Scarcity*, New York: Oxford University Press.

Schnaiberg, A. and Gould, K. (2000) *Environment and Society: The Enduring Conflict*, New York: St Martin's Press.

Schutz, A. (1965) 'The Social World and the Theory of Social Action', in D. Braybrooke (ed) *Philosophical Problems of the Social Sciences*, New York: Macmillan.

Scottish Executive (2006) *Choosing Our Future: Scotland's Sustainable Development Strategy*, Edinburgh: Scottish Government.

SDC (Sustainable Development Commission) (2010) *Sustainable Development: The Key to Tackling Health Inequalities*, London: SDC.

SEER (2013) The Surveillance, Epidemiology, and End Results (SEER) Program of the National Cancer Institute (NCI) 'Cancer Statistics', www.seer.cancer.gov.

SEHN (Science and Environmental Health Network) (1998) 'Wingspread Consensus Statement', www.sehn.org/wing.html

Sen, A.K. (1985) *Commodities and Capabilities*, Oxford: Oxford University Press.

Seo, W. (1991) 'Research of Discrimination with the Socio-Economic Factor by Environmental Pollution', Master's thesis, Seoul: Environmental Planning, Seoul National University.

Seo, W. (2001) 'The Thoughtless Development in Yongin from the Perspective of Environmental Justice', *Environmental Justice Forum*, in Lee, H. (2009) The Political Ecology of Environmental Justice: Environmental Struggle and Injustice in the Yeongheung Island Coal Plant Controversy, PhD thesis, Florida: College of Social Sciences, Florida State University.

SEPA (Swedish Environmental Protection Agency, S.R.A., and Swedish Consumer Agency) (2007) 'Index for New Cars' Influence on Climate: In the country, in the counties and in the municipalities', Report 5707, Stockholm: Naturvårdsverket.

Shah, P.S. and Balkhair, T. (2011) 'Air pollution and Birth Outcomes: A Systematic Review', *Environment International*, vol 37, no 2, pp 498–516.

Shalom, S. (2005) 'ParPolity: Political Vision for a Good Society', *Znet*, http://www.zcommunications.org/parpolity-political-vision-for-a-good-society-by-stephen1-shalom.html

Shapiro, J. (2001) *Mao's War Against Nature: Politics and the Environment in Revolutionary China*, Cambridge: Cambridge University Press.

Shapiro, T.M. et al (2010) *The Racial Wealth Gap Increases Fourfold*, Research and Policy Brief, Institute on Asset and Social Policy, The Heller School for Social Policy and Management, Brandeis University.

Shelter (2013) 'Sharp Rise in Number of Homeless Families', http://england.shelter.org.uk/news

Shen, J.A. (2006) 'Simultaneous Estimation of Environmental Kuznets Curve: Evidence from China', *China Economic Review*, vol 17, pp 383-94.

Shiva, V. (1998) *Staying Alive: Women, Ecology and Development*, London and New York: Zed Books.

Shrum, L.J. et al (2012) 'Persuasion in the Marketplace: How Theories of Persuasion Apply to Marketing and Advertising', in J. Dillard and L. Shen (eds) *The Persuasion Handbook*, Thousand Oaks, CA: Sage.

Shultz, J. (2010) 'Latin America Finds a Voice on Climate Change: With What Impact?', *NACLA Report on the Americas*, vol 43, no 4, pp 5-6.

Sideris, L. (2012) 'A Fable for Bloomington', www.carsoncenter.uni-muenchen.de/download/publications/perspectives/2012_perspectives/1207_silentspring_web_color.pdf

Silverman, R.A. et al (2010) 'Association of Ambient Fine Particles With Out-of-Hospital Cardiac Arrests in New York City', *American Journal of Epidemiology*, vol 172, no 8, pp 917-23.

Simms, A. (2013) *Cancel the Apocalypse: The New Path To Prosperity*, St Ives: Little, Brown.

Sklair, L. (2002) *Globalization: Capitalism and its Alternatives*, Oxford: Oxford University Press.

Slunge, D. and Jaldin, R. (2007) *Bolivia Environmental Policy Brief: Environmental Sustainability, Poverty and the National Development Plan*, Göteburg, Sweden: Göteburg University.

Smith, D. (2000) 'Moral Progress in Human Geography: Transcending the Place of Good Fortune', *Progress in Human Geography*, vol 24, no 1, pp 1-18.

Smith, D.M. et al (2010) 'Neighbourhood Food Environment and Area Deprivation: Spatial Accessibility to Grocery Stores Selling Fresh Fruit and Vegetables in Urban and Rural Settings', *International Journal of Epidemiology*, vol 39, no 1, pp 277-84.

Socialstyrelsen (2010) *Social Report 2010 – The national report on social conditions in Sweden*, www.socialstyrelsen.se/publikationer2010/socialreport-summary

Solt, F. (2009) 'Standardizing the World Income Inequality Database', *Social Science Quarterly*, vol 90, no 2, pp 231-42. (SWIID Version 3.1, December 2011).

Solt, F. (2011) Standardized World Income Inequality Database, Version 3.1, http://myweb.uiowa.edu/fsolt/swiid/swiid.html

Sombart, W. (1902) *Modern Capitalism*, Leipzig: Duncker and Humblot.

Spangenberg, J. (2001) 'The Environmental Kuznets Curve: A Methodological Artefact?', *Population and Environmental Politics*, vol 23, nos 1/2, pp 175-91.

Spencer (1864) *Principles of Biology*, London: Williams and Norgate.

Stanley, A. (2009) 'Just Space or Spatial Justice? Difference, Discourse, and Environmental Justice', *Local Environment*, vol 14, no 10, pp 999-1014.

State Council (China) (1994) 'Agenda 21 White Paper on China's Population, Environment, and Development in the 21st Century', China State Council.

Statewatch (2013) 'Over One Thousand Children Illegally Registered', DN.se, 23 September, www.statewatch.org/news/2013/sep/sweden-roma-register.pdf

Statistics Sweden (2012a) 'Population Statistics', http://www.scb.se/Pages/TableAndChart____25891.aspx

Statistics Sweden (2012b) 'Labour Force Survey (LFS)', www.scb.se/Pages/Product____23276.aspx

Steckel, R.H. and Floud, R. (eds) (1997) *Health and Welfare During Industrialization*, Chicago, IL: University of Chicago Press.

Stephens, C. et al (2001) 'Environmental Justice: Rights and Means to a Healthy Environment for All', Special Briefing Paper 7, London: ESRC Global Environmental Change Programme.

Stern, D.I. (2004) 'The Rise and Fall of the Environmental Kuznets Curve', *World Development*, vol 32, no 8, pp 1419-39.

Stockton, H. and Campbell, R. (2011) *Time to Reconsider UK Energy and Fuel Poverty Policies?*, York: Joseph Rowntree Foundation.

Sullivan, T. et al (2012) *State of the Dream 2012*, Boston, MA: United for Fair Economy.

Summers, L. (1991) cited in Pellow, D.N. (2007) *Resisting Global Toxics: Transnational Movements for Environmental Justice*, Cambridge, MA and London: MIT Press.

Sustainable Development Commission (2003) *Mainstreaming Sustainable Regeneration: A Call to Action*, London: SDC.

Sweden.se (2012) 'Environment: Environmental Work for Generations', www.sweden.se/eng/Home/Society/Sustainability/Facts/Environment/

SWIID (2011) Standardized World Income Inequality Database. Version 3.1, 2011, http://myweb.uiowa.edu/fsolt/swiid/swiid.html

Swyngedouw, E. (2007) *Impossible/Undesirable Sustainability and the Post-Political Condition*, London: Routledge.

Szaz, A. (2007) *Shopping our Way to Safety: How we Changed from Protecting the Environment to Protecting Ourselves*, Minneapolis: University of Minnesota Press.

Takano, T. et al (2002) 'Urban Residential Environments and Senior Citizens' Longevity in Megacity Areas: The Importance of Walkable Green Spaces', *Journal of Epidemiology and Community Health*, vol 56, no 12, pp 913-18.

Talih, M. and Fricker, R.D. (2002) 'Effects of Neighbourhood Demographic Shifts on Findings of Environmental Justice', *Journal of the Royal Statistical Society A*, no 165, pp 375-97.

Taliman, V. (1992) 'Stuck Holding the Nation's Nuclear Waste', *Race, Poverty, and Environment Newsletter* (Autumn), pp 6-9.

Tao, F. (2011) 'Breaching Barriers: Chinese Environmental NGOs Come of Age', in J. Keeley and Z. Yisheng (eds) *Green China: Chinese Insights on Environment and Development*, London: International Institute for Environment and Development.

Taylor, D.E. (2000) 'The Rise of the Environmental Justice Paradigm', *American Behavioral Scientist*, vol 43, no 4, pp 508-80.

Taylor, J.H.L. (2009) *Inside El Barrio: A Bottom-up View of Neighborhood Life in Castro's Cuba*, Sterling, VA: Kumarian Press.

The Open University (2008) *The Open University Household Waste Study: Key Findings for 2007*, London: Defra.

The Welsh Assembly (2009) *One Wales: One Planet: The Sustainable Development Scheme of the Welsh Assembly Government*, Cardiff: The Welsh Assembly Government

Thibaut, J. and Walker, L. (1975) *Procedural Justice: A Psychological Analysis*, Hillsdale, NJ: Lawrence Erlbaum.

Tofler, G.H. and Muller, J.E. (2006) 'Triggering of Acute Cardiovascular Disease and Potential Preventive Strategies', *Circulation*, no 114, pp 1863-72.

Townsend, P. (1987) 'Deprivation', *Journal of Social Policy*, vol 16, no 1, pp 125-46.

Trotsky, L. (2010 [1929]) 'The Permanent Revolution', www.marxists.org/archive/trotsky/1931/tpr/index.htm

Tsai, S. et al (2003) 'Evidence for an Association between Air Pollution and Daily Stroke Admissions in Kaohsiung, Taiwan', *Stroke*, vol 34, pp 2612-16.

Turner, S. (2006) 'Transforming Environmental Governance in Northern Ireland – Part one: The Process of Policy Renewal', *Journal of Environmental Law*, vol 18, no 1, pp 55-87.

UCC CRJ (United Church of Christ Commission for Racial Justice) (1987) 'Toxic Wastes and Race in the United States: A National Report on the Racial and Socio-Economic Characteristics of Communities with Hazardous Waste Sites', New York: United Church of Christ Commission for Racial Justice.

UK DECC (Department for Energy and Climate Change) (2011a) *Annual Fuel Poverty Statistics Report*, London: Office for National Statistics/DECC.

UK DECC (2011b) Energy Act, London: Office for National Statistics /DECC.

UK DECC (2011c) *Energy Act 2011: Green Deal*, London: Office for National Statistics /DECC.

UK ELA (UK Environmental Law Association) (2012) *The State of UK Environmental Law in 2011–12: Is there a Case for Legislative Reform?*, King's College London and Cardiff University.

UN (2012) *The Millennium Development Goals Report*, New York: United Nations.

UN Habitat (1996) 'Best Practices Programme', in A.D. Fernandez and L. Angeles (2009) 'Building better communities: Gender and Urban Regeneration in Cayo Hueso, Havana, Cuba', *Women's Studies International Forum*, vol 32, no 2, pp 80-88.

UNDP (United Nations Development Programme) (2011) 'International Human Development Indicators: Bolivia', http://hdrstats.undp.org/en/countries/profiles/BOL.html

UNDP (2011a) *Human Development Report 2011: Sustainability and Equity: A Better Future for All*, http://hdr.undp.org/en/media/HDR_2011_EN_Tables.pdf

UNECE (United Nations Economic Commission for Europe) (1998) *UNECE Convention on Access to Information, Public Participation in Decision-Making and Access to Justice in Environmental Matters*, Aarhus, Denmark: UNECE.

UNEP (United Nations Environment Programme) (1992) *Rio Declaration on Environment and Development*, The United Nations Conference on Environment and Development, Rio de Janeiro: UNEP.

UNEP (2002) *Minimizing Hazardous Wastes: A Simplified Guide to the Basel Convention*, Basel: UNEP.

UNEP (2004) *United Nations Environment Programme Vital Waste Graphics*, Nairobi, Kenya: UNEP.

UNEP (2008) *Towards Decent Work in a Sustainable, Low Carbon World*, Nairobi, Kenya: UNEP.

UNEP (2010) 'Overview of the Republic of Korea's National Strategy for Green Growth', Geneva: UNEP.

UNEP (2011) *Towards a Green Economy. Pathways to Sustainable Development and Poverty Reduction*, Nairobi, Kenya: UNEP.

UNEP (2012) *Global Chemicals Outlook*, Nairobi, Kenya: UNEP.

UNESCO (United Nations Educational, Scientific and Cultural Organization) (2009) 'Results achieved by the Republic of Bolivia in Eradicating Illiteracy as a Potentially Valuable Experience in UNESCO's Efforts during the United Nations Literacy Decade (2003–2012)', 181 EX/6, Paris, UNESCO.

UNICEF/WHO (2012) *Progressing on Drinking Water and Sanitation, 2012 Update*, based on 2010 data, www.unicef.org/media/files/JMPreport2012.pdf

Union of Concerned Scientists (1992) 'Scientist Statement: World Scientists' Warning to Humanity', www.ucsusa.org/about/1992-world-scientists.html

US DHHS (US Department of Health and Human Services) (2012) *Draft 2012 HHS Environmental Justice Strategy*, Washington, DC: US DHHS.

US Energy Information Administration (2012) http://www.eia.gov

US EPA (Environmental Protection Agency) (1998) *Definition of Environmental Justice*, http://www.epa.gov/region2/ej/overview.htm

US EPA Region 4 (1999) *Interim Policy to Identify and Address Potential Environmental Justice Areas*, Atlanta, GA: Environmental Accountability Division.

US EPA (2004) 'Toolkit for Assessing Allegations of Environmental Justice', Washington DC, EPA.

US EPA (2012) 'Air Quality Trends', www.epa.gov/airtrends/aqtrends. html

US GAO (General Accounting Office) (1983) *Siting of Hazardous Waste Landfills and Their Correlation with Racial and Economic Status of Surrounding Communities*, GAO/RCED-83–168, Washington, DC: Government Printing Office.

Valpak (2012) 'Company History', www.valpak.co.uk/AboutUs/ Company/CompanyHistory.aspx.

Van der Elst, N.J., et al (2013). 'Enhanced Remote Earthquake Triggering at Fluid-Injection Sites in the Midwestern United States', *Science*, vol 341, no 6142, pp 164-7.

Van Rooij, B. (2010) 'The People vs. Pollution: Understanding Citizen Action against Pollution in China', *Journal of Contemporary China*, vol 19, no 63, pp 55-77.

Van Rooij, B. et al (2012) 'The Compensation Trap: The Limits of Community-Based Pollution Regulation in China', *Pace Environmental Law Review*, vol 29, no 3, pp 701-45.

Värnik, P. (2012) 'Suicide in the World', *International Journal of Environmental Research and Public Health*, vol 9, pp 760-71.

Veblen, T. (1994 [1899]) *The Theory of the Leisure Class. An Economic Study in the Evolution of Institutions*, New York: Macmillan.

Vennemo, H. et al (2009) 'Environmental Pollution in China: Status and Trends', *Review of Environmental Economics and Policy*, vol 3, no 2, pp 209.

Viereck, J. (1993) 'The Newest Smallpox Blanket', *Against the Current*, vol 7, no 6, pp 17-18.

Vision of Humanity (2013) 'Global Peace Index', www.visionofhumanity. org/#page/indexes/global-peace-index/2013/CUB/OVER

Wackernagel, M. and Rees, W. (1996) *Our Ecological Footprint: Reducing Human Impact on the Earth*, Gabriola Island, BC: New Society Publishers.

Walker, G. (2007) 'Environmental Justice and the Distributional Deficit in Policy Appraisal in the UK', *Environmental Research Letters*, vol 2, no 4, 045004.

Walker, G. (2010) 'Environmental Justice, Impact Assessment and the Politics of Knowledge: The Implications of Assessing the Social Distribution of Environmental Outcomes', *Environmental Impact Assessment Review*, vol 30, no 5, pp 312-18.

Walker, G. (2012) *Environmental Justice: Concepts, Evidence and Politics*, London: Routledge.

Walker, G. and Bulkeley, H. (2006) 'Geographies of Environmental Justice', *Geoforum*, vol 37, no 5, pp 655-9.

Walker, G. and Burningham, K. (2011) 'Flood Risk, Vulnerability and Environmental Justice: Evidence and Evaluation of Inequality in a UK Context', *Critical Social Policy*, vol 31, no 2, pp 216-40.

Walker, G. et al (2003) *Environmental Quality and Social Deprivation*, Bristol: Environment Agency.

Walker, G. et al (2006) *Addressing Environmental Inequalities: Flood Risk*, Bristol: Environment Agency.

Wall, D. (2010) *The No-Nonsense Guide to Green Politics*, Oxford: New Internationalist.

Wallerstein, I. (2004) *World-Systems Analysis: An Introduction*. Durham, NC: Duke University Press.

Walmsley, R. (2009) *Prison Population List* (8th edn), London: International Centre for Prison Studies, Kings College London.

Wanderley, F. (2008) 'Beyond Gas: Between the Narrow-Based and Broad-Based Economy', in J. Crabtree and L. Whitehead (eds) *Unresolved Tensions: Bolivia Past and Present*, Pittsburgh, PA: University of Pittsburgh Press, pp 194-211.

Wang, A. (2011) 'Green Litigation in China Today', *Chinadialogue*, 18 July.

Wang, A. and Gao, J. (2010) 'Environmental Courts and the Development of Environmental Public Interest Litigation in China', *Journal of Court Innovation*, vol 3, no 1, pp 37-50.

Wang, C. (2007b) 'Chinese Environmental Law Enforcement: Current Deficiencies and Suggested Reforms', *Vermont Journal of Environmental Law*, vol 8, no 21, pp 160-93.

Wang, J. and Wang, M. (2011) 'Environmental Rule of Law in China: Why the System isn't Working', in J. Keeley and Z. Yisheng (eds) *Green China: Chinese Insights on Environment and Development*, London: International Institute for Environment and Development, pp 160-71.

Wang, J. et al (2011) 'Green GDP Accounting Research: Past Experience and Future Prospects', in J. Keeley and Z. Yisheng (eds) *Green China: Chinese Insights on Environment and Development*, London: International Institute for Environment and Development, pp 190-203.

Wang, R. (2009) 'The Welfare of Rural Migrant Workers', Working Paper, Institute of Population and Labor Economics, Chinese Academy of Social Sciences.

Wang, S. (2010) 'Steadfastly Maintain Our Direction and Explore New Roads: Sixty Years of Socialist Practice in China', *Social Sciences in China*, vol 31, no 2, pp 21-43.

Wang, Y. (2007a) 'Why Build an Incinerator at a Sensitive Spot in Beijing?', *China Business Times,* 6 April, http://business.sohu.com/20070406/n249248875.shtml

Wang, Z. (2012) 'Ecological Marxism in China', *Monthly Review,* vol 63, no 9, February.

Ware, J.H. (2000) 'Particulate Air Pollution and Mortality – Clearing the Air', *New England Journal of Medicine*, vol 343, pp 1798-9.

Warren, K.J. (1999) 'Environmental Justice: Some Ecofeminist Worries about a Distributive Model', *Environmental Ethics*, vol 21, no 2, pp 151-61.

Watts, J. (2012) 'Air Pollution Could Become China's Biggest Health Threat Expert Warns', *Guardian*, 16 March.

Webber, J.R. (2010) 'Bolivia in the Era of Evo Morales', *Latin American Research Review*, vol 45, no 3, pp 248-60.

Webber, J.R. (2011) *From Rebellion to Reform in Bolivia: Class Struggle, Indigenous Liberation, and the Politics of Evo Morales*, Chicago, IL: Haymarket Books.

Wegner, G. and Pascual, U. (2011) 'Cost-benefit Analysis in the Context of Ecosystem Services for Human Well-Being: A Multidisciplinary Critique', *Global Environmental Change*, vol 21, no 2, pp 492-504.

Wei, Y. (2007) 'Rural–Urban Migrant Workers in China: The Vulnerable Group in Cities', Paper presented at the 6th Berlin Roundtables on Transnationality, Population Politics and Migration, Berlin, Germany, 14–20 February 2007.

Wellenius, G.A. et al (2005) 'Air Pollution and Hospital Admissions for Ischemic and Hemorrhagic Stroke among Medicare Beneficiaries', *Stroke*, vol 36, no 2549, pp 2549-53.

Wen Jiabao (2011) 'China Lowers Growth Rate Target in Sustainability Drive', *BBC News Asia – Pacific*, http://www.bbc.co.uk/news/world-asia-pacific-12589757.

WGAEJ (Working Group on Access to Environmental Justice) (2008) *Ensuring Access to Environmental Justice in England and Wales*, London: WGAEJ.

Wheeler, B.W. (2004) 'Health-Related Environmental Indices and Environmental Equity in England and Wales', *Environment and Planning A*, vol 36, pp 803-22.

Whittle, D. and Rey Santos, O. (2006) 'Protecting Cuba's Environment: Efforts to Design and Implement Effective Environmental Laws and Policies in Cuba', *Cuban Studies*, vol 37, pp 73-103.

WHO (World Health Organization) (2006) *Preventing Disease through Healthy Environments: Towards an Estimate of the Environmental Burden of Disease*, Geneva: WHO.

WHO-UNICEF (2006) 'Coverage Estimates Improved Sanitation', http://www.wssinfo.org/documents-links/documents/

Wilkinson, R. and Pickett, K. (2009) *The Spirit Level: Why More Equal Societies Almost Always Do Better*, London: Allen Lane.

Williams, R. W. (2005) 'Getting to the Heart of Environmental Injustice: Social Science and its Boundaries', *Theory and Science,* vol 6, no 1, pp 1-20,

Woods, A. (2008) Reformismo o Revolución: Marxismo y Socialismo del Siglo XXI, Respuesta a Heinz Dieterich, Madrid: Fundación Federico Engels.

Woodward, D. and Simms, A. (2006) *Growth isn't Working: The Unbalanced Distribution of Benefits and Costs from Economic Growth*, Rethinking Poverty series 1, London: New Economics Foundation.

World Bank (2007) 'Cost of pollution in China', Washington, DC: World Bank.

World Bank (2008a) 'Bolivia: Environment at a Glance', www.vub. ac.be/klimostoolkit/sites/default/files/documents/bolivia_country_ env_fact_sheet.pdf

World Bank (2008b) 'Bolivian highlights', Washington, DC: World Bank

World Bank (2010) 'Environmental Data by Country', Washington, DC: World Bank.

World Bank (2011a) 'World Bank Gini Index' World Development Indicators. Washington, DC: World Bank. Gini Values, http://data. worldbank.org/indicator/SI.POV.GINI/

World Bank (2011b) 'Renewable Internal Freshwater Resources. Data Tables', Washington, DC: World Bank.

World Bank (2012a) http://data.worldbank.org/indicator/SN.ITK. DPTH

World Bank (2012b) 'World Bank Indicators 2012', based on 2009 data, http://data.worldbank.org/indicator/EG.ELC.ACCS.ZS

World Bank (2012c) 'Environment Data by Country – China', Washington, DC: World Bank.

World Public Opinion (2006) 'Presidents of Bolivia, Argentina get highest approval ratings in Latin America', www.worldpublicopinion.org/pipa/ articles/brlatinamericara/242.php?nid=&id=&pnt=242&lb=brla

Wu, X. and Treiman, D.J. (2004) 'The household registration system and social stratification in China: 1955–1996', *Demography*, vol 41, no 2, pp 363-84.

WWF (World Wildlife Fund) (2006) *Living Planet Report*, Gland, Switzerland: WWF International, http://awsassets.panda.org/downloads/1_lpr_2012_online_full_size_single_pages_final_120516.pdf

WWF (2010) *Living Planet Report*, Gland, Switzerland: WWF International.

WWF (2012a) *Living Planet Report*, Gland, Switzerland: WWF International.

WWF (2012b) 'Environmental Problems in Sweden: Persistent Bad Forestry Practices', Gland, Switzerland: WWF International.

Xiaomin, G. (2011) 'Understanding Environmental Pollution in China', in J. Keeley and Z. Yisheng (eds) *Green China: Chinese Insights on Environment and Development*, London: International Institute for Environment and Development, pp 26-45.

Xie, H. and Hou, S. (2010) 'Assessment of the Relationships Between Air Quality and Socio-Economic Factors in Sheffield, UK using GIS', *Fresenius Environmental Bulletin*, vol 19, no 9B, pp 2040-6.

Xie, L. (2009) *Environmental Activism in China*, London and New York: Routledge.

Xie, L. (2011) 'Environmental Justice in China's Urban Decision-Making', *Taiwan in Comparative Perspective*, vol 3, pp 160-79.

Xinhua News Agency (2012) 'Environmental Progress Vital for Official's Advancement', *Media News*, 14 December, http://english.mep.gov.cn/News_service/media_news/201212/t20121214_243752.htm

Yaffe, H. (2009) *Che Guevara: The Economics of Revolution*, London: Palgrave Macmillan.

Yang, G. (2005) 'Environmental NGOs and Institutional Dynamics in China', *China Quarterly*, vol 181, no 3, pp 46-66.

Yang, G. (2010) 'Brokering Environment and Health in China: Issue Entrepreneurs of the Public Sphere', *Journal of Contemporary China*, no 101, pp 118 **[one page?]**.

Yisheng, Z. (2011) 'China's Environment and Development Challenge', in J. Keeley and Z. Yisheng (eds) *Green China: Chinese Insights on Environment and Development*, London: International Institute for Environment and Development, pp 10-25.

York City Council (2012) http://www.york.gov.uk/environment/waste/recycling/4-packaging/

Young, I.M. (1990) *Justice and the Politics of Difference*, Princeton, NJ: Princeton University Press.

Young, I.M. (2002) *Inclusion and Democracy*, Oxford: Oxford University Press.

Yun, S.-J. (2010) 'Not So Green: A Critique of The Republic of Korea's Growth Strategy', *Global Asia*, www.globalasia.org/V5N2_Summer_2010/Sun-Jin_Yun.html

Zelenika, I. and Pearce, J.M. (2011) 'Barriers to Appropriate Technology Growth in Sustainable Development', *Journal of Sustainable Development*, vol 4, no 6, pp 12-22.

Zhang, Q. and Zou, H. (2012) 'Regional Inequality in Contemporary China', *Annals of Economics and Finance*, vol 13, no 1, pp 113-37.

Žižek, S. (2011) *Living in the End Times*, New York and London: Verso.

Index

Note: The following abbreviations have been used – f = figure; n = note; t = table

A

Aarhus Convention (Directive 2003/35/EC) (UN Economic Commission for Europe) 29, 114
'access to information' 29
'accumulation by dispossession' 50
Act on Disclosure of Information by Public Agencies (1998) (South Korea) 89–90
activism 39–40, 65, 92–3, 234
  China 151–2, 153
  Cuba 198, 201
advertising 52–3
ageing population 2
Agenda 21 proposals (Rio Earth Summit 1992) 46, 156
'Agricultural and Environmental Courts' (Bolivia) 172
Aguas de Tunari 165
Air Pollutants, Committee on the Medical Effects of (2010) (UK) 99
air pollution 2–3, 99, 104, 119, 122, 135
  Bolivia 164
  China 142, 143, 147
  Cuba 187
  see also pollution
ALBA *see* 'Bolivarian Alliance for the Peoples of Our America, The'
Alliance for Sweden 120
anarchist/libertarian communism 227
'Andean capitalism' 162
anthropogenic PM air pollution 99
anti-capitalism 233, 234
anti-environmental movements 60–1
appropriate technologies (ATs) 45
Arlanda airport (Sweden) 123
Arnstein, S.R. 25, 26f, 92, 133
Asamblea Nacional del Poder Popular (National Assembly of Popular Power) (Cuba) 195, 197, 200
asbestos 3, 60–1

B

Balme, R. 147
Beck, U. 38, 51
Been, V. 35
Bell, D.A. 150
Benhabib, S. 20
Beowulf Mines 132–3
Bies, R.J. 25
Black Environment Network (UK) 107, 112
black and minority ethnic communities (BME) 78n, 98, 146, 147, 191
  discrimination 33, 69, 75–6
  policy-making decisions and 109
  Sweden 125–6, 127f, 128–9, 135
  toxic waste facilities 15, 35, 36–7, 65, 73–4
Boerner, C. 35, 36
'Bolivarian Alliance for the Peoples of Our America, The' (ALBA) 162, 178n, 222
Bolivia 161–4, 213, 216, 223, 229
  capitalist/socialist spectrum 6f
  causes of environmental injustice 176–8
  citizen power 39
  distributive environmental justice 170–1
  Environmental Justice Indicator Framework (EJI) 176
  policy-making 220t
  procedural environmental justice 171–5, 176f
  substantive environmental justice 164–70
  see also socialism
Bookchin, M. 230
Bradley, K. 129, 130
Brajer, V. 147
British Petroleum (BP) 53
Brulle, R. 38–9, 233
Bullard, R.D. 37, 66
burden of proof principle 121

C

CAJE (UK) 113
Caldeira, K. 13*n*
Cameron, David 108
campaign organisations 38, 134, 234–5
cancer 2, 73–4, 144
Cancún Accord 167
'cap and trade' 56
Capacity Global (UK) 107, 112, 113
capitalism 4–5, 6*f*, 7, 9, 10, 63*t*, 231
  arguments for 223–6
  consumption 42, 50, 51, 52–3, 55,
    59–60
  Cuba and 205–6, 209–10
  Damaging Hegemonic Environmental
    Discourses and 217, 218, 219
  dematerialisation and 55
  democracy and 60–1
  Dependency Theory 51–2
  elimination of 222–3, 235
  employment 40–1
  'green capitalism' 53–4
  'green economy' 57–8
  income and wealth inequalities 58–60
  indigenous people and 75
  market mechanisms 55–6
  power relations and 37
  procedural environmental justice 71
  responsibility for environmental
    degradation 51, 77, 141, 154, 214,
    215–16, 221, 222–3
  socialism/Marxism and 61–3, 162
  technology 54–5
  'treadmill of production theory' 51
  World Systems Theory 52
  see also market dynamics; South Korea;
    Sweden; United Kingdom; United
    States
car ownership 186
carbon dioxide emissions (CO$_2$) 4, 13*n*,
  44, 68, 93
  China 13*n*, 142, 154
  Cuba 190
  Sweden 130
  United Kingdom 103, 105, 116
carbon trading projects 56, 83, 216
Carson, Rachel 47
CCEJ *see* Connecticut Coalition for
  Environmental Justice
Center for Genetic Engineering and
  Biotechnology (Cuba) 204
Centre for Legal Assistance to Pollution
  Victims (China) 151
'change the world by not taking power'
  approach 234
Chavis, Rev Benjamin 66

Chemicals Regulation Directorate
  (UK) 100
Cheung, Sze Pang 153, 159
China 141–2, 213, 218, 227
  activism 151–2, 153
  capitalist/socialist spectrum 6*f*
  carbon dioxide emissions (CO2) 13*n*,
    142, 154
  causes of environmental injustice
    154–9
  decision-making processes 150
  distributive environmental justice
    145–9
  Environmental Justice Indicator
    Framework (EJI) 154
  gross domestic production (GDP) 65
  housing 143, 145–6, 159–60*n*
  industrialisation 39, 40, 216
  policy-making 220*t*
  procedural environmental justice
    149–54
  substantive environmental justice
    142–5
  see also socialism
Chinese People's Political Consultative
  Conference (CPPCC) 149, 152, 153
Christianity 45
CIDOB 173, 174
citizens' advisory committees 131
Citizens' Movement for Environmental
  Justice (South Korea) 79, 89
CITMA *see* Ministry of Science,
  Technology and Environment
  (Cuba)
civil liberties 90
Civil Rights Act (Title VI) (1964) 67
Clean Air Act (1963) (US) 68
climate change 1, 18, 20, 44, 48, 164,
  167
Climate Change Act (UK) 100
Climate Change and the Rights of
  Mother Earth, World Peoples'
  Summit on 167
'climate justice' movement 18
coal-fired power plants 149
Coalition government (UK) 100–1,
  103, 113
colonialism 206
COMECON *see* Community for
  Economic Cooperation
Committee on Energy and Commerce
  of the US Congress 53
Committee on the Medical Effects of
  Air Pollutants (2010) (UK) 99
commodification, 221, 235
  capitalism and 50, 51, 52, 56, 57, 58,
    62

communism 182–3, 193, 194–5, 210–211*n*, 227
communitarianism 17, 30*n*
communities: lack of citizen power 36–9, 63*t*
Community for Economic Cooperation (COMECON) 183
community markets 111*f*
compensation payments 92, 94, 153, 154, 214
Conference on the Environment (UN) (1972)
Conference of the Parties in Copenhagen (COP15) (UN) 167, 179*n*
Connecticut Coalition for Environmental Justice (CCEJ) 71
Constitution (Cuba) 195
consumption 18, 41–3, 217, 232, 233
    capitalism and 50, 51, 52–3, 55, 59–60
    China 142, 145, 217
    Cuba 186, 206
    human nature 223–4
    South Korea 84
    Sweden 121, 135–6
    United Kingdom 115
'consumption-side environmentalism' 229
'contraction and convergence' 49
cooperatives 6
corporations 37–8, 53, 55, 58, 60
'correctability' 25
cost-effectiveness 29–30
CPPCC *see* Chinese People's Political Consultative Conference
Critical Theory 8–9, 24, 60
CSCB *see* Union Confederation of Bolivian Colonisers
CSUTCB *see* Sole Union Confederation of Bolivian Campesino Workers of Bolivia
Cuba 181–3, 210*n*, 214, 218, 222, 223
    activism 198, 201
    capitalist/socialist spectrum 6*f*
    causes of environmental injustice 204–10
    degrowth 229–30
    distributive environmental justice 190–3
    economic growth 39
    Environmental Justice Indicator Framework (EJI) 204
    policy-making 220*t*
    procedural environmental justice 193–202, 203*f*, 204
    substantive environmental justice 183–7, 188*f*, 189–90
    world ranking 228

'Cubanology' 181–2, 205
culture 18, 43–50, 63*t*, 217

D

Daewoo Logistics 81
Daly, H. E. 49
Damaging Hegemonic Environmental Discourses (DHEDs) 9, 10, 43–50, 63, 64, 75–6, 77
    achieving environmental justice and 217–18, 221, 228–32, 235
    Bolivia 166, 167
    China 156–8, 159
    Cuba 208, 209
    South Korea 86, 94–5
    Sweden 136, 137
    United Kingdom 115
Davis, S.J. 13*n*
Deaton, A. 48
decision-making processes 25, 28, 29, 109, 150, 205, 214
    Sweden 130–1, 133, 135, 136
decolonisation 163, 170, 171, 177
Defra *see* Department for the Environment, Food and Rural Affairs (UK)
degrowth movement 49, 64*n*, 228, 229–31, 232, 233
delegated power 26
deliberative democracy 26–7, 28
dematerialisation 55
democracy 21, 26–7, 60–1, 89, 131, 149–50, 175, 193–4
'Democracy Index' (Economist Intelligence Unit) 130
'Dennis Package' road plan (Sweden) 129, 139*n*
Department of Energy and Climate Change (UK) 83
Department for the Environment, Food and Rural Affairs (Defra) (UK) 101, 107, 116
Department of Health and Human Services (DHHS) (US) 77
Dependency Theory 51–2, 177
'developmental outsourcing' 81
'developmentalist' 175, 178
DHEDs *see* Damaging Hegemonic Environmental Discourses
DHHS *see* Department of Health and Human Services (US)
disability 40–1
Disch, L. 38
discrimination 33–5, 63*t*, 69, 75–6, 86–7, 170, 217
Discrimination Act (2009) (Sweden) 126
'distance-based' methodology 69–70

distributive environmental justice 1,
    17–19, 21, 24, 28, 31*t*, 63*t*
  Bolivia 170–1
  China 145–9
  Cuba 190–3, 214
  South Korea 86–7, 88*f*, 89
  Sweden 124–6, 127*f*, 128–30
  United Kingdom 103–4, 105*f*, 106–7,
    108*f*, 109
  United States 35, 67, 69–70
  see also procedural environmental
    justice; substantive environmental
    justice
Dobson, A. 23
Dominick, R. 62
dominion: nature and 45–6
Dorling, D. 60
'double injustice' 4
Doyal, L. 23
'Draft Guidelines for Economic and
  Social Policy' (Cuba) 196
Dryzek, J. 27
dumpster diving 129, 138*n*
Dworkin, R. 19

E

Easterlin, R.A. 48–9
Eco-Action (community-based
  organisation) 71–2
eco-socialism 227, 228, 233
'ecological civilization' 158, 228, 231,
  232
'ecological debt' 18, 229
Ecological Footprint (EF) 8, 24, 30, 81,
  244, 245*n*
  Bolivia 176
  Cuba 181, 214
  Sweden 121, 123, 130, 135
  United Kingdom 99, 100
ecological modernisation 54, 123, 136,
  137, 156
economic datasets (international) 240*t*,
  241*t*, 242*t*
economic determinism 4, 8
economic growth 9, 38, 43, 47–9, 217,
  221, 230
  Bolivia 166
  China 155, 156–8, 218
  industrialisation 39–41, 54
  South Korea 80, 82–3, 94, 95
  Sweden 120, 124, 135–6, 138*n*
  United Kingdom 115, 116
Economist Intelligence Unit (EIU) 130
ecosystems services 56, 216
ELA *see* Environmental Law Association
  (UK)
electric and magnetic fields (EMFs) 23,
  105*f*, 117*n*

electricity 122
ELF *see* Environmental Law Foundation
  (UK)
Emotional Freedom Technique 234–5
employment 61, 87
  ecological processes 228–9, 236*n*
  industrialisation and 39, 40–1
  toxic waste facilties 37, 38
'emulative consumption' 59
'end of history' thesis 225
Energy Act (2011) (UK) 106
Energy and Climate Change,
  Department of (UK) 83
Energy and Commerce of the US
  Congress, Committee on 53
energy policies 104, 105*f*, 106
Energy Revolution ('Revolución
  Energética') (Cuba) 185, 186
Engels, F. 62
England 97–8
environment
  human realm and 45–6, 123, 166
  Marxism and 62
  ownership and control of 9, 43, 50
Environment Agency (UK) 107, 108,
  112, 113, 116, 117*n*
Environment, Food and Rural Affairs,
  Department for (Defra) (UK) 101,
  107, 116
Environment, Ministry of the (Sweden)
  121
Environment Protection Act (1969)
  (Sweden) 131
Environmental Audit Committee (UK)
  2
'environmental blackmail' 37
Environmental Code (1999) (Sweden)
  121, 122–3, 130
environmental courts/tribunals 133–4,
  144, 172
Environmental Equality Indicator (UK)
  107, 114
Environmental Equity, Office of (US)
  66, 67
environmental 'goods'/'bads' 3, 18, 33,
  135, 164, 192
  substantive justice 21, 22
  United Kingdom 98, 104
Environmental Impact Assessment Act
  (2003) (China) 150
Environmental Impact Assessment Act
  (2009) (South Korea) 90–1
Environmental Impact Assessments
  (Sweden) 132
Environmental Impact Assessments
  (UK) 106
Environmental Information Disclosure
  Decree (2008) (China) 150–1

environmental injustice
  individual countries 74–8, 93–5, 114–
    16, 135–8, 154–9, 176–8, 204–10
  capitalism and 51
  Environmental Justice Indicator
    Framework (EJI) 214, 215*f*, 216–19
  inequality and 3–4
Environmental Justice Act (1992) (US)
  66
Environmental Justice Advisory
  Council, National (US) 66
Environmental Justice, Citizens'
  Movement for (South Korea) 79, 89
Environmental Justice, Connecticut
  Coalition for (CCEJ) 71
environmental justice (EJ)
  conceptualisation and use of 15–16,
    17, 30*n*
  definition 1–2, 67
  scope/limitations of research 10–11
Environmental Justice Forum (South
  Korea) 79
Environmental Justice Indicator
  Framework (EJI) 7–8, 22–5, 26*f*,
    27–30, 31*t*, 232, 235
  achieving environmental injustice 213,
    214, 215*f*, 216–19, 237–9*t*
  construction of 243–5
Environmental Justice, Interagency
  Working Group (US) 77
Environmental Justice Strategy (US) 77
Environmental Justice Summit *see*
  First National People of Color
  Environmental Justice Summit
'Environmental Kuznet's Curve' (EKC)
  thesis 48
environmental law 100, 151, 195–6
Environmental Law Association (ELA)
  (UK) 101
Environmental Law Foundation (ELF)
  (UK) 113
Environmental Non-Governmental
  Organizations (ENGOs) (China)
  152, 153
Environmental Performance Index 190
Environmental Policy Act, National
  (1970) (US) 68
Environmental Protection Agency
  (EPA) (US) 23, 34, 66, 67, 71–2, 77
Environmental Protection Agency
  (Sweden) 121, 129–30, 131
environmental quality 20, 185, 192, 193
'environmental racism' 15, 16, 18, 33,
  66, 70, 114
environmental rankings 68
environmental social work brigades
  (Cuba) 185–6, 211*n*

EPA *see* Environmental Protection
  Agency (US)
Equality Bill (2010) (UK) 107
Equality Impact Assessments (UK) 107,
  108, 114
equitable access 190
ETC group 44
'ethicality' 25
Executive Order 12898 (Federal Actions
  to Address Environmental Justice
  in Minority Populations and Low
  Income Populations) 66–7, 72–3, 77
'extractivism' 163–4, 168, 172, 174, 177,
  216

F

Faber, D. 27, 60, 71, 221
Federal Actions to Address
  Environmental Justice in Minority
  Populations and Low Income
  Populations (Executive Order
  12898) 66–7, 72–3, 77
Feed-in Tariffs (FiTs) (UK) 106
feminism 20
financial sectors 55, 57, 84
First National People of Color
  Environmental Justice Summit
  (1991) 15–16, 66, 74
Fitzpatrick, Tony 46
'floating signifier' 57
FNMCB-BS *see* National Federation
  of Bolivian Campesino Women –
  Bartolina Sisa
food 81, 104, 111*f*, 129, 138*n*, 189
Foster, J.B. 58–9, 230, 231
'Four Rivers Restoration Project' 85–6,
  91, 94
'fracking' (hydraulic fracturing) 68–9,
  71, 112
Framework Act on Environmental
  Policy (FAEP) (South Korea) 80
'Framework Law of Mother Earth and
  Integral Development for Living
  Well' (2012) 166–7, 169–70, 213
Fraser, N. 131
freedom of expression 90, 93, 172, 193,
  201–2
Freedom of Information Act (1966)
  (US) 70
Friends of the Earth Sweden 134
Friends of the Earth (UK) 112, 113
fuel poverty 104, 105–6
'fungibility' 23

G

Gallup World Poll 48
General Agreement on Tariffs and Trade
  (GATT) 79, 94, 96*n*

Genetic Engineering and Biotechnology, Center for (Cuba) 204
genetically modified organisms *see* transgenic agricultural technology
Genuine Progress Indicator 228
geoengineering projects 44–5, 216
Geographical Information Systems (GIS) software 19
Georgescu-Roegen, N. 49
GGGI *see* Global Green Growth Institute
Gibson-Graham, J.K. 53, 233
Gilmore, B. 69, 78
Gini Coefficient 69, 103, 125, 145, 170, 191, 211n
'given value' 56
glaciers 167
Global Compact (UN) 41
Global Green Growth Institute (GGGI) 84
global neoliberal capitalism 94
globalisation 155–6, 157
Gough, I. 23, 46
Gramsci, A. 177
'green capitalism' 53–4
'green cars' 42
'green consumption' 41–3
'Green Deal' (UK) 106
'green economy' 56, 57–8, 103
Green GDP 145, 228
'green growth' 56, 57
  South Korea 82, 83, 84, 85, 86, 94, 95
  Sweden 123–4, 137
'green growth education' 84
Green Growth, Presidential Committee on (South Korea) 82
'green' jobs 229
'Green New Deal' project (South Korea) 82, 85
'green revolution' (Cuba) 184, 211n
'Green Wall of China' project 145
'green washing' 42
greenhouse gas emissions 49, 54, 68, 83, 145, 190, 213
Groat, Dr Charles 71
gross domestic product (GDP) 48, 49, 65, 80, 136–7, 228
  China 145, 154, 158
  climate change and 167
  Cuba 183, 190, 230
  United States 230
Gudynas, E. 163
Guethón, Dr Reynaldo Jiménez 200

H

Habermas, J. 19–20, 27
Hahnel, R. 28

Han, M. 89
Happy Planet Index 121, 228
Hardin, G. 50
Harvey, D. 50, 234
Health and Human Services, Department of (DHHS) (US) 77
hegemony 9–10, 20, 38
'Helms-Burton Act' (1996) (US) 182
'high' technology 9, 43, 45, 208–9
high-income countries *see* Korea; Sweden; United Kingdom; United States
'Hills Fuel Poverty Review' (2012) (UK) 105
Hills, J.A. 103
Ho, P. 81
Hofman, I. 81
Holdaway, J. 147
Holifield, R. 72–3
Holloway, J. 233–4
Hou, Y. 157
Houck, O.A. 193
housing 87, 88f, 89, 101–2
  China 143, 145–6, 159–60n
  Cuba 187, 188–9, 191–2, 205
  Sweden 123, 125, 127, 128–9, 136
Høyer, K.G. 49
Hukou system (China) 148–9
human health 1–3, 9, 43, 46–7, 143–4, 151
  capitalism and 216, 218, 228, 233
human realm 9, 43, 45–6
hurricanes 70, 189
hydraulic fracturing *see* 'fracking'
hydrocarbons 165, 174

I

'ideal speech situation' 19–20, 27
illiteracy 170
ILO *see* International Labour Organisation
IMF *see* International Monetary Fund
income/wealth 35, 58–60, 87, 114
  Bolivia 170–1
  China 145, 146
  Cuba 190–1, 211n
  redistribution of 229
  Sweden 124–5, 135, 136
  see also inequalities
Index of Sustainable Economic Welfare 228
indicators *see* Environmental Justice Indicator (EJI) Framework
indigenous groups 18, 34, 37, 46, 51, 57–8
  Bolivia 162, 166, 167–8, 170–1, 172, 173–4, 175
  Sweden 126, 132–3

United States 66, 67, 70, 75–6
Indigenous Peoples Global Conference
   on Rio+20 and Mother Earth 57–8
individual behaviour 41–3, 63*t*
industrial waste 39
industrialisation 63*t*, 94, 136, 205, 216
   capitalism 39–41
   China 143, 154–5
inequalities 103, 104, 128
   basic needs 3–4
   capitalism 216
   deliberative democracy and 27
   economic growth 49, 94
   race 171
   rural/urban communities 146, 153–4
   see also income/wealth
infant mortality 164
institutional discrimination 34–5, 75
Integrated Neighbourhood
   Transformation Workshops (Talleres
   de Transformación Integral del
   Barrio) (TTIB) 201–2, 203*f*
'interactional justice' 19
Interagency Working Group on
   Environmental Justice (US) 77
International Labour Organisation
   (ILO) 3
International Monetary Fund (IMF)
   59, 163
international/intergenerational/inter-
   species indicator 31*t*
'intersectionality' 18
Isiboro Ségure Indigenous Territory and
   National Park (TIPNIS) 173–4, 175,
   179*n*
ISO 14000 (voluntary standard) 41
Iwanami, Francisco Salvatierra 165

J

Jackson Jnr, Jessie 77
Jeon, J.K. 89
'Jevons Paradox' 54
Johnson, G.S. 37
Jones, R.S. 87
Jonsson, A. 131

K

Kapcia, Anthony 199, 209
Karlsson, Jenny Wik 133
Karlsson, Mikael 134, 137
Kember, Mark 115, 223, 225
Kennet, P. 11
KEPCO 91, 92*f*
Khan, J. 131–2
Kim Dae-jung 82
Kim Young-sam 81–2
Korea Credit Guarantee Fund 83
Korea Development Bank 83

Kuylenstierna, Johan 119, 124, 128,
   136–7

L

'Ladder of Participation' (Arnstein) 25,
   26*f*, 92, 133
Lake, R.W. 38
Lambert, T. 35, 36
'land grabbing' 53, 81
landfill sites 66, 70, 104
Law 81 (The Law of the Environment)
   (Cuba) 184, 207
Law 180 (Bolivia) 174
Law on Environmental Protection
   (1979) (China) 144
Law of Low Rents (1959) (Cuba) 192
Law of Urban Reform (1960) (Cuba)
   192
Le Grand, Prof. Julian 47
Lee, H. 89, 91, 92*f*
Lee Myung-bak 79–80, 82
Lee, Yujin 91, 93, 95
legal aid centres 151
less developed countries (LDCs) 34
Leventhal, G.S. 25
Levins, R. 185, 226
libertarianism 5, 17, 30*n*, 227
Lievesley, G. 193
lifestyles 41–3, 63*t*, 77, 100, 114–15, 217
   Sweden 130, 136
linear rationality 43, 44–5
Linera, Álvaro García 162, 173, 178
Llanes- Regueiro, Dr Juan 197
lobbyists 134
Local People's Congresses (LPCs)
   (China) 149
locally unwanted land uses (LULUs) 35
Lockleaze, Bristol (UK) 105*f*, 110, 111*f*,
   115
London Sustainability Exchange (UK)
   112
'Longhouse tradition' 75
Lora-Wainwright, A. 153
Lovelock, J. 21
'Low-Carbon Green Growth' (LCGG)
   (South Korea) 82, 83, 84, 85, 86, 94,
   95
low-income communities 36–7, 38, 43,
   49, 59, 69, 213
   China 146–7
   South Korea 87, 88*f*, 89, 93–4
   Sweden 119, 125–6, 129–30, 134–5
   United Kingdom 98, 103–4, 106, 107,
   110, 111*f*, 112, 115
   United States 66–7, 72–3, 77
lower middle income countries *see*
   Bolivia
Lowndes, V. 110

Lu Feng 142, 156–7, 231
Ludlum, S. 196
LULUs *see* locally unwanted land uses (LULUs)
'luxury consumption' 52

M

Ma, C. 147
McAdam, D. 20
McConnell, Jack 98
Madagascar 81
Magdoff, F. 58–9, 230
Mamani, Matilde Delgado 173
managerialist approach 8–9
'mandat imperatif' ('instructed delegate model') 197
manipulation 25
market dynamics 35–6, 63*t*, 93–4, 115, 120, 215–16, 217
  Cuba and 183
  democratic workers' control 227
  socialism and 141
  Sweden 136, 137
  see also capitalism
market mechanisms 55–6
Martinez-Alier, J. 233
Marxism 8, 23, 50–1, 61–3, 159, 178, 182, 218
MAS *see* Movimiento al Socialismo (Movement toward Socialism) (Bolivia)
mass media: Cuba 199–201
MDGs *see* Millennium Development Goals
Measures on Environmental Administrative Reconsideration Act (2008) (China) 150
migration 125–6
Millennium Declaration 46
Millennium Development Goals (MDGs) 46
Ministry of Education, Science and Technology (South Korea) 84
Ministry of the Environment (Sweden) 121
Ministry of Science, Technology and Environment (CITMA) (Cuba) 184, 207–8
mixed economies 6, 162–3
Moag, J.S. 25
Mohai, P. 69–70
Mohawk communities 75, 76
Monbiot, G. 60
monetisation 56, 235
Morales, Evo 162, 166, 173, 176–7
morbidity/mortality rates 2
'move-in' hypothesis 35–6

Movimiento al Socialismo (Movement toward Socialism) (MAS) (Bolivia) 161–2, 163, 170, 176–7, 178
  procedural environmental justice 171–3, 175
  substantive environmental justice 165, 166, 169
Myiow, Stuart 75

N

Næss, P. 49
NAFTA *see* North America Free Trade Agreement
nation-state analysis 10–11
National Assembly (Cuba) 195, 196
National Assembly of Popular Power *see* Asamblea Nacional del Poder Popular (Cuba)
National Commission on the BP Deepwater Horizon Oil Spill and Offshore Drilling 53
National Development Plan (Bolivia) 163, 172
National Environmental Justice Advisory Council (US) 66
National Environmental Policy Act (1970) (US) 68
'National Environmental Strategy, The' (Cuba) 184
National Federation of Bolivian Campesino Women – Bartolina Sisa (FNMCB-BS) 174
National Institute of Statistics (Bolivia) 170
National People's Congress (NPC) (China) 149, 152
National Planning Policy Framework (UK) 101
National Strategy for Sustainable Development (NSSD) (South Korea) 82
National Sustainable Development Strategy (NSDS) (Sweden) 128, 138*n*
'National Vision for Sustainable Development' (South Korea) 82
nationalisation 165–6
'natural order' 9
needs (human) 23, 52, 115, 228–9, 230
Neighbourhood Renewal (UK) 110, 111
neoclassical economics 35
neoliberalism 59, 79–80, 120, 162, 175, 177
NGOs *see* non-governmental organisations
nitrous oxide (N$_2$O) 142, 159*n*
non-capitalist activities 6

non-communicable diseases 2
non-governmental organisations
    (NGOs) 152–3, 172–3, 175
non-material social goods 19
North America Free Trade Agreement
    (NAFTA) 59
Northern Ireland 98
NSSD *see* National Strategy for
    Sustainable Development (South
    Korea)
Nu River (China) 152, 160*n*
nuclear power 54, 84, 122, 135, 216

O

Oakes, J. 36
O'Connor, J. 51
OECD 94, 95, 145
Office of Environmental Equity/Justice
    (US) 66, 67
Oliveras, R. 192
'Open Government Information
    Regulations' (China) 150
open-pit mining techniques 178*n*
Orellana, Juanita Ancieta 169
organic food production 184
Osborne, George 102
Oxfam 58

P

packaging 100
Pan, Yue 156, 158
paradigm change 231–2
Park Geun-hye 80
participatory economics (parecon) 28,
    227
participatory models 20, 25, 26*f*, 109–10
participatory politics (parpolity) 28
Partido Comunista de Cuba
    (Communist Party) (PCC) 182–3,
    193, 194–5, 210–11*n*
partnership 25–6
Pastille Consortium 22
Pastor, J. 36
Pavlak, T.J. 25
'payments for ecosystems services' (PES)
    56
PCC *see* Partido Comunista de Cuba
    (Communist Party)
Pellow, D. 38–9
'People's Agreement' 167
People's Republic of China *see* China
Percussive Suggestion Technique 235
PES *see* 'payments for ecosystems
    services'
Pesticides Campaign (UK) 100
pharmaceutical industry 122, 138*n*
placation 25

Plains Exploration and Production
    Company 71
'planetary boundaries' 1–2
Planning and Building Act (Sweden)
    130
'plural economy' 163, 171
Plurinational State of Bolivia *see* Bolivia
Polanyi, K. 224
policy-making 4, 109, 114–15, 205, 219,
    220*t*, 221–7
political freedom 60
polluter pays principle 121
'polluter-industrial complex' 60, 71,
    100, 221
pollution 33–4, 36, 38, 39, 48
    China 142, 143–4, 147, 149
    core/peripheral nations 52
    Cuba 187, 190, 202
    indigenous groups 70
    oil spills 53
    permits 56
    Scotland 108*f*
    Sweden 122, 124, 131, 135
    United States 68
    see also air pollution
Pollution Victims, Centre for Legal
    Assistance to (China) 151
'poor' 21, 30*n*
Pops, G.M. 25
population growth 64*n*
Porritt, J. 63
Post-2015 Development Agenda,
    Report of the High-Level Panel of
    Eminent Persons on the 46
post-capitalism 233–4
'post-material values thesis' 43
'post-political' condition 9, 27
post-structuralist approach 8–9
poverty
    food 81, 104, 111*f*, 129, 138*n*
    fuel 104, 105–6
    rates 170, 171
power 9–10, 136, 217
    activism and 27
    Critical Theory and 24
    lack of citizen power 36–9, 76–7, 202
    non-dominant groups 20
    partnerships and 25–6
Precautionary Principle (Rio
    Declaration (1992)) 28, 29–30, 121
Presidential Commission on Sustainable
    Development (PCSD) (South
    Korea) 82
Presidential Committee on Green
    Growth (South Korea) 82
pricing mechanisms 56
prior consent 172
privatisation 39, 50, 56, 57, 59

Bolivia 163, 165
China 146
South Korea 79, 85
United Kingdom 97
United States 70
procedural environmental justice 1,
    19–21, 31*t*, 63*t*, 214
  Bolivia 171–5, 176*f*
  China 149–54
  Cuba 193–202, 203*f*, 204
  environmental indicators 24–5, 28
  South Korea 89–91, 92*f*, 93
  Sweden 130–5
  United Kingdom 98, 109–110, 111*f*,
    112–14
  United States 70–4
  see also distributive environmental
    justice; substantive environmental
    justice
'production-side environmentalism' 229
'productive justice' 22
Provincial People's Congress 149
public consultation 25, 133, 136
  Bolivia 161, 172, 175, 176*f*
  Cuba 183, 196–7, 203
'public deficit model' 109
public health *see* human health
Public Sector Equality Duty (UK) 107

R

'radioactive colonialism' 70
RCOG *see* Royal College of
    Obstetricians and Gynaecologists
REACH *see* Registration, Evaluation,
    Authorisation and Restriction of
    Chemicals (UK)
reasonableness principle 121, 124
'rebound effect' 54
'recognition justice' 19
recycling 56, 81, 100, 187, 217
  Sweden 121, 123, 130, 136
'Red Tape Challenge Environment
    Theme' (UK) 101, 117*n*
Reducing Emissions from Deforestation
    and Forest Degradation (REDD) 56
reforestation schemes 184–5
Registration, Evaluation, Authorisation
    and Restriction of Chemicals
    (REACH) (UK) 100
renewable energy sources 106, 184, 229,
    236*n*
repayment of debt 59
Report of the High-Level Panel of
    Eminent Persons on the Post-2015
    Development Agenda 46
Republic of Korea *see* South Korea
research funding 27, 51
'resource wars' 165

'Revolución Energética' (Energy
    Revolution) (Cuba) 185, 186
Ricardo Núñez, R. 192
rights for nature 166–7
Rio Declaration (1992) 28, 29–30
Rio Earth Summit (1992) 46, 156, 184
'risk society' 51, 54
Ro Mu-hyun 82
Rodríguez, J.L. 181
Roma communities 126
Roman, P. 194
Rönnbäck, K. 129
Royal College of Obstetricians and
    Gynaecologists (RCOG) 218
Royal Society for the Protection of
    Birds (RSPB) (UK) 113
rural/urban communities 146, 147–8,
    154, 164, 188*f*, 192

S

Saami communities 126–7, 132–3
Safe Drinking Water Act (1974) (US) 68
Saha, R. 69–70
Saney, I. 222
Santos, Dr Orlando Rey 208, 210
Saravia, Ramiro 175
Scandrett, E. 16–17
Schnaiberg, A. 51
Science, Technology and Environment,
    Ministry of (CITMA) (Cuba) 184,
    207–8
Scotland 16–17, 97, 98, 108*f*
SDC *see* Sustainable Development
    Commission (UK)
second home ownership 123, 136
Seo, W. 89
Seoul–Incheon Canal construction
    (South Korea) 89
SEPA *see* Swedish Environmental
    Protection Agency
Shintech Corporation 73–4
Shocco Township 66
Silent Spring (Carson) 47
'single-issue' environmental laws 144
social change 232–5
social exclusion 98–9
social movements 20, 46, 172, 177, 233
'social science' 116
socialism 5, 6*f*, 61–3, 97, 221, 222, 236*n*
  'image problem' 226
  see also Bolivia; China; Cuba
Sole Union Confederation of Bolivian
    Campesino Workers of Bolivia
    (CSUTCB) 174
Sombart, W. 50
South Korea 79–80, 96*n*, 213
  capitalist/socialist spectrum 6*f*, 79
  causes of environmental injustice 93–5

distributive environmental justice 86–7, 88*f*, 89
Environmental Justice Indicator Framework (EJI) 93, 95
industrialisation 40
policy-making 220*t*
procedural environmental justice 89–91, 92*f*, 93
substantive environmental justice 80–6
toxic waste facilities 37
see also capitalism
South-North Water Diversion project (China) 145
Soviet Union 62–3
'Special Period in Peacetime' (Cuba) 183, 185, 186–7, 188, 190, 209, 230
SPICE *see* Stratospheric Particle Injection for Climate Engineering
SSNC *see* Swedish Society for Nature Conservation
State Council (China) 156
State, The 38, 61, 142
state-based economy *see* socialism
state-subsidised food 189
Stockholm Resilience Centre 1–2
Strategic Environmental Assessments (UK) 106
Strategy for Sustainable Development (Scotland) 98
Stratospheric Particle Injection for Climate Engineering (SPICE) 44–5
'street level incivilities' 16
street protest 198
substantive environmental justice 1, 21*n*, 22, 31*t*, 63*t*
  Bolivia 164–70
  China 142–5
  Cuba 183–7, 188*f*, 189–90
  South Korea 80–6
  Sweden 121–4
  United Kingdom 99–103
  United States 68–9
  see also distributive environmental justice; procedural environmental justice
suicide rates 95
Sullivan Report (UK) 113
sulphur dioxide (SO_2) 142, 159*n*
Summers, Lawrence 34
Supreme Decree No. 28701 (Nationalisation Decree) (2006) (Bolivia) 165–6
'survival of the fittest' 224
sustainability 23, 46, 49, 57, 82, 229
  China 156
  Cuba 181, 190
  Sweden 119, 121
  United Kingdom 101, 116

Sustainability Appraisals (UK) 106
Sustainable Development Commission (SDC) (UK) 98, 113
Sustainable Development, National Strategy for (NSSD) (South Korea) 82
'Sustainable Development, National Vision for' (South Korea) 82
Sustainable Development, Presidential Commission on (PCSD) (South Korea) 82
Sustainable Development Research Network (UK) 104
Sustainable Development Strategies (England) 98
Sustainable Development Strategy, National (NSDS) (Sweden) 128, 138*n*
Sustainable Development, Strategy for (Scotland) 98
Sustainable Economic Welfare, Index of 228
Sweden 119–21, 138*n*, 213
  capitalist/socialist spectrum 6*f*
  causes of environmental injustice 135–8
  distributive environmental justice 124–6, 127*f*, 128–30
  Environmental Justice Indicator Framework (EJI) 135, 138
  policy-making 220*t*
  procedural environmental justice 130–5
  substantive environmental justice 121–4
  see also capitalism
Swedish Environmental Protection Agency (SEPA) 123–4, 133
Swedish Social Democratic Party 120, 138*n*
Swedish Society for Nature Conservation (SSNC) 134
Swyngedouw, E. 9, 27
'symbolic consumption' 52
synthetic chemicals 3, 99–100

T

'take power to change the world' approach 234
Talleres de Transformación Integral del Barrio (Integrated Neighbourhood Transformation Workshops) (TTIB) 201–2, 203*f*
Tao, F. 152
Taylor, J.H.L. 192
techonological innovation 40, 45, 54–5, 62, 83–4, 109
  Bolivia 166, 167–8

China 145
Sweden 124, 136
therapy 25
Thibaut, J. 25
timber harvesting 122
Title VI (Civil Rights Act 1964) 67
'Torricelli Law' (1992) (US) 182
Town and Country Planning Act (1990) 112
Townsend, P. 30
Toxic Substances Control Act (1976) (US) 68, 70
toxic waste facilities 15, 28, 33, 35, 36, 39, 216
  employment and 37, 38
  South Korea 89, 91
  United Kingdom 103–4
  United States 66, 69–70, 71, 73–4, 76
trade unions 46, 61, 131, 199
traditional medicine 168, 209
Traditional Medicine and Interculturality, Vice Ministry of (Bolivia) 168
'Tragedy of the Commons' (Hardin) 50
transfer payments 170
transgenic agricultural technology 55, 204, 211*n*
transportation 129, 186
'treadmill of production theory' 51, 54
'triple injustice' 4
TTIB *see* Talleres de Transformación Integral del Barrio (Integrated Neighbourhood Transformation Workshops)
Tulane Environment Law Clinic 73
'twenty-first century socialism' 162

U

UNECE *see* United Nations, Economic Commission for Europe
unemployment 58, 69, 125
Union of Concerned Scientists 47–8
Union Confederation of Bolivian Colonisers (CSCB) 174
United Kingdom 40, 55, 97–9, 100, 213, 218
  anti-environmental movements 60–1
  capitalist/socialist spectrum 6*f*
  carbon dioxide emissions (CO2) 103, 105, 116
  causes of environmental injustices 114–16
  climate change policies 4
  distributive environmental justice 103–4, 105*f*, 106–7, 108*f*, 109
  Environmental Justice Indicator Framework (EJI) 114
  policy-making 220*t*

procedural environmental justice 109–110, 111*f*, 112–14
substantive environmental justice 99–103
top 10 values of people living in 225
see also capitalism
United Nations 145, 232
  Conference on the Environment (1972)
  Conference of the Parties in Copenhagen (COP15) 167, 179*n*
  Economic Commission for Europe (UNECE) 29
  Global Compact 41
  water as human right 167
United States 38–9, 59, 60, 65–8, 69, 213, 230
  capitalist/socialist spectrum 6*f*
  carbon dioxide emissions (CO2) 13*n*
  causes of environmental injustice 74–8
  Cuba and 182, 194, 200, 207, 209, 210*n*, 211*n*
  'democracy promotion' 173
  distributive environmental justice 69–70
  Environmental Justice Indicator Framework (EJI) 74
  environmental racism 15, 16, 34, 37, 69, 70
  policy-making 220*t*
  procedural environmental justice 70–4
  research funding 27
  social movement advocacy 233
  substantive environmental justice 68–9
  see also capitalism
universality 190
University of Texas Energy Institute 71
upper middle income countries *see* China; Cuba
Urasawa, S. 87
Urban Reform Law (1960) (Cuba) 188
USAID 173, 175

V

Van Rooij, B. 144
Vargas, Leonida Zurita 169
Veolia Water 155
Vice Ministry of Traditional Medicine and Interculturality (Bolivia) 168
Vilela, Martin 161, 177
'Vivir Bien' (Living Well) 166–7, 168–9, 175, 177, 178, 213, 228, 231
'voluntary simplicity' 41, 42

W

Walker, G. 103–4
Walker, L. 25
Walley, Joan 102, 115

Wang, J. and Wang, M. 144, 151
'war of position' 177–8
Warren, K.J. 18
Wasserman, Joe 71
waste collection services 187
Waste Directive (1997) (EU) 100
water 143, 164, 167, 207
  pollution 135, 142, 144, 155, 164, 187
'water war' (*guerra del agua*) 165
Welsh Assembly Government 98
Wen Jiabao 158
Western countries 5, 45–6, 218
'Western Development Program' ('Go
  West' policy) (China) 146
WGAEJ *see* Working Group on Access
  to Environmental Justice (UK)
Wheeler, B.W. 235
WHO *see* World Health Organization
Wong, Judy Ling 107, 109
Working Group on Access to
  Environmental Justice (WGAEJ)
  (UK) 113
World Bank 59, 143, 145, 147, 163
World Health Organization (WHO) 3
World Peoples' Summit on Climate
  Change and the Rights of Mother
  Earth 167
World Prison Population List (2009)
  198–9
World Systems Theory 51, 52, 155, 177
World Trade Organization (WTO) 94,
  96*n*
Worldwatch Institute 229
Worldwide Fund for Nature (WWF)
  113, 122, 181

X

Xiamen paraxylene (PX) petrochemical
  project (China) 153–4
Xie, Dr Lei 150, 151

Y

Yeampierre, Elizabeth 75
Yeongheung coal plant 91, 92*f*
Yisheng, Z. 158
Young, I.M. 19, 27–8, 131
Yun, S.-J. 86

Z

Žižek, S. 225